PC Scheme

User's Guide
&
Language Reference Manual

Student Edition

by
Texas Instruments

foreword by
David H. Bartley, John C. Jensen, & Donald W. Oxley

▲ *The Scientific Press* • 507 Seaport Court • Redwood City, CA 94063-2731 • (415) 366-2577

Texas Instruments Incorporated
ATTN: Data Systems Group, M/S 2151
P.O. Box 2909
Austin, Texas 78769-2909

Printed in the United States of America

10 9 8 7 6 5 4 3 2 1

ISBN 0-89426-114-2

Publisher: The Scientific Press
Production: Texas Instruments, Data Systems Group
Cover Design: Rogondino & Associates

contents

Foreword

Programming languages, like just about everything else these days, seem to come in two kinds. There are the large, ponderous, something-for-everybody languages that seem to be saying, "Try me, surely you'll find something you like!" Somehow, these languages all seem to be designed by committee to fit the perceived needs of big business or big government. And, somehow, the language that tries to be something for everyone is too much for anyone.

Then there's the other kind—small and focused, often with academic beginnings, revolutionary ideas, and humble aspirations—that surprise just about everyone with their power, expressiveness, and grass-roots popularity.

Niklaus Wirth's Pascal is a textbook example of the latter case. Though clearly an evolving member of the Algol family of programming languages, Pascal grew out of Wirth's dissatisfaction with the "creeping featurism" that threatened the evolution of Algol-68. Once considered only a pedagogical tool, Pascal forged its own identity and tradition, countering the complexity to be found on the PL/1 and Ada side of the Algol family.

Scheme's role in the Lisp family of languages is a bit like that. Conceived in the mid-70s at Massachusetts Institute of Technology by Guy Lewis Steele and Gerald Jay Sussman as a testbed for the study of programming language theory, it soon became the research and teaching vehicle of choice at MIT and, soon after, Indiana and Yale universities and elsewhere. An explosion of commercial implementations ensued, stimulated by the fortuitous widespread appearance of personal computers in the hands of hobbyists and educators and abetted by the publication of *Structure and Interpretation of Computer Programs* by Harold Abelson and Gerald Jay Sussman with Julie Sussman.

We at Texas Instruments adopted Scheme as a research tool in 1984. We first viewed Scheme as a model for the design of new computer architectures for symbolic computing. Other experiments involved Scheme as an intermediate representation for compiling other languages and as the host language for research in realtime embedded systems and symbolic mathematics. One project to study compilation techniques and the byte-coded emulation of an idealized computer instruction set evolved into the PC Scheme product.

Like Pascal, Scheme has come into its own with a devoted following and a wide variety of implementations available for most PCs and major mainframe computer systems. We hope you too will discover the joy of programming with this deceptively simple, yet powerful language.

> *David H. Bartley*
> *John C. Jensen*
> *Donald W. Oxley*

April, 1988
Dallas, Texas

Acknowledgments

We would like to thank the many individuals and groups who have helped us develop TI Scheme and this book.

Dan Friedman of Indiana University was responsible for introducing Scheme to TI. He was patient and persuasive in helping us understand the nature of the language and the importance of the concepts in Scheme. Chris Haynes and Mitch Wand, also of Indiana University, joined us early and provided a great deal of advice and support. Of course, other faculty and graduate students at Indiana University also provided both direct and indirect support for which we are grateful.

Hal Abelson, Gerry Sussman, and Julie Sussman of the Massachusetts Institute of Technology gave us all a critical boost with the publication of their superb book, *Structure and Interpretation of Computer Programs*. That text is bringing the power of Scheme to a new generation of students, and sets an exceptionally high standard of quality to which all of us can aspire.

Will Clinger and Jonathan Rees, editors of the *Revised Report on Scheme,* and all the participants and supporters of the Brandeis Workshop and subsequent meetings deserve credit for their cooperative spirit and willingness to compromise. This manual and TI Scheme itself have benefited immensely from that work.

The MIT Scheme group has freely provided code, advice, and support. We gratefully acknowledge the use of parts of their Scheme manual as a basis for parts of this manual and of TI Scheme itself. Special thanks go to Chris Hanson for a superb job in his implementation of the Edwin editor which we have modified and incorporated.

We wish to thank Dan Friedman, Chris Haynes, Mitch Wand, Eugene Kohlbecker, and other members of the Indiana University Scheme group for the use of their implementations of Scheme 84 and permission to borrow material from their documentation. We particularly appreciate Chris Haynes' contribution to parts of this manual.

- Rusty Haddock, Paul Kristoff, and Amitabh Srivastava assisted us in the development of the initial version of *PC Scheme*.

- Our special thanks go to Jan Stevens for her patience and diligence in pulling this manual together. Its quality, style, and form have all been improved immensely by her efforts as editor.

- TI's Computer Science Center has had a number of summer students from Indiana University and from MIT. These include Bruce Duba, John Gateley, Eugene Kohlbecker, John Lash, Joe Loyall, Mark Meyer, John Nienart, and Glenn Slick. They have contributed significantly to the implementation.

- Bob Beal, Keith Carlson, Terry Caudill, Jennifer Hao, Mike McGiffin, and Bill Turpin were responsible for its release as a product and its subsequent development.

- Finally, we acknowledge the influence of other dialects of Scheme and Lisp. Both the work on T by Jonathan Rees and Norman Adams and the entire Common Lisp effort have been particularly influential.

User's Guide

CONTENTS

Chapter	Paragraph	Title	Page

Chapter	Paragraph	Title	Page

Appendix	Paragraph	Title	Page

INTRODUCTION 1

This book is a user's guide for PC Scheme (PCS), an implementation of TI Scheme. For a complete description of the TI Scheme language, see the *TI Scheme Language Reference Manual — Student Edition*. This user's guide is not intended to be a tutorial or language reference manual. Instead, it provides an overview of the facilities provided by PC Scheme, including descriptions of implementation-specific features that are not discussed in the language reference manual. For additional help learning PC Scheme, see the paragraph entitled Instructional Uses in this chapter.

The remainder of this chapter describes the highlights of the PC Scheme system and outlines the remainder of the book.

Scheme—the Language

1.1 The features of Scheme include the following:

■ Scheme is a modern dialect of LISP, noteworthy for its simplicity, elegance, and power.

■ The design of the language is exceptionally clear and simple, with a small, select set of powerful facilities.

■ Its interactive operation provides an effective environment for learning and application development.

■ The lexical scoping of variables facilitates program development and makes programs more maintainable.

■ Since procedures are "first-class" objects, they are treated in exactly the same way as other data objects, thus simplifying the language and its implementation.

■ Tail recursion allows looping via procedure calls without sacrificing performance.

■ Continuations provide a very general control mechanism.

PC Scheme—the Implementation

1.2 This implementation of TI Scheme does the following:

■ Adheres faithfully to the Scheme standard.

■ Runs on members of both the TI and IBM® personal computer families, as well as their compatible computers.

■ Provides an optimizing incremental compiler for ease of programming and efficient execution.

- Includes EDWIN, an EMACS-like text editor (requires 512K of memory).

- Provides extensions for debugging, graphics, and windowing.

- Can suspend PC Scheme, execute DOS-based programs, and then return to PC Scheme.

- Includes the Scheme Object-Oriented Programming System (SCOOPS) for developing object-oriented applications.

- Supports international applications; therefore, it handles 8-bit characters.

- Supports environments, thus providing a convenient encapsulation mechanism.

- Supports engines, which allow process abstractions to be implemented.

A LISP System for Personal Computers

1.3   The Scheme programming language is a lexically scoped dialect of LISP originally developed at the Massachusetts Institute of Technology (MIT) to demonstrate that a single language could efficiently support the major programming paradigms in use today, including imperative, functional, and message-passing styles.

Scheme is small and simple. It provides general facilities for addressing a broad range of symbolic applications, yet it can be mastered easily. This makes Scheme suitable for both instructional use and system software development. It is particularly suitable in personal computer environments.

Like Pascal, which developed a decade earlier, Scheme was created originally as a distillation of proven concepts and was first used in research and teaching. It now has emerged in several implementations as a serious tool for producing applications and system software. Many of the ideas in Scheme were incorporated into the Common Lisp specification, making Scheme a close relative to Common Lisp that nevertheless retains a simple and streamlined nature.

Scheme has proven to be particularly effective for symbolic computing on small personal computers, where full implementations of Common Lisp are difficult to construct and are relatively inefficient. Scheme's use of lexical scoping, block structure, call by value, and tail-recursive semantics permits it to be compiled efficiently, whereas most personal computer implementations of LISP are interpretive in nature.

The implementation of PC Scheme has been finely tuned for maximum performance, given the computing and memory resources available on most personal computers. An incremental compiler provides both the advantages of interactive programming and the run-time speed of a compiler. To conserve the memory required by compiled programs, the compiler produces low-level byte codes rather than native machine code. The byte codes are executed by a virtual machine (VM) emulator. PC Scheme optimizes the trade-off between speed and memory to provide an efficient modern LISP system for personal computers.

Application and System Software Development

1.4 For symbolic applications, PC Scheme offers ease of development, high performance, and a broad base of delivery machines. The base language itself is simple, powerful, and carefully implemented for optimal performance on a personal computer (PC). Although PC Scheme is a compiled language, interactive development is supported with effective debugging and editing tools.

Extensions for windowing and graphics may be utilized. Applications may be delivered on disk in a fast-load format, and a single copy of the application can run on the TI Professional Computer (TI PC), the IBM PC, and their compatibles, providing a broad delivery base.

PC Scheme is based on the recent Scheme standard defined in the *Revised*[3] *Report on the Algorithmic Language Scheme*, a joint technical report of Indiana University and the MIT AI Laboratory.[1] Extensions to the Scheme standard and detailed implementation decisions that are not covered by the standard generally conform to Common Lisp. Texas Instruments has been an active participant in the standardization efforts for both Scheme and Common Lisp. The stability of Scheme as a language, combined with its similarities to Common Lisp, make PC Scheme a solid foundation on which to build applications.

The TI expert systems development tools Personal Consultant™ Easy and Personal Consultant Plus and EDWIN, an EMACS-like text editor, are implemented in PC Scheme, demonstrating the suitability of PC Scheme for the development of substantial applications programs.

DOS-based programs can be accessed quickly without exiting from PC Scheme, a capability that is described in the next paragraph.

Creating an Interface

1.5 You can create an interface between PC Scheme and other languages on 8086/80286-class machines through use of the DOS-CALL procedure.

The DOS-CALL procedure executes an MS®-DOS program. Using DOS-CALL is advantageous in situations where time is not critical (for example, you want to run a database program and are not planning to use PC Scheme until the database program has completed).

For further information concerning the DOS-CALL procedure, refer to the chapter in this manual entitled Advanced Features. DOS-CALL is fully described in the *TI Scheme Language Reference Manual — Student Edition*.

---

[1] W. Clinger and J. Rees, ed., "The Revised[3] Report on the Algorithmic Language Scheme," Massachusetts Institute of Technology AI Memo 848a (September, 1986).

Instructional Uses

1.6 The attributes that make PC Scheme a valuable tool for software development are also useful in instructional environments. Using PC Scheme and reading the textbook *Structure and Interpretation of Computer Programs*[2] provide an excellent basis for learning LISP and effective programming techniques. Advance review copies of *Programming in Scheme — An Introduction*[3] indicate an exceptional match between the text and PC Scheme.

The SCHEME Programming Language[4] contains examples written in Chez Scheme. However, since PC Scheme supports the Scheme standard, many of the examples will run successfully.

PC Scheme is particularly suited for use in courses in artificial intelligence, principles of programming languages, software engineering, simulation, operating systems, and introductory programming.

System Requirements

1.7 The following list gives the system requirements needed for PC Scheme:

- Texas Instruments Professional, Portable Professional, or BUSINESS-PRO™ computers: IBM PC, IBM PC/XT™, or IBM Personal Computer AT™; or compatible computers

- MS-DOS 2.1 (or greater) or PC-DOS 2.0 (or greater)

- 320K bytes of memory

- Dual diskette drives

Note that additional memory and a hard disk are recommended, particularly for software development. The EDWIN text editor requires a minimum of 512K bytes of memory. Also, graphics hardware support is required to use the graphics features of PC Scheme.

---

[2] Harold Abelson and Gerald Jay Sussman with Julie Sussman, *Structure and Interpretation of Computer Programs*, MIT Press, Cambridge MA, 1985.

[3] Michael Eisenberg, *Programming in Scheme — An Introduction*, Scientific Press, Redwood City, CA, to be published in 1988.

[4] R. Kent Dybvig, *The SCHEME Programming Language*, Prentice-Hall, Englewood Cliffs, NJ, 1987.

Conventional Memory

1.8 The IBM PC, the TI Professional Computer, and their compatibles use the Intel® 8088 processor, which can directly address up to 1 megabyte of conventional memory. However, conventional memory reserves a certain amount of space for read-only memory and video memory, leaving the remainder as user memory.

In short, conventional memory allows a maximum user memory space of 640K on an IBM PC or 768K on a TI Professional Computer.

Overview of This Manual

1.9 Chapter 2 of this manual, Getting Started, explains how to install PC Scheme on your computer system and begin to use it. It also describes how the system uses autoloaded files to avoid loading seldom-used features into memory until they are needed. Read this chapter carefully before you attempt to use the system.

Chapter 3 describes the interactive debugging facilities provided in PC Scheme. These include the Inspector, the error handler, a set of procedures for tracing and setting break-points, the pretty-printer, and the structure editor.

Chapter 4 describes EDWIN, an interactive, real-time, display-oriented file editor based on the MIT EMACS editor. As a Scheme program, EDWIN is integrated fully into the PC Scheme environment, allowing easy transition between the coding and testing phases of program development.

Chapter 5 explains how to create and manipulate windows to enhance interactive screen input/output (I/O). It also describes the system's use of windows for its standard I/O port and status display line.

Chapter 6 describes the graphics facilities and their operation on both TI and IBM hardware.

Chapter 7 provides information on several advanced features and topics of the PC Scheme system, including garbage collection, fast-load and autoloaded files, and linking to DOS.

Chapter 8 contains a complete list of error messages, along with descriptions of their meanings and suggestions for corrective action.

Chapter 9 describes the machine and implementation constraints that limit the maximum program and data sizes that can be accommodated by the system.

Appendix A presents a Scheme session where you execute TI Scheme expressions in order to familiarize yourself with the Scheme language and unique features of PC Scheme.

Appendix B explains some of the functions associated with the %GRAPHICS primitive.

GETTING STARTED 2

This chapter tells you how to install PC Scheme on your computer and begin to use it.

Installation

2.1   The PC Scheme system is packaged on one disk. You must execute an installation program to load PC Scheme onto your system before using it. The following paragraphs present the procedures for installing PC Scheme according to the type of drives you have. Note that you do not need to create back-up installation diskettes because the installation diskette itself serves as a back-up.

Installing PC Scheme on a Winchester Disk System

2.1.1   Use the following installation procedure if you have a Winchester drive.

1. Insert the PC Scheme Installation diskette in disk drive A and close the drive door.

2. Enter the command

   `a:install d: \`*directory* `W`

   where `d:` is the designation for the Winchester disk drive that is to contain the PC Scheme system and *directory* is the name of the directory under which you want to place PC Scheme. If *directory* does not already exist, it will be created. If *directory* does exist, DOS prints an error message, but you can ignore it. Note that there is a space between the disk drive designation and the backslash preceding the PC Scheme directory name. The third parameter (W) must be present to indicate that you are installing PC Scheme onto a Winchester.

3. Follow the instructions that appear on the screen during the interactive execution of the installation command.

4. When the installation program concludes, the message `Installation of PC Scheme is complete` is displayed on the screen. The installation procedure has put the version of PC Scheme for conventional memory on your Winchester.

You also may want to create other directories to contain your Scheme program and data files. PCS may be executed with any of these files as your current directory if you add the PC Scheme system directory to your PATH declaration. This is done with the DOS PATH command, which is the way you specify which directories are to be searched when trying to execute a DOS command. For example, if you have installed PC Scheme in the directory \pcs, you would enter the following command:

```
path ...; \pcs
```

This command requests that DOS search \pcs, as well as the other directories you have specified previously.

Installing PC Scheme on a Dual Diskette System

2.1.2 The installation procedure builds the disks for the conventional memory version of PC Scheme only.

1. Prepare three diskettes by using the DOS FORMAT command.

2. Insert the PC Scheme Installation diskette in disk drive A and close the drive door.

3. Place a formatted diskette in disk drive B and close the drive door.

4. Enter the following command:

```
a:install b: \ F
```

Note that there is a space between the disk drive designation and the backslash. The third parameter (F) must be present to indicate that you are installing PC Scheme onto floppy diskettes.

5. Follow the instructions that appear on the screen during the interactive execution of the installation command.

6. When the installation program concludes, the message `Installation of PC Scheme is complete` is displayed on the screen.

7. Ensure that the disks are labeled as follows:

`PCS Boot Diskette for Conventional Memory.`

`PCS Autoload Diskette`

`PCS Sources Diskette`

Execution

2.2 If you are using a floppy-only system, first insert the PCS Boot Disk (which you created during the installation procedure) into the default disk drive.

You execute the PC Scheme system by entering the following command:

PCS

As PC Scheme starts to load, it displays a banner message on the screen. The initial loading of the PC Scheme compiler and run-time systems take approximately 8 seconds on IBM-AT-class machines, after which the [1] prompt appears, followed by the cursor. Whenever the cursor appears, PC Scheme is waiting for keyboard input.

The display on the screen is divided initially into two rectangular areas called windows. The single-line window at the bottom of the screen is called the *status line*, or status window, and displays system status information. The large window occupying the rest of the screen is called the *console*. The console is the default window in which all input and output occurs.

If you are using a floppy-only system, remove the PCS Boot Disk from the default disk drive and replace it with the PCS Autoload Disk after the [1] prompt is displayed. This disk, or a copy of it, must remain in the drive throughout the PCS session to allow the system to access procedures and other definitions that are autoloaded as needed (see the paragraph entitled Autoloading).

You can now enter any valid Scheme expression for evaluation. As you type, you may edit the line of input characters using the function and arrow keys in a manner similar to the DOS line editor. The following table summarizes the keys used to edit a single command line. After you type the expression to be evaluated, press the RETURN key.

Key	Meaning
F3	Recalls the last command entered
F5	Stores the current command into the keyboard buffer and clears the input line
→	Recalls the next character from the keyboard buffer
←	Backspaces over the last character typed
INS	Inserts characters into the keyboard buffer
DEL	Deletes characters from the keyboard buffer

The break key may be used at any time to interrupt the system and enter the PC Scheme debugger. On the TIPC, hold down the SHIFT key and press the BRK/PAUS key. On the IBM PC, hold down the CTRL key and press the Scroll Lock key. Similarly, the pause key may be used to suspend output to the screen temporarily. On the TIPC, press the BRK/PAUS key. On the IBM PC, hold down the CTRL key and press the Num Lock key. To resume output to the screen after suspending it with the pause key, press any key.

The break key may be used to interrupt output operations, such as the printing of a circularly linked list. However, when an output operation is interrupted using the break key, the remainder of the output for that operation is lost. Read operations must read a complete syntactic object before the break key is acknowledged. Therefore, you must enter at least one character on the current line and press the RETURN key before the interrupt is serviced (if you are typing in a character string, you must enter the closing double quote (") before pressing the RETURN key).

Expressions typed in at the console are evaluated in the context of a global environment called the *user initial environment*. This environment frame is initially empty but becomes populated in time with the definitions that you enter. Environment-extending operations like LET and LAMBDA that you type in at the top level create new environment frames that are nested within the user initial environment.

The user initial environment frame is itself nested within an environment called the *user global environment*, the environment in which the standard PC Scheme variables are bound. New definitions at the top level are added to the user initial environment.

The variables USER-INITIAL-ENVIRONMENT and USER-GLOBAL-ENVIRONMENT are bound in the user global environment to the corresponding environment objects.

Unlike SETQ in most dialects of LISP, SET! in Scheme is used only to modify already bound variables and is unable to define new ones. At the top level, DEFINE may be used to define new variables or to modify existing ones. Restricting SET! in this way helps catch typing and spelling errors.

To leave PC Scheme and return to DOS, enter the following command:

(EXIT)

If you have not read the *TI Scheme Language Reference Manual — Student Edition* yet, please do so at this time. Many of the features of Scheme are different from those of other LISP dialects you may know already.

Loading and Compiling Files

2.2.1 Although PC Scheme is primarily an interactive system, the development of non-trivial programs quickly becomes impossible without the ability to save programs and data on disk as files. A source file is a disk file containing one or more Scheme expressions. Source files may be created with the EDWIN editor[1] or any editor of your choice. The PC Scheme (LOAD *source-file*) operation reads and evaluates the expressions in *source-file* exactly as if they had been typed in at the console.

It is desirable to divide a large source file containing a program under development into several smaller files. As changes are made with EDWIN, only the changed files need to be reloaded for testing.

After the contents of a source file have stabilized, you may want to compile it into object-file form to speed up the loading process. To create an object file, use the following Scheme procedure:

(COMPILE-FILE *source-file object-file*)

where *source-file* is a string[2] that names the source file to be compiled, and *object-file* is a string that names the file to which the compiled expressions in *source-file* are to be written. The COMPILE-FILE procedure overwrites any previous contents of *object-file*.

COMPILE-FILE reads each expression in *source-file*, evaluates it, and writes its compiled form to *object-file*. The expressions in the source file are evaluated as they are compiled to ensure that each expression is compiled in the proper environment of macro and global variable bindings.

Compiled files also may be converted to *fast-load* format, as described in the chapter of this manual entitled Advanced Features. The LOAD procedure can load files of all three kinds—source, object, and fast-load—with the last being significantly faster.

You should use the following extensions when naming files:

.so — Scheme object

.fsl — fast-load

Also, the extension *.app* is reserved, so **do not** use it when naming a file.

---

[1] The EDWIN editor also allows you to evaluate expressions directly from an edit buffer without necessarily writing them to a file first.

[2] The file name must be bracketed between double quotes (" ") and any backslash characters (\) that are part of the file name must be typed in twice.

Autoloading   **2.2.2** Only the essential and most frequently used features of PC Scheme are loaded into memory during the initial program load. Others, including the pretty-printer, EDWIN, the transcendental math routines, and so on, are autoloaded as needed. This generally saves space since, for example, many features needed during program development are unnecessary for end-user execution of an application. The system autoload files are installed on the standard PC Scheme system directory by the procedure specified in the paragraph entitled Installation.

(The SCOOPS system is the one system file that cannot be autoloaded. To use SCOOPS, you first must load the file *SCOOPS.FSL*.)

Autoloading may be confusing initially because of the additional delay caused when the disk is accessed to bring definitions into memory. Mysterious run-time errors will arise if the system autoload files are removed from the standard PC Scheme system directory or if the diskette containing that directory in a floppy-only system has been removed from the drive.

The chapter in this manual entitled Advanced Features explains how to set up your own files for automatic loading on demand.

Customization

2.3 You can control PC Scheme's initial program load at many levels, ranging from fully automatic to complete manual control.

When PC Scheme is invoked, up to three initialization files are loaded, each one controlling a different aspect of initialization. These three files are:

COMPILER.APP
PATCH.PCS
SCHEME.INI

Only the .APP file is required. An .APP file is a fast-load file containing the predefined system functions and is used to bootstrap PC Scheme to the point where the top-level read-eval-print loop becomes active. PC Scheme will search the DOS path for the .APP file and will abort and return to DOS if it cannot find the file.

After locating the .APP file, PC Scheme loads PATCH.PCS. This file, if it exists (and it need not) must reside in the same directory in which the .APP file was found. PATCH.PCS contains expressions in source, object, or fast-load formats. Source and object expressions can be freely intermixed, but the entire file must be in fast-load format if any part of it is; however, the file can LOAD other files in any of the three formats. The expressions are executed in the context of the user global environment.

Finally, PC Scheme loads the .INI file. This file, if it exists (and it need not) is in the current directory. It contains expressions in source, object, or fast-load formats. Source and object expressions can be freely intermixed, but the entire file must be in fast-load format if any part of it is; however, the file can LOAD other files in any of the three formats. The expressions are executed in the context of the user initial environment.

After the .INI file is loaded, a SCHEME-RESET is done, making the top-level read-eval-print loop active.

Normally, all the files listed above are loaded automatically by PC Scheme when you type only PCS at the command line. Alternate ways of invoking PC Scheme allow you to override the default initialization files with other files and also let you give command-line arguments to your functions.

The full syntax of the PCS command line is:

PCS   *files arg1 ...*

The *files* argument is either one filename or up to three filenames inside parentheses. The filenames must be in either the current directory or be completely specified pathnames. .APP files must have those extensions to be overridden. A filename that does not end in .APP is taken to be the override of the .INI file. If such a file does not exist, no error occurs and SCHEME.INI is not loaded. The PATCH.PCS file cannot be overridden.

An *arg* is a group of characters delimited by blanks or by parentheses that are themselves delimited by blanks. Each element of the command line, *files* and *args* becomes a string and is grouped together into a list that becomes the value of the variable PCS-INITIAL-ARGUMENTS. Its value can be examined by PATCH.PCS and/or an .INI or equivalent file.

Although the syntax of the command line may look somewhat Scheme-like because parentheses can be used to group items together into one argument, other aspects of Scheme parsing are missing. Special reader features, such as quasiquote syntax or backslash handling are not present. Nevertheless, simple usage of the arguments likely can be treated as string representations of Scheme expressions. For example, if A, B, and C represent flags of some kind, the following shows one way these may be captured in Scheme:

The command line invocation: `PCS my.ini (a b c)`.

PCS-INITIAL-ARGUMENTS gets the value `("my.ini" "(a b c)")`

A function in MY.INI executes the following expression:

`(read (open-input-string (cadr pcs-initial-arguments)))`

with the result being a list of three symbols:

`--> (A B C)`

DEBUGGING

PC Scheme provides several interactive facilities to aid in the debugging of Scheme programs. Among these facilities are the ability to trace calls to procedures, set breakpoints, and inspect the environment at breakpoints. The four principal components of the system relative to debugging are the top-level *Read-Eval-Print* loop, the Inspector, the error handler, and the set of program advisory procedures. This chapter explains how these components interact with each other and with the user.

The Scheme Evaluator

3.1 The user's primary interface with the PC Scheme system is through the top-level *Read-Eval-Print* (or REP) loop, which reads expressions from the console, evaluates them in the current global environment, and prints the results. The evaluation mechanism for Scheme is embodied in the procedure EVAL, which computes and returns the value of an expression in a specified environment. Earlier versions of PC Scheme implemented EVAL in terms of the compiler. All arguments to EVAL were compiled, with the resulting code then executed. Beginning with version 3.0, EVAL was modified to be partially interpretive and partially compiled. In particular, arguments to EVAL are interpreted until an expression containing a lambda-binding construct is encountered, at which time the compiler will be called because it can perform a more thorough job. This mixed strategy of evaluation will result in better execution performance for relatively straight-forward operations such as variable value lookups and function application.

For compiled expressions, it is possible to control the degree of optimization performed by the compiler by manipulating the values of the system variables PCS-DEBUG-MODE, PCS-INTEGRATE-INTEGRABLES, PCS-INTEGRATE-PRIMITIVES, and PCS-INTEGRATE-T-AND-NIL.

The value of PCS-DEBUG-MODE controls whether debugging information is collected and stored with compiled object code. When PCS-DEBUG-MODE is *false*, only the names of procedures that can be called externally[1] are stored with the object code. When it is set to *true*, all procedures are compiled with both names and source code information, and optimization is disabled.[2] The system variables PCS-INTEGRATE-INTEGRABLES, PCS-INTEGRATE-PRIMITIVES, and PCS-INTEGRATE-T-AND-NIL also may be reset to *false* to disable their associated compiler optimizations.

---

[1] These procedures are also known as "full closures" because a closure object must be created for them at run time. When optimization is enabled, the compiler often can avoid generating code to create closures for procedures that are accessible only from within an expression.

[2] Expressions compiled with optimization disabled typically execute three or four times slower but are easier to debug because the compiler is not as free to rearrange the way the expression is executed.

The standard top-level REP loop begins execution immediately after the PC Scheme system is loaded by prompting you for input with a sequentially assigned command number within brackets. Thus, the first prompt is " [1] ". At top level, you may refer to a previously entered expression with the procedure %C, whose argument is the command number for that expression. Similarly, the value returned for a previously entered expression may be accessed with the procedure %D. This can be helpful if you forget to assign the result of a calculation to a variable.

For example:

```
[1] (+ 2 2)              ;  enter an expression
4
[2] (%c 1)              ;  recall the input to the first prompt
(+ 2 2)
[3] (%d 1)              ;  recall the value returned
4
[4] (eval (%c 1))       ;  re-evaluate the input to the first prompt
4
```

You can specify your own top-level REP loop by rebinding the fluid identifier SCHEME-TOP-LEVEL. The new loop remains in effect until the procedure SCHEME-RESET is invoked.

During the evaluation of a program, invoking EXIT, RESET, or SCHEME-RESET terminates execution immediately. EXIT lets you leave the system and returns to DOS. The others abandon the current computation and return to the top-level REP loop; RESET returns to the current top-level loop, which is bound to (FLUID SCHEME-TOP-LEVEL), while SCHEME-RESET invokes the standard top-level loop that was in effect when the system first started. SCHEME-RESET also discards the command history that can be accessed by the %C and %D procedures.

The Inspector

3.2 The Inspector is a PC Scheme system program that interacts with the user to investigate the context, or state, of a program at an arbitrary breakpoint. It may be entered directly by invoking the procedure INSPECT or indirectly due to error traps or breakpoints that are set by the programmer, as described in the paragraph entitled Breakpoints.

The context at a breakpoint in a program's execution includes the current environment in which identifiers are looked up, the point of execution, and the trace of unreturned procedure calls to that point. For reasons of efficiency, PC Scheme does not provide resolution below the level of a procedure, so the interesting components at a breakpoint are the procedure that is executing, the user who called it, and the current environment.

The Inspector uses a keystroke-driven REP loop, where each command is a single keystroke that is acted upon immediately. A summary of these commands is listed in the following table and may be obtained by pressing "?" in response to the Inspector's prompt.

Command	Description
?	Display this command summary
!	Reinitialize INSPECT
CTRL-A	Display All environment frame bindings
CTRL-B	Display procedure call Backspace
CTRL-C	Display the Current Environment frame bindings
CTRL-D	Move Down to callee's stack frame
CTRL-E	Edit a variable's binding
CTRL-G	Go (resume execution)
CTRL-I	Evaluate one expression and Inspect the result
CTRL-L	List the current procedure
CTRL-M	Repeat the breakpoint Message
CTRL-P	Move to the Parent environment's frame
CTRL-Q	Quit (RESET to top level)
CTRL-R	Return from BREAK with a value
CTRL-S	Move to the Son environment's frame
CTRL-U	Move Up to the caller's stack frame
CTRL-V	EValuate one expression in the current environment
CTRL-W	Where (Display the current stack frame)

Most of the commands are entered as *control characters*; therefore, the command listed as CTRL-A in the table is entered by holding down the CTRL key while pressing the A key. The "?" and "!" commands are not entered with the CTRL key. The space bar can be pressed as a convenient alternative to entering the CTRL-V command.

Errors that occur inside the Inspector do not cause PCS to invoke a new copy of the Inspector. Instead, PCS resumes execution at the top of the existing Inspector's REP loop.

The Lexical Environment

3.2.1 Each point of execution in a Scheme program is associated with an environment in which variables are bound. PC Scheme environments are structured in contours called *frames*, which mirror the nested levels of binding constructs in the program (such as LAMBDA and LET). When a breakpoint occurs, the Inspector establishes the environment at the breakpoint as the Current Environment. If the code at the breakpoint was compiled in debug mode (PCS-DEBUG-MODE was set to true), you can access all of the variables whose scope includes the breakpoint. If debug mode was not used, only a subset, or perhaps none, of the variables is accessible because of compiler optimization.

The contents of the innermost frame of the Current Environment may be displayed with the CTRL-C (Current) command. The contents of all of the frames of the Current Environment may be displayed with the CTRL-A (All) command. In listing the bindings in a frame, the Inspector conserves space on the screen by denoting pairs and lists as "-- list --" and vectors as "-- vector --". You may stop the listing as it is scrolling simply by pressing any key on the keyboard.

The CTRL-V (EValuate) command allows you to enter a single expression, which is evaluated in the Current Environment. The result is "pretty-printed." The Current Environment may be modified or extended by entering expressions containing side-effecting forms like SET!, DEFINE, and SET-CAR!. For convenience, you also may press the space bar instead of entering the CTRL-V command.

A value can also be edited with the CTRL-E (Edit) command, which invokes the structure editor EDIT described in the paragraph entitled The Structure Editor. If the argument to the CTRL-E command evaluates to a closure object that has been compiled in debug mode, the source for the procedure is edited and the result recompiled. If the argument is an identifier, it is rebound to the value returned from EDIT.

The *parent* of an environment frame is the frame immediately enclosing it in scope. The CTRL-P (Parent) command resets the Current Environment to the parent of the existing Current Environment. This is useful when the value of an identifier in a higher lexical level is needed and is masked by a rebinding of the identifier in the Current Environment. The CTRL-S (Son) command restores the environment that was in effect prior to the most recent unrestored CTRL-P command. These two commands allow you to move up and down the relevant branch of the environment tree at will. The '!' (pronounced "bang") command reinitializes the Inspector to the context in effect (except for intervening side effects) when it was first invoked. This includes resetting the Current Environment to its initial value.

To inspect other environments besides those reachable with the CTRL-P or CTRL-S commands, the Inspector can be invoked recursively on arbitrary environment objects with the CTRL-I (Inspect) command. This command prompts you for an expression that evaluates (in the Current Environment) to either an environment object or a closure object from which an environment may be extracted and then calls INSPECT with that value. When the recursive invocation of the Inspector is exited with a CTRL-G command, the existing Inspector and its context is resumed.

The Dynamic Call Stack

3.2.2 The *call stack* is a record of all the procedure invocations in the current execution that have not yet been completed. A procedure invocation is initiated when the procedure is called and is completed when the procedure is exited[3]. Like environments, which are structured as lexically scoped frames of bindings, the call stack is a sequence of dynamically entered frames of runtime information. The Inspector provides several commands for examining the call stack to determine where a breakpoint has occurred and how the program got to that point.

---

[3] By definition, a tail recursive call exits the calling procedure and therefore completes its invocation. Therefore, tail recursive calls have iterative behavior in Scheme and result in no net growth of the stack.

The CTRL-W (Where?) command displays the current call stack frame by printing the name of the called procedure, if known, and the contents of the innermost frame of the environment over which the procedure was closed at its creation. This environment is often different from the Current Environment at the breakpoint, since breakpoints often occur within the scope of the procedure's argument variables or other nested environment frames. CTRL-W is somewhat analogous to the CTRL-C command but should not be confused with it. CTRL-W displays the environment closed over by the called procedure, but CTRL-C displays the possibly nested environment in effect at the breakpoint.

The CTRL-L (List) command lists the source representation for the procedure associated with the current call stack frame. This information is stored with the procedure if it is compiled in debug mode. If the information is not available, the CTRL-L command merely prints the representation of the closure object itself, which appears as #<PROCEDURE name>.

A backtrace of all the call frames on the dynamic call stack is produced by the CTRL-B (Backtrace) command. The backtrace lists the names, where known, of the procedures involved in the sequence of calls but omits the listing of environment bindings for clarity.

The commands CTRL-U (Up) and CTRL-D (Down) move up and down the dynamic call stack. CTRL-U moves to the frame of the caller of the current frame, and CTRL-D moves to the frame invoked from the current frame. When you move up, the Current Environment is rebound to the environment in effect at the time of the call; it is restored when the corresponding move down occurs. Thus, the CTRL-U and CTRL-D commands can be used with the CTRL-P and CTRL-S commands to examine the environments in effect at all levels of the dynamic call stack. In addition to restoring the original environment, the "!" command also restores the Inspector's context to the original call frame in which the breakpoint occurred.

Miscellaneous Commands

3.2.3   There are three commands that leave the Inspector and resume execution: Go, Return, and Quit.

The CTRL-G (Go) command attempts to continue execution from the point at which the breakpoint occurred. This may not be possible if the breakpoint was caused by a call to the ERROR special form or if the condition that caused the breakpoint to occur has not been corrected. Also, CTRL-G terminates a current invocation of the Inspector (which was initiated with CTRL-I) and returns you to the previous invocation.

The CTRL-R (Return) command is similar to CTRL-G but returns a specified value from a procedure call that has been trapped into the Inspector by a BREAK, BREAK-ENTRY, or BREAK-EXIT. When CTRL-R is used, the value you specify when prompted for an expression to be evaluated is returned instead of the value the "broken" routine would have returned.

The CTRL-Q (Quit) command invokes RESET, thus terminating not only the Inspector but also the current execution cycle in the top-level REP loop. You also can leave the Inspector by entering the CTRL-V command and evaluating a SCHEME-RESET or EXIT procedure call.

The CTRL-M (Message) command reminds you of the error or breakpoint message that was displayed when the Inspector was invoked. There is no message to be displayed when the Inspector is called explicitly.

Breakpoints

3.3 A *breakpoint* is a point in a program where execution is halted because of an error condition or a programmer-specified trap. The handling of breakpoints is necessarily implementation-dependent and, therefore, is not prescribed by the Scheme standard. The implementation in PC Scheme uniformly suspends execution, displays an informative message, and invokes the Inspector. In most cases, the Inspector can execute in the lexical environment that was in effect at the point of the break and has access to its dynamic call frame.

You can set an unconditional breakpoint at any point in your program with the special form (BKPT *message irritant*), which displays its arguments and enters the Inspector. When the CTRL-G command is entered to leave the Inspector, BKPT returns an unspecified value and execution continues. The CTRL-R command cannot be used to return from BKPT.

Similarly, the special form (ASSERT *predicate message* . . .) sets a conditional break-point. If *predicate* evaluates to *false*, a breakpoint occurs, the messages are evaluated and displayed, and the Inspector is entered; otherwise, execution continues. When the CTRL-G command is entered to leave the Inspector, ASSERT returns an unspecified value and execution continues. The CTRL-R command cannot be used to return from ASSERT.

The special form (ERROR *message* exp_1 exp_2 . . .) is similar to BKPT but signals an unrecoverable error. You cannot proceed from this kind of breakpoint with the Inspector's CTRL-G or CTRL-R command.

The special forms BKPT, ASSERT, and ERROR are macros defined in terms of the procedures BREAKPOINT-PROCEDURE, ASSERT-PROCEDURE, and ERROR-PROCEDURE, respectively.

A breakpoint occurs when errors such as division by zero occur within the lower levels of the PC Scheme system itself. The effect is either that of BKPT or ERROR, depending on whether the error is recoverable. The Inspector's CTRL-G command may be used in some cases to resume execution after these errors, depending on their severity. However, you cannot proceed from this kind of breakpoint with the CTRL-R command.

To define your own error handler for PC Scheme errors, you must rebind the global variable *USER-ERROR-HANDLER* to a procedure of four arguments. When bound to such a procedure, *USER-ERROR-HANDLER* will be called by the system instead of the normal system error. This enables the user error handler to trap errors and provide diagnostics or error recovery. The arguments are as follows:

- *error-number* — When non-nil, *error-number* will contain a number that can be useful in distinguishing some of the more frequent errors. In particular, all the DOS I/O errors will be represented. Error-number codes from 1 through 88 indicate DOS I/O error return codes. The error numbers shown below contain the corresponding error message in *error-msg*. The numbers between 1 and 88 that are not shown below will contain the general message "DOS I/O error number *xx*" (where *xx* is the DOS I/O error return code) in *error-msg*. For more information on the error return codes, see the chapter entitled Error Messages. Error numbers 100 and 200 are currently the only error codes above 88.

```
  2 — "DOS I/O error - File not found"
  3 — "DOS I/O error - Path not found"
  4 — "DOS I/O error - Too many open files"
  5 — "DOS I/O error - Access denied"
 12 — "DOS I/O error - Invalid access"
 16 — "DOS I/O error - Invalid disk drive"
 19 — "DOS I/O error - Disk write protected"
 21 — "DOS I/O error - Drive not ready"
 28 — "DOS I/O error - Printer out of paper"
100 — "User keyboard interrupt"
200 — "DOS I/O error - Disk Full"
```

CAUTION: Error-number 100 is the only error that is restartable. All others should be aborted through the procedure RESET or handled through your own error recovery system. Failure to handle the errors as such can cause catastrophic failure of Scheme, which may either return to DOS or require a system reboot.

- *irritant* — This argument will contain the Scheme object that caused the error.

- *error-msg* — This argument will contain the error message text for the error encountered.

- *sys-error-handler* — This argument is a procedure of no arguments which, when invoked, calls the normal system error handler (that is, the inspector). This error handler should be invoked for errors that cannot be handled by the user-error-handler.

The following code is an example of an error handler for I/O errors. The function my-open-input-file attempts to open filename for input. Note that a continuation is saved in the fluid variable my%ioerr before the call to *open-input-file*. Upon return from the open, the variable *port* is interrogated, to retry the operation with the same filename, retry the operation with a different filename, or return the port object. *USER-ERROR-HANDLER* has been designed to trap on all I/O errors, pop up a window to indicate the error, and elicit a response from the user. The result is then returned via the continuation bound to the fluid variable my%ioerr. The system error handler is called for all other errors.

```
(define (my-open-input-file filename)
  (let ((port (call/cc
                (fluid-lambda (my%ioerr) (open-input-file filename)))))
    (cond ((eq? port 'retry)
           (my-open-input-file filename))
          ((string? port)
           (my-open-input-file port))
          (else
           port))))

(set! (access *user-error-handler* user-global-environment)
 (lambda (error-num error-msg irritant sys-error-handler)
   (if (and (number? error-number)
            (>= error-number 1)
            (<= error-number 88))
       (let ((win (make-window error-msg #t))
             (result '()))
         (window-set-position! win 10 10)
         (window-set-size! win 6 50)
         (window-set-cursor! win 2 5)
         (window-popup win)
         (case error-number
           ((2 3)                                ;file/path not found
            (display "File/Path not found : " win)
            (display irritant win)
            (newline win)
            (display "Enter new pathname (or return to exit) - " win)
            (set! result (read-line win))
            (if (string=? result "")
                (set! result '())))
           ((21)                                 ;drive not ready
            (display "Drive not ready - Retry (y/n)?" win)
            (set! result
                  (if (char=? (char-upcase (read-char win)) #\Y)
                      'retry
                      '())))
           (else
            (display "Extended Dos I/O Error - " win)
            (display irritant win)
            (newline win)
            (newline win)
            (char-upcase (read-char win))
            (set! result '())))
         (window-popup-delete win)
         ((fluid my%ioerr) result))
       ;else
       (sys-error-handler))))
```

Advisory Procedures

3.4 You can modify the effect of a call to a procedure by *advising* the procedure with the facilities described in this chapter. These facilities are powerful debugging aids capable of implementing dynamic tracing and breakpointing of calls as well as other arbitrary actions.

The *advice* given to a procedure is itself a procedure that is invoked whenever the advised procedure is called. With the procedure call (ADVISE-ENTRY *proc advice*), the procedure *advice* is called every time the procedure *proc* is entered. Similarly, ADVISE-EXIT causes its advice to be invoked whenever a procedure is exited. Advice may be removed from a procedure with UNADVISE-ENTRY, UNADVISE-EXIT, and UNADVISE. The first two remove all advice at entry or exit from a procedure, while UNADVISE removes all advice from both.

The standard procedures TRACE-ENTRY and TRACE-EXIT are used to define advice that traces procedure calls upon entry or exit. The standard procedures BREAK-ENTRY and BREAK-EXIT are used to define advice that sets breakpoints upon entry or exit from calls. In addition, TRACE-BOTH sets trace advice, and BREAK-BOTH sets breakpoints upon both entering and exiting a procedure. TRACE and BREAK are short names for TRACE-ENTRY and BREAK-ENTRY, respectively. UNTRACE-ENTRY and UNTRACE-EXIT remove trace advice upon entering or exiting a procedure. UNTRACE removes both. UNBREAK-ENTRY, UNBREAK-EXIT, and UNBREAK remove breakpoint advice.

You can add advice to a procedure from within the Inspector by using the Inspector's CTRL-V command. This command is often the only convenient way to advise procedures that are lexically hidden within other procedure definitions.

You may notice extra call frames when backtracing an advised procedure. They are identified with the advised procedure's name, but they actually correspond to routines that apply the advice. Although this may be confusing, it does not impair the execution of your program. Note that unadvising a procedure from the Inspector while that procedure is in execution may have undesirable consequences and should be avoided.

The procedures *PROC*, *ARGS*, and *RESULT* may be evaluated from within the Inspector (using CTRL-V) at entry and exit breakpoints caused by BREAK, BREAK-BOTH, BREAK-ENTRY, and BREAK-EXIT. The *PROC* procedure pretty prints the procedure that was broken, the *ARGS* procedure returns its list of arguments, and the *RESULT* procedure returns the value of the call (BREAK-EXIT only). The CTRL-R command returns a user-supplied value from a broken procedure.

The Pretty-Printer

3.5 The PC Scheme pretty-printer is another useful debugging tool. The procedure PP prints its argument as WRITE does, with strings enclosed in double quotation marks, characters preceded with the '#\' prefix, and symbols appropriately "backslashed." However, PP attempts to display the expression with additional line breaks and indentation to improve its readability.

Unlike WRITE, the pretty-printer attempts to print the source form for a procedure when given its compiled closure object as an argument. However, the source is available only for procedures compiled in debug mode.

Performance Testing

3.6 The rate at which PCS executes Scheme code depends on several factors, many of which are under the programmer's control. PCS evaluates an expression by compiling it and executing the resulting low-level code. The size and speed of the compiled code are affected primarily by the programmer's choice of programming paradigms and algorithms and whether or not PCS-DEBUG-MODE is set to true. Programs compiled with PCS-DEBUG-MODE set to *true* are typically larger and up to four times slower than normal.

The following procedure measures the execution speed of a Scheme expression:

```
(define timer
  (lambda (thunk number-of-iterations)
    (let ((time0 (runtime)))
      (do ((counter 1 (+ counter 1)))
          ((>? counter number-of-iterations)
           (/ (- (runtime) time0) 100.0))
        (thunk)))))
```

TIMER computes the number of seconds needed to execute a given expression a given number of times. It evaluates the expression by invoking a procedure of no arguments (a *thunk*) that contains the expression as its body. For example, to compute the time needed for *n* evaluations of the expression *exp*. the call would be (timer (lambda () exp) n). The overhead costs associated with the invocation of the thunk and other costs of the looping code inside TIMER can be determined by calling TIMER for the same number of iterations of a trivial thunk, as in (timer (lambda () #F) n). A large number of iterations may be needed to obtain a meaningful estimate of the cost to evaluate simple expressions, since the PC Scheme RUNTIME procedure is capable of only 100 millisecond precision, and the overhead is on the order of one millisecond.

Timing figures should be gathered and interpreted carefully. The execution rate of a program compiled with PCS-DEBUG-MODE set to *true* is especially misleading since compiling in debug mode affects different language features in different ways.

Timing results also may be skewed by garbage collections and autoloading of definitions. Running a test several times and discarding the time whenever the Garbage Collecting message appears prevents the first problem. The second is solved by ignoring the results for the first test, which forces into memory all referenced variables that are autoloaded.

Compiler optimization also may give misleading results. Consider the following thunk:

```
(lambda ()
  (car x)
  (cdr x)
  (cadr x)
  (caddr x))
```

Timing this thunk to ascertain the average execution time for the four procedures does not work since the compiler knows that none of them have side effects and that all but the last expression in the body may be removed. In addition, the execution speed of a simple expression like (CADDR X), where X is a global variable, is dependent on the time it takes to look up the variable, not on the execution speed of the procedure CADDR, which is an in-line *instruction* in the compiled code.

The Structure Editor

3.7 The PC Scheme structure editor EDIT edits memory-resident data structures and returns their modified values. Unlike more conventional text-oriented editors like EDWIN, a structure editor edits a *tree* comprised of pairs and atoms instead of strings or files of characters. Although a structure editor may be somewhat more difficult to learn and use than a screen-oriented text editor, it has three important advantages. First, it is usually smaller and less likely to run out of memory. Second, it is able to edit circular (self-referential) data structures. Third, structure editors are inherently immune to errors like unbalanced parentheses. The main disadvantage is that the changes made to data with EDIT do not persist across Scheme sessions unless you save them in a file with WRITE. The structure editor should be invoked from within the Inspector. First, invoke the procedure INSPECT and then press CTRL-E to bring up the structure editor.

PC Scheme procedures are compiled objects that cannot be edited by EDIT. However, when debug mode is on (PCS–DEBUG–MODE is set to *true*), a list representation of the procedure is available to the Inspector. Pressing CTRL–E invokes EDIT with this representation, which is then compiled.

Overview

3.7.1 Editing data with EDIT consists of *walking through* the structure and displaying or modifying its nodes, or *elements*. Each element is either a pair or an atom. Pairs are displayed as they would be printed with WRITE, so it is convenient (possibly improper) to think of each pair as representing the entire list that it begins. Each list is the *parent* of the elements within it. For example, the list (A (B C) (D E) . F) is the parent of the elements A, (B C), (D E), and F. However, the structure's top-level element has no parent.

Most of the structure editor's commands refer to the Focus Point (FP), which always points to the Current Element (CE). The FP and CE *always* change together; repositioning the Focus Point simply redefines which subtree of the edited expression is considered the Current Element. The FP points initially to the entire tree passed as the argument to EDIT. The editor executes each command relative to the FP and then displays the CE. If it cannot execute a command, it displays an error message.

Each command is entered on a new line after the editor prompt "EDIT->". Commands that take arguments are entered as a list enclosed in parentheses, similar to a procedure call in Scheme. The command name is entered without parentheses when no arguments are required.

There are two classes of arguments to editor commands. Positioning arguments specify which element of the structure is being addressed by the command and are of the following types:

■ Positive integers, which reference elements of the CE counting from the left. For example, (D E) is the third element from the left of (A (B C) (D E) . F).

- Negative integers, which reference elements of the CE from the right. A "dotted" atomic element, such as Y in (X Y), is not counted in this numbering scheme. For example, (B C) is the second element from the right of (A (B C) (D E) . F).

- Zero, which references the CE itself.

- '*', which references the cdr component of the last pair of the CE. For example, () is referenced when the CE is (A (B C) (D E)), but F is referenced when the CE is (A (B C) (D E) . F). This is the only way to access F, since the other positioning arguments assume that the CE is a proper list.

The other class of command argument is an element value. This type of argument is used in commands for searching and replacing.

The editor commands are grouped into four categories: commands that display the Current Element, commands that reposition the Focus Point, commands that modify the structure, and a command to leave the editor. These categories are discussed in the following paragraphs.

Name	Command	Description
Print	P or '?'	Prints the Current Element
Pretty-Print	PP or '??'	Pretty-Prints the Current Element
Move	integer or '*'	Repositions the Focus Point
Beginning	B	Moves the FP to the parent of the Current Element
Next	N	Moves the FP to the next element to the right
Previous	PR	Moves the FP to the next element to the left
Top	T	Moves the FP to the Top Element
Find	(F *elem*)	Searches for a matching element
Replace	(R *pos elem*)	Replaces an element with a new value
Substitute	(S *elem₁ elem₂*)	Substitutes $elem_2$ for all occurrences of $elem_1$
Delete	(D *pos*)	Deletes the specified element
Delete Parens	(DP *pos*)	Deletes the parentheses surrounding the specified element
Add Parens	(AP *pos₁ pos₂*)	Surrounds the specified sequence of elements with parentheses
Insert Before	(IB *pos elem*)	Inserts a new value before an element
Insert After	(IA *pos elem*)	Inserts a new value after an element
Splice Before	(SB *pos elem*)	Splices new values before an element
Splice After	(SA *pos elem*)	Splices new values after an element
Quit	Q	Returns from the call to EDIT

Displaying the Current Element

3.7.2 The Current Element can be printed or pretty-printed with the following commands.

Print — The Print command is entered as the symbol P or '?', with no arguments. P displays the CE in its entirety with Scheme's WRITE procedure. '?' displays the CE to a level of two and a length of 10, representing elements below level two with the character #\# and elements in a list beyond a length of 10 with ellipses. The following is an example:

```
[1] (edit '(a (b (c) d) e f g h i j k l m n))
(A (B #\# D) E F G H I J K L ...)
EDIT-> p
(A (B (C) D) E F G H I J K L M N)
EDIT-> ?
(A (B #\# D) E F G H I J K L ...)
```

Pretty-Print — The Pretty-Print command is entered as the symbol PP or '??', with no arguments. PP displays the CE in its entirety with PC Scheme's PP procedure. '??' pretty-prints the CE to a level of two and a length of 10, representing elements below level two with the character #\# and elements in a list beyond a length of 10 with ellipses.

```
[1] (edit '(let ((a 1)(b 2))(if x (+ a b)(- a b))))
(LET (#\# #\#)(IF X  #\# #\#))
EDIT-> pp
(LET ((A 1)
      (B 2))
   (IF X (+ A B)(- A B)))
EDIT->   ??
(LET (#\#
      #\#)
   (IF X #\# #\#))
```

Moving and Searching

3.7.3 The FP can be repositioned by specifying a particular move or by searching for a matching element.

Move — The move commands are entered as integer values or as the character '*', with no arguments. It is an error to specify a Move command when the Current Element is not a pair. After the FP is moved, it defines a new Current Element.

A positive integer value *n* moves the FP to the *nth* element from the left in the CE. If n is greater than the number of elements in the CE, the FP is moved to the last element.

```
[1] (edit '(a b c))
(A B C)
EDIT-> 3
C
EDIT-> b
(A B C)
EDIT-> 99
C
```

A negative integer value *n* moves the FP to the *n(th)* element from the right in the CE, ignoring any non-null atomic value in the last cdr of the list. If the magnitude of *n* is greater than the number of elements in the CE, the FP moves to the first element.

```
[1] (edit  '(a b c))
(A B C)
EDIT-> -1
C
EDIT-> b
(A B C)
EDIT-> -99
A
```

The '*' command moves the FP to the cdr component of the last pair of the CE.

```
[1] (edit  '(a b . c))
(A B . C)
EDIT-> *
C
```

Beginning — The *B* command moves the FP to the parent of the CE.

```
[1] (edit  '(a b c))
(A B C)
EDIT-> 3
C
EDIT-> b
(A B C)
```

Next — The *N* command moves the FP to the next element to the right in the parent of the CE. If the FP currently points to the last element of the parent of the CE, the FP does not move.

```
[1] (edit  '(a b c))
(A B C)
EDIT-> 2
B
EDIT-> n
C
EDIT-> n
C
```

Previous — The *PR* command moves the FP to the next element to the left in the parent of the CE. If the FP currently points to the first element of the parent of the CE, the FP does not move.

```
[1] (edit '(a b c))
(A B C)
EDIT-> 2
B
EDIT-> pr
A
EDIT-> pr
 ?      There is no Previous from this position
A
```

Top — The *T* command moves the FP to the top-level element of the structure being edited.

```
[1] (edit '(a b (c d e) f g))
    (A B (C D E) F G)
    EDIT-> 3
    (C D E)
    EDIT-> 2
    D
    EDIT-> t
    (A B (C D E) F G)
```

Find — The (F *elem*) command searches forward in the structure from the FP, looking for an element that matches the argument *elem*, using the Scheme predicate EQUAL?. If no argument is specified, the previous search is continued. If the search is successful, the FP moves to the matched element. Otherwise, the FP does not move. An unsuccessful search through a circular data structure can loop indefinitely until stopped with the break key.

```
[1] (edit '(a b (c d) (c e)))
(A B (C D) (C E))
EDIT-> (f c)
C
EDIT-> b
(C D)
EDIT-> 1
C
EDIT-> f
C
EDIT-> b
(C E)
```

Modifying the Structure

3.7.4 The following commands modify the original data structure given to EDIT with the destructive procedures SET-CAR! and SET-CDR!. If you want to preserve the original structure, make a copy of it before you call EDIT.

Replace — The (R *pos elem*) command replaces the element in the CE specified by *pos* with the new value *elem*. The CE must be a list. The FP does not move.

```
[1] (edit '(a b . c))
(A B . C)
EDIT-> (r 2 (q s))
(A (Q S) . C)
EDIT-> (r * zzz)
(A (Q S) . ZZZ)
```

Substitute — The (S *elem₁ elem₂*) command substitutes the value *elem₂* for all occurrences of *elem₁* in the CE. The FP does not move.

```
[1] (edit '(a b (d c d) f d))
(A B (D C D) F D)
EDIT-> 3
(D C D)
EDIT-> (s d (a b))
((A B) C (A B))
EDIT-> b
(A B (#\# C #\#) F D)
EDIT-> p
(A B ((A B) C (A B)) F D)
```

Delete — The (D *pos*) command deletes the element at the specified position in the CE. If *pos* is '*', the cdr of the last pair in the CE is replaced by the empty list, () ; otherwise, the specified element is destructively *spliced out* of the CE. The CE must be a list. The FP does not move.

```
[1] (edit '(a b c . d))
(A B C . D)
EDIT->   (d *)
(A B C)
EDIT-> (d 2)
(A C)
EDIT-> 2
c
EDIT-> (d 0)
()
EDIT-> b
(A ())
```

Delete Parentheses — The (DP *pos*) command deletes the parentheses surrounding the element at the specified position in the CE. The element must be a proper list. The CE must be a list. The FP does not move.

```
[1] (edit  '(a b (c d) e))
(A B (C D) E)
EDIT-> (dp 3)
(A B C D E)
```

Add Parentheses — The (AP *pos*$_1$ *pos*$_2$) command adds parentheses around the elements between the specified positions in the CE. If *pos*$_1$ is zero or '*', *pos*$_2$ is ignored. Otherwise, *pos*$_1$ must specify the same position as *pos*$_2$ or one that precedes *pos*$_2$. The CE must be a list. The FP does not move.

```
[1] (edit  '(a b c d . e))
(A B C D . E)
EDIT-> (ap 3 -1)
(A B (C D) . E)
EDIT-> (ap *)
(A B (C D) E)
```

Insert Before — The (IB *pos elem*) command inserts *elem* into the CE just before the element specified by *pos*. The value for *pos* may not be zero or '*'. The CE must be a list. The FP does not move.

```
[1] (edit '(a  b  c  d))
(A B C D)
EDIT-> (ib 1 z)
(Z A B C D)
```

Insert After — The (IA *pos elem*) command inserts *elem* into the CE just after the element specified by *pos*. The value for *pos* may not be zero or '*'. The CE must be a list. The FP does not move.

```
[1]  (edit '(a b c d))
(A B C D)
EDIT-> (ia -1 z)
(A B C D Z)
```

Splice Before — The (SB *pos elem*) command splices the proper list *elem* into the CE just before the element specified by *pos*. The value for *pos* may not be zero or '*'. The CE must be a list. The FP does not move.

```
[1] (edit '(a b (c d) e))
(A B (C D) E)
EDIT-> (sb 3 (z z))
(A B Z Z (C D) E)
```

Splice After — The (SA *pos elem*) command splices the proper list *elem* into the CE just after the element specified by *pos*. The value for *pos* may not be zero or '*'. The CE must be a list. The FP does not move.

```
[1] (edit  '(a b (c d) e))
(A B (C D) E)
EDIT-> (sa 3 (z z))
(A B (C D) Z Z E)
```

Leaving the Editor

3.7.5 The Q command leaves the structure editor and returns the top-level value, possibly modified, as the value of the call to EDIT.

THE EDWIN EDITOR

EDWIN is a version of EMACS that was written in Scheme by the Scheme project at MIT. However, the original MIT version has been modified substantially for use with the PC Scheme system. Although the original MIT version and the version available with PC Scheme are very similar, many changes have been made to accommodate the limited capabilities of personal computers. This manual specifically describes the PC Scheme version of EDWIN and may not accurately describe the features or behavior of any other implementation.

EDWIN is an interactive, real-time, display-oriented editor. It features a set of commands that support a variety of text editing operations. This manual assumes that the user is familiar with the concepts of a text editor and is comfortable in an interactive environment. Although this manual does not assume that the user has previous experience with EMACS, it is more a reference than a tutorial.

EDWIN is integrated into the PC Scheme system to allow the user to move freely between PC Scheme (or other applications running in PC Scheme) and the editing environment. It also allows code to be edited and then executed without requiring that it be saved and read in again. However, EDWIN consumes substantial memory resources for its code and data space (often 100K to 200K bytes, depending on the size of the file being edited and the nature of the changes).

The terminology and notation used in this manual are similar to that used in other EMACS documentation.[1]

EDWIN supports the 8-bit ASCII character set, which enables it to handle international characters. This means EDWIN can handle national versions of MS-DOS, such as Swedish and German.

EDWIN treats a personal computer that it does not recognize as an IBM computer.

---

[1] For a more complete description of EMACS, see MIT AI Memo #519 or "EMACS, The Extensible, Customizable, Self–Documenting Display Editor" in the proceedings of the June 1981 SIGPLAN Text Manipulation Symposium. Both are by Richard Stallman, the inventor of EMACS. Where possible, command names have been chosen to be consistent with GNU EMACS by Richard Stallman and UNIX EMACS by James Gosling.

General Concepts 4.1 This paragraph briefly describes some of the basic concepts that are important for understanding EDWIN.

Interactive, Real-time, Display 4.1.1 EDWIN is an interactive, real-time, display-oriented editor. It is interactive in that an edit session consists alternately of commands entered by the user and responses to those commands by EDWIN. It is real-time in that it updates the display frequently (usually after each character entered by the user), thus providing immediate response to user commands. It is a display editor in that the text being edited is displayed on the screen and is updated automatically as the user enters commands.

Edit Buffer 4.1.2 EDWIN performs all editing operations in a buffer. Initially, the buffer is empty. Text may be entered directly in the buffer. It is also possible to *visit* a file, which means the file is loaded into the buffer (replacing whatever is in the buffer at the time). It is also possible to insert text from a file into the buffer at any point without affecting the rest of the buffer's contents. When you want to retain a permanent copy of the current contents of the buffer, it must be saved in a file.

It is important to distinguish between files and the buffer. Files are supported by the operating system and provide permanent storage. The buffer is used by EDWIN to modify the contents of files, but it is temporary. The buffer is lost when you reset EDWIN (exit EDWIN permanently) or when something catastrophic happens such as a power failure or system error. Thus the buffer must be saved at the end of each edit session, and it should also be saved at regular intervals during the session.

Point, Cursor, and Mark 4.1.3 Editing operations, such as inserting and deleting, are done at the current position in the buffer, which is called the *point*. The position of the point is indicated by the cursor. (The cursor may be an inverse video character or an underline, perhaps flashing, depending on the type of display.) When the cursor is *on* a character, it indicates that the point is just before the character. The point is always *between* characters. The character following the point is sometimes said to be "at the point."

Occasionally it is necessary to make note of another position in the buffer besides the point. This is done with the *mark*. The mark may be used to remember the point's current position so that you can return to it later. Also, for some commands it is necessary to indicate a *region* of text that is to be deleted, written to a file, and so forth. The region is taken to be the characters between the point and the mark.

Edit Modes 4.1.4 An editing *mode* adjusts the behavior of the editor to the particular nature of the text being edited. EDWIN supports two modes: *Fundamental mode* and *Scheme mode*.

Fundamental mode is suitable for most editing. *Scheme mode* provides specific support for editing of Scheme or LISP code, including automatic indentation and matching of parentheses. See the paragraph entitled Modes for a more detailed explanation of the two modes.

Types of Commands   **4.1.5** An editing session involves a user entering a series of *commands* (short sequences of keystrokes) that are executed by EDWIN. The five basic types of commands that can be entered are as follows: simple, control, meta, meta-control, and control-x.

Simple commands are entered by typing a single character. Normally, these commands just insert the character into the buffer. However, some may have more complex behavior (e.g., TAB is often used to control indentation).

Control commands are entered by holding down the CTRL key while typing another character. Control commands are notated by the prefix CTRL-; for example, CTRL-F is the notation for holding down the CTRL key while typing F.

Meta commands were originally entered by holding down a META key while typing another character. However, because there is no META key on most keyboards, including the TI BUSINESS-PRO, TIPC and IBM PC, EDWIN's meta commands are entered by either pressing the ESC key or by typing the CTRL-Z prefix and then typing another character. The use of CTRL-Z as an alternative to typing ESC is useful on keyboards where the ESC is inconveniently placed. Meta commands are notated by the prefix *meta-*.

Meta-control commands are entered on most keyboards, including the TIPC and IBM PC, by typing the meta prefix and then holding down the CTRL key while typing another key. Meta-control commands are notated by the prefix *meta-CTRL-*.

Control-x commands are entered by typing CTRL-X as a prefix, so they are always multi-keystroke commands. For example, the command CTRL-X CTRL-S saves a buffer to a file.

It is important to distinguish the control-x commands from the control, meta, and meta-control commands. Control-x commands introduce a general class of extended commands that often require many keystrokes (such as a file name). Control, meta, and control-meta commands usually are related to one another, so it is useful to think of them as an ordered set of modifiers to a basic command. For example, CTRL-F moves forward a character, meta-F moves forward a word, and meta-CTRL-F moves forward an S-expression.

With the exception of the simple commands, EDWIN commands are insensitive to case. Therefore, CTRL-F and CTRL-f invoke the same command.

It is possible to customize the assignment of key sequences to specific commands by calling the procedure REMAP-EDWIN-KEYS after EDWIN has been loaded. REMAP-EDWIN-KEYS is a procedure that takes two arguments: the new key sequence and the old key sequence. The effect is that the new key sequence assumes the function of the old key sequence while within EDWIN (to determine the key codes for particular key sequences, reference the technical reference manual associated with your particular machine). Remapping keys for EDWIN can be performed automatically by including their definitions in the EDWIN.INI file (see the paragraph in this chapter entitled Customizing EDWIN). For examples of remapping the keys for EDWIN, see the example file EDWIN.INI on your autoload diskette.

Remembering Marks and Deleted Information

4.1.6 EDWIN uses *rings* to remember information that may be needed again. The *mark ring* is a circular list of the last 10 marks that have been set. Because it is possible to set the mark to any element of the mark ring, a number of different locations in the buffer can be tracked simultaneously.

The *kill ring* is similar in concept. Rather than recording positions, its contents are text blocks that have been deleted. When a block of text is deleted, EDWIN stores it as an entry in the kill ring so that it can be retrieved, if necessary.

The kill ring is used extensively in EDWIN as the mechanism for copying or moving text from one place to another. There are no commands to move text directly from place to place. Instead, moving is accomplished by killing (deleting) the text that then goes into the kill ring, moving the point to the location where the text is to be placed, and recovering the text from the kill ring. For more information on copying and moving text, see the paragraph entitled Killing and Unkilling.

Using EDWIN

4.2 This paragraph discusses the basic techniques needed to enter, use, and exit from EDWIN.

Entering EDWIN

4.2.1 The EDWIN editor is entered from the Scheme *read-eval-print* loop at any time by invoking the PC Scheme procedure EDWIN with no arguments.

```
(edwin)
```

The PC Scheme console window is saved and replaced by the EDWIN window.

Interacting with EDWIN

4.2.2 To use EDWIN, you should understand how it communicates through the keyboard and display.

The EDWIN Display — EDWIN divides its screen window into three subwindows. The large *Edit Window* displays the visible portion of the buffer. The other two EDWIN windows are each single-line windows. The *Mode Line* displays general information about the buffer's state. The *Echo Area* displays messages and other feedback.

The Edit Window displays a portion of the buffer surrounding the point. As the point is moved around in the buffer, the position of the Edit Window in the buffer is changed, if necessary, to ensure that the point remains within the window. The Edit Window is redisplayed after each command to reflect accurately the contents of the buffer. When the entire buffer fits completely within the Edit Window, it is displayed at the top of the window followed by enough blank lines to fill the window.

The Mode Line is shown in reverse video immediately below the Edit Window. The format of the Mode Line is:

** EDWIN *Version Mode File*

The two asterisks at the beginning of the mode line indicate that the buffer has been modified since it was first read or last saved to a file. If no changes have been made or all changes have been saved, no asterisks are shown. *Version* gives the version number of EDWIN itself. *Mode* tells the current mode (Scheme or Fundamental), and *file* gives the name of the file, if any, associated with the buffer.

The Echo Area window at the bottom of the screen displays prefix characters of multiple-character commands or command arguments if you stop typing for a half-second or longer. The Echo Area is also used to display special messages and to prompt you for the arguments required by some commands.

EDWIN Keyboard Response — Since EDWIN is an interactive, real-time editor, most keystrokes result in an immediate response on the display. It is possible, however, to *type ahead* of EDWIN in some cases, particularly when garbage collection takes place or when EDWIN executes a lengthy command. In these cases, the input is buffered by the operating system. The size of the type-ahead buffer depends on the operating system. When the type-ahead buffer is full, the system beeps and ignores that keystroke.

If you enter several commands rapidly, EDWIN may execute more than one command before updating the display. Although this may make EDWIN's response appear a bit erratic, this grouping of command responses significantly reduces the work that EDWIN must do to keep up with user input. This greatly improves the overall responsiveness of the system.

Lines — Unlike so-called "line-oriented" or "record-oriented" editors, EDWIN views the text in the buffer as a single long string. Embedded in the string are any number of line separators. In EDWIN, a line is a sequence of characters between line separators. Note that a line separator is an operating-system-dependent character or sequence of characters. Even though a line separator may be a sequence of characters (such as a LINEFEED followed by a CARRIAGE RETURN), EDWIN treats the sequence as a single character.

When text is displayed, the occurrence of a line separator causes the text following the line separator to be displayed on the next line of the Edit Window. Inserting a line separator in the middle of a line splits the line into two lines. Deleting a line separator joins two adjacent lines into a single line.

Customizing EDWIN   **4.2.3** EDWIN may be customized in terms of the key assignments and display characteristics by including code in the file EDWIN.INI. Whenever EDWIN is loaded, the system will look in the directory in which PC Scheme was loaded for the file EDWIN.INI. If it exists, it will be loaded and executed before entering EDWIN. See the EDWIN.INI file located on your installation diskette for examples of how to customize EDWIN.

Commands   **4.2.4** The following paragraphs discuss the EDWIN command set. Commands are generally grouped by type and are presented approximately in order of increasing complexity. It is possible for you to do useful editing by starting with the basic editing commands. After you become comfortable with one set of commands, the next (more complex) set can be learned.

The terms *cursor* and *point* are often used interchangeably. In general, the term *cursor* is used in the context of the physical position of text on a screen. The term *point* is used to refer to the underlying position in the buffer. *Cursor* will normally be used when a reference means both the point and the cursor. Remember that the cursor is displayed on top of the character following the point.

A summary of all the commands is given at the end of this chapter.

Exiting from   **4.2.5** The commands to exit EDWIN are as follows:
EDWIN

Command	Description
CTRL-X CTRL-C	Reset EDWIN and return to Scheme
CTRL-X CTRL-Z	Save EDWIN and return to Scheme

Resetting EDWIN before returning to Scheme erases EDWIN data structures, including the buffer and the kill ring, but leaves more free space available for other programs. If the buffer has been modified since it was last saved, you are prompted to save it before EDWIN resets.

Using CTRL-X CTRL-Z to exit to PC Scheme allows you to return to EDWIN at exactly the same point in the editing session.

Basic Editing   **4.2.6** The basic editing commands are the simplest commands. They allow
Commands   the user to insert and erase text, move the cursor around, perform simple file I/O, and abort other commands.

Inserting and Deleting Text — The simplest commands for inserting and deleting text are as follows:

Command	Description
Any printing character	Insert character before point
CTRL-Q	Quote insert character (such as TAB)
BACKSPACE	Erase previous character
CTRL-T	Transpose characters

To insert a printing character at the point, just type the character. The cursor and all the text to its right (on the same line) move one position to the right. Thus characters appear to be inserted *before* the cursor. For example, assume the current line is 'PQSTUV' and the cursor is positioned on the 'S'. If you type an 'R', the line reads 'PQRSTUV', with the cursor still positioned on the 'S'.

To delete the character to the left of the cursor, press the BACKSPACE (or CTRL-H) key. The cursor and all the text to its right (on the same line) move to the left one space. For example, the current line is 'PQRSTUV' and the cursor is positioned on the 'S'. If you press BACKSPACE, the line becomes 'PQSTUV'.

To insert non-printing characters (control, TAB, and BACKSPACE characters) into the text, type CTRL-Q followed by the non-printing character to be inserted. CTRL-Q is the *quote* command that causes the next character input to be accepted without further interpretation. Control characters are displayed in the text by a two-character sequence. A caret (^) is followed by the appropriate identifying character.

To transpose two characters use the CTRL-T command.[2] The CTRL-T command transposes the character before the point with the character after the point. If the point is at the end of a line, CTRL-T transposes the two preceding characters.

Simple Cursor Movement — There are several commands for moving one position left, right, up or down.

---

[2] In larger versions of EMACS, there is a whole set of transpose commands. In this version of EDWIN, higher level transpose commands have not been implemented in order to conserve space.

Command	Description
CTRL-F	Move forward one character (→)
CTRL-B	Move backward one character (←)
CTRL-N	Move down one line (↓)
CTRL-P	Move up one line (↑)

CTRL-F moves the point (cursor) one character forward, and CTRL-B moves the point one character backward. (Recall that the end of a line is treated as a single character; for example, a CTRL-F while at the end of a line will position the point at the beginning of the next line.) While at any position on a line, CTRL-N moves the point to the next line, and CTRL-P moves the point to the previous line. On many systems the arrow keys (↑, ↓, ←, →) may be used instead of CTRL-P, CTRL-N, CTRL-B and CTRL-F, respectively.

EDWIN tries to keep the cursor in the same column when executing the vertical line motion commands CTRL-N and CTRL-P, but sometimes this is not possible or desirable. If the new line does not have enough characters to reach the desired column, then the point is positioned at the end of the new line. When a sequence of CTRL-N or CTRL-P commands is given in a row, it is desirable for the cursor to stay in the column in which the sequence started. Thus, if a CTRL-N command is issued with the cursor in column 50, and there are only 40 characters in the next line, the cursor will be positioned in column 41 of the next line. But if another CTRL-N command follows immediately, and the following line has 60 characters, the cursor will be positioned back in column 50 of that line. EDWIN remembers the column in which a vertical motion sequence starts and returns to that column whenever possible.

Ending Lines and Inserting Blank Lines — There are two commands that are useful for ending lines and inserting blank lines into the buffer.

Command	Description
RETURN	Insert an end-of-line sequence before the point
CTRL-O	Insert an end-of-line sequence after the point

To end a line and start a new one, press the RETURN key. RETURN puts an end-of-line sequence before the point and moves the cursor and any text to its right onto a new line. The cursor is then positioned at the beginning of the new line. If BACKSPACE is pressed immediately after a RETURN, the cursor and all the text on the line are rejoined with the line above.

RETURN inserts the end-of-line sequence before the point. This causes the cursor to be positioned at the beginning of the new line. This is the normally expected behavior for RETURN. The CTRL-O command, on the other hand, inserts the end-of-line sequence after the point, with the cursor remaining on the original line (now at the end).

To insert a line before the current line, it is best to type CTRL-O at the beginning of the line. This is better than typing the line and then pressing RETURN because it is much faster to insert characters at the end of a line.

Visiting a File — The command CTRL-X CTRL-V followed by a filename is used to *visit* the named file. This causes the file to be loaded into the edit buffer and the filename to be associated with the buffer. For instance, if the file named 'AAA.BBB' is to be edited, the command 'CTRL-X CTRL-V AAA.BBB' is used. The file is read into the buffer (replacing anything that was previously in the buffer), and the cursor is placed at the beginning of the buffer. If 'AAA.BBB' does not exist and the buffer is saved, a new file is created, and the buffer is emptied. After editing the file, type the command CTRL-X CTRL-S to replace it.

Aborting a Command — The CTRL-G command is used to abort a multi-keystroke command as it is being entered. For example, after you type CTRL-X CTRL-V to visit a file, a prompt is displayed that asks for the file-name. Entering CTRL-G, you can abort the command, returning EDWIN to the same state it was in before CTRL-X CTRL-V was entered.

Arguments to EDWIN Commands

4.2.7 Any EDWIN command can be given a numeric argument. However, these arguments are interpreted differently by different commands. Most commands interpret an argument as a repetition count. For example, giving an argument of five to the CTRL-F (forward character) command moves the cursor forward five characters. With these commands, omitting the argument is equivalent to specifying an argument of one.

A numeric argument for a command is specified by preceding the command by CTRL-U followed by the digits of the argument. Negative arguments are entered by typing a CTRL-U followed by '-' and the digits of the argument. The action of many commands may be reversed by using a negative argument.

There is a special interpretation for CTRL-U when it is followed directly by a command (rather than a digit or minus sign): the argument of the following command is multiplied by four.[3] Thus an argument of 16 for a command can be generated by typing two CTRL-U's in succession. Combinations like CTRL-U CTRL-N or CTRL-U CTRL-N move the cursor down a good fraction of the screen.

Some commands do special things when no argument is specified. For example, the CTRL-K command (kill line) with an argument of five kills five lines and the line separators that follow them. But CTRL-K with no arguments kills the text up to the line separator. Or, if the point is at the end of the line, CTRL-K kills the line separator itself. Thus either two successive CTRL-K commands with no arguments or a single CTRL-K command with an argument of one will kill a non-blank line.

---

[3] The actual parsing of universal arguments is somewhat more complicated. The argument may consist of multiple digits and CTRL-U's. The digits are taken as a number and are multiplied by 4 for each occurrence of a CTRL-U except the first. Thus CTRL-U 22 CTRL-U CTRL-U produces the argument 352. Complex arguments such as this are rarely used.

Moving the Cursor

4.2.8 In order to move the point (and cursor), EDWIN must be given both the direction of movement and the distance to move. All movement is relative to the current position of the point.

The direction of movement is specified as *forward*, *backward*, *beginning*, or *end* (*next* and *down* are forward movements; *previous* and *up* are backward movements). In forward and backward moves, the point moves in the given direction by a specified quantity. In beginning or end moves, the point is moved to the beginning or end of the quantity in which it currently points. If the point is between two quantities, beginning and end become synonymous with backward and forward, respectively.

Movement may be performed with respect to any of the following quantities:

- Character. Any single character (including a line separator).

- Word. Any sequence of alphabetic or numeric characters or one of '$', '.', or '%'.

- Sentence. A sequence of characters ending with a '.', '?', or '!' followed by an arbitrary number of ')', ']'. '"', or '"' characters followed by two spaces or line separators (or a combination of them). A blank line also terminates a sentence. A paragraph terminator (see below) also terminates a sentence.

- Line. Any sequence of characters from the point up to a line separator (in either direction) or any sequence of characters between two line separators (if the point is not positioned in that line).

- Paragraph. Any sequence of lines separated by a blank line or a line beginning with a blank, '.', '"', '"', '@', or '-'. In Scheme mode, only blank lines separate paragraphs (see the paragraph entitled Scheme Mode).

- List. Any sequence of characters enclosed in matching parentheses. The sequence itself may contain sublists.

- S-expression. Either a list or an atom. An atom is either a Scheme identifier or a quoted string. The algorithm for discriminating Scheme identifiers is a heuristic that is correct in most cases; however, it can be confused by things such as quote characters that do not introduce or terminate strings.

- Screen. The displayed portion of the buffer.

- Buffer. The entire editing buffer.

The following table summarizes the movement commands with respect to each of the above quantities and directions.

	Forward	Backward	Beginning	End
Character	CTRL-F	CTRL-B	CTRL-B	CTRL-F
Word	meta-F	meta-B	meta-B	meta-F
Sentence	—	—	meta-A	meta-E
Paragraph	meta-]	meta-[	meta-[	meta-]
Line	CTRL-N	CTRL-P	CTRL-A	CTRL-E
List	meta-CTRL-N	meta-CTRL-P	meta-CTRL-P	meta-CTRL-N
S-Expr	meta-CTRL-F	meta-CTRL-B	meta-CTRL-B	meta-CTRL-F
Screen	CTRL-V	meta-V	—	—
Buffer	—	—	meta-<	meta->

On many systems, the →, ←, ↑, and ↓ keys are synonymous with CTRL-B, CTRL-F, CTRL-P, and CTRL- N, respectively.

The following table gives more detail on point movement commands other than the list and S-expression movement commands. List and S-expression commands are treated in the following paragraph.

Command	Description
CTRL-F	Move forward one character
meta-F	Move forward one word
CTRL-B	Move backward one character
meta-B	Move backward one word
meta-A	Move to beginning of sentence
meta-E	Move to end of sentence
CTRL-N	Move down one line
CTRL-P	Move up one line
CTRL-A	Move to the beginning of the line
CTRL-E	Move to the end of the line
CTRL-V	Display the next screen (The cursor is moved to the beginning of the first line of the screen.)
meta-V	Display the previous screen (The cursor is moved to the beginning of the first line of the screen.)
CTRL-L	Redraw the screen, centering the point
meta-<	Move to the beginning of the buffer
meta->	Move to the end of the buffer

The commands CTRL-V and meta-V differ from the other movement commands in that they are primarily concerned with changing the display to the next or previous "screen" of text. CTRL-V moves forward to the next screen or to the end of the buffer if it is encountered first. Meta-V moves to the previous screen or the beginning of the buffer. The point is positioned before the first character on the screen. If an argument is given to either CTRL-V or meta-V the screen is scrolled by the number of *lines* specified in the argument.

The CTRL-L command is useful when the text being edited is near the top or bottom of the screen so that some of it is not visible on the screen. This command redraws the screen with the line containing the point in the middle of the screen (assuming that the file extends far enough past the point in both directions to make this possible).

Moving over Lists and S-expressions — The list and S-expression motion commands are very similar except that the list motion commands will skip over atoms (words) until a parenthesis is encountered. Thus, list motion commands deal only with parenthesized lists, while S-expression motion commands deal with both lists and atoms.

The commands for moving the point over lists and S-expressions are given in the following table.

Command	Description
meta-CTRL F	Move forward over an S-expression
meta-CTRL-B	Move backward over an S-expression
meta-CTRL-N	Move forward over a list
meta-CTRL-P	Move backward over a list
meta-CTRL-D	Move down one level of structure, forward
meta-CTRL-U	Move up one level of structure, backward

The commands dealing with lists or S-expressions are meta-CTRL-X commands. With lists and S-expressions, which may have many levels of nesting, the terms *up* and *down* refer to movement into less deeply nested levels and more deeply nested levels of the list or S-expression, respectively.

The meta-CTRL-F command moves the point over an S-expression. If the first significant character is '(', the point moves past the matching closed parenthesis. If the character is an atom, the point moves to the end of the atom. The meta-CTRL-B command is similar to meta-CTRL-F, except that it moves backwards.

The meta-CTRL-N and meta-CTRL-P commands are similar to meta-CTRL-F and meta-CTRL-B except that they ignore atoms. Thus meta-CTRL-N moves the point until a left parenthesis is encountered and then moves the point across that list. If meta-CTRL-N is invoked while the point is inside of a list, the point moves to the end of the list.

The previous list commands stay at the *same level* of parentheses or nesting. Meta-CTRL-U moves the point up one level (namely, to an outer or surrounding level) in the backward direction. The meta-CTRL-D command moves down into a subordinate list in the forward direction. The command is used with a negative argument to move down into a preceding list. If the closing parenthesis of the current level (in either direction of movement) is encountered before a subordinate list is found, a beep from the terminal signals the error, and the point remains unchanged.

Marks and Regions

4.3 It is sometimes necessary to specify a portion of the buffer to be modified. This specified portion of the buffer is called a *region* and is defined to be that portion of the buffer between the point and the mark. Either the point or the mark may appear first in the buffer.

The user specifies the region by putting a mark at one end and setting the point at the other. The following commands are used to set the mark.

Command	Description
CTRL-@	Set a mark
meta-@	Mark a word
meta-CTRL-@	Mark an S-expression
meta-H	Mark whole paragraph
CTRL-X H	Mark the whole buffer
CTRL-X CTRL-X	Exchange the positions of the point and the mark
CTRL-U CTRL-@	Move the point to the previous mark in the mark ring

The most common method of setting a mark is CTRL- @. This sets the mark at the current location of the point. The point may then be moved, leaving the mark behind.

In marking a word or S-expression, the mark is set at the end of the word or S-expression. If the point is not at the beginning of the word or S-expression, then the region includes only a portion of the word or S-expression.

In marking a paragraph, the point is moved to the beginning of the paragraph and the mark is set at the end of the paragraph. If the point is already between paragraphs, it is not moved, and the mark is placed after the following paragraph.

CTRL-X CTRL-X exchanges the point and the mark. This is useful for checking the position of the mark, since it is not visible on the screen.

The Mark Ring

4.3.1 In addition to defining regions, marks are used to keep track of specific locations in the text. EDWIN keeps track of the 10 most recently established marks in a circular list (ring). The point can then be moved automatically to positions remembered in the mark ring.

When new marks are created, they are added at the *front* of the ring, and a mark at the *back* of the ring is discarded (if there were 10 marks). The mark used by commands is the mark at the front of the ring.

The CTRL-U CTRL-@ command rotates the ring of previous marks from the front toward the back. Thus, one invocation of CTRL-U CTRL-@ makes the second most recently established mark the current mark, with the current mark assuming the role of the oldest mark. Repeated use of this command moves the point through all the previous marks one by one. Since this is a ring, the point eventually comes back to its original position.

Killing and Unkilling

4.4 Text is removed from the buffer by either *killing* it or *deleting* it. The effect on the buffer is the same in both cases, but text that is killed is remembered in the kill ring so that it can be retrieved later. Only single characters and blank spaces are deleted. Any other erasure of text is considered to be a kill and is saved in the kill ring.

Text that is saved in the kill ring is retrieved by unkilling it, which involves copying it from the kill ring into the buffer at the point.

Deleting

4.4.1 The following commands delete text:

Command	Description
BACKSPACE	Delete the character before the point
CTRL-H	Delete the character before the point (same as BACKSPACE)
CTRL-D	Delete the character after the point
meta-\	Delete all spaces and tab characters around the point
meta-*space bar*	Delete all spaces and tab characters, leaving one space

CTRL-D deletes the character *after* the point; that is, the character *under* the cursor. The cursor remains in the same location but highlights the next character. BACKSPACE and CTRL-H delete the character *before* the cursor. The cursor and the text under and following it on the line move to the left. Line separators are treated as single characters. If an end-of-line is deleted, the current line is joined with the next line.

If an argument is given to these commands, they act like kill commands, and the erased text is saved in the kill ring.

Killing

4.4.2 The kill commands are listed in the following table:

Command	Description
meta-D	Kill the next word
meta-BACKSPACE	Kill the preceding word
CTRL-K	Kill a line
meta-K	Kill forward to the end of the sentence
CTRL-X BACKSPACE	Kill backward to the beginning of the sentence
meta-CTRL-K	Kill the next S-expression
CTRL-W	Kill region
meta-W	Copy region to kill ring
meta-CTRL-W	Append next kill

The CTRL-K command kills lines from the point to the end of the line. If the point is at the end of the line, CTRL-K kills the line separator and merges the next line with the current line. Tabs and spaces are ignored in deciding if the point is at the end of the line.

If an argument is included, CTRL-K kills that many lines and line separators. If the argument is negative, it kills previous lines.

The CTRL-W command kills a region (see the paragraph entitled Marks and Regions) from the mark to the point. Meta-W is equivalent to CTRL-W CTRL-Y. It copies a region to the kill ring without removing it from the buffer.

Each kill command stores a new block of text on the kill ring. However, two or more kill commands in a row combine their text in a single entry. If a kill command is separated from the preceding kill command by other commands, the text goes into a new entry in the kill ring. To append the text to the previous entry instead of creating a new entry, use the meta-CTRL-W command before the second kill.

Unkilling **4.4.3** Unkilling retrieves text that has been killed previously but still remains in the kill ring. This is useful when text is killed accidentally. However, the primary use of unkilling is to move and copy text. The technique for moving text is to kill it and then unkill (*yank*) it back into its new location. Text that has been yanked from the kill ring also remains in the kill ring, allowing it to be yanked back into many different locations.

The unkill commands are summarized here.

Command	Description
CTRL-Y	Unkill text from the most recent kill
meta-Y	Unkill text from less recent kills
CTRL-X CTRL-K	Expunge a kill ring entry

CTRL-Y yanks the text of the most recent kill, leaving the cursor at the end of the inserted text. Meta-Y moves backwards through the kill ring to retrieve less recent kills. After CTRL-Y is invoked, each use of meta-Y replaces the yanked text with an earlier instance from the kill ring. The meta-Y command can be used only after a CTRL-Y command has been executed at least once. As with the mark ring, each use of meta-Y makes an earlier kill the "most recent kill," and what was previously the most recent kill becomes the oldest one.

EDWIN's kill ring keeps track of the last 10 kills. Because killed text can take up a substantial amount of data space, the kill ring may be an especially large consumer of limited memory resources. However, the CTRL-X CTRL-K command can be used to expunge entries from the kill ring. CTRL-X CTRL-K expunges the top element of the kill ring. With an argument of 10 (namely, CTRL-U 10 CTRL-X CTRL-K), it expunges the entire kill ring. It is a good practice to discard large items that have been killed when they are no longer needed.

File Handling

4.5 The text that EDWIN edits is stored permanently in files. File commands control the movement of data between EDWIN's buffer and the data file.

Command	Description
meta-~	Mark buffer as unmodified
CTRL-X CTRL-V *filename*	Visit (read) a file into the buffer
CTRL-X CTRL-S	Save the buffer to a file
CTRL-X CTRL-W *filename*	Write the buffer to a file
CTRL-X CTRL-I *filename*	Insert a file into the buffer
CTRL-X CTRL-P *filename*	Put (write) a region to a file
CTRL-X CTRL-Q	Toggle file's read-only flag

The meta-~ command marks the buffer as being unaltered. The asterisks on the mode line are removed. This is sometimes useful if a file has been modified accidentally and repaired in place—or if some changes have been made that have no net effect on the buffer (such as a kill followed by a yank).

The command CTRL-X CTRL-V prompts for a filename and loads the named file into the buffer after erasing anything that was in the buffer. This file *visiting* command also associates the file name with the buffer, so it may be used later in saving (replacing) the file on disk. If the file does not exist, a new file is created if the buffer is saved. If the buffer already contains a file that has been modified but not saved, the user is prompted to save the file before the new file is read. The mark ring is cleared when a file is visited. Any text in the kill ring is not affected.

CTRL-X CTRL-V accepts an argument that causes either the file or the buffer to be marked as *read only*. A positive argument to CTRL-X CTRL-V marks the file as read only so that extra confirmation is required in order to save the file, but the buffer may be modified. A negative argument to CTRL-X CTRL-V marks the buffer as read only also, so that commands that modify the buffer are not allowed. CTRL-X CTRL-Q changes the state of the file's read-only flag from read-only to writeable or vice versa.

The buffer is *saved* back in the visited file with the CTRL-X CTRL-S command. A message appears at the bottom of the window indicating that the file has been saved. The file replaces the current version of the file on the disk (no backups are made automatically).

The CTRL-X CTRL-W command writes the buffer to a specified file. The user is prompted for the name of the file into which the buffer is to be saved. The new file name is associated with the buffer so that if the buffer is later saved with the CTRL-X CTRL-S command, it is saved under the new name, rather than under the name of the file that was originally visited.

When only a portion of the buffer is to be written to a file, use the CTRL-X CTRL-P command. It writes the region (between the point and mark) to a file after prompting for the file name.

The CTRL-X CTRL-I command inserts a file into the buffer at the point.

Incremental Search   **4.6** EDWIN provides a sophisticated facility called *incremental search*. This means that EDWIN begins searching for a matching string in the buffer as soon as a character in the search string is typed. If the current partial match is not sufficient, EDWIN will look for another match as additional characters are typed. If an error is made in typing the search string, characters can be erased and EDWIN will return to appropriate earlier matches.

The incremental search commands are as follows:

Command	Description
CTRL-S search-string	Search forward incrementally
CTRL-R search-string	Search in reverse incrementally

The CTRL-S command reads characters from the keyboard and echoes them in the Echo Area. The cursor is positioned at the end of the first occurrence of a match on the current search string. If the current search string is not long enough to locate the desired position, then additional search string characters may be typed. In this way, typing a longer search string than necessary is avoided. Subsequent occurrences of the search string are located by typing CTRL-S again during the search. BACKSPACE returns the cursor to the previous occurrence of the search string.

CTRL-R is similar to CTRL-S but searches in the reverse direction. The cursor points to the beginning of the current match.

The direction of a search can be changed by entering CTRL-R in the middle of a forward search—or CTRL-S in the middle of a backwards search.

Any character that is not meaningful to the search (such as a movement command) terminates the search and is executed. After a search is completed, another search for the same string can be initiated by typing CTRL-S CTRL-S or CTRL-R CTRL-R.

If a search fails, a message is displayed in the echo area. If failure was caused by a typing error, the string can be corrected by typing CTRL-G (Abort Character). This causes the characters that were not matched to be discarded, leaving only those that were matched. A second CTRL-G cancels the search, and the point moves back to the place where the search originated.

Modes   **4.7** There are two editing modes supported by EDWIN: Scheme mode and Fundamental mode. Most commands work exactly the same in either mode; however, it is useful to interpret some commands (such as TAB) differently when editing Scheme code than when editing ordinary text. Modes allow EDWIN to make useful assumptions about the nature of the data being edited.

The command CTRL-X CTRL-M toggles between Scheme mode and Fundamental mode. The current mode is shown in the Mode Line. Modes may be switched at any time by entering CTRL-X CTRL-M.

Fundamental Mode

4.7.1 Fundamental mode provides commands for basic text editing. EMACS traditionally differentiates between Fundamental mode and Text mode, which provides some extra knowledge about the structure of prose text, such as paragraphs and indenting. However, in EDWIN there is no separate text mode.[4]

Scheme Mode

4.7.2 All of the commands described in this chapter behave differently in Scheme mode than in Fundamental mode. Some other commands (such as the cursor movement commands for S-expressions) are particularly useful in Scheme mode but do not need a different behavior in Fundamental mode. Therefore, they are not exclusively a part of Scheme mode.

Paragraph commands (meta-[, meta-] ,and meta-H), behave differently in Scheme mode than in Fundamental mode. In Scheme mode, a paragraph boundary is denoted by a blank line. This generally corresponds to individual procedure definitions.

Matching parentheses — Whenever a closing parenthesis is typed, its matching open parenthesis is highlighted. If a matching parenthesis is not found, a beep is sounded. If the matching parenthesis is visible on the screen, the cursor moves to it for half a second and returns. If the matching parenthesis is not visible on the current screen, the portion of the line starting with the matching parenthesis is displayed in the Echo Area.

Detection of an unmatched parenthesis can be extremely slow because a reverse search through the entire file may be required. In order to reduce this overhead, EDWIN uses a heuristic to determine when there is no matching parenthesis. If an open parenthesis is encountered in the first column and is preceded by a blank line, EDWIN assumes that there is no matching opening parenthesis. This works well in most cases.

Indenting — EDWIN understands a number of Scheme forms such as LET and LAMBDA. This knowledge is used to support a simplified heuristic to help in maintaining code in a *pretty-printed* form during the editing process.

Maintaining edited Scheme code in a neat and readable form is one of the most complicated tasks EDWIN performs. Most of this is done automatically for the user. However. it is possible to change a line without causing EDWIN to adjust the indentation. It is also possible to make changes that affect the correct indentation for subsequent lines. In these cases, EDWIN must be told to correct the indentation on one or more lines.

The commands for maintaining the indentation of Scheme code are presented here.

---

[4] This considerably reduces the size and complexity of EDWIN, a reduction that was felt to be an acceptable trade-off for most editing.

Command	Description
TAB	Indent the line according to the Scheme syntax
LINEFEED	Insert a new line and indent it
meta-CTRL-Q	Indent the next S-expression

TAB adjusts the indentation of the current line. In Scheme mode, if LINEFEED [5] is used instead of the RETURN key to open a new line, the cursor is automatically indented on the new line; it is equivalent to RETURN followed by TAB.

Meta-CTRL-Q reindents the contents of the S-expression following the point. The line on which the S-expression starts is not indented, so the indentation of the following lines of the S-expression is relative to the first line's indentation.

Evaluating Scheme Code — It is useful to evaluate Scheme expressions directly from within EDWIN. This is accomplished by marking the code to be evaluated and invoking the PC Scheme system from within EDWIN to evaluate it. Control is also transferred from EDWIN to PC Scheme. This causes EDWIN's window to be replaced by PC Scheme's console window (unless the screen is split, see the paragraph entitled Splitting the Screen). EDWIN may be reentered later to resume editing at the same place.

These are the commands to evaluate Scheme expressions:

Command	Description
meta-CTRL-Z	Evaluate a marked region and enter Scheme
meta-CTRL-X	Evaluate the next S-expression and enter Scheme
meta-O	Evaluate the whole buffer and enter Scheme

EDWIN writes the expression to a temporary file that is then read by PC Scheme (no explicit user I/O is required to support this process). Passing a large data structure (such as the whole buffer) to PC Scheme may present a problem if there is little available disk space.

---

[5] On an IBM PC, CTRL-J must be used instead, as there is no LINEFEED key. CTRL-J is also equivalent to LINEFEED on a TI PC.

System Level Considerations

4.8 With the exception of file handling issues and starting and stopping EDWIN itself, EDWIN operates with only a minimal knowledge of the underlying PC Scheme system. This paragraph discusses two additional considerations in using EDWIN.

Splitting the Screen

4.8.1 The display screen can be divided into two major parts, with EDWIN in one half and Scheme in the other. The Edit window shrinks to 11 lines followed by the Mode Line and the Echo Area. The remaining 12 lines (on a TIPC) form the console window and the Scheme status line.

The command CTRL-X ! is used as a toggle to switch between split screen and full screen display. From a full screen display, CTRL-X ! splits the screen, with EDWIN at the top and the last (most recent) 11 lines of the console window at the bottom. PC Scheme's status line is on the bottom. Another CTRL-X ! returns EDWIN to a full screen.

While in Scheme, the console window can be expanded to a full screen with the procedure call (EDWIN-RESET-WINDOWS). On reentry to EDWIN, however, it is still necessary to use the CTRL-X ! command to expand the EDWIN Edit window to a full screen (the console window is not affected). EDWIN-RESET-WINDOWS is useful when EDWIN has been exited via a CTRL-X CTRL-C while using the split screen feature.

The EDWIN split screen feature works well with the PC Scheme console window. However, it must be used with caution if there are other user-developed or application windows on the screen. EDWIN manages the window changes itself (there is no underlying window manager) and assumes that the only window that needs to be protected is the console. Consequently, other windows will not be managed properly. This problem exists only when the split screen feature is being used.

Checkpointing

4.8.2 It is possible to fill memory completely, thus making it impossible for EDWIN to proceed. This does not occur in most normal situations, but it may occur when code is being alternately edited and debugged, when the application (particularly a large one) builds substantial data structures, or when there is considerable use of the kill ring.

When this happens, PC Scheme makes every attempt to free space by resetting some system structures to allow processing to continue. Once the garbage collector finishes, a PC Scheme error handler is invoked. If there are substantial data structures that can be freed (for example, by setting appropriate variables to ()), this is helpful. After any storage is freed, EDWIN may be reinvoked. If EDWIN successfully restarts, the buffer should be saved immediately.

Since it is possible that there will still not be enough space for EDWIN to restart successfully, *make sure to save the buffer frequently*. This also provides protection from other forms of catastrophic failure, such as system power loss. Running out of space should be a very rare occurrence in most normal situations. However, it is easy to forget the relatively small capacity of personal computers.

**Command
Summary**

4.9 *Control* commands (denoted by CTRL-) are entered by holding down the CTRL key and typing the identifying character.

Meta commands (denoted by meta-) are entered by pressing the ESC key (or CTRL-Z) and then typing the identifying character for the command.

Meta-Control commands (denoted by meta-CTRL-) are entered by pressing ESC (or CTRL-Z) and then holding down the CTRL key as you type the identifying character.

Control-X commands are invoked by entering the CTRL-X command followed by the appropriate subcommand.

WARNING: Some third-party software may interfere with some of these commands. For instance, some users of PC Scheme report that CTRL-@ is ignored if certain keyboard software packages (such as Borland's Side Kick™ and Super Key™) are installed.

**Simple Motion
Commands**

4.9.1

Command	Description
CTRL-F	Move forward one character
CTRL-B	Move backward one character
meta-F	Move forward one word
meta-B	Move backward one word
CTRL-N	Move down one line
CTRL-P	Move up one line
CTRL-A	Move to the beginning of the line
CTRL-E	Move to the end of the line
meta-A	Move to the beginning of the sentence
meta-E	Move to the end of the sentence
meta-<	Go to the beginning of the buffer
meta->	Go to the end of the buffer
CTRL-V	Display the next screen
meta-V	Display the previous screen

The arrow keys (→, ←, ↑, and ↓) can be used instead of CTRL-F, CTRL-B, CTRL-P, and CTRL-N, respectively.

List Commands 4.9.2

Command	Description
meta-CTRL-F	Move forward over an S-expression
meta-CTRL-B	Move backward over an S-expression
meta-CTRL-N	Move forward over a list
meta-CTRL-P	Move backward over a list
meta-CTRL-D	Move down one level of list structure
meta-CTRL-U	Move backward and up one level of list structure

Line Commands 4.9.3

Command	Description
CTRL-O	Insert a new line after the point
RETURN	Insert a new line before the point

Mark Commands 4.9.4

Command	Description
CTRL-@	Set a mark
meta-@	Mark a word
meta-CTRL-@	Mark an S-expression
meta-H	Mark the whole paragraph
CTRL-X H	Mark the whole buffer
CTRL-X CTRL-X	Exchange the positions of the point and the mark

Kill/Unkill Commands 4.9.5

Command	Description
BACKSPACE	Delete the character before the cursor
CTRL-D	Delete the character at the cursor
meta-\	Delete all spaces and tab characters around the point
meta-SPACE	Delete all spaces and tab characters around the point, leaving one space
meta-D	Kill the next word
meta-BACKSPACE	Kill the preceding word
CTRL-K	Kill a line
meta-K	Kill forward to end of the sentence
CTRL-X BACKSPACE	Kill backward to beginning of the sentence
meta-CTRL-K	Kill the next S-expression
CTRL-W	Kill a region
meta-W	Copy a region
CTRL-Y	Unkill
meta-Y	Unkill using previous Kill Ring entry
meta-CTRL-W	Append next kill to preceding kill
CTRL-X CTRL-K	Expunge Kill Ring entry

Incremental Search Commands 4.9.6

Command	Description
CTRL-S	Search forward incrementally
CTRL-R	Search in reverse incrementally

File Commands 4.9.7

Command	Description
CTRL-X CTRL-V	Visit (read) a file in the buffer
CTRL-X CTRL-S	Save the buffer to a file
CTRL-X CTRL-W	Write the buffer to a file
CTRL-X CTRL-I	Insert a file into the buffer
CTRL-X CTRL-P	Put (write) a region to a file
meta-~	Ignore changes made to the buffer
CTRL-X CTRL-Q	Make file read only or read/write

Modes 4.9.8

Command	Description
CTRL-X CTRL-M	Toggle mode

Indentation Commands 4.9.9

Command	Description
TAB	Indent the line according to the Scheme syntax (Scheme mode only)
LINEFEED	Insert a new line and indent it
meta-CTRL-Q	Indent the next S-expression

Window Commands 4.9.10

Command	Description
CTRL-X !	Toggle between split screen and full screen

While in Scheme, the procedure invocation (EDWIN-RESET-WINDOWS) returns EDWIN and Scheme to full screen display.

Miscellaneous Commands 4.9.11

Command	Description
CTRL-X CTRL-Z	Exit the editor and return to Scheme
CTRL-X CTRL-C	Reset the editor and return to Scheme
CTRL-L	Redraw the screen, centering the point
CTRL-U	Repeat a command
CTRL-G	Abort the current command
CTRL-Q	Insert the next character (including control characters) into the buffer
CTRL-T	Transpose characters

Evaluation Commands 4.9.12

Command	Description
meta-CTRL-Z	Evaluate a marked region and enter Scheme
meta-CTRL-X	Evaluate the next S-expression and enter Scheme
meta-O	Evaluate the buffer and enter Scheme

WINDOWS

PC Scheme extends the I/O capabilities of the Scheme language to support windows and graphics. Although these facilities share the screen, they are logically independent in their operation. Windows are not affected by graphics operations that occur within their boundaries and vice versa.

PC Scheme supports windows as an extension to the standard input/output capabilities of the Scheme language. A *window* is a rectangular region on the screen to which character-oriented I/O operations may be performed. Each window is independent of every other window, and it is the programmer's responsibility to coordinate how multiple windows interact.

A window may be viewed as a miniature version of the screen. Each window has its own boundaries, video attributes, and a cursor position. When characters are written past the end of a line, the window scrolls up and the output is continued on the next line of the window.

When PC Scheme begins execution, two windows appear as the system begins to load. The major portion of the screen is occupied by the *console*, a window that occupies 24 of the 25 lines of the screen. The console is the default window to which all input and output occur. The console window is referenced explicitly using the special symbol 'CONSOLE as a port object. The second window on the initial screen is the *status window*, which displays information about the PC Scheme system's execution. It is a single-line window, and it appears as a reverse video line at the bottom of the screen. The Scheme variable PCS-STATUS-WINDOW may be used to reference the status window.

When multiple windows appear on the screen, make sure they do not overlap. Windows are independent, and I/O to a window that covers another causes the data in the covered window to be overwritten. Similarly, portions of a window that are covered by another window scroll when the overlapping window scrolls.

On the TIPC, the text and graphics planes of the screen are separate, allowing both text and graphics to appear on the screen simultaneously.

Text and graphics cannot be mixed on the IBM PC and IBM-compatible hardware (including the TI BUSINESS–PRO computer in IBM mode). PC Scheme windows are designed to operate in 80-column text mode and may fail to work as expected when the screen is executing in a graphics mode or a text-and-graphics mode. When you are operating in a graphics mode on these computers, do not use the WINDOW-SAVE-CONTENTS and WINDOW-RESTORE-CONTENTS procedures.

Windowing Support

5.1 Windows are created by the constructor procedure MAKE-WINDOW, which returns a default window object representing the entire screen. Once created, a window object can be modified to change its size, position, and appearance.

The WINDOW-SET-POSITION! procedure specifies the screen coordinates for the upper left hand corner of the window. WINDOW-SET-SIZE! specifies the number of lines and columns of data in the window. WINDOW-SET-ATTRIBUTE! changes the appearance of a window's border and of the text within the window. WINDOW-SET-CURSOR! changes the location of the cursor within the window to position it for the next input or output operation.

After the window object has been modified as desired, the WINDOW-CLEAR procedure draws the window on the screen, along with any specified borders. Once a window is visible, any of the Scheme I/O procedures may transmit characters to and from a window by specifying the window object as the port operand. WINDOW-DELETE deletes a window when it is no longer needed.

Several procedures return information about a window object. The WINDOW? predicate determines whether an object is a window. WINDOW-GET-ATTRIBUTE returns the current attribute settings for the text and border characters. WINDOW-GET-CURSOR returns the current position of the cursor within a window. WINDOW-GET-POSITION returns the screen coordinates of the upper left hand corner of the window, and WINDOW-GET-SIZE returns the number of lines and columns of data in the window.

To display information momentarily on top of windows existing on the screen, a *pop-up* window may be used. A pop-up window saves the data on the portion of the screen that it covers so that the data may be restored when the pop-up window is removed. Pop-up windows must be displayed and deleted in a last in, first out manner. A pop-up window is created and modified as any other window, except the WINDOW-POPUP procedure is called to display the pop-up window, and WINDOW-POPUP-DELETE is used to remove it and restore the screen to its previous state.

Two functions save and restore the contents of windows. WINDOW-SAVE-CONTENTS captures the characters and their attributes for a window, and WINDOW-RESTORE-CONTENTS restores a window to the same state as when the WINDOW-SAVE-CONTENTS captured the window image.

A Simple Window Example

5.2 In addition to the procedures that create and manipulate windows, any of the standard Scheme I/O procedures may be used to perform I/O to a window. For example, consider the following sequence of Scheme expressions that create a small, bordered window in the upper left-hand corner of the screen:

```
(define wind (make-window "test" #!true))
(window-set-position! wind 1 1)
(window-set-size! wind 5 15)
(window-clear wind)
(display "Hello" wind)
```

After entering the above example, press the RETURN key a number of times and watch what happens. Notice how I/O to overlapping windows can cause interference. Eventually, I/O to the console window causes the test window to be scrolled off the screen, border and all. To correct this, shrink the console window as follows so that it occupies only the lower portion of the display:

```
(begin
  (window-clear 'console)
  (window-set-position! 'console 7 0)
  (window-set-size! 'console 17 80))
```

Now you can display the test window without interference from console I/O. For example, try the following:

```
(let ((key #\?))
  (begin
    (window-clear wind)
    (display "Press Any Key" wind)
    (newline wind)
    (set! key (read-char wind))
    (display "You Pressed" wind)
    (print key wind)))
```

Now you can save and restore the contents of a window. For example, try the following:

```
(window-clear wind)
(display "hello" wind)
(define store-screen (window-save-contents wind))
(window-set-cursor! wind 0 0)
(display "goodbye" wind)
(window-restore-contents wind store-screen)
```

To restore the console to its original dimensions and erase the experiment, execute the following:

```
(begin
  (window-set-position!  'console 0 0)
  (window-set-size! 'console 24 80)
  (window-clear 'console))
```

Bordered Windows

5.3 A window may have a border to set it off from the other data on the screen. Since the border is drawn using text graphics characters, it does not require the use of graphics modes or graphics hardware. Also, the size of a window is not affected by whether the window has a border. If a border is specified, it is drawn in the character positions just outside of the data area of the window. When arranging windows on the screen, be sure to account for the extra line above and below and the extra column on the left and right that are used to display the borders. When the borders of two adjacent windows overlap, special characters are used to connect the intersecting borders.

If a window label is specified in the MAKE-WINDOW procedure call and the window is bordered, the label is displayed in the upper left-hand corner of the top border. The borders are drawn only by the WINDOW-CLEAR procedure. If a window is positioned so that a border is off the edge of the screen, that particular border is not drawn. This feature may be used to create windows that appear open on one or more sides.

Text and Border Attributes

5.4 Text and border attributes are specified by using machine-dependent video attributes. These attributes include color, flashing characters, reverse video, and underlining. In the case of border attributes, a value of -1 indicates that a window is not bordered.

Text and border attributes are specified as integer values that correspond to a set of attribute bits. The following diagram shows how character attributes are defined for the TIPC and for the TI BUSINESS-PRO computer in TI mode:

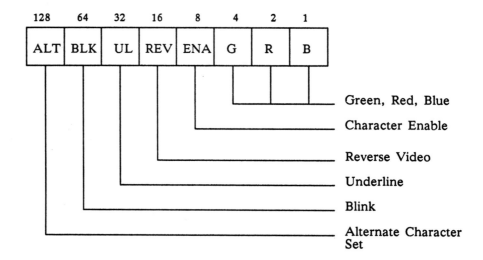

The next diagram shows the Extended Graphics Adapter (EGA) attribute bit settings for the IBM PC, IBM compatibles, and the TI BUSINESS-PRO computer in IBM mode:

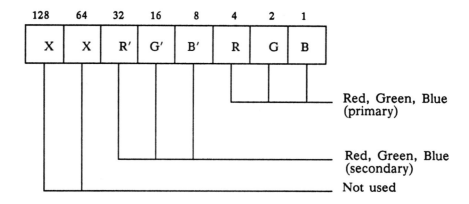

The next diagram shows the Color Graphics Adapter (CGA) attribute bit settings for the IBM PC, IBM compatibles, and the TI BUSINESS-PRO computer in IBM mode.

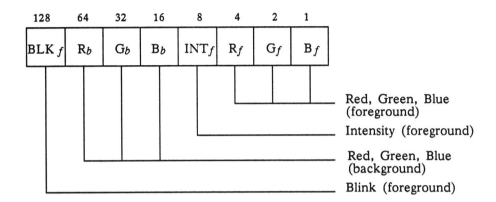

The settings for an IBM monochrome monitor are given in the following table. Consult the technical reference manual for your system for additional information about character attributes.

Background			Foreground			Monochrome Monitor Function
R	G	B	R	G	B	
0	0	0	0	0	0	Non-display
0	0	0	0	0	1	Underline
0	0	0	1	1	1	White on black background
1	1	1	0	0	0	Reverse video

GRAPHICS 6

PC Scheme provides graphics facilities suitable for most instructional and application purposes, including routines to draw points, lines, and rectangles on the screen, change pen colors, and test the color of a point. These graphics facilities do not function in the same way on the TIPC and the IBM PC; therefore, both computers are discussed in the following paragraphs. Note that any unrecognized computers are treated as IBM computers with a Color Graphics Adapter (CGA) by the graphics procedures.

Graphics Hardware on the TIPC

6.1 To use graphics on the TIPC, a one-plane or three-plane graphics card is required. If a graphics card is not installed, no graphics are displayed. Also, if fewer than three graphics planes are available, the number of available colors is reduced. On a monochrome monitor, the different color settings appear as varying levels of intensity.

The graphics hardware on the TIPC or the TI BUSINESS-PRO computer running in TI mode provides a resolution of 720 pixels (picture elements) horizontally and 300 pixels vertically in eight colors. The graphics planes are separate from the text plane, thus permitting the text to scroll while leaving the graphics untouched. This allows the text or graphics to be disabled individually while leaving the other displayed. The procedure SET-VIDEO-MODE! controls this. No additional resolutions are available on the standard TI color graphics card, unlike the IBM PC color graphics adapters, which allow a variety of resolution and color combinations.

Graphics Hardware on the IBM PC

6.2 A wide variety of graphics hardware is available for the IBM PC or the TI BUSINESS-PRO computer running in IBM mode. Currently, PC Scheme graphics are supported only for the IBM CGA in graphics mode 4 and the Enhanced Graphics Adapter (EGA) in modes 4, 14 and 16. Many of the newer boards from IBM emulate the various display modes of the CGA while adding newer modes of their own. Graphics operations performed in other modes will work, but functionality may be reduced or the operation of a function may differ from the way it works in mode 4. The PC Scheme graphics routines assume a resolution of 320 pixels horizontally and 200 pixels vertically in mode 4.

Graphics are not supported on the IBM monochrome display. Also, if you are using a monochrome display with another IBM display controller, you cannot switch from one display to the other while in PC Scheme.

General Graphics Support

6.3 PC Scheme's graphics support procedures are modeled after those in MIT Scheme. The screen is viewed as a grid, with the origin, (0,0), in the center of the screen. Screen coordinates are specified as a pair of values, (x, y), where x is the displacement in the horizontal dimension, and y is the displacement in the vertical dimension. Positive displacements indicate pixels to the right and up for x and y, respectively; and negative displacements indicate pixels to the left and down.

The graphics display acts as a plotter. An invisible pen is positioned initially at the origin (in the center of the screen) and is set to the color white. Graphics procedure calls specify how the pen is to be moved and how the display is to be modified.

An invisible rectangle called the clipping rectangle controls the actual area where drawing is performed. The output of drawing functions appears on the screen only if it falls inside the clipping rectangle. The SET-CLIPPING-RECTANGLE! procedure changes the size or position of the clipping rectangle. The intersection of the specified rectangle and the full screen is used for the final clipping rectangle. If this would put the clipping rectangle entirely off-screen, the clipping rectangle is set to the full screen — its area is never allowed to be totally off-screen. SET-VIDEO-MODE! and CLEAR-GRAPHICS reset the clipping rectangle to the full screen.

The POSITION-PEN procedure places the invisible pen at a specified pixel location. The pen's position is not restricted to the screen area. The x,y coordinates can take on, roughly, any fixnum value, positive or negative. (The exact bounds depends on the screen resolution; values with absolute values of 16384 −max (x-resolution, y-resolution) or greater may be subject to over-flow.) The pen's position is maintained independent of the clipping rectangle. This enables figures to be clipped without distortion. The procedure GET-PEN-POSITION returns the coordinates of the pen.

The color of the pen is changed by the SET-PEN-COLOR! procedure. The list of colors that are valid arguments to SET-PEN-COLOR! are defined in the Scheme variable *GRAPHICS-COLORS*. Note that on IBM color monitors these colors are valid either for CGA mode 4 or for EGA modes 14 or 16. GET-PEN-COLOR returns the pen's current color.

DRAW-POINT draws a single pixel of the current pen color at a given location on the screen. CLEAR-POINT erases a pixel (draws it in black). Either function works only inside the clipping rectangle. IS-POINT-ON? determines if a pixel at a specified location is on or returns false if the pixel is outside the clipping rectangle. POINT-COLOR returns a pixel's color value or −1 if the pixel is outside the clipping rectangle.

DRAW-LINE-TO draws a line in the current pen color from the current pen position to a specified point, clipping the line if necessary. DRAW-BOX-TO draws an outlined rectangle using the current pen position and a specified location as opposite corners. Clipping a box is not done in the obvious way, as that would produce a figure not closed on all four sides. Instead, the coordinates for the clipped edges are readjusted to be those of the clipping rectangle. Therefore, if the side of a box falls outside the clipping rectangle, the side is drawn with the clipped edges running snugly against the side of the clipping rectangle.

Some graphics operations differ depending on which machine is used. These routines are listed in the following table and are described in the following paragraphs.

Procedure	Description
GET-VIDEO-MODE	Get the current video mode
SET-PALETTE!	Change the color mappings
SET-PEN-COLOR!	Change the pen color
SET-VIDEO-MODE!	Change the video mode

Before you attempt to use any of the preceding graphics operations, be sure to execute the CLEAR—GRAPHICS procedure.

Graphics Support on the TIPC

6.4 The following paragraphs describe how the PC Scheme graphics procedures behave on the Texas Instruments Professional Computer and on the TI BUSINESS—PRO computer in TI mode.

Before issuing any graphics commands, the graphics hardware of your PC must be put into the appropriate graphics mode using the CLEAR-GRAPHICS procedure. In addition to clearing the graphics display, CLEAR-GRAPHICS resets the palette and the clipping rectangle.

The graphics procedures address the pixels of the TIPC's screen as (x,y), where x specifies the horizontal axis, and y specifies the vertical axis. The origin, $(0,0)$, is located in the center of the screen. Maximum visibility ranges for x-coordinates on the TIPC are -360 through 359; for y-coordinates, -150 through 149.

Set Video Mode

6.4.1 The graphics procedure SET-VIDEO-MODE! allows you to turn on or off any combination of the text and graphics planes. Also provided is a means to erase the graphics planes (namely, set all the pixels to zero, which defaults to black) and reset the graphics palettes. The clipping rectangle is set to the full screen.

The valid modes for the TIPC are 0 through 3, as described in the following table. The default video mode on the TIPC is 3.

TIPC Mode	Operation
0	Clear/reset graphics
1	Enable text
2	Enable graphics
3	Enable text and graphics

Read Video Mode 6.4.2 The graphics procedure GET-VIDEO-MODE is the complement of the procedure SET-VIDEO-MODE!. It returns the mode number of the most recent SET-VIDEO-MODE! operation or the default value set when PCS begins execution. The graphics planes need not be enabled to use this procedure. GET-VIDEO-MODE provides the capability for a program to determine in what mode it is running, and to save and restore the video mode as needed. On the TIPC, the value returned by the GET-VIDEO-MODE procedure is in the range 0 through 3.

Set Graphics Palette 6.4.3 The procedure SET-PALETTE! allows you to change the mapping of a particular pixel value to display a different color. The color values for the TIPC are shown in the following table.

Value	Color
0	Black
1	Blue
2	Red
3	Magenta
4	Green
5	Cyan
6	Yellow
7	White

This SET-PALETTE! procedure does not modify the pixel values stored within the graphics planes. What is modified are the hardware latches that translate the pixel values to their respective displayed colors as they are displayed on the screen. As an example, if (SET-PALETTE! 0 7) were invoked with the default palette in use, all pixels with a value of zero (which are normally displayed as black) would be displayed as color seven or white. Note, however, that those pixels remain stored in memory as zeros while they are displayed as white. Thus, if you want to modify the display so that all the pixels with values of seven are displayed as black, execute (SET-PALETTE! 7 0). The pixels with a value of seven that were displayed as white are now redisplayed as black, but pixels with a value of zero continue to be displayed as white.

Change Pen Color 6.4.4 The procedure SET-PEN-COLOR! changes the pen color for subsequent graphics commands. On the TIPC, the new pen color may be specified using the integer value for the desired color or by using the symbol that represents the color. For example, the pen color can be changed to red by specifying an argument of 2 or 'RED.

Graphics Support on the IBM PC

6.5 The following paragraphs describe how the PC Scheme graphics procedures behave on the IBM Personal Computer, IBM compatibles, and the TI BUSINESS–PRO computer in IBM mode.

On the IBM PC, text and graphics share the display planes. Thus, graphics operations overwrite the text and vice versa. Also, whenever text is scrolled, any graphics that are displayed are scrolled as well. Whenever a new video mode is selected (even if it is the same as the current mode), the screen is cleared.

The graphics procedures address the pixels of the IBM PC screen as (x,y) where x specifies the horizontal axis, and y specifies the vertical axis. The origin, $(0,0)$, is located in the center of the screen. Maximum visibility ranges for x-coordinates in mode 4 are –160 through 159; for y-coordinates, –100 through 99.

A coordinate that is outside the legal range is mapped to the nearest boundary value for the appropriate axis. For example, $(-500,0)$ is mapped to $(-160,0)$ in mode 4.

With an Enhanced Graphics Adapter, maximum visibility ranges for x-coordinates in modes 14 and 16 are –320 through 319; for y-coordinates, –100 through 99 in mode 14 and –175 through 174 in mode 16.

Before issuing any graphics commands, the graphics hardware of your PC must be put into the appropriate graphics mode using the SET-VIDEO-MODE! procedure. That procedure will call CLEAR-GRAPHICS to clear the graphics display, reset the palette[1], reset the clipping rectangle to the full screen, and reset the graphics functions. You may, likewise, reset graphics without switching video modes by calling CLEAR-GRAPHICS.

Set Video Mode

6.5.1 The graphics procedure SET-VIDEO-MODE! allows you to select between the various text or graphics modes available on an IBM PC with an appropriate display adapter. The various modes available on the IBM Color Graphics Adapter, EGA, or the Professional Graphics Adapter are accessible from within PCS, although full functionality is available only in modes 4, 14 and 16. You need to be aware of the capabilities of each of the various modes to use them properly, especially where graphics modes are used.

Note that in a graphics mode, the number of characters per line may be reduced. The following table lists the mode numbers and their corresponding meaning for the CGA and EGA. The default video mode on the IBM PC varies according to which video card is selected as the default display adapter. If the CGA or EGA is available, the default mode is 3.

---

[1] The IBM CGA in graphics mode 4 reduces the line length to 40 characters. If you are using text and graphics, you should execute (SET-LINE-LENGTH! 40) so your monitor will scroll correctly.

IBM Mode	Resolution	Color	Capability
0	40x25	B/W	Text
1	40x25	Color	Text (16 colors)
2	80x25	B/W	Text
3	80x25	Color	Text (16 colors)
4	320x200	Color	4-color graphics/bitmap
5	320x200	B/W	Graphics/bitmap
6	640x200	B/W	Graphics/bitmap
7	80x25	Mono	Text

The following table lists the mode numbers and their corresponding meaning for the EGA.

IBM Mode	Resolution	Color	Capability
13	320x200	Color	4-color graphics/bitmap
14	640x200	Color	16-color graphics/bitmap
15	640x350	Mono	Graphics/bitmap
16	640x350	Hi Res	16-color graphics/bitmap

Read Video Mode

6.5.2 The graphics procedure GET-VIDEO-MODE is the complement of the procedure SET-VIDEO-MODE!. It returns the mode number passed by the last SET-VIDEO-MODE! call or the default value set when PCS begins execution. A graphics mode need not have been selected in order to use this procedure. GET-VIDEO-MODE provides the capability for a program to determine in what mode it is running, and to save and restore the video mode as needed.

Set Graphics Palette

6.5.3 The procedure SET-PALETTE! allows you to select the colors to be used in graphics mode 4 (320 x 200 pixels), mode 14 (640 x 200 pixels), and mode 16 (640 x 350 pixels).

In mode 4 on the IBM PC, if the first argument to SET-PALETTE! is zero, a background color is being selected by the second argument. The background color is specified as an integer whose value is in the range 0 through 127.

In mode 4, if the first argument to SET-PALETTE! is one, one of two color palettes is selected by the second argument. These palettes determine the colors you can choose when drawing. Each palette contains four colors. When the second argument is zero, the palette contains black (background), red, green, and yellow. A value of one selects a palette containing black (background), cyan, magenta, and white.

When a new palette is selected, the variable *GRAPHICS-COLORS* is updated to contain the current selection of color symbols and the values associated with the colors.

The following table lists the values for each of the colors available in graphics modes 14 and 16.

Value	Color
0	Black (background)
1	Blue
2	Green
3	Cyan
4	Red
5	Magenta
6	Brown
7	White
8	Gray
9	Light-Blue
10	Light-Green
11	Light-Cyan
12	Light-Red
13	Light-Magenta
14	Yellow
15	Intense-White

Change Pen Color   **6.5.4** The procedure SET-PEN-COLOR! changes the pen color for subsequent graphics commands. The available colors depend upon the graphics mode and the current palette selection. On the IBM PC, the argument to SET-PEN-COLOR! may be an integer value or the symbol that names a color. For example, if you are using palette one, the color magenta can be specified as 2 or 'MAGENTA. Only the colors in the list bound to *GRAPHICS-COLORS* are valid arguments to SET-PEN-COLOR! at a given time. The following table lists the values for each of the colors of the two color palettes in graphics mode 4.

Value	Palette 0 Color	Palette 1 Color
0	Black (background)	Black (background)
1	Green	Cyan
2	Red	Magenta
3	Yellow	White

ADVANCED FEATURES 7

This chapter explains several advanced aspects of the PC Scheme system.

Garbage Collection and the Heap

7.1 When PC Scheme begins executing, it determines the amount of memory available on your personal computer and allocates all of it for use by the Scheme memory management routines. Memory for any object created by a Scheme program is taken from this pool of available memory, called the *heap*. As a program executes, it constantly creates new objects. Old objects that are no longer needed by the program accumulate in the heap and must be reclaimed periodically. The memory management processes whereby these unneeded objects are recycled are called *garbage collection* (GC).

Garbage collection occurs automatically whenever PC Scheme determines that the heap is full and memory for an object cannot be allocated. The operation that is unable to allocate space for an object is suspended, and the garbage collector is invoked. When the garbage collection is complete, the suspended operation is restarted from the point where it stopped. The GC process has no logical effect on the execution of your program. When GC occurs, you may notice a delay of a few seconds in the execution of your program, and the message Garbage Collecting appears in the status window at the bottom of the screen while GC is in progress.

PC Scheme uses a two-phase garbage collection strategy. The first phase uses a *mark and sweep* algorithm. Objects that are no longer needed are identified so that their memory can be used to allocate new objects. Objects are not moved in the heap during this phase of GC, but the holes in memory that contain unreferenced objects are identified for later reuse.

After GC has occurred a number of times, the holes of available memory between referenced objects may become too small for reuse. At this point, the second phase of garbage collection is invoked. During this phase, *memory compaction* takes place, causing objects in heavily fragmented areas of memory to be copied to new locations to create larger contiguous areas of available memory. Memory compaction is invoked only when the mark and sweep phase of garbage collection is unable to reclaim enough usable memory to continue execution.

If there is not enough memory to create a new object after both phases of GC, the message Out of memory is displayed, and a SCHEME-RESET is executed in an attempt to free up enough memory to continue. SCHEME-RESET transfers control to the top-level *read-eval-print* command loop.

Normally, garbage collection is handled automatically, and it is not necessary for the programmer to request a GC explicitly. However, for timing and performance reasons, it may be desirable to force a GC so that memory is clear at the beginning of a computation. The GC procedure is used to force a garbage collection to take place at a specific time. A call to the GC procedure with no arguments invokes the mark and sweep phase of garbage collection; a call with an optional argument of #T invokes the compaction phase as well. Note that a GC with compaction takes approximately twice as long as a GC without compaction. For consistent results during a timing test, you should always force a GC before running the test.

To change the text of the Garbage Collecting message that appears in the status window during a GC, define the variable PCS-GC-MESSAGE to be the string you want displayed. Similarly, the message that is displayed after the GC is complete can be changed by defining PCS-GC-RESET. Setting these variables to #F restores their default message.

Fast-Load Files

7.2 A *fast-load* facility to speed up loading of previously compiled files is supplied with PC Scheme. Besides loading faster than source or object programs, fast-load files do not create any garbage (memory that must be reclaimed). Programs containing integer constants larger than 32 bits ($\pm 2,147,483,647$) cannot be converted to fast-load format.

To create a file in fast-load format, follow these steps:

1. Use the COMPILE-FILE procedure to compile the file and write the object to a disk file.

2. Use either the procedure call (EXIT) or the DOS-CALL procedure to exit PCS.

3. Run the PCS utility program MAKE_FSL. Enter:

   MAKE-FSL *object-file fast-load-file*

   where *object-file* is the name of the object file produced by COMPILE-FILE and *fast-load-file* is the name of the file to which the fast-load program representation is to be written. The MAKE_FSL utility can reference any file in your system.

   The MAKE_FSL utility displays the message module *n* complete each time an expression in your compiled program is processed successfully. If any other message appears, it means that the MAKE_FSL step failed and the fast-load file is unusable.

4. Load the program in fast-load format by entering either of the following Scheme commands:

   (FAST-LOAD *fast-load-file*)
   (LOAD *fast-load-file*)

   In this command, *fast-load-file* is a string giving the filename of your program in fast-load format.

Autoloaded Files

7.3 Rather than setting up your program to load explicitly all of the files that define it, you may want to arrange for them to be loaded implicitly as needed. By using incremental loading, you may save space by avoiding unnecessary loads.

Autoloading is keyed to references to unbound variables. When a program references an unbound variable, PC Scheme looks to see if the name of the variable has been declared in an AUTOLOAD-FROM-FILE operation prior to considering the reference to be in error. If the variable's definition can be autoloaded, a specified file is loaded and execution continues.

A call to AUTOLOAD-FROM-FILE specifies the name of a file, usually in fast-load format, and the identifiers of variables that are defined within that file. A typical call to autoload the bindings of variables FOO, BAR, and BAZ is as follows:

```
(autoload-from-file "NEWDEFS.FSL" '(foo bar baz))
```

Whenever any of the variables FOO, BAR, and BAZ are referenced for the first time, the file NEWDEFS.FSL is loaded into the user initial environment. It is your responsibility to ensure that the file actually contains definitions for the specified variables.

Autoloading of macro definitions is not possible with this mechanism, since uses of macros need to be recognized at the time they are compiled, not at execution time. *SCOOPS.FSL*, for example, is not autoloaded by PC Scheme, since most of its definitions are macros.

Linking to DOS

7.4 The DOS-CALL procedure provides a general mechanism to interface with DOS. With DOS-CALL, you can execute a specific program, execute a DOS command, or start a new copy of DOS. When the operation is complete, control returns to your Scheme program. For additional information, see the *TI Scheme Language Reference Manual — Student Edition*.

WARNING: The DOS facility underlying the PC Scheme DOS-CALL feature must be used with great care to avoid damage to the system and the directory structure on your disks. Please read the next two paragraphs carefully before using DOS-CALL.

When executing within DOS during an invocation of DOS-CALL, do not delete any file that is currently open for input or output by your Scheme program. DOS allows you to delete a file that is active, but a subsequent write to that file *may destroy your disk's directory structure*. For example, if you are using the TRANSCRIPT-ON capability of PC Scheme at the time you invoke DOS-CALL, do not delete the transcript file and return to Scheme. Turn off the transcript with a call to TRANSCRIPT-OFF before invoking DOS-CALL.

Some DOS tasks execute and stay resident in memory when they terminate. An example of such a task is the PRINT command. If such a task is executed using DOS-CALL, Scheme cannot restore its memory without overwriting the resident task. When this situation is detected, PC Scheme issues the message DOS-CALL error: Unable to restore PC Scheme memory. This error condition causes PC Scheme to terminate and return control to DOS. If you wish to execute a DOS task that terminates and stays resident, you must invoke it before you enter PC Scheme so that it does not have to be loaded at the time of the DOS-CALL.

DOS-CALL saves the state of the PC Scheme execution by copying the contents of the Scheme memory to a temporary checkpoint file. Since the amount of data copied may be large, it is recommended that this feature be used only on a system with a Winchester disk. The optional third argument to DOS-CALL indicates the amount of memory that you wish to make available to execute the command. This argument is an integer value that specifies the number of paragraphs (16-byte units) of memory to be freed. If the memory argument is not specified, is zero, or is larger than the amount of available memory, all possible memory is freed. Approximately 130K bytes of the Scheme system code remain in memory during the execution of the DOS-CALL procedure.

If the DOS-CALL operation completes successfully, it returns a value of zero. If a non-zero value is returned, it indicates that an error has occurred and the operation has been aborted. The error numbers are usually those returned by the DOS function calls that are used during the DOS-CALL processing. The following table lists the error codes that may be returned from DOS-CALL:

DOS Error Codes

Code	Explanation
1	Function number invalid
2	File not found
3	Path not found
4	Too many open files (no handles left)
5	Access denied
6	Handle invalid
7	Memory control blocks destroyed
8	Not enough memory
9	Memory block address invalid
10	Environment invalid
11	Format invalid
12	Access code invalid
13	Data invalid
15	Invalid drive specified
16	Attempt to remove current directory
17	Not same device
18	No more files

PC Scheme Code

Code	Explanation
0	No error
20	Could not write checkpoint file (disk probably full)

Using Your Own Editor

7.5 PC Scheme provides the ability to execute other programs that run under DOS; therefore, it is a straightforward procedure to use any PC text editor with which you feel comfortable. The following Scheme expression defines a procedure, EDIT-FILE, which executes the text editor named by the DOS EDIT command:

```
(define (edit-file filename)
  (if (string? filename)
      (dos-call "" (string-append "EDIT " filename))
      (error "Invalid Operand to EDIT-FILE")))
```

Environmental Inquiries

7.6 PC Scheme provides a number of global variables that give information about the execution environment.

PCS-MACHINE-TYPE

7.6.1 The Scheme global variable PCS-MACHINE-TYPE indicates the type of personal computer on which PC Scheme is running. By testing this variable at run time, applications may be created that execute differently depending on the host computer. Such differences are especially important for applications that exploit the graphics facilities of PC Scheme. Shown below are defined values for PCS-MACHINE-TYPE.

Value	Machine Type
0	Unknown
1	TIPC or TI BUSINESS-PRO in TI mode
252	IBM PC/AT or TI BUSINESS-PRO in AT mode
254	IBM PC/XT
255	IBM PC

Changing the value of PCS-MACHINE-TYPE does not affect the execution of the PC Scheme run–time support. Once PC Scheme has determined the make (and mode) of the computer on which it is running, the appropriate set of service calls is selected. This selection makes it impossible to switch between TI mode and IBM mode on the TI BUSINESS-PRO during a single Scheme session.

PCS-SYSDIR   **7.6.2**   The variable PCS-SYSDIR gives the directory name in which the PC Scheme system files are located. The system defines this variable at the time the PC Scheme system is loaded by searching for the compiler file (*COMPILER.APP*) in the current default directory and the directories specified in the DOS path declaration. The character string bound to PCS-SYSDIR may be appended to the front of file names to be loaded from the PC Scheme directory.

ERROR MESSAGES 8

This chapter lists the messages that PC Scheme displays in response to user and system errors. Listed with each message are a brief description and suggestions for possible action to be taken to correct or avoid the error situation. The error messages are listed alphabetically within four categories: READ errors, Syntax errors, Execution errors, and PCS errors. READ error messages are issued by the procedure READ in response to improperly specified input expressions. Syntax errors are detected by the PC Scheme compiler. Execution errors are detected during the evaluation of an expression after it has been compiled. PCS errors result from internal resource allocation problems in the PC Scheme system itself.

READ Errors

8.1 The standard input procedure READ converts Scheme data from their external to their internal representations using the syntactic notations specified in the *TI Scheme Language Reference Manual — Student Edition*. READ issues an error message in the event of an improperly specified input expression. Each message is displayed along with the text [ERROR encountered!]. READ errors are as follows:

■ `Invalid outside of QUASIQUOTE expression:` *item*

Commas are not meaningful to READ except within backquoted, or QUASIQUOTE, expressions. Check for a missing backquote character (') or a quote character (') that should be a backquote.

■ `Unexpected ')' encountered before '('`

The READ procedure has read a right parenthesis that has not been preceded by a matching left parenthesis. The EDWIN editor has several features that simplify finding and balancing parentheses in an expression. Pretty-printing the previous expression also may be helpful because mismatched parentheses are displayed as improperly indented subexpressions.

■ `WARNING – EOF encountered during READ`

The READ procedure has reached the end of its input file without finding a right parenthesis to match a preceding left parenthesis. The EDWIN editor has several features that simplify finding and balancing parentheses in an expression. Pretty-printing the expression also may be helpful (after adding sufficient right parentheses at its end to make it readable) because mismatched parentheses display as improperly indented subexpressions.

When READ is called with no expressions remaining in the input file, it returns an end-of-file token that may be recognized with the predicate EOF-OBJECT?. This is not an error.

■ WARNING — Invalid use of `.' encountered during READ

A period is understood by READ only as a constituent of a real number or symbol and in the dotted notation for pairs and improper lists. Check for an incorrectly written atom or an isolated period that is not contained within a list or followed by exactly one subexpression.

Syntax Errors

8.2 The Scheme evaluator issues messages whenever it detects errors in the specification of a Scheme program. These messages are displayed with the additional text [Syntax Error] to distinguish them from execution errors. If the evaluator cannot continue, it displays the message [Compilation terminated because of errors] and returns to the top-level *read-eval-print* loop. Syntax errors are as follows:

■ Expression ends with `dotted' atom *exp*

The indicated expression is syntactically required to be a proper list, but the improper list *exp* was supplied.

■ Expression has too few subexpressions *exp*

The indicated expression syntactically requires more component subexpressions than were supplied.

■ Expression has too many subexpressions *exp*

The indicated expression syntactically requires fewer component subexpressions than were supplied.

■ Incorrectly Placed DEFINE *exp*

A DEFINE placed within the body of a LAMBDA, LET, LET*, LETREC, or NAMED-LAMBDA special form must appear at the very beginning of the body, preceded only by other DEFINE forms.

■ Invalid bound variable name *exp*

The expression *exp* was found where a valid variable name was expected, such as in a pair binding list. Identifiers that name special forms are not valid variable names. The identifiers T and NIL are not valid variable names unless the global variable PCS-INTEGRATE-T-AND-NIL is set to false.

■ Invalid DO list item: *item*

The DO special form includes a specification of the iteration variable names, their initial values, and iteration forms; *item* is an improperly specified item in a list of such triples.

- `Invalid DO triples list: form`

  The DO special form includes a specification of the iteration variable names, their initial values, and iteration forms; *form* is a DO expression with an improperly specified list of such triples.

- `Invalid function name exp`

  The specified *exp* is not a valid procedure identifier but was used in an apparent procedure call. This error is usually caused by failing to quote a constant list in an expression, such as (3 "abc" x), so that the list appears to be an invalid procedure call.

- `Invalid identifier for DEFINE : exp`

  The first argument for DEFINE must be a valid variable name or a proper or improper list of identifiers.

- `Invalid identifier for SET!: exp`

  The first argument to SET! must be a valid variable name; an ACCESS, FLUID, or VECTOR-REF special form; or an accessor procedure defined with DEFINE-STRUCTURE.

- `Invalid identifier in expression exp₁ exp₂`

  The expression exp_2 incorrectly contains an occurrence of exp_1 where an identifier is required.

- `Invalid identifier list list`

  The indicated expression, *list*, is syntactically required to be a list of identifiers; but an atom or a list containing some element that was not an identifier was supplied. Such a list is required for the FLUID-LAMBDA, LAMBDA, and NAMED-LAMBDA special forms, among others. Depending on the context, the list may be required to be a proper list.

- `Invalid option list list`

  DEFINE-STRUCTURE has been called with an incorrect option list argument.

- `Invalid pair binding list list`

  The indicated expression, *list*, is syntactically required to be a list of sublists with each sublist containing two elements, the first of which must be an identifier. Such a list is required for the LET, LET*, and LETREC special forms.

- `Invalid special form form`

  The indicated expression is an incorrect use of a special form previously defined with SYNTAX.

■ Invalid SYNTAX form: *form*

The first argument to the SYNTAX special form in *form* is specified improperly. It should be a list representing a template for an expression.

■ Invalid QUASIQUOTE expression *form*

The indicated QUASIQUOTE expression *form* contains an incorrectly placed ',@' or ',.' specifier.

■ List expected *exp*

The indicated expression is syntactically required to be a proper list, but the atom *exp* was supplied.

■ Macro or special form name used as variable *name*

Identifiers that have been reserved as names for special forms cannot be used to name variables.

■ [WARNING: modifying an `integrable´ variable: *name*]

The specified variable *name* has been defined previously with DEFINE-INTEGRABLE and is now being redefined by the current expression. This message is issued only as a warning since this situation occurs frequently when the file containing the original definition of the variable is reloaded. It also occurs during the development of a program when variable bindings are changing constantly.

■ Wrong number of arguments *exp*

The number of arguments passed in the procedure call *exp* does not match the specification of the procedure. This error is detected by the compiler whenever the called procedure is visible lexically from the point of call or has been defined with DEFINE-INTEGRABLE; otherwise, it is detected during execution. If no expression value is displayed with the message text, the error is not detected until a point in the compilation when the source form of the expression is no longer available for display.

Execution Errors

8.3   The messages that follow are issued when errors are detected during the execution of a program. There are three categories of execution-time errors.

■ Assertion failures result when the argument to an ASSERT special form evaluates to false. The text [ASSERT failure!] is displayed along with the messages specified in the ASSERT form.

■ Run-time errors detected by the virtual machine underlying PC Scheme are reported along with the text [VM ERROR encountered!] or [VM FATAL ERROR].

■ Errors detected by system routines written in Scheme are reported along with the text [ERROR encountered!].

The Inspector's BACKTRACE command is helpful in finding the sequence of calls that resulted in one of these errors, although tail recursive calls are not necessarily shown in the backtrace listing.

The execution errors are as follows:

■ `Attempt to call a non-procedural object with n argument(s) as follows:` *expression*

An *expression* that evaluated to something other than a closure or continuation object appeared as the first element of an application. The first entry in *expression* shows the value of the first element of the Scheme expression in question.

■ `Divide by zero` *exp*

A division operation was given a value of zero as a divisor. Division operations include '/', QUOTIENT, REMAINDER, and MODULO as well as the procedures that call them.

■ `DOS-CALL error: unable to restore PC Scheme memory`

PC Scheme is unable to reload memory after a DOS-CALL because the memory it used before the DOS-CALL is no longer available. This situation occurs when a DOS task is executed that terminates and stays resident (such as with the DOS PRINT command). PC Scheme cannot recover from this error. Upon encountering this situation, PC Scheme terminates execution and control returns to DOS.

■ `DOS I/O error - Access denied`

An attempt was made to write to a file that is marked read-only. The file name you are using is protected.

■ `DOS I/O error - Disk Full`

There is no more room on disk to handle the current write request. You will need to retry the operation on a disk with sufficient room.

■ `DOS I/O error - Disk write protected`

You attempted to write to a write-protected disk. Either insert another disk, or remove the write tab and retry the operation.

■ `DOS I/O error - Drive not ready`

An attempt to perform I/O occurred to a drive that doesn't respond. Ensure that the drive door is fully closed on diskette drives, and retry the operation.

■ `DOS I/O error - File not found`

The filename specified for the current I/O operation does not exist in the current or specified directory. Retry the operation with the correct file name.

■ DOS I/O error – Invalid access

Access to a file was denied by DOS due to a sharing violation. Consult your DOS manual on file sharing.

■ DOS I/O error – Invalid disk drive

An invalid drive was specified on the current I/O operation. Retry the operation with a valid drive specifier.

■ DOS I/O error – Path not found

An invalid pathname was specified for the current I/O operation. Retry the operation with a valid pathname.

■ DOS I/O error – Printer out of paper

The printer is out of paper. Reload the printer and retry the operation.

■ DOS I/O error – Too many open files

The maximum number of files that can be opened at one time has been exceeded. Either close some files not in use, or increase the maximum number of files by modifying config.sys (see your DOS manual).

■ DOS I/O error number *xx*

An error occurred during the execution of an I/O operation. The error number xx is a DOS error return code between 1 and 88. Following is a current list of error codes; for more information refer to your DOS manual(s).

DOS Error Codes

Code	Explanation
1	Function number invalid
2	File not found
3	Path not found
4	Too many open files (no handles left)
5	Access denied
6	Handle invalid
7	Memory control blocks destroyed
8	Not enough memory
9	Memory block address invalid
10	Environment invalid
11	Format invalid
12	Access code invalid
13	Data invalid
15	Invalid disk drive specified
16	Attempt to remove current directory
17	Not same device
18	No more files

Code	Explanation
19	Disk write-protected
20	Unknown unit
21	Drive not ready
22	Unknown command
23	Data error (crc)
24	Bad request structure length
25	Seek error
26	Unknown medium type
27	Sector not found
28	Printer out of paper
29	Write fault
30	Read fault
31	General failure
32	Sharing violation
33	Lock violation
34	Disk change invalid
35	FCB unavailable
80	File already exists
85	Already assigned
86	Invalid password
87	Invalid parameter
88	Net write fault

■ `Engine already running`

An engine has attempted to call another engine. Nested engine calls are not permitted.

■ `ENGINE-RETURN not invoked`

The only valid way to terminate an engine's execution is with a call to ENGINE-RETURN. It is an error to return from the thunk executed by an engine.

■ `Environment object expected:` *object*

ENVIRONMENT-BINDINGS has been called with an argument that did not evaluate to an environment object.

■ `Expanded Memory Manager error` *xx*

The Expanded Memory Manager (EMM) software has detected an error. Ensure that the EMM software and expanded memory board hardware are functioning properly. An error code xx indicates the type of error and will be one of the following:

80	Malfunction in EMM software
81	Malfunction in EMM hardware
82–8F	Application error, call TI Customer Support Line

Upon encountering this situation, PC Scheme terminates execution and control returns to DOS after you press any key.

■ `FAST-LOAD file does not exist` *filename*

The argument given to the FAST-LOAD procedure did not name an existing file. Be sure to include the proper extension with the filename, as well as the directory information if the file is not in the current default directory.

■ `FAST-LOAD nesting too deep. Maximum is` *number*

During the loading of Scheme expressions with the FAST-LOAD procedure, the maximum nesting depth for fast-load files was exceeded. When this condition occurs, an end-of-file status is returned for the offending FAST-LOAD invocation.

■ `File not found: compiler.app`

The PC Scheme compiler cannot be found. Ensure that the `compiler.app` file exists in your PCS directory, which was set up by the installation batch stream.

■ `FLONUM overflow or underflow` *exp*

An arithmetic operation on floating point values has resulted in an overflow or underflow.

■ `Invalid argument count: Function expected` *n* `argument(s) but was called with` *m* `argument(s) as follows:` *expression*

The procedure that appears in *expression* has been called with the wrong number of arguments. The called procedure requires *n* arguments, but *m* were specified at the time of invocation as shown by *expression*.

■ `Invalid argument list for` *procedure exp*

The specified procedure was called with one or more arguments of the wrong type or value. In some cases, it is the combination of arguments that is incorrect, rather than the value of any one in particular. For this reason, all of the arguments usually are displayed in *exp*, not just those in error.

■ `Invalid argument to <engine>` *ticks success-k failure-k*

One of the arguments to an engine invocation is of the wrong type. All three argument values are listed. Note that *ticks* must be an integer, and *success-k* and *failure-k* must be procedures.

■ `Invalid argument to` *procedure argument*

The specified procedure was called with an argument of the wrong type or value. Only the incorrect argument is displayed although the procedure may have been called with others.

■ Invalid character constant *string*

During a READ operation, an invalid sequence of characters (*string*) was encountered following the #\ prefix used to denote character constants. If execution is allowed to continue, a question mark character (#\?) is substituted for the invalid character constant.

■ Invalid Column Number to *window-proc*

One of the following procedures was called with an invalid third argument: WINDOW-SET-CURSOR!, WINDOW-SET-POSITION!, or WINDOW-SET-SIZE!. The third argument must evaluate to an integer column number or column count in the range of zero through 80, inclusive.

■ Invalid FAST-LOAD module

During the execution of the FAST-LOAD procedure, a fast-load file with an invalid format was encountered. Fast-load modules should not be edited with a text editor or concatenated using the COPY command for DOS. To correct this problem, recompile the Scheme module that produced this message and rerun the MAKE_FSL utility.

■ Invalid Line Number to *window-proc*

One of the following procedures was called with an invalid second argument: WINDOW-SET-CURSOR!, WINDOW-SET-POSITION!, or WINDOW-SET-SIZE!. The second argument must evaluate to an integer line number or line count in the range zero to 25, inclusive.

■ Invalid operand to VM instruction *exp*

The specified primitive procedure (virtual machine instruction) was called with one or more arguments of the wrong type or value. In some cases, it is the combination of arguments that is incorrect rather than the value of any one in particular. For this reason, all of the arguments usually are displayed in *exp*, not just those in error.

■ Invalid Window Argument to *window-proc*

One of the following procedures was called with an invalid second argument: WINDOW-SET-CURSOR!, WINDOW-SET-POSITION!, or WINDOW-SET-SIZE!. The first argument must evaluate to a window object.

■ MAKE-STRING size limit exceeded *exp*

The size specified as an argument to MAKE-STRING was larger than the implementation limit. The current implementation limit is 16,383 character elements.

■ `MAKE-VECTOR size limit exceeded` *exp*

The size specified as an argument to MAKE-VECTOR was larger than the implementation limit. The current implementation limit is 10,921 elements.

■ `Memory paging error number` *n*

The movement of a block of data between conventional and extended memory has caused an error. ROM BIOS returns a value *n*, which normally denotes one of the following types of errors:

1	RAM parity error
2	Exception interrupt error
3	Gate address (line 20) error

A hardware error is probable. Upon encountering this situation, PC Scheme terminates execution, and control returns to DOS after you press any key.

■ `No fluid binding for SCHEME-TOP-LEVEL`

The fluid variable SCHEME–TOP–LEVEL could not be bound to the value of the top–level *read–eval–print* loop.

■ `Non-numeric operand to arithmetic operation` *exp*

One of the arguments to an arithmetic operation evaluated to a non-numeric value.

■ `Null continuation invoked`

ENGINE-RETURN has been invoked when no engine is running.

■ `NUMBER->STRING: integer too large for float conversion` *number*

The magnitude of the specified integer is too large to be represented as a floating point value.

■ `NUMBER->STRING: Invalid argument` *exp*

The first argument to NUMBER->STRING must evaluate to a number.

■ `NUMBER->STRING: Invalid format specification` *exp*

The second argument to NUMBER->STRING must evaluate to a valid format specification. Verify that the constant format expression is quoted.

■ `NUMBER->STRING: number too large for format` *number*

The format specified as the second argument to NUMBER->STRING did not suffice to represent the number.

■ Object module incompatible with this version — Recompile from source

The Scheme expression being executed was compiled under a version of PC Scheme that is incompatible with the current version. The program should be recompiled from its source representation using the current version of PC Scheme.

■ Out of memory

The program being executed has used up all available memory, and garbage collection cannot reclaim enough memory to permit the program to continue. This error condition causes a SCHEME-RESET to be executed and produces the message Attempting to execute SCHEME-RESET [Returning to top level]. By aborting execution and executing a SCHEME-RESET operation, enough memory may be freed to allow PC Scheme to return to the top-level read-eval-print loop. However, it is possible that the SCHEME-RESET will not succeed and you will have to terminate PC Scheme by rebooting the PC.

■ PC stack overflow during FAST-LOAD

An expression being read from a fast-load file is too complex to be read in fast-load format. Deeply nested list (linked through the car field) and vector structures may cause this problem to occur. This error condition causes a SCHEME-RESET to be executed and produces the message Attempting to execute SCHEME-RESET [Returning to top level].

■ Recursion too deep: Stack overflow

During the execution of a recursive program, PC Scheme's internal stack is holding so much state information that it is about to overflow. Check your program to see if there is an infinite loop or if a termination condition is incorrect. This error condition causes a SCHEME-RESET to be executed and produces the message Attempting to execute SCHEME-RESET [Returning to top level].

■ SET! of an unbound lexical variable *id*

The specified identifier is not bound to a variable in the lexical environment in which it was accessed by a SET!. Look for a misspelling or missing binding. Note that SET! modifies existing variable bindings and does not extend the environment with new bindings. Use DEFINE to define new global variables and LET, LET*, or LETREC for new local variables.

■ SET! of an unbound variable *name*

The specified identifier is not bound to a variable in the environment in which it was accessed by a SET!. Look for a misspelling or missing binding. Note that SET! modifies existing variable bindings and does not extend the environment with new bindings. Use DEFINE to define new global variables and LET, LET*, or LETREC for new local variables.

■ SET-FLUID! of an unbound fluid variable *name*

The specified identifier is not bound to a variable in the fluid environment in which it was accessed by a SET-FLUID!. Look for a misspelling or missing binding. Note that SET-FLUID! modifies existing fluid bindings and does not extend the environment with new bindings. Use FLUID-LAMBDA or FLUID-LET to create new fluid bindings.

■ Stack overflow during GC

This condition occurs during garbage collection when a data structure is too complex. Deeply nested list (linked through the car field) and vector structures may cause this situation to occur. It may be possible to execute an expression that temporarily creates such a structure by forcing a garbage collection using the GC procedure before executing the expression. PC Scheme cannot recover from this error. Upon encountering this situation, PC Scheme terminates execution, and control returns to DOS after you press any key.

■ Stack overflow in EQUAL? — Expression lists circular or too complex

The expressions passed as arguments to EQUAL? were circularly linked lists or were too deeply nested to be evaluated. Deeply nested list (linked through the car field) and vector structures can cause this error to occur. This error condition causes a SCHEME-RESET to be executed and produces the message Attempting to execute SCHEME-RESET [Returning to top level].

■ String index out of range *exp*

The index specified to a STRING-REF or STRING-SET! operation was outside of the bounds of the specified string argument. The valid range of indices for a string of N characters is from zero through N − 1, inclusive.

■ STRING>NUMBER: Invalid exactness specifies exp

The exactness argument to STRING>NUMBER must be either 'E or 'I.

■ STRING>NUMBER: Invalid radix exp

Either the argument that specifies the radix is not one of 'B, 'O, 'D, or 'X, or the string specified cannot be converted to the desired radix.

■ Structure component unknown to *type*

The structure instance constructor procedure MAKE-*type* was called with an initialization value for a component name. However, that component name is undefined for structures of that type.

■ Timer already running

An attempt was made to start the PC Scheme internal timer (used to support engines) when it was already running. If execution is allowed to continue, the second request to start the timer is ignored.

■ Unable to allocate memory for PC Scheme

You do not have enough memory on your system to run PC Scheme.

■ User keyboard interrupt

The user has interrupted execution by causing a break. On the TIPC, a break key is selected by holding down the SHIFT key and pressing the BRK/PAUS key. On the IBM PC, hold down the CTRL key and press the SCROLL LOCK key.

■ Variable not defined in current enviroment *id*

The specified identifier is not bound to a variable in the environment in which it was accessed. Look for a misspelling or missing binding.

■ Variable not defined in lexical environment *name*

The specified identifier is not bound to a variable in the lexical environment in which it was accessed. Look for a misspelling or missing binding.

■ Variable not defined in fluid environment *name*

The specified identifier is not bound to a variable in the fluid environment in which it was accessed. Look for a misspelling or missing binding.

■ Vector index out of range *exp*

The index specified to a VECTOR-REF or VECTOR-SET! operation was outside the bounds of the specified vector argument. The valid range of indices for a vector of N elements is from zero through N − 1, inclusive.

Because structures are defined in terms of vectors, this error also may result from a structure component accessor procedure that has been given an argument of the wrong type. It is common for other abstract data types to be defined in terms of vectors also.

■ [WARNING: Output aborted by SHIFT-BREAK]

This message indicates that an output operation was terminated because the user issued a break to force an interrupt. Execution may proceed from the interrupt, but the output operation is not resumed or restarted (that is, the remainder of the output is lost).

8.4 The following error messages result from internal resource allocation problems in the PC Scheme system itself:

■ `*** Compiler ran out of registers ***`

The compiler translates Scheme programs into a byte-coded virtual machine that is oriented around 64 emulated general-purpose registers. Because these registers are allocated to user variables as well as temporary expressions, it is possible for the compiler to run out of registers to allocate to a program. This problem rarely happens unless the number of local variables in a routine approaches 64 or a procedure call is made with a very large number of arguments (which are passed in the registers).

The most practical correction is to reduce the number of local variables or the number of arguments passed. For example, the following routine consumes five registers for the local variables A, B, C, D, and E plus three more for the arguments of the call:

```
(lambda (a b c)
  (let ((d (+ a b))
        (e (+ b c)))
    (if (=? a b)
        (* d d)
        (foo b e))))
```

Because the value of D is needed only in the true branch of the IF and the value of E is needed only in the false branch, those variables can be made to share the same register by defining them in parallel LET environment frames, as follows:

```
(lambda (a b c)
     (if (=? a b)
         (let ((d (+ a b)))
          (* d d))
         (let (e (+ b c)))
           (foo b e))))
```

Of course, such manipulations are only important when dozens of variables are involved and the out-of-registers error forces such extreme measures.

■ `Constants table overflow in compiler`

The format of compiled Scheme object programs permits a maximum of 256 distinct literal expressions for each top-level expression that is compiled. This limit is rarely reached except in contrived examples, but it is possible with very large program modules or expressions that contain a large number of quoted expressions.

It is difficult to tell by looking at the source for an expression how many constant table entries will be required in its object form. In many cases, small integer values are folded into immediate instruction operands. In other cases, the compiler determines that two constants are equivalent (using EQV?) and uses a single table entry for both.

The most practical correction when this error is reported is to break up a large expression into two smaller ones.

■ `Register overflow — Too many arguments to closure`

The second argument to APPLY was a list whose length exceeded the implementation limit for the maximum number of arguments allowed in a procedure call. The limit for this situation is 62 arguments.

IMPLEMENTATION CONSTRAINTS

The implementation of PC Scheme on small personal computers necessarily has imposed constraints on the maximum program and data sizes that can be accommodated. This chapter lists those machine and implementation constraints and explains some of the reasons for them.

Data Type Size Constraints

9.1 The number of objects that may exist in memory at any time is a function of the total amount of memory space available and the size of each object. The following table lists the maximum size limits for those data types that are implemented in PC Scheme as heap-allocated, variable-length objects. (The heap is the area of Scheme memory from which objects with indeterminate extent are allocated as described in the chapter entitled Advanced Features).

The table also lists the maximum and minimum values for floating point and small integer (FIXNUM) values. The actual limit on the size of an object is either the value given in the table or the amount of free memory remaining in the PC Scheme heap, whichever is smaller.

Data Type	Size Limation
BIGNUM integer	9,520 decimal digits (see notes 1 and 2)
FIXNUM integer	−16,384 to +16,383 (see note 4)
Floating point number	±2.226e-308 to ±1.797e308
List	Unbounded (see note 3)
String	0 to 16,380 characters (see note 1)
Symbol	0 to 16,376 characters (see notes 1 and 2)
Vector	0 to 10,921 elements

NOTES:

1. The maximum length of a string, symbol, or BIGNUM (arbitrary precision integer) is constrained fundamentally to be less than 64K bytes because only 16 bits are used to represent the size information. In addition, many operations on these objects allocate additional space outside the PC Scheme heap area for storage of temporary results. For example, the calculation of the product of two BIGNUM values requires sufficient temporary space to hold the multiplier, the multiplicand, and the product. Currently, the space allocated for such temporary results is less than 64K bytes. These considerations dictate the maximum values listed in the table.

2 The I/O routines use the temporary workspace area to format symbols and numbers for printing. Symbols are preprocessed in this way to ensure that they are prefixed by slashes. Thus, the largest symbol that can be printed depends on the number of characters in its representation which must be preceded by backslash (\) characters in the output. Although BIGNUM values of up to 9,520 digits can be manipulated by the PC Scheme arithmetic procedures, only 8,960 digits can be accommodated in the temporary output buffer.

3. A list is comprised of linked pairs, with each pair consisting of 6 bytes of heap storage. The maximum length of a noncircular list is determined by the amount of heap storage available. Circular lists, which contain cyclic substructures, appear to have infinite length. The LENGTH procedure assumes that no list has more than 16,383 elements; the value it returns for longer lists is unspecified.

4. PC Scheme implements integer values between −16,384 and +16,383 using a FIXNUM representation and values with larger magnitudes with a BIGNUM representation. The conversion between FIXNUM and BIGNUM representations is automatic. Calculations with FIXNUM results are more efficient since BIGNUM values are variable-length objects allocated from the heap.

Program Size Constraints

9.2 The PC Scheme compiler imposes large, but fixed, limits on the number of constants and variables that may appear in various components of a program. Efficient use of the operating system and microprocessor that underlie PC Scheme also dictates certain restrictions on a program's size and its dynamic behavior. These constraints are listed in the following table:

Item	Size Limitation
Constants	256 constants per top-level expression
Arguments on a call	62 maximum (see note 1)
Local lexical variables	62 maximum (see note 1)
Call/return stack size	65,536 bytes (see note 2)
OBJECT-HASH calls	65,536 calls (see note 3)
Open I/O ports	DOS dependent (see note 4)

NOTES:

1. The compiler translates Scheme programs into a byte-coded virtual machine oriented around 64 emulated general-purpose registers. Since these registers are allocated to user variables as well as temporary expressions, it is possible for the compiler to run out of registers to allocate to a program. This problem rarely happens unless the number of local variables in a routine approaches 64 or a procedure call is made with a very large number of arguments (which are passed in the registers).

2. The Scheme equivalent to the traditional call/return stack is a tree of linked continuation objects. For efficiency, these continuations are manipulated internally in standard linear stack fashion until an overflow occurs or CALL/CC is invoked. The stack contents then are moved into a heap-allocated continuation object, and the stack growth is continued. The upper limit for stack growth is 65,536 bytes, the addressability of a single segment in the underlying hardware. The minimal stack frame size for a procedure call is 15 bytes, and 3 additional bytes are allocated (in the worst case) for each local variable. Thus, up to 4,000 stack frames can accumulate from unreturned recursive calls before the stack overflows.

3. The procedure OBJECT-HASH returns a unique identifying integer value for each distinct argument it is given. These values are maintained internally as 16-bit unsigned integers. When OBJECT-HASH is called with the 65,537 distinct value, the internal counter wraps around, and the returned value is no longer uniquely associated with the argument value.

4. The number of ports that can be open simultaneously depends on the underlying operating system. For example, MS-DOS has a system configuration command called FILE that specifies the maximum number of open files. To increase the allowable number of open ports in PC Scheme, consult the manual for your operating system to determine how to increase the file allocation accordingly.

A SCHEME SESSION

Introduction

A.1 In this session, you execute TI Scheme expressions in order to familiarize yourself with the Scheme language and unique features of PC Scheme.

Note the following things before starting:

■ The system may need to recover memory during a session. At such times, a Garbage Collecting message appears momentarily in the PCS-STATUS-WINDOW.

■ The key referred to as the RETURN key may be the ENTER key on your keyboard.

You must load the PC Scheme software before starting this session. Refer to Section 2, Getting Started, for these instructions.

First steps:

1. If you have not already done so, set the drive designator to the fixed disk and the current directory to the directory containing the PC Scheme software.

2. Type PCS and press the RETURN key. The Texas Instruments copyright statement appears.

3. PC Scheme has finished loading when the following message appears:

```
[PCS-DEBUG-MODE is OFF]
[1]
```

You are now ready to begin entering Scheme expressions.

The Session

A.2 Now you begin the actual session. Each of the commands used during the session is fully described in the *TI Scheme Language Reference Manual — Student Edition*.

1. One of the first things you usually do during a session is to define a variable. To do this in Scheme, you use the DEFINE procedure. Enter the following expression after the [1] prompt:

```
(define size 5)
```

2. Press the RETURN key. Scheme responds as follows:

```
SIZE
```

Notice that the response SIZE was returned in uppercase characters. Scheme, like the Pascal language, is insensitive to case, so almost everything you enter is converted into uppercase.

3. Since you have defined SIZE, we can now use it in expressions. Enter the following and press the RETURN key. (Now that you are in the habit, press the RETURN key every time you are told to enter an expression.)

```
(* SIZE 3)
```

Scheme responds by returning the value 15.

4. Note that the space between * and SIZE in the expression (* SIZE 3) is important, as its omission would generate an error. However, to show you how errors are handled in Scheme, generate an error by entering the following:

```
(*SIZE 3)
```

Scheme responds by returning the following message:

```
[VM ERROR encountered!] Variable not defined in lexical
 environment
*SIZE

[INSPECT]
```

You receive this message because Scheme did not recognize what you entered. Whenever Scheme cannot evaluate an expression, it enters the Inspector. The Inspector is fully described in the section of this manual that is entitled Debugging. For now, just remember that the way to get out of the Inspector and back to PC Scheme is to press CTRL–Q (press the CTRL key and the Q key at the same time).

5. Now is a good time to consider how Scheme uses *prefix notation*. The first element in an expression, which is called the *operator*, always denotes a procedure. For example, if you enter (+ 1 4), '+' is the operator (or name of the procedure), and 1 and 4 are the parameters of the procedure.

If you are not already comfortable with LISP, prefix notation may take some getting used to. A key advantage to prefix notation is its ability to handle any number of parameters with one operator. For example, the expression (5 * 4 * 3 * 2 * 1) in Pascal is simply (* 5 4 3 2 1) in Scheme.

6. In Scheme, you also use the DEFINE procedure to define other procedures. Enter the following:

```
(define (square x) (* x x))
```

Scheme responds by returning SQUARE. What you have done is to define a procedure called SQUARE that has x as its parameter. Scheme will take x and evaluate it according to the expression (* x x). For example, if you enter (square 2), Scheme will respond by returning the value 4. If you enter (square size), the value 25 is returned.

7. Now that you have a procedure that calculates the square of a number, you can define a procedure that uses SQUARE to calculate the cube of a number. Enter the following:

```
(define (cube x) (* (square x) x))
```

Note that you have used one procedure (SQUARE) within the definition of another procedure (CUBE). Enter the following:

```
(cube 4)
```

Scheme returns the value 64.

You should now be comfortable with entering Scheme expressions at the top-level of PC Scheme. Hopefully, you have not grown too attached to the work that you have created in this session, as there is no way to save procedures that are defined at PC Scheme's top level. Go on to the next paragraph to learn how to use the EDWIN editor to create programs and save them on disk.

Creating and Saving Programs

A.3 This paragraph tells you how to create and save programs with the EDWIN editor. EDWIN is fully described in the chapter of this manual entitled The EDWIN Editor.

1. To execute EDWIN from the top level of PC Scheme, enter the following:

```
(edwin)
```

2. After EDWIN has been loaded, the status line at the next-to-the-bottom line of your screen reflects the change of control to EDWIN:

```
Edwin 2.0     [Scheme]
```

3. Watch the screen carefully as you enter the following expression:

```
(define (average x y) (/ (+ x y) 2))
```

As you can see, EDWIN is tailored to the needs of a Scheme programmer. Did you notice how EDWIN moved the cursor back to each opening parenthesis for a moment after you entered its corresponding closing parenthesis?

Also, did you notice how EDWIN displayed each component of the complete expression at the bottom of the screen as soon as the component was a valid expression in itself? First the expression (average x y) appeared at the bottom of the screen, followed by (+ x y), followed by (/ (+ x y) 2), which in turn was followed by the complete expression (define (average x y) (/ (+ x y) 2)).

If you did not catch all of this, reenter the expression. As you can see, EDWIN helps you easily wade through the mass of parentheses that is LISP programming.

4. Now that we have defined the procedure AVERAGE, we can save it to disk as a source file by pressing CTRL-X, then CTRL-S. At the bottom of the screen, you are prompted with the following line:

```
Write buffer to file:
```

5. Respond by entering `average.s`. Scheme uses the convention of having the extension `.s` stand for source files. (While on the subject, `.so` stands for compiled files and `.fsl` stands for fast-load files.)

Scheme responds with the following message:

```
Writing file average.s -- done
```

6. After having successfully saved the file, you can now return to the top level of PC Scheme by pressing CTRL-X, then CTRL-C.

Loading Source Files

A.4 To have a source file evaluated, you need to bring it up to the top level of PC Scheme.

1. To have the AVERAGE procedure that you previously saved to a file, enter the following expression:

```
(load "average.s")
```

Scheme responds with the message OK.

2. You can now have PC Scheme evaluate the expression contained in the source file. Enter the following:

```
(average 90 80)
```

Scheme responds with the correct answer of 85.

A Recursion Example

A.5 Recursion, the ability of a procedure to call itself, is just as important to Scheme as it is to any LISP dialect. To demonstrate recursion in Scheme, you will be asked to write a recursive procedure to calculate factorials. Namely, for any number n, its factorial $n!$ is calculated as follows:

$$n * (n-1) * (n-2) ... * 1$$

For example, 5! is equal to 5 * 4 * 3 * 2 * 1, which is equal to 120.

1. Enter the EDWIN editor by entering the following from the top level of PC Scheme:

```
(edwin)
```

2. Type in the following program:

```
(define (factorial x)          ; define procedure
  (if (= x 1)                  ; is x equal to 1?
      1                        ; if so, return 1
      (* x (factorial (- x 1)))))) ; if not, call factorial
                                   of x-1
```

What this procedure does first is check whether x is equal to 1. If it is, the procedure returns 1. If not, the procedure multiplies x by the factorial of x-1 . Notice how the procedure uses recursion to call itself in the last line.

3. Instead of saving the program, leaving EDWIN, and returning to PC Scheme, you can evaluate the definition of the procedure factorial by pressing META-O (which is the ESC key, followed by the O key). This evaluation causes the procedure to be compiled. After the procedure is compiled, control passes back to PC Scheme.

4. To save the factorial procedure to disk, reenter EDWIN and press CTRL-X, then CTRL-W. When prompted for a filename, enter factorial.s.

5. Enter CTRL-X, then CTRL-Z to exit EDWIN and return to PC Scheme.

Compiling Source Files

A.6 Once you have defined a procedure and saved it to a source file, you can compile it by using the COMPILE-FILE procedure. To compile factorial.s, enter the following:

```
(compile-file "factorial.s" "factorial.so")
```

PC Scheme takes the source file factorial.s and puts it into the compiled file factorial.so.

Making Fast-Load Files

A.7 Fast-load files (.fsl) take much less time to load than source files (.s). To make fast-load files, you must first be completely familiar with the DOS-CALL procedure, which allows you to execute DOS commands from Scheme. Make sure you read the warning contained in the description for DOS-CALL that is found in Section 7 of the *TI Scheme Language Reference Manual — Student Edition*.

1. Enter the following:

```
(DOS-CALL "" "" 4095)
```

Note that the MS-DOS prompt (such as A> or E>) appears.

2. Next, you need to use the MAKE_FSL utility. Since DOS has a maximum of eight characters for filenames, you would enter the following to make a fast-load file out of the compiled file factoria.so:

```
make_fsl factorial.so factorial.fsl
```

3. To leave DOS and return to PC Scheme, enter the following:

```
exit
```

Automatic Loading

A.8 To automatically load procedures that you often use, you can use the *SCHEME.INI* file, which is a text file that you can create with any editor that produces text files, such as EDWIN. The objective is to put instructions into this file to tell PC Scheme to load your favorite procedures. You should put a load instruction for each desired source file.

For example, if you wanted the factorial function above to be available each time that you brought up Scheme, you could enter the following line of code in your *SCHEME.INI* file:

```
(load "factorial.s")
```

THE %GRAPHICS PRIMITIVES

The %GRAPHICS Primitives

B.1 The %GRAPHICS primitives allow you to use some alternative graphics functions to set points, set palettes, draw lines, and draw boxes.

These are the primitives upon which the MIT Scheme graphics functions (described in the chapter of this manual entitled Graphics) are built. MIT Scheme views the screen as a grid, with the origin (0,0) at the center of the screen, while the %GRAPHICS primitives view the origin as the upper left corner of the screen. The %GRAPHICS primitives are also somewhat faster than the regular MIT Scheme functions.

NOTE: The %GRAPHICS primitives are low-level routines whose function may change in future releases without notice. They are for use strictly at your own risk. Also, any color argument to a procedure must be a fixed number and not a symbol that represents a color (for example, use 2, not red).

Keep the following points in mind when you are using %GRAPHICS functions:

■ All coordinates are in the range −16384 .. 16383, where (0,0) is the upper left pixel.

■ Images are displayed only if they fall inside the clipping rectangle. The clipping rectangle is the full screen initially and reverts to the full screen on video mode changes.

■ If your computer is in TI mode, the clear graphics mode resets the graphics palette as well. Also, the default graphics mode is 3.

■ If your computer is in IBM mode, selecting a graphics mode automatically clears the screen. Both text and graphics share the screen in graphics mode. (Namely, if your text scrolls, your graphics will scroll.) The default graphics mode depends on the type of video card that is selected as the default display adapter. If the Color Graphics Adapter (CGA) or the Enhanced Graphics Adapter (EGA) is available, the power–up mode is 3.

■ You can create your own Scheme function to invoke the %GRAPHICS primitives. This appendix includes examples of such functions after the description of each primitive. The advantage of defining such functions is that you do not need to supply the placeholder zeroes.

Explanation of Primitives

B.2 This section explains some of the %GRAPHICS primitives. Because several of the %GRAPHICS primitives are simply duplicates of functions that were covered in the chapter of this manual entitled Graphics, they are not included in this appendix. A complete example of the use of the %GRAPHICS primitives is at the end of this appendix.

Set Point

B.2.1 The following function sets the pixel at coordinates x, y to the value of color if the point lies inside the clipping rectangle.

```
(%graphics 1 x y color 0 0 xor)
```

The 1 following %graphics denotes that this is %GRAPHICS function #1. The arguments 0 0 that follow color are simply placeholders to match the number of arguments expected for the function. The actual color that is displayed as a result of the integer argument that you give for color depends on the graphics color palette. A computer in TI mode will use only the lower three bits of the value of color. In IBM mode, the appropriate portion of the value is used, depending on the number of colors that are available in the current graphics mode (if the computer is in graphics mode).

The xor argument indicates how this graphic is to be added to the existing graphics on the screen.

The xor argument may have one of two values: 0 or 1. A value of 0 indicates that the pixels of this graphic should replace all current values of those pixels. A value of 1 indicates that the pixels of this graphic should be merged with the current values of these pixels (this is known as exclusive or). Two successive applications of exclusive or should return the pixels to their original values.

Example:

```
; Set point
(define-integrable setp
   (lambda (x y color xor)
      (%graphics 1 x y color 0 0 xor)))
```

Set Palette

B.2.2 The following function allows you to change the mapping of a particular pixel value to display a different color:

```
(%graphics 2 cc nc 0 0 0 0)
```

The 2 following %graphics denotes that this is %GRAPHICS function #2. The argument cc means the current color that is used, and the argument nc means the new color to display. The arguments 0 0 0 0 that follow nc are simply placeholders to match the number of arguments expected for the function.

This function does not modify the pixel values that are stored within the graphics planes. Rather, the hardware latches that map the pixel values to the proper displayed colors are modified.

For the TIPC and for IBM computers running EGA modes 14 and 16, cc is the palette register number and nc is the color to be assigned to the register.

When a point is plotted in some color, what is put into memory is actually a palette register number. The hardware then maps the number to the color.

As an example, if palette register n contains color n, color 0 is black, and 7 is white (this is true for both TIPC and IBM in EGA modes 14 or 16), then the expression (%graphics 2 0 7 0 0 0) assigns to palette register 0 the color 7. All pixels having a value of 0 in the graphics memory that were black are now displayed as white. The expression (%graphics 2 7 0 0 0 0) assigns to palette register 7 the color 0, so all pixels with a value of 7 in the graphics memory that were white now become black. However, pixels with a value of 0 continue to be displayed as white.

The TIPC has 8 palette registers and the IBM EGA has 16 palette registers. Eight colors are available on the TIPC, and 64 colors are available on the EGA. The color values for the TIPC appear in the following table:

Value	Color
0	Black
1	Blue
2	Red
3	Magenta
4	Green
5	Cyan
6	Yellow
7	White

For the IBM EGA, color values have the format rgbRGB, where each letter represents one bit, lowercase values represent high intensity, and uppercase values represent low intensity. The following table lists the color values of the EGA:

Value	Color
0	Black
1	Blue
2	Green
3	Cyan
4	Red
5	Magenta
6	Brown
7	White
56	Gray
57	Light-blue
58	Light-green
59	Light-cyan
60	Light-red
61	Light-magenta
62	Yellow
63	Intense-white

In IBM CGA mode, the function allows you to select the colors to be used in graphics mode 4. The argument cc signifies select function and nc signifies select color.

In mode 4, the functions cc and nc are misnomers, as cc signifies *select function* and nc signifies *select color*. If you give the cc argument a value of 0, a background color is being selected by the nc argument. The background color is specified as an integer whose value is in the range 0 through 127. For mode 4 only, if cc has the value 1, one of two color palettes is selected by nc. These palettes determine the colors you can choose when drawing. Each palette contains four colors. When nc is 0, the palette contains black (background), red, green, and yellow. A value of 1 selects a palette containing black (background), cyan, magenta, and white.

Example:

```
; Set palette
(define-integrable resetp
   (lambda (cc nc)
      (%graphics 2 cc nc 0 0 0 0)))
```

Draw Line   **B.2.3** The following function draws a solid line from one point to another (parts of the line lying outside the clipping rectangle are not drawn):

```
(%graphics 3 x1 y1 x2 y2 color xor)
```

The 3 following %graphics denotes that this is %GRAPHICS function #3. The arguments x1 y1 give you the coordinates of the first point; x2 y2 give you the coordinates of the second. The actual color that is displayed as a result of the integer argument that you give for color depends on the graphics color palette. A computer in TI mode will use only the lower three bits of the value of color. In IBM mode, the appropriate portion of the value is used, depending on the number of colors that are available in the current graphics mode (if the computer is in graphics mode).

Example:

```
; Draw Line
(define-integrable line
   (lambda (x1 y1 x2 y2 color xor)
      (%graphics 3 x1 y1 x2 y2 color xor)))
```

Read Point   **B.2.4** The following function reads the pixel value at coordinates x y.

```
(%graphics 4 x y 0 0 0 0)
```

The 4 following %graphics denotes that this is %GRAPHICS function #4. The arguments 0 0 0 0 that follow x y are simply placeholders to match the number of arguments expected for the function.

The value returned for the pixel may not correspond with the color displayed if the color palette has been modified on your computer. If your computer is in IBM mode, the range of values that can be returned for the point depends on the graphics mode that you selected. If the point is outside the clipping rectangle, −1 is returned.

Example:

```
; Read Point (return color of point)
(define-integrable point
    (lambda (x y)
        (%graphics 4 x y 0 0 0)))
```

Draw Box **B.2.5** The following function draws a box between two opposite corners, which are given by the arguments x1 y1 and x2 y2.

```
(%graphics 6 x1 y1 x2 y2 color xor)
```

The 6 following %graphics denotes that this is %GRAPHICS function #6. The argument color determines what color the perimeter of the box takes on.

Unfilled boxes are not clipped as such, as the result may not be a closed figure. Instead, the coordinates for the clipped edges are readjusted to be those of the clipping rectangle. Therefore, if the side of a box falls outside the clipping rectangle, the side is drawn with the clipped edge running snugly against the side of the clipping rectangle.

Example:

```
; Draw Box
(define-integrable draw-box
    (lambda (x1 y1 x2 y2 color xor)
        (%graphics 6 x1 y1 x2 y2 color xor)))
```

Draw Filled Box **B.2.6** The following function draws a filled box between two opposite corners, which are given by the arguments x1 y1 and x2 y2. The edges of a filled box are clipped to the edges of the clipping rectangle.

```
(%graphics 7 x1 y1 x2 y2 color xor)
```

The 7 following %graphics denotes that this is %GRAPHICS function #7. The argument color determines what color the box takes on.

Example:

```
; Draw Filled Box
(define-integrable draw-filled-box
    (lambda (x1 y1 x2 y2 color xor)
        (%graphics 7 x1 y1 x2 y2 color xor)))
```

Set Clipping Rectangle **B.2.7** The following function sets the screen's clipping rectangle between two opposite corners, which are given by the arguments x1 y1 and x2 y2.

```
(%graphics 8 x1 y1 x2 y2 0 0)
```

The 8 following %graphics denotes that this is %GRAPHICS function #8. The arguments 0 0 that follow y2 are simply placeholders to match the number of arguments expected for the function.

The coordinates of the two corners are in the range −16384 .. 16383, where the origin is the screen's upper left pixel. The intersection between the requested clipping rectangle and the full screen is calculated, and the result becomes the final clipping rectangle. If this would put the rectangle completely off the screen, the full screen is used instead. The clipping rectangle is never allowed to become totally invisible (off-screen).

SET-VIDEO-MODE! resets the clipping rectangle to the full screen for the video mode selected.

Example:

```
; Set clipping rectangle
(define-integrable set-clipping-rectangle
        (lambda (x1 y1 x2 y2)
           (%graphics 8 x1 y1 x2 y2 0 0)))
```

Complete Example   **B.2.8** The file GRAPHICS.S contains an example that uses most of the functions described in this appendix. To obtain the example that is appropriate for your hardware configuration, select the appropriate command from the following three choices:

TI mode:	`(ti-example x y)`
IBM, CGA:	`(cga-example x y)`
IBM, EGA:	`(ega-example x y)`

where x and y are the coordinates of the upper left corner of the clipping rectangle that you want.

The command loads GRAPHICS.S from the PC Scheme system directory onto your computer. The example contains the following code:

```
(define-integrable setp
  (lambda (x y color xor)
    (%graphics 1 x y color 0 0 xor)))
(define-integrable resetp
  (lambda (cc nc)
    (%graphics 2 cc nc 0 0 0 0)))
(define-integrable line
  (lambda (x1 y1 x2 y2 color xor)
    (%graphics 3 x1 y1 x2 y2 color xor)))
(define-integrable point
  (lambda (x y)
    (%graphics 4 x y 0 0 0 0)))
(define-integrable draw-box
  (lambda (x1 y1 x2 y2 color xor)
    (%graphics 6 x1 y1 x2 y2 color xor)))
(define-integrable draw-filled-box
  (lambda x1 y1 x2 y2 color xor)
    (%graphics 7 x1 y1 x2 y2 color xor)))
(define-integrable clipping-rectangle
  (lambda (x1 y1 x2 y2)
    (%graphics 8 x1 y1 x2 y2 0 0)))
    ; x and y are coordinates of upper left corner of picture
    ; a and b are coordinates of upper left corner of clipping
      rectangle
    ; c and d are coordinates of lower right corner of clipping
      rectangle
(define cga-example
  (lambda (x y a b c d)
    ; set video mode to graphics
    (set-video-mode! 4)
    (ti-example x y a b c d)
    (display "Type a key to return to mode 3")
    (read-char `console)
    ; return to text mode
    (set-video-mode! 3)))
(define ega-example
  (lambda (x y a b c d)
    ; set video mode to graphics
    (set-video-mode! 16)
    (ti-example x y a b c d)))
(define ti-example
  (lambda (x y a b c d)
    ; x and y are coordinates of upper left corner of clipping
      rectangle
    ; set clipping rectangle
    (clipping-rectangle (a b c d)
    ; draw box (replace)
    (draw-box (+ x 10) (+ y 20) (+ x 50) (+ y 50) 3 0)
    ; draw filled box (exclusive or)
    (draw-filled-box (+ x 30) (+ y 30) (+ x 90) (+ y 120) 2 1)
    ; draw line (exclusive or)
    (line (+ x 10) (+ y 20) (+ x 90) (+ y 120) 1 1)
    ; set point
    (setp (+ x 20) (+ y 20) 2 0)
    ; set palette
    (resetp 2 6)
    ; read color of point
    (point (+ x 20) (+ y 20))))
```

INDEX

EDWIN commands (continued)
  CTRL-X CTRL-I 4-16
  CTRL-X CTRL-K 4-15
  CTRL-X CTRL-M 4-17
  CTRL-X CTRL-P 4-16
  CTRL-X CTRL-Q 4-16
  CTRL-X CTRL-S 4-16
  CTRL-X CTRL-V 4-9, 4-16
  CTRL-X CTRL-W 4-16
  CTRL-X CTRL-X 4-13
  CTRL-X H 4-13
  CTRL-Y 4-15
  CTRL-Z CTRL-Z 4-6
  CTRL-X BACKSPACE 4-14
  LINEFEED 4-19
  meta commands 4-3
  meta-< 4-11
  meta-> 4-11
  meta-@ 4-13
  meta-\ 4-14
  meta-- 4-16
  meta-A 4-11
  meta-B 4-11
  meta-BACKSPACE 4-14
  meta-D 4-14
  meta-E 4-11
  meta-F 4-11
  meta-H 4-13
  meta-K 4-14
  meta-O 4-19
  meta-*space bar* 4-14
  meta-V 4-11
  meta-W 4-14—4-15
  meta-Y 4-15
  meta-control commands 4-3
  meta-CTRL-@ 4-13
  meta-CTRL-B 4-11, 4-12
  meta-CTRL-D 4-12
  meta-CTRL-F 4-12
  meta-CTRL-K 4-14
  meta-CTRL-N 4-12
  meta-CTRL-P 4-12
  meta-CTRL-Q 4-19
  mèta-CTRL-U 4-12
  meta-CTRL-W 4-14
  meta-CTRL-X 4-19
  meta-CTRL-Z 4-19
  RETURN 4-8
  simple commands 4-3
  TAB 4-19
EXIT 2-5
inspector commands 3-3, 3-4, 3-5
  miscellaneous commands 3-5—3-6
PCS 2-2—2-3

structure editor commands:
  add parentheses (AP) 3-16
  beginning (B) 3-14
  delete (D) 3-16
  delete parentheses (DP) 3-16
  find (F) 3-15
  insert after (IA) 3-16
  insert before (IB) 3-16
  move 3-13
  next (N) 3-14
  pretty print (PP) 3-13
  previous (PR) 3-14
  print (P) 3-13
  Q command 3-17
  replace (R) 3-15
  splice before (SB) 3-17
  splice after (SA) 3-17
  substitute (S) 3-15
  top (T) 3-15
Common Lisp, relationship of
      Scheme to 1-2
COMPILE-FILE procedure 2-5
compiling files:
  COMPILE-FILE procedure 2-5
  fast-load format 2-5
  filename extensions 2-5
  source files tutorial A-4—A-5
console 2-3
  in windows 5-1
control characters 3-3
creating programs, tutorial A-3—A-4
CTRL-@ 4-13
CTRL key 3-3
CTRL-A 3-3, 4-11
CTRL-B 3-3, 3-5, 4-8, 4-11
CTRL-C 3-3, 3-5
CTRL-D 3-3, 3-5, 4-14
CTRL-E 3-3, 3-4, 4-11
CTRL-F 4-8, 4-11
CTRL-G 3-3, 3-4, 3-5, 3-6, 4-9
CTRL-H 4-14
CTRL-I 3-3, 3-4
CTRL-K 4-14
CTRL-L 3-3, 3-5, 4-11
CTRL-M 3-3, 3-6
CTRL-N 4-8, 4-11
CTRL-O 4-8
CTRL-P 3-3, 3-4, 3-5, 4-7, 4-11
CTRL-Q 3-3, 3-5, 4-7
CTRL-R 3-3, 3-5, 3-6, 3-8, 4-17
CTRL-S 3-3, 3-4, 3-5, 4-17
CTRL-T 4-7
CTRL-U 3-3, 3-5
CTRL-X CTRL-X 4-13
CTRL-X CTRL-Z 4-6

PART **2**

Language Reference Manual

CONTENTS

Chapter	Paragraph	Title	Page

INTRODUCTION

The Scheme programming language is a lexically scoped dialect of LISP developed at MIT to demonstrate that a language inspired by Church's lambda calculus could efficiently support the major programming paradigms in use today, including imperative, functional, and message passing styles.

Like Pascal a decade earlier, Scheme was created originally as a distillation of proven concepts and was first used in research and teaching. It has now emerged in several implementations as a serious tool for producing applications and system software. Many of the ideas in Scheme were incorporated into the Common Lisp specification, making Scheme a close relative to this language that nevertheless retains a simple and streamlined nature.

Scheme has proven to be particularly effective for symbolic computing on small personal computers, where full implementations of Common Lisp are difficult to construct and are relatively inefficient. Scheme's use of lexical scoping, block structures, call by value, and tail-recursive semantics permits it to be compiled efficiently, whereas most personal computer implementations of LISP are interpretive in nature. Scheme's treatment of all procedures and continuations as "first-class" data objects makes it a remarkably extensible language. The efficient implementation of continuations makes it an effective systems programming language as well.

Purpose

1.1 This book is a language reference manual for TI Scheme and is not intended to be a user's guide or tutorial. Chapter 7 contains an alphabetic list of all TI Scheme procedures, forms, variables, and literals along with their descriptions. Its alphabetical organization is designed to facilitate searching for specific information rather than reading from cover to cover. The sources of all text references to other documentation are listed in the bibliography.

The TI Scheme language specification has been developed concurrently with a specific implementation at Texas Instruments called PC Scheme. Although the purpose of this manual is to describe TI Scheme in general rather than for a specific implementation, several implementation dependencies are discussed. When these dependencies are not obvious, language details are separated from specific implementation details. Refer to the *PC Scheme User's Guide — Student Edition* [23] for information specific to the PC Scheme implementation.

In this manual, the name "Scheme" refers to the Scheme language in general, particularly as described in the *Revised*[3] *Report on the Algorithmic Language Scheme* [16]. The name "TI Scheme" refers to the specific dialect described in this manual, and the name "PC Scheme" refers to the specific implementation of this dialect for the TI Professional Computer (TIPC), TI Portable Professional Computer, TI BUSINESS-PRO™ Computer, IBM® PC, PC/XT, Personal Computer AT™, and compatibles.

Notational Conventions

1.2 This manual uses differing type styles to clarify various terms and concepts. Uppercase TYPEWRITER typeface is used for the names of actual Scheme identifiers and expressions such as CAR and (CAR FOO) when they appear within surrounding text. Lowercase typewriter typeface is used for examples of Scheme code set off from the text as follows:

```
(define (fibgen a b)
   (cons-stream a (fibgen b (+ a b))))
```

Italics are used to highlight the introduction of new technical terms and to represent arbitrary values in code samples, as in (FOO *a b*). Italics are also used for the boolean values *true* and *false*. The value *true* represents any value that is not explicitly false (any value except #F).

The paragraph entitled Variables in Chapter 3 of this manual describes conventions used in naming Scheme procedures.

Language Overview

1.3 Scheme is a dialect of LISP that incorporates many features of ALGOL and its descendants. Scheme has inherited LISP's metalinguistic power, latent (or dynamically checked) data types, an interactive user interface, automatic storage management, and the convenient representation of programs as data. From the ALGOL tradition, Scheme has borrowed block structure and lexical scoping of variables. Like LISP and ALGOL, Scheme uses the applicative order of argument evaluation.

In addition, TI Scheme provides procedures, continuations, environments, and engines as first-class data objects. These objects can be passed as arguments to procedures, returned as results, incorporated in composite data structures, and stored indefinitely while still retaining their environment of definition. This feature significantly increases the expressive power of the language with little additional complexity. TI Scheme also provides a rich set of data types including lists, strings, vectors, characters, symbols, integers of arbitrary precision, and floating point numbers.

Unlike most dialects of LISP, Scheme does not prescribe the order of evaluation of arguments in a procedure call. In particular, parallel evaluation of arguments is not prohibited. The compiler can thus generate optimized code. Scheme also differs from other LISP dialects in its treatment of the operator position of a procedure call. Scheme evaluates the identifier or expression in the operator position just as it does each expression in the operand positions. This system simplifies the rules for evaluation and eliminates the need for two namespaces (one for function values and another for data values).

A continuation is a general semantic mechanism for representing the future of any computation. Instead of hiding continuations in the implementation, Scheme provides for explicit access to them through the language. This capability provides powerful control facilities such as coroutines, exception handlers, and nonblind backtracking, without requiring additional mechanisms in the language (see the paragraph entitled Continuations in Chapter 4).

An environment makes explicit the association of variable names with values and provides a simple, general construct for implementing many different program packaging mechanisms. Although environments can be used to implement packaging systems similar to those in Common Lisp, the first-classness of environments in TI Scheme supports more sophisticated applications. For example, an environment can serve as a user-defined data type containing the operations on that type (see the paragraph entitled Environments in Chapter 4).

An engine is a mechanism for allowing a computation to proceed for a limited amount of time. By abstracting timed pre-emption, engines avoid the implementation-dependent complexities associated with timers and interrupt handlers. Engines are particularly useful in developing task scheduling capabilities and in implementing process abstractions (see the paragraph entitled Engines in Chapter 4).

Unlike conventional dialects of LISP, Scheme is specified to be properly tail recursive. In Scheme, tail recursive procedure invocations are executed without consuming control stack space. This execution allows iteration to be expressed as recursion without a loss of efficiency.

Lexical scoping and tail recursion encourage a functional programming style. By constructing higher order procedures, the Scheme programmer has access to alternate ways to accomplish many computations that require side effects in other languages. Side effects are not prohibited, however, and the imperative programming style natural to languages like Pascal and FORTRAN is supported efficiently. Side effects are also an essential part of object-oriented programming in Scheme, in which the "information hiding" abstraction of an encapsulated state is implemented with Scheme's lexically-scoped block structures.

As an extension to the standard language, TI Scheme also provides a dynamic inheritance facility called SCOOPS (Scheme Object-Oriented Programming System). SCOOPS is related to the Flavors system in ZetaLisp and in the TI Common Lisp implementation for the Explorer™ Lisp Machine. SCOOPS is described in the Chapter 5 of this manual.

Scheme achieves its conciseness and expressive power in a relatively small language through the generality and uniformity of its mechanisms. Simplicity has been a critical concern of Scheme developers, who have resisted the temptation to add new features to the language unless they significantly improve its utility and expressive power.

The simplicity and elegance of Scheme make it particularly well suited for use in educational environments. With the availability of good supporting texts and growing support among leading researchers, Scheme shows considerable promise for having a significant impact on the computer science community in coming years. However, Scheme is in no sense a toy language. Its expressive power substantially exceeds that of other dialects of LISP in use today. It is well suited to crisp, high performance implementations and is semantically clean enough to provide a good basis for continued evolution.

Evolution of the Scheme Language

1.4   The theoretical basis for Scheme is Alonzo Church's lambda calculus [3]. Scheme was inspired further by the object-oriented programming model of Greif and Hewitt [8]. Guy Lewis Steele Jr. and Gerald Jay Sussman of the Massachusetts Institute of Technology designed Scheme to be "a simple, concrete experimental domain for certain issues of programming semantics and style" [22].

The first description of Scheme appeared in 1975 [22]. The 1978 *Revised Report on Scheme* [21] described the evolution of the language as its MIT implementation was upgraded to support an innovative compiler [19]. Three distinct projects began in 1981 and 1982 to use dialects of Scheme for courses at MIT [14], Yale [15], and Indiana University [4]. An excellent computer science textbook using Scheme was published in 1984 [1].

Like other languages used primarily for education and research, Scheme has evolved rapidly. This rapid change was no problem when Scheme was used only within MIT. As Scheme became more widespread, however, local dialects diverged until students and researchers occasionally found it difficult to understand code written at other sites. In response to this problem, 15 representatives of the major implementations of Scheme met at Brandeis Universisity in October, 1984 to work toward a more consistent standard for Scheme. Their unanimous recommendations, augmented by committee work in the areas of arithmetic, characters, strings, and input/output, are contained in the 1985 *Revised Revised Report Scheme*. This evolution has continued and is reflected in the 1986 *Revised³ Report on the Algorithmic Language Scheme* [16], which is generally accepted by the Scheme community.

Although there is consensus in the Scheme community on the notion of an essential Scheme, the language continues to evolve. TI Scheme supports the language defined at the Brandeis workshop along with several extended features taken from other dialects of Scheme, primarily those developed at MIT and Indiana University. Programmers interested in writing portable programs are encouraged to become familiar with the *Revised³ Report*.

In any evolving language, there is some risk of code obsolesence. This risk is a natural consequence of progress in the computer science community as a whole. If a language fails to progress, the language in its entirety may become obsolete. The *Revised³ Report on Scheme* specifically accommodates some traditional LISP features for compatibility reasons but reserves the right to abandon them in the future. TI Scheme will also reflect such changes. In addition, TI may promote standardization of other features developed for TI Scheme. TI has no current plan or schedule to change the language; if changes become necessary, TI will follow a policy of making the change over an extended period of time to minimize disruption to users.

Scheme and Common Lisp

1.5 Like Common Lisp [18], Scheme was developed as a core language common to several implementations. Scheme differs from Common Lisp by emphasizing simplicity of form and function over compatibility with older LISP dialects. At the Brandeis workshop, participants agreed that Scheme should avoid gratuitous differences with Common Lisp. Although the definition of a gratuitous difference is obviously open to interpretation, there was a strong feeling that as much compatibility should be maintained as possible. TI Scheme strongly subscribes to this philosophy.

Although it often takes much more than minor syntactic changes to revise a Common Lisp program to run under Scheme, the process is generally straightforward. The result of such a mechanical transformation, while functionally correct, is not likely to exploit the unique features that make Scheme so attractive for program development.

Similarly, because Scheme shares the ALGOL heritage, it is relatively straightforward to translate many programs from languages like Pascal into Scheme.

SYTNAX

This chapter reviews the form of Scheme programs and data and explains the rules for converting between their internal and external representations. In addition, it defines the formal grammar for Scheme programs.

Representation of Programs and Data

2.1 Scheme programs and data are represented in files and on display devices as a sequence of characters. The lexical and syntactical rules of the language determine which sequences of characters are meaningful to Scheme and are thus valid representations of Scheme programs or data. Like most dialects of LISP, Scheme represents programs using the syntax of general-purpose data structures. Unlike LISP, Scheme distinguishes a program object, which is an executable entity at runtime, from the program's internal or external representation.

Characters are used for the external representation of Scheme data, and a tree constructed from lists, vectors, and atomic elements is used for the internal representation. The procedures READ and WRITE transform Scheme data between the external and internal representations. Special characters such as parentheses, periods, and quotation marks are used as punctuation in external representations to indicate corresponding internal structures.

Unlike traditional languages such as Pascal and C, TI Scheme reads programs and other data from a file or keyboard into an internal representation as a list (or tree) called an *S-expression*. Thus, a program's internal representation is like any other data in the language except that it can be *evaluated* by the procedure EVAL. See Chapter 3 for a description of the semantics of programs.

Not all Scheme data have useful external representations. For example, procedure objects created by executing the LAMBDA special form are written simply as #<PROCEDURE name>. These notations are not valid input to READ, since the internal details of the internal object are lost in translation.

Syntactic Elements

2.2 This chapter describes each of the fundamental components of a program such as numbers and identifiers and explains how they are built up from the characters read from a file or the keyboard.

TI Scheme uses the standard 8-bit ASCII character set. Consult the appropriate manuals for your computer system to determine the keyboard keys and displayed representations for ASCII characters.

The following characters have special meanings to the system:

```
\   |   (  )   [  ]  {  }   #   ´  `   ,   @   "   ;   blank
```

Backslash characters (\ ) and vertical bars (|) are used as escape mechanisms to accept any character as alphabetic. This use is called *slashification*. Backslash is used to accept the single character following it. A pair of vertical bars can be used to enclose a sequence of arbitrary characters that are to be taken as alphabetic. Backslash behaves as an escape character when used inside a vertical bar pair, thus allowing backslash and vertical bar to be included in such an identifier. For example, the following identifiers are all valid:

```
\(
\\
| ( ) # @ .,\\\||
```

For further information, see chapter 2.2.5.

Except when included in strings and characters or escaped by backslash or vertical bars, alphabetic characters are case-insensitive. Thus, 1.234E-5 and 1.234e-5, #T and #t, and X and x are identical, respectively; however, each of the following items is distinct:

```
"ABC"
"abc"
#\A
#\a
```

Left and right parentheses are used for grouping and to notate lists as described in chapter 2.2.6. Left and right brackets [ ] and left and right braces { } are reserved for future use.

The sharp sign (#) is used for a variety of purposes, depending on the character that follows it. A sharp sign followed by any of several letters is used to notate numbers (see chapter 2.2.1), and a sharp sign followed by a backslash is used to notate characters (see chapter 2.2.2). A sharp sign followed by a left parenthesis signals the beginning of a vector (see chapter 2.2.7), and a sharp sign followed by T or F indicate *true* or *false*.

Quote (') and backquote (') are used in quoting S-expressions, as described in chapter 3.3.1. Comma (,) and at-sign (@) have special interpretations inside a backquoted expression.

Numbers   **2.2.1** TI Scheme supports integer and floating point numerical constants. Numbers can be written with binary, octal, decimal, or hexadecimal bases. In the grammar for numbers on the next page, X* means zero or more occurrences of X. Spaces never appear inside a number; all spaces in the grammar are used for legibility. The term <empty> represents the empty string.

```
number --> real | real + ureal i | real - ureal i
          | real @ real
real   --> sign ureal
ureal  --> prefix2 bit bit* #* suffix
         | prefix2 bit bit* #* / bit bit* #* suffix
         | prefix2 . bit bit* #* suffix
         | prefix2 bit bit* . bit* #* suffix
         | prefix2 bit bit* #* . #* suffix
         | prefix8 oct oct* #* suffix
         | prefix8 oct oct* #* / oct oct* #* suffix
         | prefix8 . oct oct* #* suffix
         | prefix8 oct oct* . oct* #* suffix
         | prefix8 oct oct* #* . #* suffix
         | prefix10 dit dit* #* suffix
         | prefix10 dit dit* #* / dit dit* #* suffix
         | prefix10 . dit dit* #* suffix
         | prefix10 dit dit* . dit* #* suffix
         | prefix10 dit dit* #* . #* suffix
         | prefix16 hit hit* #* suffix
         | prefix16 hit hit* #* / hit hit* #* suffix
         | prefix16 . hit hit* #* suffix
         | prefix16 hit hit* . hit* #* suffix
         | prefix16 hit hit* #* . #* suffix
suffix --> <empty>  |  e sign dit dit*  |  E sign dit dit*
sign   --> <empty>  |  +  |  -
prefix2  --> radix2 exactness precision
         | radix2 precision exactness
         | exactness radix2 precision
         | exactness precision radix2
         | precision radix2 exactness
         | precision exactness radix2
prefix8  --> radix8 exactness precision
         | radix8 precision exactness
         | exactness radix8 precision
         | exactness precision radix8
         | precision radix8 exactness
         | precision exactness radix8
prefix10 --> radix10 exactness precision
         | radix10 precision exactness
         | exactness radix10 precision
         | exactness precision radix10
         | precision radix10 exactness
         | precision exactness radix10
prefix16 --> radix16 exactness precision
         | radix16 precision exactness
         | exactness radix16 precision
         | exactness precision radix16
         | precision radix16 exactness
         | precision exactness radix16
```

```
precision --> <empty>  |  #s  |  #S  |  #l  |  #L
exactness --> <empty>  |  #i  |  #I  |  #e  |  #E
radix2 --> #b  |  #B
radix8 --> #o  |  #O
radix10 --> <empty>  |  #d  |  #D
radix16 --> #x  |  #X
bit --> 0  |  1
oct --> bit  |  2  |  3  |  4  |  5  |  6  |  7
dit --> oct  |  8  |  9
hit --> dit  |  a  |  b  |  c  |  d  |  e  |  f
              |  A  |  B  |  C  |  D  |  E  |  F
```

Characters   2.2.2 Graphic character objects are indicated by preceding the character with #\ as shown in the following examples:

```
#\a                   ; lowercase letter
#\A                   ; uppercase letter
#\(                   ; left parenthesis as a character
#\                    ; space character
```

Certain nongraphic characters also have names with the #\ prefix, as shown in the following examples:

```
#\backspace           ; ASCII backspace
#\escape              ; ASCII escape
#\newline             ; end-of-line character sequence
#\page                ; ASCII form-feed
#\return              ; ASCII carriage return
#\rubout              ; ASCII delete
#\space               ; ASCII space
#\tab                 ; ASCII tab
```

The character #\newline actually may represent more than one character, depending on the representation for line breaks in the underlying operating system.

Strings   2.2.3 Strings are written as a sequence of characters enclosed within double quotation marks. The inclusion of a backslash or double quotation mark within a string requires that it be preceded with another backslash.

A string can continue across multiple lines. An end-of-line marker terminating a line is included in the string as a sequence of characters (determined by the underlying operating system).

Other Literals   2.2.4 The special literal values #T and #F denote the corresponding boolean values *true* and *false*.

Identifiers **2.2.5** Identifiers in Scheme are similar to those in most languages, although they can consist of a wider range of characters. A TI Scheme identifier is any sequence of characters chosen from the following set (except sequences that can be interpreted as denoting numbers):

```
a b c d e f g h i j k l m n o p q r s t u v w x y z
A B C D E F G H I J K L M N O P Q R S T U V W X Y Z
0 1 2 3 4 5 6 7 8 9
!   $   %   &   *   /   :   <   =   >   ?   _   -   +   ~   @   #   ^
```

For identifiers, Scheme is not case-sensitive. Foo, for example, is the same identifier as FOO.

Pairs and Lists **2.2.6** A pair (or dotted pair) is a data structure containing two components traditionally called the *car* and *cdr*. A pair whose car and cdr components are a and b is written within parentheses and separated by a dot as follows:

```
(a . b)
```

The spaces on either side of the dot are required. A list is either the special object called the empty list, denoted by ( ), or a pair, such as the following:

```
(a . (b . (c . (d . (e . ( ) ) ) ) ) )
```

When the cdr component of a pair is itself a pair or list, it is customary to omit both the dot and the parentheses surrounding the cdr. The last example, therefore, can be written as follows:

```
(a  b  c  d  e)
```

When the innermost cdr component of a list is the empty list (as in the last example), the entire structure is called a *proper list*. Proper lists are so common that the term *list* usually refers to a proper list. Other lists are commonly called *improper*, or *dotted*, lists.

Vectors **2.2.7** A vector is a data structure with an arbitrary number of components. Its representation is much like that of a proper list, but with a prefixed #(as in the following example:

```
#(a  b  c  d  e)
```

Comments **2.2.8** A semicolon indicates the start of a comment, which continues to the end of the line on which the semicolon appears. Comments are ignored by Scheme, but the end of the line is visible as white space. This prevents a comment from appearing in the middle of an identifier or number. A semicolon appearing between the double quotation marks of a string or after a backslash does not indicate a comment.

A Grammar for Scheme Programs

2.3 The grammar that follows is ambiguous because special forms are indistinguishable from applications or procedure calls. This ambiguity is resolved by reserving the names that serve as keywords of special forms. It is possible to use an identifier to name a variable and subsequently define a special form using a keyword with the same spelling. Such uses of identifiers, however, should be avoided. Once a special form has been defined, the name always refers to the keyword of the special form rather than to the identifier.

```
expression      -->     literal
                |       identifier
                |       special-form
                |       application

literal         -->     number | string | character | vector
                |       #T       | #F      |  #!NULL
                |       (QUOTE object)      | 'object
                |       (QUASIQUOTE object)| `object

application     -->     (expression expression . . .)

special-form    -->     (keyword syntactic-component . . . . )
```

In the grammar, `object` stands for any written representation of a Scheme object; `identifier`, `number`, `string`, `vector`, and `character` have been described already; and `special-form`, `application`, and the syntactic components of special forms are described in Chapter 3.

SEMANTICS 3

This chapter describes the rules that determine the meaning of a program represented as an S-expression. These rules define the semantics of TI Scheme. The procedure EVAL gives meaning to an S-expression by executing it according to the defined semantics of the language and returning its value. This execution may be either through interpretation or through compilation to an intermediate form, which is then interpreted or executed directly.

General Characteristics

3.1 This chapter reviews Scheme's major characteristics and compares Scheme to other languages and dialects of LISP.

Lexical Scoping and Block Structure

3.1.1 Scheme is a *lexically* (or *statically*) scoped programming language with block structure. Each use of an identifier refers to a lexically enclosing binding of that identifier. Thus, for each use of an identifier, its associated binding can be determined by simply inspecting the program text. In this respect, Scheme is like ALGOL 60, Pascal, and Common Lisp but is unlike dynamically scoped languages such as APL and traditional LISP.

A *block* is a region of program text that defines the scope of a lexical identifier. The special forms DO, LAMBDA, LET, LET*, LETREC, and REC impose a structure on Scheme programs that makes it possible to determine the scope of identifiers.

Applicative Order

3.1.2 Arguments to Scheme procedures are always passed by value; that is, the actual argument expressions are evaluated before the procedure is invoked. Scheme uses this order whether the procedure needs the result of the evaluation or not. This order is known as *applicative order evaluation*. The order of evaluating arguments of a procedure application is unspecified and may vary from call to call.

Sometimes it is necessary to delay the evaluation of an argument until it is actually used. This order is called *normal order evaluation*. Some of the characteristics of normal order evaluation can be obtained through explicit use of the FREEZE and DELAY special forms.

Tail Recursion

3.1.3 Scheme is defined to be *properly tail recursive*. This means that Scheme handles all tail recursive procedure calls with no net growth of the stack. A tail recursive call is one in which no further computation is to be performed by the calling procedure and therefore the called procedure may return directly to the calling procedure's caller.

Proper tail recursion allows the compiler considerable flexibility in optimization. Its most important advantage, however, is that it allows recursion to subsume iteration completely without losing efficiency. Iterative special forms such as DO are transformed into equivalent recursive code.

Latent Typing

3.1.4 Scheme uses latent types instead of manifest types. Whereas manifest types are associated with variables, latent types are associated with values (also called objects). Languages with latent types are sometimes classified as weakly typed or dynamically typed languages. Other languages with latent types are APL, SNOBOL, and other dialects of LISP. (Languages with manifest types, sometimes referred to as strongly typed or statically typed languages, include Pascal, ALGOL 60, and C.)

Latent typing is more flexible and convenient than manifest typing, since declarations are not required. However, latent typing generally requires that objects carry tags identifying their types and that these tags be checked at runtime.

Data types are not necessarily discrete. For example, TI Scheme does not distinguish between the empty list and the boolean value *false*. This characteristic has been retained for compatibility with Common Lisp.

First-Classness

3.1.5 In general, a *first-class object* has no unnecessary restrictions on its use. In most programming languages, only simple objects such as numbers, characters, and strings are first-class; restrictions are placed on the use of other objects. In Pascal, for example, arrays, records, and functions cannot be returned by functions or stored in arrays or records. In most LISP systems, functions require special treatment when they are passed as arguments.

All objects in Scheme are first-class. In TI Scheme, first-class objects include procedures, continuations, engines, and environments. Any first-class object has the following capabilities:

■ It can be stored in compound data structures.

■ It can be returned by a procedure.

■ It can be bound to a variable by being passed to a procedure (LAMBDA bound), by entering a lexical scope (as with LET), or by being globally bound (with DEFINE).

Treating all objects as first-class objects greatly increases the expressive power of Scheme, since it minimizes restrictions on program design.

Unlimited Extent

3.1.6 All objects created in a Scheme computation, including all procedures and variables, have an unlimited *extent*, or lifetime. This means, in effect, that Scheme objects are never destroyed. The reason that Scheme implementations seldom run out of storage is that they can reclaim the storage occupied by an object if they can prove that the object cannot possibly be used in any future computation. These proofs are performed by the "garbage collector," which is invoked automatically when no free storage is available. Other languages in which most objects have unlimited extent include APL and LISP.

Side Effects

3.1.7 Most Scheme expressions are evaluated only for their value. However, expressions that perform I/O, assign values to variables, or change values stored in compound data structures not only return values but also have *side effects* on the computation environment. Frequently, such expressions are evaluated solely for effect, and the value returned is ignored. For this reason, values returned are often unspecified for operations that perform side effects.

It is difficult to understand programs that use side effects, so they should be avoided whenever reasonable. To make the use of side effects more obvious, names of Scheme operations that perform them (except I/O) end with an exclamation mark, as in the name SET!. (This exclamation mark is sometimes called a "bang".) The purely functional subset of Scheme (which does not include side-effect-producing operations) is very powerful, so side effects can and should be avoided in many cases where they would be required in other languages [1].

Identifiers, Variables, and Environments

3.2 Identifiers have two uses within Scheme programs. When an identifier appears within a quoted literal, it is being used as a symbol (a data object); otherwise, it is being used as a name. In Scheme, an identifier can name a special form or a variable. A special form is a syntactic class of expressions, and an identifier that names a special form is called the *keyword* of that special form. A variable, on the other hand, has an associated value that can be changed at runtime (using, for example, SET!). An identifier that names a variable is said to be *bound* to that variable.

A set of identifier-to-variable bindings is known as an *environment*. TI Scheme supports two kinds of identifier bindings — lexical and fluid. Each kind has an associated environment. An expression that consists of only an identifier is a reference to a lexical environment variable. The lexical environment is used far more often than the fluid environment; therefore, the terms *identifier* and *environment* usually refer to a lexical identifier and the lexical environment.

Lexical Environment

3.2.1 Ordinary TI Scheme variables have lexical scope and indefinite extent. These variables are lexically bound by the binding forms of the language, which include LAMBDA and LET. In most cases, the scope of the bindings is the set of expressions in the bodies of these forms.

In its *lexical (or static) scope* and *block structure*, Scheme is similar to ALGOL, Pascal, and Common Lisp and is dissimilar to most other dialects of LISP. To each place where an identifier is bound in a program, there corresponds a region of the program within which the binding is effective. The region varies according to the binding construct that establishes the binding. If the binding is established by a lambda expression, for example, the region is the entire lambda expression. Every use of an identifier in a variable reference or assignment refers to the binding of the identifier that established the innermost of the regions containing the use. If the identifier is not bound in a region that contains its use, the use refers to a binding, if any, in the *global environment*. The global environment is established in the call to EVAL from the top-level read-eval-print loop. If there is no binding for the identifier, it is said to be unbound.

In Scheme, all lexical identifier references are resolved using the single lexical environment in effect at the point of reference. In many other languages such as ALGOL, Pascal, and Common Lisp, references are not resolved in this manner. In Common Lisp, for example, the bindings of identifiers in the first position of a procedure application are resolved in a different environment from those in argument position.

An environment is *extended* within binding forms like LAMBDA and LET to include newly introduced bindings. An environment might best be thought of as a sequence of *frames* mirroring the block structure of the program. Although the same identifier may be bound in different frames of the environment, a reference to identifier X refers to the innermost binding of X. This binding is contained in the most recently added frame that binds X and is associated with the nearest lexically enclosing binding of X.

A procedure object, or *closure*, is created by the evaluation of the LAMBDA special form. Since procedure objects must be able to access the bindings in effect at the time of their creation, the environment in effect at that time is *closed over* (preserved with the object) for future use.

When a closure is applied to a set of arguments, references to free identifiers in the body of the closure are resolved using the environment preserved with the closure (the environment of the definition). This environment is used even when the environment of application does not bind the identifier or binds it to a different variable. This use ensures that static scope rules are obeyed.

As mentioned previously, environments are first-class objects in TI Scheme. The special forms THE-ENVIRONMENT and MAKE-ENVIRONMENT convert identifier-to-variable bindings, which are normally maintained automatically by the system, into Scheme data objects. Environment objects can be manipulated by the programmer and searched with the ACCESS operator.

Fluid Environment

3.2.2 TI Scheme provides special forms that produce and access *fluid* (or *dynamic*) bindings. FLUID-LAMBDA and FLUID-LET are analogous to LAMBDA and LET, except that they create fluid bindings rather than lexical bindings. These bindings are in effect only while the expressions in the bodies of these forms are being evaluated. The special forms FLUID and SET-FLUID! are used to access and change, respectively, the values of fluidly bound variables. The fluid variable associated with a given identifier is the *identifier's* most recently created fluid binding that is still in effect. The fluid bindings in effect at a given time are stored in the *fluid environment*.

Just as closures capture the lexical environment in which they are closed, continuations capture the fluid environment in which they are created and restore this environment when they are invoked (see the paragraph entitled Continuations in chapter 4). This process is facilitated in PC Scheme by using *deep binding* in the fluid environment. Therefore, context switches are quite fast, although it becomes less efficient to access distant bindings if many fluid bindings are in effect. Since relatively few identifiers are fluidly bound in Scheme, as compared to most dialects of LISP, this efficiency loss is seldom a serious problem.

Expressions

3.3 A Scheme program can be any expression that follows the rules given in the paragraph entitled A Grammar for Scheme Programs in Chapter 2. Expressions are literals, identifiers, procedure calls, or special forms.

Literals

3.3.1 Literals are expressions in a program that are self-evaluating; that is, each expression evaluates to a data object whose printed representation is equivalent to that of the expression. Numbers, characters, and strings are self-evaluating forms, as are the boolean literals #T and #F.

The literal #F represents the boolean value *false*, or the empty list, or ( ). TI Scheme does not distinguish the empty list from #F; thus, WRITE prints the value of #F as the empty list, or ( ); EQ? returns true when comparing them, and NULL? and NOT? returns *true* for either.

For similar historical reasons, the variable NIL has the initial value (), and the variable T has the initial value #T in TI Scheme. Using these variables instead of literals is strongly discouraged for both theoretical and performance reasons.

The special form QUOTE returns its argument without evaluating it. The form (QUOTE x) can be abbreviated as ´x. QUASIQUOTE is similar to QUOTE, but specifies a compound data template that may contain both literal elements and elements whose values are to be determined by evaluating subexpressions at runtime. The form (QUASIQUOTE x) can be abbreviated as `x. Subexpressions with values to be instantiated into the template are prefixed by a comma or enclosed by UNQUOTE. Subexpressions that evaluate to proper lists that are to be spliced into the template are prefixed by ,@ or enclosed by UNQUOTE-SPLICING (for a non-destructive splice) or by , . (for a destructive splice).

Since literals are intended to evaluate to themselves always, it is important that they not be modified by the program. For example, evaluating (set-car! ´(a . b) ´c) or (string-set! "abc" 1 #\x) may cause side effects in other occurrences of the literals ´(a . b) and "abc" in the program and should be avoided.

Variables

3.3.2 An expression consisting of only an identifier that is not the keyword of a special form is a lexical variable reference. The value of the identifier is the value of the variable associated with the identifier by the innermost binding in the current lexical environment. Referencing an unbound identifier is an error.

TI Scheme follows some simple naming conventions common to most implementations of Scheme. The naming conventions that follow help to make key aspects of the behavior of a procedure or special form clear from its name.

... ? The suffix ? indicates a predicate. Procedures such as EQ? (which typically are evaluated for control) have the suffix ? to indicate that they return a truth value.

... ! The suffix ! indicates an operation that modifies its argument or the environment. However, such constructs as SET! or REVERSE! cannot be characterized fully by the results that are returned (indeed, in many cases, results are unspecified). This convention is not followed in the case of procedures such as PRINT and WRITE, whose side effects are external to the Scheme environment.

...->... An infix -> is used in the names of procedures such as SYMBOL->STRING to indicate that the procedure converts its argument from one object data type to another.

MAKE- The prefix MAKE- indicates a routine that creates an instance of some object such as a string or a vector.

... Q The suffix Q is appended to procedures like MEMQ to indicate that the predicate EQ? is used in performing a comparison.

... V The suffix V is appended to procedures like MEMV to indicate that the predicate EQV? is used in performing a comparison.

In addition, identifiers starting with % or PCS- are reserved for system use by implementations of TI Scheme.

Procedure Applications

3.3.3 A sequence of one or more expressions enclosed within parentheses denotes a procedure call, or *application*. A special form is syntactically the same as an application but is distinguished by the presence of a reserved *keyword* in the first position of the sequence. Note that a special form is not an application.

The value of an application is determined by first finding the value of each of its subexpressions. The first subexpression, said to be in *function position*, must evaluate to a functional object (a procedure or continuation). Then, that functional object is invoked by passing the other subexpression values as arguments. The value returned from the functional object is the value of the application.

Scheme does not distinguish between user-defined procedures and those provided by the system as standard routines. For efficiency, however, PC Scheme normally treats certain standard procedures like + as *primitive operations* and assumes that the standard meaning of + is intended. For example, in the following program the innermost + is understood to be a new lexical binding, but the outer + is assumed to refer to the addition operation:

```
(+ a
   (let ((+ 4))
      (* b +)))
```

The PC Scheme variable PCS-INTEGRATE-PRIMITIVES may be set to #F to override these assumptions if the global bindings of these identifiers are to be changed.

Probably the most significant difference between Scheme and Common Lisp is in the way the expression in the function position of an application is evaluated. Common Lisp requires this expression to be an identifier or a lambda expression. Unlike Scheme, in which the first position must evaluate to a procedure, Common Lisp looks up the identifier in a separate namespace of procedure name bindings. Thus, in Common Lisp, LIST may be both a procedure name and a variable name at the same time.

Common Lisp does provide the ability to use the actual value of an expression as a procedure with the procedure FUNCALL. This procedure applies the value of its first argument, a procedure object, to the other arguments, thus making it possible, although awkward, to use first-class procedures in Common Lisp.

Steele [21] argues against the use of FUNCALL to implement first-class procedures by observing that the method causes the space of meaningful S-expressions to be very sparse. He further points out that applications occur about as often as all other atomic forms combined. Therefore, over half of all S-expressions would probably begin with FUNCALL.

Special Forms

3.3.4 Special forms are expressions distinguished by a leading *keyword*, or reserved word, that is known specifically to the Scheme system. All other compound expressions designate procedure calls. Special forms provide capabilities that are not expressible as procedure calls. Sometimes they are used to avoid the evaluation of arguments in forms that otherwise appear to be procedure calls. QUOTE is the simplest example of this.

Special Forms for Binding The *binding forms* DO, LAMBDA, LET, LET*, LETREC, NAMED-LAMBDA, and REC extend the lexical environment by creating a new frame of lexical bindings. Similarly, the special forms FLUID-LAMBDA and FLUID-LET extend the fluid environment by creating new fluid bindings.

Special Forms for Sequencing and Control The special forms AND, APPLY-IF, BEGIN, BEGIN0, CASE, COND, DO, IF, OR, SEQUENCE, and WHEN provide a mechanism for obtaining a specified or conditional flow of control within a program. Each special form defines the order in which some (or all) of its arguments are to be evaluated and the value that is to be returned for the form.

Special Forms for Error Handling The special forms ASSERT, BKPT, and ERROR are used to trap to an error handler or debugger under certain conditions. Their use is discussed in detail in the implementation-specific *PC Scheme User's Guide — Student Edition.*

Special Forms for Syntactic Extension TI Scheme provides a limited means for extending the syntax of the language with aliases and macros. An *alias* is an identifier that is invariably substituted for another identifier whenever it appears in a Scheme expression (except within quoted literals). A *macro* is a procedure that maps from one form of an S-expression to another. After repeated macro expansion, all program forms are reduced to a subset of Scheme, called *core Scheme*, which consists only of identifiers, literals, applications, and a few essential special forms.

The special forms MACRO and SYNTAX are used to define macros. MACRO associates a keyword with a specified procedure that takes one argument, an S-expression representing the original macro call, and returns a transformed expression. SYNTAX specifies a transformation through pattern matching. MACRO is more flexible than SYNTAX but is less convenient to use for simple transformations.

Most of the special forms in PC Scheme are actually implemented as macros.

DATA TYPES AND OPERATIONS ▪4

This chapter specifies the TI Scheme data types and briefly describes the procedures and special forms that create and manipulate them. In addition to numbers, characters, strings, vectors, and I/O ports, which are common to many languages, Scheme supports symbols, lists, and procedural objects. Unlike most LISP dialects, TI Scheme fully supports continuations, environments, engines, and streams as first-class data types.

Boolean Objects and Equivalence Predicates

4.1 The standard boolean objects representing *true* and *false* are written as #T and #F, respectively. However, the Scheme conditional expressions AND, COND, IF, and so forth treat any value other than #F as *true*. Since TI Scheme does not distinguish the empty list, written as ( ), from #F (see the paragraph entitled Literals in Chapter 3), the empty list also is treated as *false*. The procedure BOOLEAN? can be used to determine if an object is *true* or *false*.

A predicate is a procedure that always returns #T or #F. The general equivalence testing predicates in Scheme are EQ?, EQV?, and EQUAL?. EQ? is the most discriminating of these, EQV? is slightly less discriminating, and EQUAL? is the most liberal.

EQ? returns #T if and only if its two arguments are identical objects. Generally EQ? is used only when comparing symbols where spelling uniqueness is guaranteed by READ. The predicate EQ? can also test whether two references to an object are to the same instantiation of that object. However, this use of EQ? is highly implementation dependent since systems are free to make copies of objects at times that may not be obvious to the users. Using EQ? to compare small integers and characters may work in some systems but not in others. However, these data types have their own appropriate identity predicates.

Since #F and the empty list evaluate to the same distinguished object, EQ? suffices to distinguish this value. Other base values, such as zero, the empty string, and the empty stream, do not necessarily have unique values and must be tested with their type-specific predicates.

EQV? is like EQ? but EQV? recognizes *exact* numbers that are identical (see the paragraph entitled Numeric Types in this chapter). TI Scheme extends the domain of EQV? to include character objects and all numbers, making it equivalent to the Common Lisp EQL predicate, as well as strings.

EQUAL? returns #T if its arguments are identical objects or equivalent numbers, lists, characters, strings, or vectors. Two objects are generally considered to be equivalent if they print the same. EQUAL? may fail to terminate if either argument is a circular data structure.

Symbols

4.2 *Symbols* are data objects with two important characteristics:

■ They are represented simply by their names.

■ Two symbols are identical (in the sense of the EQ? predicate) only if their names are spelled the same way (ignoring the capitalization of alphabetic characters).

The READ command ensures that matching occurs by maintaining a table of associations between spellings and symbols. This process is called *interning* the symbol. READ also maps all alphabetic characters to uppercase letters unless they are preceded by a backslash (\) or enclosed within vertical bars (|). Thus, the syntax for symbol names is the same as that for identifiers.

The data type *symbol* is disjoint from other data types in TI Scheme. The predicate SYMBOL? determines if an object is a symbol.

The procedures ASCII->SYMBOL, GENSYM, STRING->SYMBOL, and STRING->UNINTERNED-SYMBOL also may be used to create symbols. These procedures do not coerce alphabetic characters to uppercase letters. For example, (STRING->SYMBOL "abc") produces the symbol |abc| instead of ABC, and (eq? '|abc| 'ABC) evaluates to *false*. GENSYM and STRING->UNINTERNED-SYMBOL produce new symbols guaranteed to be different from any other symbols with the same spelling. This uniqueness is ensured by ignoring the table that READ maintains. ASCII->SYMBOL and STRING->SYMBOL intern the symbols they produce just as READ does.

A symbol's name can be obtained with the procedure SYMBOL->STRING, which is the inverse of STRING->SYMBOL. Since READ coerces a symbol to uppercase letters, (SYMBOL->STRING 'abc) evaluates to ABC. Similarly, the procedure SYMBOL->ASCII is the inverse of ASCII->SYMBOL.

Like Common Lisp, TI Scheme provides each symbol with a component called its *property list*, or *plist*. The procedures GETPROP, PROPLIST, PUTPROP, and REMPROP are used to manipulate the property list of a symbol.

For compatibility with older dialects of LISP, TI Scheme provides the procedures EXPLODE and IMPLODE, which transform between symbols and lists of their constituent characters.

Numbers

4.3 Numerical computation traditionally has been neglected by the LISP community. Until Common Lisp, no carefully planned strategy existed for organizing numerical computation. In addition, with the exception of the MacLisp system, little effort had been made to execute numerical code efficiently. Common Lisp has set the standard for specification of numeric data types and operations in LISP systems. In some ways, Scheme simplifies and generalizes this work.

In Scheme, numerical operations treat numbers as abstract data, which are as independent of their representation as possible. Thus, it is possible to write simple programs without having to know that the implementation may use fixed-point, floating-point, and perhaps other representations for the data. Unfortunately, this illusion of uniformity can be sustained only approximately because the implementation of numbers leaks out of its abstraction whenever control of precision, accuracy, or construction of especially efficient computations is required.

Distinguishing between abstract numbers, their machine representations, and their written representations is important. The mathematical terms NUMBER, COMPLEX, REAL, RATIONAL, and INTEGER describe the properties of abstract numbers. Words like *FIXNUM*, *BIGNUM*, and *FLONUM* are used to describe the machine representations of abstract numbers. The words INT, FIX, FLO, HEUR, and SCI specify numeric formats for input/output conversion.

Numeric Types **4.3.1** The most general numerical type provided in Scheme is NUMBER, a union type implemented in terms of *FIXNUM*, *FLONUM*, and other primitive representations. The system automatically selects the correct operation for each representation.

Mathematically, numbers may be arranged into a tower of subtypes with natural projections and injections relating adjacent levels of the tower:

NUMBER
COMPLEX
REAL
RATIONAL
INTEGER

The uniform rule of downward coercion is that a number of one type is also of a lower type if the injection (up) or the projection (down) of a number leaves the number unchanged. Since this tower is a mathematical structure, Scheme provides predicates and procedures to access it.

The Scheme standard does not require all implementations of Scheme to provide the entire tower, but a coherent subset consistent with both the purposes of the implementation and the spirit of the Scheme language must be included. Currently, PC Scheme does not support the numeric types COMPLEX and RATIONAL. However, the predicates COMPLEX? and RATIONAL? are provided. COMPLEX? is equivalent to NUMBER? and RATIONAL? is equivalent to INTEGER?.

Scheme numbers are either *exact* or *inexact*. A number is exact if it is derived from exact numbers using only exact operations. A number is inexact if it models a quantity known only approximately, if it is derived using inexact ingredients, or if it is derived using inexact operations. Thus, inexactness is a contagious property of a number.

Some operations, such as square root (of nonsquare numbers), must be inexact because of the finite precision of the representation. Others may be inexact because of implementation requirements. However, it must be emphasized that exactness is independent of the position of the number on the tower, making it possible to have an inexact INTEGER or an exact REAL. Also, a value such as 355/113 may be an exact RATIONAL, or it may be an inexact RATIONAL approximation to π, depending on the application.

PC Scheme presently implements all numbers as inexact. The predicates EXACT? and INEXACT? always return #F and #T, respectively. Programmers are strongly advised not to rely on this behavior. Other implementations, including future implementations of TI Scheme, are expected to comply more fully with the spirit of the Scheme standard in this respect.

The written representation for Scheme numbers is given in the paragraph entitled Numbers in Chapter 2.

NOTE: As is true of many computer languages, the results of mathematical operations may not be exactly equal to numbers entered through the keyboard even though you might perceive them to be equal.

Integers

4.3.2 TI Scheme supports arbitrary precision integers restricted in size only by physical implementation constraints. PC Scheme implements integers between −16384 and +16383 using a *FIXNUM* representation and integers with larger magnitudes with a *BIGNUM* representation. The conversion between *FIXNUM* and *BIGNUM* representations is automatic.

Rational Numbers

4.3.3 PC Scheme reserves the data type RATIONAL for possible future implementation as typed pairs of arbitrary precision integers with no non-trivial common factors. Note that integers are considered to be rational numbers.

Real Numbers

4.3.4 Real numbers are represented in TI Scheme as integers and as floating point values, or *FLONUMs*. In PC Scheme, all floating point operations are implemented using the 64-bit IEEE floating point standard. This standard provides approximately 16 decimal digits of precision for values with magnitudes in the range 2.226E-308 to 1.797E+308 (approximately).

Complex Numbers

4.3.5 PC Scheme reserves the data type COMPLEX for possible future implementation as typed pairs of real numbers. Note that integers and real numbers are also considered to be complex numbers.

Input and Output of Numbers	4.3.6 The grammar for the written representation of Scheme numbers is presented in the paragraph entitled Numbers in Chapter 2. The procedure NUMBER->STRING takes a number and a format and returns the written representation of the given number in the given format as a string. The procedure STRING->NUMBER takes a string, a format, and a radix and returns the maximally precise numerical representation. The procedures WRITE and DISPLAY output numbers using formats chosen according to the types and magnitudes of their arguments.

Operations on Numbers	4.3.7 The numerical type predicates NUMBER?, COMPLEX?, REAL?, RATIONAL?, and INTEGER? may be applied to any kind of object. Each predicate returns #T if the object is of the named type. When one of these predicates is true for a number, the higher type predicates are also true. FLOAT? determines whether its argument is a floating point value; unlike REAL?, it returns #F for rationals and integers.

The predicates EXACT?, INEXACT?, EVEN?, ODD?, POSITIVE?, NEGATIVE?, and ZERO? test a number for a particular property.

The numerical comparison predicates are <, <=, =, <>, >, and >=. The redundant names <?, <=?, =?, <>?, >?, and >=? are provided for compatibility with earlier versions of Scheme but may not be supported in future versions.

The fundamental arithmetic operations are provided by the procedures +, −, *, and /. MINUS negates its argument, and ABS takes the magnitude of its argument. MAX and MIN return the maximum and minimum values from among their arguments, respectively.

QUOTIENT, REMAINDER, and MODULO perform number-theoretic (integer) division. CEILING, FLOOR, ROUND, and TRUNCATE create inexact integers from other numbers. FLOAT creates floating point values.

GCD and LCM compute the greatest common divisor and least common multiple of their arguments, respectively. RANDOMIZE initializes the random number generator, and RANDOM returns pseudorandom arbitrary precision integers.

The procedures ACOS, ASIN, ATAN, COS, EXP, EXPT, LOG, SIN, SQRT, and TAN operate on real numbers according to the meanings specified by the Common Lisp standard.

Characters

4.4 A TI Scheme character is an object that represents an ASCII character code. Character objects are created with coercion procedures like INTEGER->CHAR or by specifying them with the #\ notation discussed in the paragraph entitled Numbers in Chapter 2.

The TI Scheme character data type is disjoint from other data types. However, since the Scheme standard does not require this of implementations, programmers should not rely on it. For example, some implementations may represent character objects as integers. The Scheme procedures CHAR->INTEGER and INTEGER->CHAR convert between character objects and their numeric ASCII codes. The predicate CHAR? determines whether an object is a character.

The procedures CHAR<?, CHAR<=?, CHAR=?, CHAR>?, and CHAR>=? impose an order on the set of characters. This ordering ensures the following:

- Uppercase characters are in alphabetical order.

- Lowercase characters are in alphabetical order.

- The digits 0 through 9 are in descending order.

- Either all digits precede all uppercase letters or vice versa.

- Either all digits precede all the lowercase letters or vice versa.

TI Scheme characters use the ASCII encoding and thus are ordered accordingly.

CHAR-CI<? and CHAR-CI=? are case-insensitive versions of CHAR<? and CHAR=?, respectively. For case-insensitive comparisons, all alphabetic characters are considered to be uppercase letters. Characters can be coerced into the desired case with the procedures CHAR-DOWNCASE and CHAR-UPCASE.

WRITE-CHAR writes a character (not the written representation of the character in #\ notation) to a given port and returns an unspecified value. DISPLAY uses WRITE-CHAR for characters in the structures it writes. WRITE writes characters using the #\ notation.

Strings

4.5 Strings are mutable sequences of characters. In TI Scheme, strings are disjoint from other data types. The predicate STRING? determines if an object is a string. The maximum length of a string in PC Scheme is 16,380 characters.

Strings may be created as literals enclosed in double quotation marks (") or with the constructors MAKE-STRING, STRING-APPEND, and STRING-COPY. STRING-FILL! initializes all the elements of a string with a given character value.

The empty string, denoted by a pair of quotation marks (""), is distinguished by the STRING-NULL? predicate. STRING-LENGTH returns the number of characters in a string. The character elements in a string may be accessed with STRING-REF and modified with STRING-SET!. The first element is indexed by zero and the last element is indexed by one less than the value returned by STRING-LENGTH. Indexing a string outside this range is an error.

The procedures STRING<?, STRING<=?, STRING=?, STRING>?, STRING>=?, STRING-CI<?, and STRING-CI=? are the lexicographic extensions to strings of the corresponding orderings on characters. For example, STRING<? is the lexicographic ordering on strings induced by the ordering CHAR<? on characters.

STRING->LIST returns a list of the characters that make up a given string. Its converse, LIST->STRING, returns a string formed by concatenating the characters in a list. These procedures are inverses in terms of the predicates EQUAL? and STRING=?.

Scheme also has operations on subsequences, or substrings, of strings. SUBSTRING returns a new string comprised of a subsequence of the characters in a given string. SUBSTRING-FILL! stores a given character in the specified sequence of elements of a string. SUBSTRING-MOVE-LEFT! and SUBSTRING-MOVE-RIGHT! move the elements of one subsequence into another subsequence, possibly within the same string.

The predicates SUBSTRING<?, SUBSTRING=?, SUBSTRING-CI<?, and SUBSTRING-CI=? perform lexicographic comparisons on substrings.

SUBSTRING-FIND-NEXT-CHAR-IN-SET searches a substring for the first occurrence of any character contained in a specified set. The search progresses from left to right (from lower to higher indices). Similarly, SUBSTRING-FIND-PREVIOUS-CHAR-IN-SET searches a substring from right to left.

DISPLAY writes strings without their enclosing double quotation marks and embedded escape characters (\). WRITE writes strings with the double quotation marks and escape characters so that strings can be read in again.

Pairs and Lists

4.6   The list is the characteristic data structure in LISP systems. Lists are composed of pairs, which are compound structures consisting of two components, traditionally called the car and cdr. A pair is constructed by the primitive procedure CONS, which accepts two arguments and returns a unique pair object. The car and cdr components are accessed by the CAR and CDR primitive procedures. CONS, CAR, and CDR obey these identities:

```
(car (cons 'a 'b)) => 'A
(cdr (cons 'a 'b)) => 'B
```

The procedures SET-CAR! and SET-CDR! modify the car and cdr components of a pair, respectively. These and other operations with side effects on pairs are capable of creating circular, or self-referential, data structures. Such structures should be handled carefully, since they have an infinite written representation and may tie up structure-walking algorithms in infinite loops.

The predicate PAIR? determines whether a given object is a pair. Since other data types in TI Scheme may be implemented in terms of pairs, PAIR? may return *true* for other objects as well. The TI Scheme predicate ATOM? returns *true* when given an object that is not a pair. All such objects are considered atomic, even though some, like vectors, are compound data structures. Since no real consensus can be found in the LISP community concerning the meaning of ATOM?, the Scheme standard does not specify it at all.

Compositions of pairs linked through their cdr components are called lists. The empty list, a unique system object denoted by ( ), is also a list. When a chain of cdr links from a pair terminates in the empty list, the pair is called a proper list. The procedure LIST produces a proper list composed of the values of its arguments. LIST* produces a similar list but places the value of its last argument in the cdr component of the last pair in the chain, possibly resulting in an improper list.

LENGTH returns the number of elements in a proper list. NULL? determines whether its argument is the empty list. The nth pair of a list may be accessed with LIST-TAIL. The procedure LIST-REF returns the car component of that pair. LAST-PAIR returns the last pair in a nonempty list.

The procedure COPY returns a new list with the same elements as its argument. The elements are not copied. APPEND takes an arbitrary number of proper lists and returns a new list consisting of the elements of its arguments in order. APPEND! is like APPEND but modifies the cdr component of each argument except the last to point to the following argument. REVERSE returns a copy of its argument with the elements in reversed order. REVERSE! modifies its argument to reverse the linking of its elements through the cdr components.

MEMBER, MEMQ, and MEMV search for a given value among the elements of a proper list, and ASSOC, ASSQ, and ASSV search a proper list of pairs for an element whose car component contains a given value, using the predicates EQUAL?, EQ?, and EQV?, respectively.

DELETE! and DELQ! search for a given value in a proper list using EQUAL? and EQ?, respectively. All matching elements that are found are then destructively removed from the list.

The general name for a compound structure composed of pairs is a *tree*. Nested calls to CAR and CDR to access elements of a tree to a depth of four or fewer may be abbreviated with procedures with the names CAAR, CADR and so forth through CAAAAR and CDDDDR. For example, (CDDAR x) is an abbreviation for (CDR (CDR (CAR x))).

Vectors

4.7 Vectors are heterogenous mutable structures whose elements are indexed by integers. The predicate VECTOR? determines whether a given object is a vector. Since some other data types in TI Scheme may be implemented in terms of vectors, VECTOR? may return true for other objects as well.

Vectors differ from lists in that accessing the nth element of a vector takes constant time, whereas accessing the nth element of a list requires time proportional to n. Conversely, changing the order, length, or other structural characteristics of a list is quick and simple. Similar modifications to a vector generally require creating a new vector and copying information to it.

Vectors are created by the constructor procedure MAKE-VECTOR. The elements are accessed and modified by the procedures VECTOR-REF and VECTOR-SET!, respectively. The procedure VECTOR-LENGTH returns the number of elements in a vector. Vectors of length zero are permitted. The first element, if any, in a vector is indexed by zero, and the last element is indexed by one less than the length of the vector. Indexing outside this range is an error.

Vectors also may be created with the procedures VECTOR and LIST->VECTOR procedures. VECTOR returns a new vector containing the values of its arguments. LIST->VECTOR returns a new vector containing the same values as its argument, which is a proper list. The inverse operation, VECTOR->LIST, returns a list of the elements of a vector. VECTOR-FILL! initializes all the elements of a vector with a given value.

Procedures

4.8 The procedure is the fundamental mechanism for abstraction in Scheme. TI Scheme has three kinds of procedure objects:

- Lexical closures

- Continuations

- Engines

Lexical closures, continuations, and engines are discussed in this chapter. A lexical closure is a procedure object that encapsulates a computation to be performed and defines the environment in which it is to be performed.

Scheme's ability to treat procedures as first-class objects transcends the more common ability to treat *representations* of procedures as objects. This latter capability is traditionally associated with LISP, where functions are represented as list structures [19]. TI Scheme provides both capabilities. For example, in the following lines, FOO is defined to be the identity function and BAR is defined to be a list representation of the identity function:

```
(define foo (lambda (x) x))
(define bar '(lambda (x) x))
```

(EVAL BAR) returns a closure that behaves exactly like the closure bound to FOO. However, no general test can determine whether two such procedures are identical. In traditional LISP, the S-expression (lambda (x) x) is itself a procedural object.

Both the LAMBDA and FLUID-LAMBDA special forms create lexical closures when they are evaluated. However, while LAMBDA binds its list of identifiers (parameters) in the lexical environment, FLUID-LAMBDA binds its identifiers in the fluid environment. The body of the closure is executed in the defining environment in both cases. The closure data type is disjoint from other data types in TI Scheme. The predicate CLOSURE? determines whether an object is a closure, while the predicate PROCEDURE? returns true for continuations and engines, as well as closures.

The procedure MAP applies a given procedure to each of the elements of a proper list and returns a list of the results. FOR-EACH applies a given procedure to the elements of the list solely for effect and therefore ignores the values returned.

Closure objects read into Scheme have no written representation that reconstructs the closure. WRITE writes closures using the notation #<PROCEDURE *name*>, which is an invalid input for READ but conveys some information to human readers.

Streams

4.9 A *stream* is a sequence of data objects similar to a list or vector. Unlike these other data types, the components of a stream are evaluated when they are accessed rather than when they are stored in the object. This evaluation permits the representation of large, even infinite, data structures in finite space.

The practical implementation of streams involves the concept of delayed evaluation, which was first implemented in the ALGOL 60 call-by-name parameter-passing method. The natural mechanism for delayed evaluation in Scheme is the closure object, which suspends the evaluation of an expression until it is invoked and then performs the evaluation in the defining environment. ALGOL 60 implementers introduced the term *call-by-name thunks* for such closures. The TI Scheme special form (FREEZE *exp*) provides a mnemonic way to abbreviate the form (LAMBDA ( ) *exp*), which produces such thunks. The mnemonic procedure call (THAW *thunk*) is likewise equivalent to the application (*thunk*), which evaluates the delayed *exp*.

Repeated *thawing* of a delayed expression can be inefficient in cases where the expression returns the same value each time. An optimized form of delayed object for this situation is the *call-by-need thunk*, which thaws its value only once and remembers, or *memoizes*, the value for subsequent references. The TI Scheme special form DELAY is analogous to FREEZE but memoizes its argument. The procedure FORCE, analogous to THAW, obtains the value of a delayed expression. The predicate DELAYED-OBJECT? determines whether its argument is a memoized delayed object.

Like pairs, streams have two components, called the head and the tail. Unlike pairs, the tail of a stream is a memoized delayed object. The constructor for streams is the procedure CONS-STREAM, which evaluates its first argument but delays the evaluation of its second argument. The components of a stream are accessed with the procedures HEAD and TAIL.

Because the individual elements of a stream are not evaluated until they are actually accessed, streams are useful for representing infinite data structures. (Refer to *The Structure and Interpretation of Computer Programs*[1] for an excellent introduction to the power and use of streams.) For example, the following simple procedure constructs the infinite stream of Fibonacci numbers:

```
(define (fibgen a b)
   (cons-stream a (fibgen b (+ a b))))

(define fibs
   (fibgen 0 1))

(head fibs)                         => 0
(head (tail fibs))                  => 1
(head (tail (tail fibs)))           => 1
(head (tail (tail (tail fibs))))    => 2
```

The predicate STREAM? determines whether a given object is a stream. However, since streams generally are implemented in terms of other data types in TI Scheme, other type predicates may return *true* for streams also. Likewise, since there is no written representation for closures, which would allow them to be read back into Scheme, streams and other delayed objects have no useful written representation.

A stream containing no elements is represented by a special system value called the *empty stream* and is accessed as the value of the variable THE-EMPTY-STREAM. The empty stream plays the same role for streams that the empty list does for proper lists. The predicate EMPTY-STREAM? determines whether its argument is the empty stream.

The procedures LIST->STREAM and STREAM->LIST convert between proper lists and finite streams.

Because streams incorporate delayed evaluation and memoization, defining a stream in which a delayed expression interacts with its environment through side effects can be extremely confusing. Therefore, it is recommended that the use of such side effects be avoided in delayed expressions.

The *stream* data type in Common Lisp is somewhat different from that in Scheme, and is used primarily for external and internal I/O. The Scheme data type named *port* is closer to the Common Lisp stream data type.

Continuations

4.10 A continuation is a first-class data object which represents the future of a computation. It is used most frequently to implement escape procedures, such as those supported by CATCH and THROW in Common Lisp. However, a continuation is a much more general mechanism that can be used to implement a wide variety of control constructs.

Whenever a Scheme expression is evaluated, there is a continuation wanting the result of the expression. The continuation represents an entire (default) future for the computation. If the expression is evaluated at the top level, for example, the continuation takes the result, prints it on the screen, prompts for the next input, evaluates it, and so on. Most of the time, the continuation includes actions specified in the code, as in a continuation that takes the result, multiplies it by the value stored in a local variable, adds seven, and gives the answer to the top-level continuation to be printed.

Normally, these continuations are hidden behind the scenes, and programmers do not think much about them. On rare occasions, however, when programmers need to do something fancy, they may need to deal with continuations explicitly. CALL-WITH-CURRENT-CONTINUATION allows Scheme programmers to do that by creating a continuation object that acts just like the current continuation.

The procedure CALL-WITH-CURRENT-CONTINATION, usually abbreviated CALL/CC, must be passed a procedure of one argument. This argument is in turn passed a continuation object that represents the continuation of the CALL/CC application. Informally, this continuation object represents the remainder of the computation from the CALL/CC application point. At any future time, this continuation object may be invoked as a procedure of one argument with any value, with the effect that this value is taken as the value of the CALL/CC application.

Like all objects in Scheme, continuation objects are first-class: therefore, they can be passed to and returned by procedures and stored in data structures. At some risk of confusing them with the underlying system continuations that they represent, continuation objects usually are referred to simply as continuations.

Consider the expression (CALL/CC (LAMBDA (K) *exp*)), which behaves the same as (CALL/CC (LAMBDA (K) (K *exp*))). In either case, if the evaluation of *exp* does not invoke the continuation K, the entire CALL/CC application is equivalent to the expression *exp* alone. If K is invoked with some value *v* at any time during the evaluation of *exp*, *v* is returned immediately as the result of the entire CALL/CC application. For example, the following evaluates to 8, and the addition is never performed:

```
(* 2 (call/cc (lambda (k) (+ 3 (k 4)))))
```

The simplest use of continuations is for nonlocal exits in the event of errors or other exceptional conditions. For example, consider a procedure that computes the product of a list of numbers. If the list contains a zero, the entire product is zero. By obtaining the continuation of the invocation of the PRODUCT procedure, as shown here, zero can be returned as the result of the invocation as soon as the zero is discovered, without performing any multiplications.

```
(define product
  (lambda (lyst)
    (call/cc
      (lambda (k)
        (let loop ((lyst lyst))
          (if (null? lyst)
              1
              (if (zero? (car lyst))
                  (k 0)                 ; return 0 immediately
                  (* (car lyst)
                     (loop (cdr lyst)))))))))))
```

Continuation objects sometimes are called *escape procedures* because they are so useful for escaping from computations in this way.

A number of languages provide control mechanisms, such as the escape procedures of traditional LISP systems, which may be used to jump *out* of computations. However, since Scheme continuation objects are first-class, they have a significant additional dimension of use: they also may be used to jump *into* computations. Perhaps the simplest example of such upward use of continuations is to accomplish looping without functional recursion or an explicit iteration mechanism. Using such a continuation, the PRODUCT procedure defined previously may be implemented in an imperative style as in the following example:

```
(define product
  (lambda (lyst)
    (call/cc
      (lambda (return)
        (let ((loop 'any-value)
              (p 1))
          (call/cc
            (lambda (k)
              (set! loop k)))
          (when (null? lyst) (return p))
          (when (zero? (car lyst)) (return 0))
          (set! p (* p (car lyst)))
          (set! lyst (cdr lyst))
          (loop 'any-value))))))
```

The continuation of the inner CALL/CC expression evaluates the expressions that follow in the LET form's body. Thus, LOOP functions as a backwards *goto* label with (LOOP 'ANY-VALUE) as the *goto* statement.

Other, more practical, uses of first-class continuations include event simulation, nonblind backtracking[11], multiprocessing[24], and coroutines[12]. Friedman and Haynes[5] discuss techniques for constraining the power of continuations for security and efficiency, including generalizations of the Common Lisp UNWIND-PROTECT. For more explanation of CALL/CC and its uses, see *Programming Language: Abstractions and Their Implementations*[6].

Continuations are disjoint from other data types in PC Scheme. The predicate CONTINUATION? determines whether its argument is a continuation. The predicate PROCEDURE? returns *true* for closures and engines as well as for continuations.

There is no written representation for continuation objects that, when read into Scheme, reconstruct the continuation. WRITE writes continuations using the notation #<CONTINUATION>, which is an invalid input for READ but conveys some information to human readers.

Environments

4.11 An *environment* is a data object that maintains the bindings of identifiers to variables and their values. The Scheme evaluator uses environments to implement the lexically scoped block structure of Scheme programs so that every expression is evaluated with respect to some environment. By providing environments as first-class objects, Scheme gives the programmer the flexibility to specify which variables an expression sees during evaluation.

The environment objects of TI Scheme provide the basic packaging mechanism of the language. Abelson and Sussman [1, Chapter 4] illustrate this concept with the example of a generic arithmetic system in which procedure names are encapsulated in environments and accessed with a message-passing style of procedure call.

An environment is a sequence of *frames*, where each frame contains a table of bindings and a reference to the environment that is its lexical parent, if it has one. Environment frames are created by such special forms as LAMBDA and LET. Each frame corresponds to a block, or lexical level, of the program. Although the same variable name may occur in more than one frame, duplicate names are not permitted within the same frame.

Environments are disjoint from other data types in PC Scheme. The predicate ENVIRONMENT? determines whether its argument is an environment. The special form THE-ENVIRONMENT returns as its value the environment in which it is evaluated. The special form MAKE-ENVIRONMENT produces a new environment that is contained statically in the environment in which it is evaluated and typically contains definitions that extend that environment. The special form DEFINE extends the current environment by adding a new binding and initial value. The special form SET! assigns a new value to a previously bound variable.

EVAL evaluates its first argument, an S-expression, in the environment specified by its (optional) second argument. Since EVAL is a procedure rather than a special form, its first argument is evaluated twice: first by the parameter-passing mechanism in the environment containing the call to EVAL and then by EVAL itself in the specified environment. When no environment is passed to EVAL, the first argument is evaluated in the current global environment.

The special form ACCESS retrieves the value bound to an identifier in a specified environment. The extended special form (SET! (ACCESS *id env*) *exp*) modifies the binding of *id* in the environment *env*. The special form UNBOUND? determines whether an identifier is bound in a given environment.

The procedure ENVIRONMENT-BINDINGS returns an association list representing the bindings in a given environment. ENVIRONMENT-PARENT returns the environment in which the given environment was created. PROCEDURE-ENVIRONMENT returns the environment over which the given procedure was closed. These three procedures are intended primarily for system use.

The global environment in which the PC Scheme top-level read-eval-print loop evaluates user expressions is bound to the variable USER-INITIAL-ENVIRONMENT. This global environment is initially empty but becomes filled with bindings created by user DEFINE expressions. The lexical parent of USER-INITIAL-ENVIRONMENT contains the system global bindings and is bound to the variable USER-GLOBAL-ENVIRONMENT.

For environment objects, there is no written representation that, when read into Scheme, reconstructs the environment. WRITE writes environments using the notation #<ENVIRONMENT>, which is an invalid input for READ but conveys some information to human readers.

Engines

4.12 In TI Scheme, engines are first-class functional objects that abstract timed preemption. In conjunction with continuations, engines allow Scheme to be extended with a variety of process abstraction facilities.

Metaphorically, an engine embodies a computation that is run by giving it a quantity of fuel. If the engine completes its computation before running out of fuel, it returns the result of its computation and the quantity of remaining fuel. If it runs out of fuel, a new engine is returned that, when run, continues the computation.

Engine fuel is measured in *ticks*. In the general engine abstraction, the unit of computation associated with a tick is unspecified and is required only to satisfy a few general constraints (see [11] for details). In the current implementation of PC Scheme, ticks are associated with the PC's hardware clock interrupts.

Engines are created by the procedure MAKE-ENGINE, which takes a *thunk* (a procedure of no arguments) as its argument. The body of the thunk contains the computation to be performed, which is terminated by invoking the procedure ENGINE-RETURN with the value to be returned for the computation. The engine returned from MAKE-ENGINE is a procedure of three arguments: a positive integer specifying the number of ticks for which the computation is to be run, a *success procedure*, and a *failure procedure*. If ENGINE-RETURN is called before the specified number of ticks is exhausted, the success procedure is invoked with the value of the computation and the number of ticks remaining. If the engine exhausts the ticks before ENGINE-RETURN is invoked, the failure procedure is invoked with a new engine that continues the original engine's computation when it is run. Any value returned by the success or failure procedure becomes the value of the engine invocation.

TI Scheme does not allow a running engine to invoke another engine. This does not result in any loss of generality; see [10] for techniques that may be used to implement such nested engines in terms of the standard engine mechanism.

As a very simple example of the use of engines, the following procedure takes an engine, runs it repeatedly until its computation completes, and then returns the value of the computation:

```
(define finish
  (lambda (eng)
    (let loop  ((eng eng))
      (eng 100             ; arbitrary number of ticks per run
          (lambda (value ticks)     ; success procedure
            value)
          loop))))                  ; failure procedure
```

As a second example, the next procedure takes a thunk and returns the number of ticks required to complete its computation. This procedure might be used to make relative performance measurements to compare alternative algorithms.

```
(define ticks-to-finish
  (let  ((ticks/run 1000))
    (lambda (thunk)
      (let loop ((eng  (make-engine thunk))
                 (run-count 0))
        (eng ticks/run
            (lambda (value ticks)
              (+ (* ticks/run run-count) ticks))
            (lambda (eng)
              (loop  eng (+ run-count  1)))))))))
```

Engines may be used for a variety of applications for which operating system dependent timed preemption mechanisms usually are required. These include discrete time simulators and the implementation, via time sharing, of traditional process abstractions. See [10] for examples.

Since engines are simply closures, the only predicates that can determine whether an object is an engine are CLOSURE? and PROCEDURE?. Also, for engines there is no written representation that, when read into Scheme, reconstructs the engine.

Input/Output Ports

4.13 Scheme provides a wide variety of facilities for performing input/output (I/O) to files and other devices. All I/O is performed through ports, which are associated with input and output devices. To Scheme, an input device is a Scheme object that can deliver characters upon demand, while an output device is a Scheme object that can accept characters. TI Scheme permits ports to be opened for I/O with the files and devices supported by the underlying operating system, as well as with interactive windows representing the console screen and keyboard.

Ports

4.13.1 The port data type is disjoint from the other data types in PC Scheme. The predicate PORT? determines whether a given object is a port.

For port objects, there is no written representation that, when read into Scheme, reconstructs the port. WRITE writes ports using the notation #<PORT>, which is an invalid input for READ but conveys some information to human readers.

For programming convenience, the Scheme I/O procedures operate on default input and output ports, although most take an optional argument so that the port to be used can be specified. The current default ports may be obtained with the procedures CURRENT-INPUT-PORT and CURRENT-OUTPUT-PORT. The procedures WITH-INPUT-FROM-FILE and WITH-OUTPUT-TO-FILE provide for the execution of code with the current default ports rebound to specified files. The procedures CALL-WITH-INPUT-FILE and CALL-WITH-OUTPUT-FILE are similar to WITH-INPUT-FROM-FILE and WITH-OUTPUT-TO-FILE, except that the port for the file is bound to a user-supplied variable.

Files may be opened explicitly and ports assigned to them with the procedures OPEN-INPUT-FILE, OPEN-OUTPUT-FILE, and OPEN-EXTEND-FILE. A string may be opened as if it were an input file with OPEN-INPUT-STRING. These open ports then may be closed with CLOSE-INPUT-PORT and CLOSE-OUTPUT-PORT.

Opening a file may incur any of several error conditions, depending on the facilities of the underlying operating system. Consult the *PC Scheme User's Guide* for details. The procedure FILE-EXISTS? may be used to determine whether a file exists before attempting to open it for input.

An open port has state information associated with it, including the record length of the device and the current position within it. LINE-LENGTH and SET-LINE-LENGTH! are used to fetch and modify the maximum record length of a file for output, respectively; CURRENT-COLUMN returns the column number associated with an output port.

Random I/O is supported by GET-FILE-POSITION and SET-FILE-POSITION!, which are used to fetch and modify a byte offset within a file.

The READ procedure converts written representations of Scheme objects into the objects themselves. READ-ATOM reads arbitrary atoms and returns special values for any punctuation marks it encounters, such as parentheses, periods, and forward and backward quotation marks (' and '); it is intended primarily as a tool for implementing READ. READ-CHAR reads and returns characters, while READ-LINE reads all of the remaining characters in the current line and returns them as a string object. FLUSH-INPUT discards characters in the input port up to and including the next end-of-line. The input procedures signal an end-of-file condition by returning a distinguished eof-object, which is recognized by the predicate EOF-OBJECT?.

WRITE and DISPLAY are the principal output procedures. WRITE writes a representation of its argument to the output port in such a way that it may be read in again by READ (where possible). Thus, strings are enclosed in double quotation marks, and embedded backslash and double quotation mark characters are escaped with backslashes. Similarly, symbols containing exceptional characters are written between vertical bars or with backslashes, as needed. Character objects are written using the #\ notation.

DISPLAY writes its argument in a form more readable by humans. Strings are not enclosed in double quotation marks, characters are written as themselves, and exceptional characters in strings and symbols are not escaped. The traditional names PRIN1 and PRINC are provided as alternate names for WRITE and DISPLAY, respectively.

The primitive procedure WRITE-CHAR writes a character (not the written representation of the character in #\ notation) to a given port and returns an unspecified value. NEWLINE terminates the current output line in a system-dependent way, usually by writing an end-of-line character sequence to the port. FRESH-LINE terminates the current line only if it is not empty. PRINT is a variant of WRITE that first emits a new line, and then writes its argument followed by a space. WRITELN writes each of its arguments from left to right, and then emits a new line. The procedure PP is a variant of WRITE that attempts to pretty-print its argument with aesthetically pleasing line breaks and indentation. PRINT-LENGTH returns the number of output character positions that would be needed to print its argument with WRITE.

Windows

4.13.2 Windows are port objects representing rectangular areas on the screen. The predicate WINDOW? determines whether a given object is a port representing a window on the console's screen. All interactive screen I/O is performed through windows, including I/O through the ports STANDARD-INPUT and STANDARD-OUTPUT. New window ports are created and opened with MAKE-WINDOW; their attributes are accessed with WINDOW-GET-ATTRIBUTE and modified with WINDOW-SET-ATTRIBUTE!.

Windows are not placed on the screen until the space for them is cleared with WINDOW-CLEAR, which also draws optional borders around them. WINDOW-DELETE erases the area of screen covered by a window and its borders. WINDOW-POPUP and WINDOW-POPUP-DELETE display several overlapping windows in a "last in, first out" fashion.

The position of a window on the screen and its size in lines and columns are accessed with WINDOW-GET-POSITION and WINDOW-GET-SIZE, respectively, and are modified with WINDOW-SET-POSITION! and WINDOW-SET-SIZE!, respectively. Modifications to the position or size of a window should be made before the window is initially displayed with WINDOW-CLEAR. The position of the cursor is accessed with WINDOW-GET-CURSOR and modified with WINDOW-SET-CURSOR!. The cursor is displayed on the screen only when input is expected from the keyboard.

Structures

4.14 TI Scheme provides a facility similar to the Common Lisp facility DEFSTRUCT for creating named record structures with named components. In effect, this facility allows new data types to be defined, with each object of a structure type having components with specified names. Structures are heterogeneous data objects, which are similar to the Pascal record data type.

The special form DEFINE-STRUCTURE is used to create a new structured data type. From the user's specification, DEFINE-STRUCTURE generates new special forms and procedures that construct object instances, access the components, and test whether an object is an instance of the type. For example, if foo is the name to be given to a new type and bar and baz are its components' names, DEFINE-STRUCTURE would generate the special forms MAKE-FOO, FOO-BAR, FOO-BAZ, and the procedure FOO?. MAKE-FOO then would be used to create objects of type foo. FOO? would recognize those objects, and FOO-BAR and FOO-BAZ would be the accessor operations. The components of a structure are modified using the SET! special form, as in (SET! (FOO-BAR *obj*) *value*).

Objects created with MAKE-*name* have their components initialized to the values of expressions optionally specified in the DEFINE-STRUCTURE definition. These initialization expressions are evaluated each time an instance of *name* is created. If no initial value is specified for a component, its value is unspecified until an assignment is made with SET!.

A new structure type may be defined as an extension, or subtype, of another structure type using the INCLUDE option of DEFINE-STRUCTURE. Objects of the subtype share the components of the existing type as well as the newly defined ones. The existing type's accessor forms and recognition predicate also work as expected with instances of the new type.

Some implementations of TI Scheme may define other data types in terms of structures. Typical examples might be streams, ports, and rational and complex numbers.

Printer Output

4.15 To send output to a printer, simply treat the printer as an output file and give the file the name PRN.

SCOOPS

SCOOPS is an object-oriented programming system for TI Scheme based on first-class environments and on multiple and dynamic inheritance. Although it is similar in concept and syntax to the object-oriented paradigms of the LOOPS [2] and Flavors [25] systems, the implementation of SCOOPS relies heavily on the features of the Scheme language. Note that in PC Scheme, it is necessary to load the file SCOOPS.FSL before using SCOOPS.

If you are not familiar with SCOOPS, a tutorial is available to help you get started. The tutorial is contained on the file *tutorial.fsl*, which you can load into PC Scheme.

```
(load "tutorial.fsl")
```

The file *scpsdemo.s* contains the source code for the SCOOPS classes that are used in the tutorial. Printing off and reading a copy of *scpsdemo.s* may help you better understand SCOOPS as you go through the tutorial.

Overview

5.1 The object-oriented programming world consists of objects, which represent abstract entities. An object is comprised of variables, which determine the local state of the object, and methods, which define the object's behavior. Higher levels of abstraction are built up through inheritance; that is, higher level classes of objects may inherit the properties of other classes. Large systems can thus be divided naturally into coherent parts that can be developed and maintained separately. Programmers can also avoid the specification of redundant information.

The only way to interact with an object or to influence its state is by sending a message to it. However, the message passing style need not be adhered to internally within an object. Methods may use normal lexical scoping and procedure calls to access variables and to invoke other methods of the same class. Method definition is, therefore, both convenient and efficient.

Before you use any of the SCOOPS facilities, be sure to load the SCOOPS environment by entering the following:

```
(load "scoops.fsl")
```

Defining Classes

5.2 A *class* contains the description of one or more similar objects; an *object* is an instance of a class. The definition of a class consists of *class variables*, *instance variables*, *methods*, and *mixins*. Class variables contain information that is shared by all instances of the class. Instance variables are local to each instance and contain information specific to that instance. Methods are procedures that determine the behavior of instances of the class. A class may inherit the variables and methods of other classes through mixins. Inheritance has proven to be a useful way to organize information in complex systems.

The following code is an example of class definition in SCOOPS:

```
(define-class employees
  (classvars (no-of-employees 0))
  (instvars name emp-no manager salary (overtime 0))
  (mixins personal-info education-experience)
  (options (gettable-variables name emp-no no-of-employees)
           settable-variables
           inittable-variables))
```

The class EMPLOYEES has a class variable, NO-OF-EMPLOYEES, which is initialized to zero. It also contains five instance variables, NAME, EMP-NO, MANAGER, SALARY, and OVERTIME. This class inherits class variables, instance variables, and methods from its mixins, PERSONAL-INFO and EDU-CATION-EXPERIENCE.

Methods are generated automatically for *gettable* and *settable* variables. The *inittable* variables can be given initial values when an instance of a class is created. In the class EMPLOYEES, all the variables are settable and inittable, while only NAME, EMP-NO, and NO-OF-EMPLOYEES are gettable.

In object-oriented programming systems, it is traditional to allow class variables, instance variables, methods, and mixins to be added or deleted from the definition of the class at any time. In the current version of SCOOPS in PC Scheme, only methods can be added or deleted. Methods do not have to be recompiled when the class definition is changed.

The special form MAKE-INSTANCE is used to create new objects. Since instances are not created with names, it is necessary to keep references to them in variables or other data structures.

Methods

5.3   Methods are defined for a class with DEFINE-METHOD. If a method by a given name already exists, the new definition replaces the existing one.

The following example illustrates the addition of two methods, EARNINGS-GREATER-THAN and EARNINGS, to the class EMPLOYEES:

```
(define-method (employees earnings)  ( )
 (+ salary overtime))
```

```
(define-method (employees earnings-greater-than)  (val)
    (if (>? (earnings)  val)
    (writeln name emp-no)
    '( )))
```

The method EARNINGS computes an employee's earnings as the sum of OVERTIME and SALARY. The method EARNINGS-GREATER-THAN prints the name and employee number of the employee if the earnings are greater than a given value. Note that methods can refer to instance variables as if they were lexically enclosing variables.

An object's methods are invoked by sending a message to the object with the SEND special form. However, if a method in a class needs to invoke another method in the same class, including methods inherited from mixins, it may call the other method directly as a procedure. This call is illustrated in the previous example, where the method EARNINGS-GREATER-THAN calls EARNINGS, another method in the same class, as a procedure.

Variables

5.4 An object contains two kinds of variables: class variables and instance variables. Class variables contain information that is shared by all objects of the same class. Instance variables are local to each object and contain the object's local state.

Within an object, these variables may be treated as ordinary lexical variables. This treatment is illustrated in the example in the previous chapter, where the method EARNINGS adds the values of the instance variables SALARY and OVERTIME.

If the variables have been defined with the option GETTABLE-VARIABLES, methods to access their values are generated automatically. The names of these methods are constructed by prefixing the names of the variables with GET-. For example, in the class EMPLOYEES in the first example, the variables NAME, EMP-NO, and NO-OF-EMPLOYEES are gettable. The value of a gettable variable is obtained by sending a message such as (SEND EMP1 GET-NAME) to an instance. Similarly, for settable variables, the names of the methods are prefixed with SET-, and the value of a settable variable may be modified by sending a message such as (SEND EMP1 SET-SALARY 4000) to an instance.

The values of gettable class variables also may be accessed or set through the class itself without referring to an instance of the class. The special forms GETCV and SETCV get and modify the value of a class variable, respectively.

Active Values

5.5 Active values [2] are used to trigger procedure invocations whenever the value of a variable is accessed or updated. Currently, only instance variables can have active values. An instance variable is given an active value with the special form (ACTIVE *initial-value getfn setfn*).

The keyword ACTIVE informs the system that this is an active value. The procedure *getfn* is invoked whenever the value of the variable is accessed, and the procedure *setfn* is invoked whenever the value of the variable is modified. The procedures *getfn* and *setfn* may be external procedures, methods in the same class, or #F, if no procedure is to be specified.

Variables with active values are both gettable and settable, and access and update methods are generated automatically for them.

To trace references to an instance variable POSITION, you could define POSITION as follows:

```
(define-class shipn
  (instvars (position (active 0 traceget traceset)) ...)
      ...)
```

Whenever the value of POSITION is accessed, the current value is passed to TRACEGET, and the value returned from TRACEGET is returned as the value of POSITION. Whenever a value is assigned to the variable POSITION, TRACESET is invoked with the new value, and POSITION is set to the value returned from TRACESET.

Active values may be nested to an arbitrary depth by specifying another active value as the *initial-value* of an active value:

```
(active (active initial-value getfn1 setfn1) getfn2 setfn2)
```

Whenever the value of the variable bound to this active value is set, the *setfn* procedures are invoked in order from the outermost to the innermost. Likewise, whenever the value of the variable is accessed, the *getfn* procedures are invoked from the innermost to the outermost.

SCOOPS also provides a way to access or modify active values without invoking the *getfn* and *setfn* procedures.

Within an object, the value of a class or instance variable can be accessed in two ways — as a lexical variable and with its SET- and GET- methods. The simplest way is to access it as a lexical variable, using SET!, for example. When an active value is modified in this manner, its *setfn* procedures are not invoked.

The other way to modify an active value is with a procedure call, such as (SET-POSITION 10). This call invokes the *setfn* procedures for the active value in the manner described previously. Similarly, if POSITION is simply referenced as a lexical variable, the current value is returned, and the *getfn* procedures are not invoked. However, if the GET-POSITION procedure is used to retrieve the value, the *getfn* procedures in the active value are invoked in order.

Inheritance

5.6   Inheritance is used to build higher levels of abstractions. Large systems can be organized through an inheritance structure of classes, thus permitting a modular design and avoiding the specification of redundant information.

In SCOOPS, an inheritance structure is built by "mixing in" other classes to form an acyclic directed graph. Classes that are made to be components of other classes in this way are called *mixins*. A class inherits the class variables, instance variables, and methods from its component classes. The order in which the component classes are combined determines which variables and methods are inherited when naming conflicts arise. The inheritance graph is searched in *depth-first* order, omitting any nodes that have been visited previously. For example, if CLASS1 has mixins CLASS2 and CLASS3, CLASS2 has mixins CLASS4 and CLASS5, and CLASS3 has mixins CLASS4 and CLASS6, the order in which the classes are combined is CLASS1, CLASS2, CLASS4, CLASS5, CLASS3, CLASS6.

The set of class variables and instance variables of a class is the union of class variables and instance variables of its component classes. However, the class variables that CLASS1 inherits from its component classes are shared by all instances of CLASS1 but are not shared by instances of its component classes.

Methods also are combined in a simple manner. If two classes contain a method with the same name, the method whose class is closer to the root in the depth-first order is inherited. Methods may be added or deleted at any time. The changes made to any classes are propagated throughout the inheritance structure.

The actual inheritance structure for a class is not constructed until the class is compiled with the COMPILE-CLASS operation. This operation is performed automatically the first time MAKE-INSTANCE is used to create an object that is an instance of the class. COMPILE-CLASS builds the inheritance graph for a class by inspecting each of its mixins. Until a class is "compiled" in this way, the procedure DESCRIBE is unable to describe completely all of its class variables, instance variables, and mixins.

This use of the term "compile" should not be confused with the compilation step of the Scheme evaluator, EVAL. The term describes the process of collecting the pieces of the class definition into one place. Compiling a class with COMPILE-CLASS does not prohibit further method definitions for the class, and adding method definitions to a class does not require that it be recompiled.

The order in which the classes in the inheritance graph are compiled with COMPILE-CLASS is immaterial. Compiling a class does not automatically cause its mixins to be compiled, although the full graph containing them as nodes is built in order to collect all the components of the compiled class. Once a mixin has been added to the inheritance graph in this way, the procedure DESCRIBE is able to describe all its components, although it may not have been compiled itself.

Although a class is automatically compiled the first time MAKE-INSTANCE is used to create an instance of the class, it frequently is desirable to compile the class explicitly. For example, when a source file containing class definitions is to be compiled into object form with COMPILE-FILE, explicit calls to COMPILE-CLASS cause the class to be compiled and the inheritance structure to be constructed at the time the file is compiled. Otherwise, the class is compiled every time the file is loaded and the first MAKE-INSTANCE occurs.

Note that all the mixins of a class need to be defined before the class is compiled or its first instance object is created.

DEFINITIONS BY CATEGORY

To help you locate related definitions, this chapter categorizes the procedures, forms, variables, and literals listed in Chapter 7. The four categories are Data Types and Operations, Semantics, User's Packages, and Miscellaneous. These major categories are divided into subcategories; procedures, forms, variables, and literals are then listed under appropriate subcategories in alphabetical order.

Data Types and Operations

6.1 Data types and operations are divided into fifteen subcategories shown in the following list:

Booleans and Equivalence Predicates

'()	FALSE
BOOLEAN?	NIL
EQ?	NOT
EQUAL?	T
EQV?	#T
#F	TRUE

Characters

#\BACKSPACE	CHAR=?
CHAR->INTEGER	CHAR>?
CHAR-CI<?	CHAR>=?
CHAR-CI<=?	CHAR?
CHAR-CI=?	#\ESCAPE
CHAR-CI>?	INTEGER->CHAR
CHAR-CI>=?	#\NEWLINE
CHAR-DOWNCASE	#\PAGE
CHAR-UPCASE	#\RETURN
CHAR<?	#\RUBOUT
CHAR<=?	#\SPACE
	#\TAB

Continuations

CALL-WITH-CURRENT-CONTINUATION	CONTINUATION?
CALL/CC	

Engines

ENGINE-RETURN	MAKE-ENGINE

Environments

ACCESS	PROCEDURE-ENVIRONMENT
DEFINE	SET!
ENVIRONMENT-BINDINGS	THE-ENVIRONMENT
ENVIRONMENT-PARENT	UNBOUND?
ENVIRONMENT?	USER-GLOBAL-ENVIRONMENT
EVAL	USER-INITIAL-ENVIRONMENT
MAKE-ENVIRONMENT	

Input and Output of Numbers

INTEGER->STRING	NUMBER->STRING
STRING->NUMBER	

Numbers

*	FLOOR
+	GCD
-	INEXACT?
-1+	INTEGER?
/	LCM
1+	LOG
<	MAX
<=	MIN
<>	MINUS
=	MODULO
>	NEGATIVE?
>=	NUMBER?
ABS	ODD?
ACOS	POSITIVE?
ADD1	QUOTIENT
ASIN	RANDOM
ATAN	RANDOMIZE
CEILING	RATIONAL?
COMPLEX?	REAL?
COS	REMAINDER
EVEN?	ROUND
EXACT?	SIN
EXP	SQRT
EXPT	SUB1
FLOAT	TAN
FLOAT?	TRUNCATE
	ZERO?

Pairs and Lists

APPEND	LENGTH
APPEND!	LIST
ASSOC	LIST*
ASSQ	LIST-REF
ASSV	LIST-TAIL
ATOM?	MEMBER
C....R	MEMQ
CAR	MEMV
CDR	NULL?
CONS	PAIR?
COPY	REVERSE
DELETE!	REVERSE!
DELQ!	SET-CAR!
LAST-PAIR	SET-CDR!

Ports

CALL-WITH-INPUT-FILE
CALL-WITH-OUTPUT-FILE
CHAR-READY?
CLOSE-INPUT-PORT
CLOSE-OUTPUT-PORT
CURRENT-COLUMN
CURRENT-INPUT-PORT
CURRENT-OUTPUT-PORT
DISPLAY
EOF-OBJECT?
FILE-EXISTS?
FLUSH-INPUT
FRESH-LINE
GET-FILE-POSITION
INPUT-PORT?
LINE-LENGTH
MAKE-WINDOW
NEWLINE
OPEN-BINARY-INPUT-FILE
OPEN-BINARY-OUTPUT-FILE
OPEN-EXTEND-FILE
OPEN-INPUT-FILE
OPEN-INPUT-STRING
OPEN-OUTPUT-FILE
OUTPUT-PORT?
PORT?
PP
PRIN1
PRINC
PRINT

PRINT-LENGTH
READ
READ-ATOM
READ-CHAR
READ-LINE
SET-LINE-LENGTH!
SET-FILE-POSITION!
STANDARD-INPUT
STANDARD-OUTPUT
WINDOW-CLEAR
WINDOW-DELETE
WINDOW-GET-ATTRIBUTE
WINDOW-GET-CURSOR
WINDOW-GET-POSITION
WINDOW-GET-SIZE
WINDOW-POPUP
WINDOW-POPUP-DELETE
WINDOW-RESTORE-CONTENTS
WINDOW-SAVE-CONTENTS
WINDOW-SET-ATTRIBUTE!
WINDOW-SET-CURSOR!
WINDOW-SET-POSITION!
WINDOW-SET-SIZE!
WINDOW?
WITH-INPUT-FROM-FILE
WITH-OUTPUT-TO-FILE
WRITE
WRITE-CHAR
WRITELN

Procedures

APPLY
CLOSURE?
FOR-EACH
MAP

MAPC
MAPCAR
PROC?
PROCEDURE??

Streams

CONS-STREAM
DELAY
DELAYED-OBJECT?
EMPTY-STREAM?
FORCE
FREEZE
HEAD

LIST->STREAM
STREAM->LIST
STREAM?
TAIL
THAW
THE-EMPTY-STREAM

Strings

LIST->STRING
MAKE-STRING
STRING->LIST
STRING-APPEND
STRING-CI<?
STRING-CI=?
STRING-COPY
STRING-FILL!
STRING-LENGTH
STRING-NULL?
STRING-REF
STRING-SET!
STRING<?
STRING<=?

STRING=?
STRING>?
STRING>=?
STRING?
SUBSTRING
SUBSTRING-CI<?
SUBSTRING-CI=?
SUBSTRING-FILL!
SUBSTRING-FIND-NEXT-CHAR-IN-SET
SUBSTRING-FIND-PREVIOUS-CHAR-IN-SET
SUBSTRING-MOVE-LEFT!
SUBSTRING-MOVE-RIGHT!
SUBSTRING<?
SUBSTRING=?

Structures

```
DEFINE-STRUCTURE
```

Symbols

```
ASCII->SYMBOL          REMPROP
EXPLODE                STRING->SYMBOL
GENSYM                 STRING->UNINTERNED-SYMBOL
GETPROP                SYMBOL->ASCII
IMPLODE                SYMBOL->STRING
PROPLIST               SYMBOL?
PUTPROP
```

Vectors

```
LIST->VECTOR           VECTOR-LENGTH
MAKE-VECTOR            VECTOR-REF
VECTOR                 VECTOR-SET!
VECTOR->LIST           VECTOR?
VECTOR-FILL!
```

Semantics

6.2 The six subcategories of semantics are as follows:

Binding-Forms

```
DO                     LETREC
LAMBDA                 NAMED-LAMBDA
LET                    REC
LET*
```

Error Handling

```
ASSERT                 ERROR
BKPT
```

Fluid Environment

```
FLUID                  FLUID-LET
FLUID-BOUND?           SET-FLUID!
FLUID-LAMBDA
```

Literals

```
QUASIQUOTE             UNQUOTE
QUOTE                  UNQUOTE-SPLICING
```

Sequencing and Control

AND	COND
APPLY-IF	IF
BEGIN	OR
BEGIN0	SEQUENCE
CASE	WHEN

Syntactic Extension

ALIAS	SYNTAX
MACRO	

User's Packages

6.3 The three subcategories of user's packages are as follows:

Debugging Tools

ADVISE-ENTRY	TRACE-ENTRY
ADVISE-EXIT	TRACE-EXIT
ARGS	UNADVISE
BREAK	UNADVISE-ENTRY
BREAK-BOTH	UNADVISE-EXIT
BREAK-ENTRY	UNBREAK
BREAK-EXIT	UNBREAK-ENTRY
INSPECT	UNBREAK-EXIT
PROC	UNTRACE
RESULT	UNTRACE-ENTRY
TRACE	UNTRACE-EXIT
TRACE-BOTH	

Graphics

CLEAR-GRAPHICS	*GRAPHICS-COLORS*
CLEAR-POINT	IS-POINT-ON?
DRAW-BOX-TO	POINT-COLOR
DRAW-FILLED-BOX-TO	POSITION-PEN
DRAW-LINE-TO	SET-CLIPPING-RECTANGLE
DRAW-POINT	SET-PALETTE!
GET-PEN-COLOR	SET-PEN-COLOR!
GET-PEN-POSITION	SET-VIDEO-MODE!
GET-VIDEO-MODE	

SCOOPS

ALL-CLASSVARS	GETCV
ALL-INSTVARS	INSTVARS
ALL-METHODS	MAKE-INSTANCE
CLASS-COMPILED?	METHODS
CLASS-OF-OBJECT	MIXINS
CLASSVARS	NAME->CLASS
COMPILE-CLASS	RENAME-CLASS
DEFINE-CLASS	SEND
DEFINE-METHOD	SEND-IF-HANDLES
DELETE-METHOD	SETCV
DESCRIBE	

Miscellaneous

6.4 Miscellaneous definitions are as follows:

```
AUTOLOAD-FROM-FILE
COMPILE
COMPILE-FILE
DEFINE-INTEGRABLE
DOS-CALL
DOS-CHDIR
DOS-CHANGE-DRIVE
DOS-DELETE
DOS-DIR
DOS-FILE-COPY
DOS-FILE-SIZE
DOS-RENAME
EDIT
EDWIN
EXIT
FAST-LOAD
FREESP
GC
LOAD
OBJECT-HASH
OBJECT-UNHASH
PCS-DEBUG-MODE
PCS-INTEGRATE-INTEGRABLES
PCS-INTEGRATE-PRIMITIVES
PCS-INTEGRATE-T-AND-NIL
RESET
RESET-SCHEME-TOP-LEVEL
RUNTIME
SCHEME-RESET
SCHEME-TOP-LEVEL
SORT!
*THE-NON-PRINTING-OBJECT*
TRANSCRIPT-OFF
TRANSCRIPT-ON
```

ALPHABETIC CATALOG OF LANGUAGE ELEMENTS

This chapter describes the standard procedures, special forms, variables, and constants provided in the PC Scheme implementation of TI Scheme. These features are listed in alphabetic order, ignoring the presence of nonalphabetic characters.

The header for each feature's description consists of the name of the feature and its category. Then the description provides the format of the feature's use and all parameters (where applicable). In describing the format of a procedure or special form, the following notations are used:

exp...	Indicates zero or more occurrences of an expression
*exp*₁...	Indicates at least one occurrence of an expression
*exp*₁ *exp*₂...	Indicates two or more occurrences of an expression
{*exp*}	Indicates an optional expression

Following the format and parameters, a technical explanation of the feature appears, followed by examples of its use.

Multiple features that differ in some systematic way are grouped together if they are contiguous in the collating sequence. Thus, CHAR<? and CHAR>? appear together, but CAR and CDR do not.

This chapter uses the following conventions to clarify the use of various terms and concepts and to distinguish the special values *true*, *false*, and *unspecified value*:

■ The italicized words *true* and *false* represent any values that count as true or false in conditional expressions. In PC Scheme, the values #F and ( ) are *false*; everything else is *true*. WRITE always displays the *false* value as ( ).

■ The term *unspecified value* indicates that no particular value is specified; therefore, programmers should not rely on the values returned in any particular implementation or instance.

■ The names of standard features, such as LAMBDA, are written in uppercase letters. Names representing formal values to be supplied by the programmer, as in (+ *num* ...), are written in *lowercase italic*.

■ Lowercase typewriter style is used to represent input to the Scheme system and **boldface** type is used to indicate output in the examples. The result of evaluating an expression, as in (+ 2 2) ⇒ 4, is indicated with ⇒.

'( )   *Constant*

'( ) is the empty list.

Format   '( )

Explanation   '( ) is the empty list, which is a list with no elements. In some implementa-
                    tions of Scheme, including this version, ( ) is self-evaluating; that is, ( ) evalu-
                    ates to ( ). It is strongly recommended that '( ) be used instead of ( ) since
                    '( ) is standard Scheme.

Examples   (define a '())   ⟹ *unspecified value*
                    (null? a)   ⟹ *true*
                    (pair? a)   ⟹ *false*
                    (length a)   ⟹ 0

---

*   *Procedure*

* calculates the arithmetic product of its arguments.

Format   (* num...)

Parameters   *num* ... — Any Scheme numbers

Explanation   * multiplies its arguments together in an unspecified order and returns the
                    product. If only one *num* is given, it is multiplied by 1 and the result is
                    returned. If no arguments are specified, 1 is returned.

Examples   (* 11 2)   ⟹ 22
                    (* 20 0.5 3)   ⟹ 30.
                    (* 5 0)   ⟹ 0
                    (* 99)   ⟹ 99
                    (*)   ⟹ 1

+   *Procedure*

+ calculates the arithmetic sum of its arguments.

Format	(+ *num*...)
Parameters	*num*... — Any Scheme numbers
Explanation	+ adds its arguments together in an unspecified order and returns the sum. If only one *num* is given, it is added to zero and the result is returned. If no arguments are given, 0 is returned.

Examples

```
(+ 11 13)              ⟹ 24
(+ 42 -15 100 3)       ⟹ 130
(+ 99 -14)             ⟹ 85
(+ 42)                 ⟹ 42
(+)                    ⟹ 0
```

—   *Procedure*

– calculates the arithmetic difference of its arguments.

Format	(– *num*$_1$ ...)
Parameters	*num*$_1$ ... — Any Scheme numbers
Explanation	With two or more arguments, — repeatedly subtracts the arguments after the first one from the first argument in left associative order and returns the result. This is equivalent to the following binary operation:

$$(- (- (- num_1\ num_2)\ num_3)\ ...\ num_n)$$

With a single argument, — returns the negative of its input.

Examples

```
(- 42 21)              ⟹ 21
(- 13 42.0)            ⟹ -29.
(- 42 13 -5 12)        ⟹ 22
(- 42)                 ⟹ -42
```

−1+ *Procedure*

−1+ subtracts 1 from its argument.

Format	(−1+ *num*)
Parameter	*num* — Any Scheme number
Explanation	−1+ subtracts one from *num* and returns the difference.
Examples	(−1+ 8) $\Rightarrow$ 7
	(−1+ −14.0) $\Rightarrow$ −15.

/ *Procedure*

/ calculates the quotient of its arguments.

Format	(/ *num₁* ...)
Parameters	*num₁* ... — Any Scheme numbers
Explanation	With two or more arguments, / repeatedly divides the arguments after the first one into the first argument in left associative order and returns the result. This is equivalent to the following binary operation:

$$(/ \; (/ \; (/ \; num_1 \; num_2) \; num_3) \; ... \; num_n)$$

With a single argument, / returns the reciprocal of its input. Division by zero is an error and causes a breakpoint.

Examples	(/ 4 2) $\Rightarrow$ 2
	(/ 21 42) $\Rightarrow$ 0.5
	(/ 21 7 3 2) $\Rightarrow$ 0.5
	(/ 10) $\Rightarrow$ 0.1

1+ *Procedure*

1+ adds one to its argument.

Format	(1+ *num*)
Parameter	*num* — Any Scheme number
Explanation	1+ adds one to *num* and returns the sum.
Examples	(1+ 99) ⟹ 100
	(1+ -5.0) ⟹ -4.

<, *Procedure*
<=, <>, =, >, >=

These procedures perform arithmetic comparisons.

Format	(< *num₁* *num₂*)
	(<= *num₁* *num₂*)
	(<> *num₁* *num₂*)
	(= *num₁* *num₂*)
	(> *num₁* *num₂*)
	(>= *num₁* *num₂*)
Parameters	*num₁* — Any Scheme number
	num₂ — Any Scheme number
Explanation	These predicate procedures compare two numbers using the specified relational operator. Each procedure returns *true* if the comparison is true; otherwise, *false* is returned. The procedures are defined as follows:

<	Less than
<=	Less than or equal to
<>	Not equal to
=	Equal to
>	Greater than
>=	Greater than or equal to

Examples	(< 1 2)	$\Rightarrow$ *true*
	(< -3 -5.6)	$\Rightarrow$ *false*
	(= 3 3.0)	$\Rightarrow$ *true*
	(> 5.1 5)	$\Rightarrow$ *true*
	(>= 77 2)	$\Rightarrow$ *true*
	(<= 44 43.9)	$\Rightarrow$ *false*
	(<> 3 44)	$\Rightarrow$ *true*
	(= 'foo 4)	$\Rightarrow$ *error*

ABS

Procedure

ABS returns the absolute value of a number.

Format	(ABS *num*)
Parameter	*num* — Any Scheme number
Explanation	ABS returns the absolute value of *num*.

Examples	(abs -5)	$\Rightarrow$ 5
	(abs -42.03)	$\Rightarrow$ 42.03
	(abs 7.5)	$\Rightarrow$ 7.5
	(abs 0)	$\Rightarrow$ 0

ACCESS

Special Form

ACCESS returns the value of a variable in a particular environment.

Format	(ACCESS *sym$_1$* {... *env*})
Parameters	*sym$_1$* ... — Symbols (not evaluated)
	env — An environment (evaluated)
Explanation	ACCESS returns the value of *sym$_1$* in an environment.
	If *env* is not specified, ACCESS returns the value of *sym$_1$* in the current environment.
	If only *sym$_1$* and *env* are specified, ACCESS returns the value of *sym$_1$* in *env*.

If more than one *sym* is specified, ACCESS gets the value of sym_n in *env*. This value must be an environment. Next, sym_{n-1} is looked up in that environment and an environment is returned. Then sym_{n-2} is looked up in that environment and so forth. When sym_1 is looked up in the environment returned when sym_2 is looked up, the value of sym_1 is returned.

Examples

```
(define env1
  (make-environment (define x 5)))
                                    ⇒ unspecified value
(define env2
  (make-environment (define y env1)))
                                    ⇒ unspecified value
(access x env1)                     ⇒ 5
(access y env2)                     ⇒ environment
(access x y env2)                   ⇒ 5
```

ACOS   *Procedure*

ACOS returns the arc cosine of a number.

Format   (ACOS *num*)

Parameter   *num* — Any Scheme number between −1 and +1

Explanation   ACOS returns the arc cosine of *num* in radians. This is a value between zero and π, inclusive.

Examples

```
(acos -1)                 ⇒ 3.14159265358979
(acos 0)                  ⇒ 1.57079632679489
(acos 1)                  ⇒ 0.
(acos 0.499997879272544)  ⇒ 1.0472
```

ADD1   *Procedure*

ADD1 adds one to its argument.

Format   (ADD1 *num*)

Parameter   *num* — Any Scheme number

Explanation   This procedure is the same as 1+. ADD1 adds one to *num* and returns the sum.

Examples

```
(add1 99)                 ⇒ 100
(add1 -5.0)               ⇒ -4.
```

ADVISE-ENTRY, ADVISE-EXIT   *Procedure*

These procedures include advice in a procedure.

Format	(ADVISE-ENTRY *proc advice-in*) (ADVISE-EXIT *proc advice-out*)

Parameters   *proc* — A procedure name. Since *proc* must evaluate to a procedure, it must be defined before ADVISE-ENTRY or ADVISE-EXIT is used.

advice-in — A procedure that takes three arguments. It is invoked when the procedure specified by *proc* is entered.

advice-out — A procedure that takes four arguments. It is invoked when the procedure specified by *proc* is exited. This argument is responsible for returning a value on behalf of *proc*.

Explanation   These procedures give advice upon entry to or exit from a procedure. An unspecified value is returned. Specifically, these procedures behave as follows:

■ ADVISE-ENTRY invokes *advice-in* each time *proc* is entered. When *advice-in* is invoked, three arguments are passed to it: *proc*, a list of the arguments to *proc*, and the current environment.

■ ADVISE-EXIT invokes *advice-out* each time *proc* is exited. When *advice-out* is invoked, four arguments are passed to it: *proc*, a list of the arguments to *proc*, the result computed by *proc*, and the current environment. The value returned by *advice-out* is the value returned by *proc*.

These are general advising procedures. Some examples of entry-advising procedures are BREAK-ENTRY and TRACE-ENTRY; examples of exit-advising procedures are BREAK-EXIT and TRACE-EXIT.

For information on removing advice from a specified procedure, see UNADVISE, UNADVISE-ENTRY, and UNADVISE-EXIT.

Example   A procedure named FOO is defined as follows:

```
(define foo (lambda (a b) (+ a b 3)))    ⇒ unspecified value
```

Then a procedure named MY-TRACE-ENTRY is defined to trace the entry to FOO. In the ADVISE-ENTRY procedure, the argument proc is *proc* and (lambda (p a e) ...) is *advice*.

MY-TRACE-ENTRY is defined as follows:

```
(define my-trace-entry
  (lambda (proc)
    (advise-entry proc (lambda (p a e)
                         (writeln "The procedure" p
                          " is being called with "
                         a)))))
```
$\Rightarrow$ *unspecified value*

Next, the trace entry point is set as follows:

```
(my-trace-entry foo)
```
$\Rightarrow$ *unspecified value*

The FOO procedure is called, and the advice is displayed as follows when FOO is entered:

```
(foo 3 4)
```
**The procedure #<PROCEDURE foo>
is being called with (3 4)**
$\Rightarrow$ 10

ALIAS
Special Form

ALIAS creates a special form.

Format	(ALIAS *name1* *name2*)
Parameters	*name1* — A new name
	name2 — A name
Explanation	ALIAS declares *name1* to be a special form that has the same behavior as *name2*. Therefore, *name2* must exist when *name1* is used. An unspecified value is returned.

Examples

```
(define x '( )          ⟹ unspecified value
(alias := set!)         ⟹ unspecified value
(:= x 2)                ⟹ unspecified value
x                       ⟹ 2
```

ALL-CLASSVARS

ALL-CLASSVARS returns a list of all the class variables in a SCOOPS class.

Format	(ALL-CLASSVARS *class*)
Parameter	*class* — A SCOOPS class
Explanation	ALL-CLASSVARS returns a list of the names of all the class variables in *class*, including the inherited class variables (if *class* is compiled or is in the inherited structure).
	To exclude the inherited class variables from the listing, use CLASSVARS.
Example	Assume that the class employees exists (as shown in the example for DEFINE-CLASS) and that it has been compiled with the inherited class variable soc-sec-no.

```
(all-classvars employees)    ⇒ (NO-OF-EMPLOYEES SOC-SEC-NO)
```

ALL-INSTVARS

ALL-INSTVARS return a list of all the instance variables in a SCOOPS class.

Format	(ALL-INSTVARS *class*)
Parameter	*class* — A SCOOPS class
Explanation	ALL-INSTVARS returns a list of the names of all the instance variables in *class*, including the inherited instance variables (if *class* is compiled or is in the inherited structure).
	To exclude the inherited instance variables from the listing, use INSTVARS.
Example	Assume that the class employees exists (as shown in the example for DEFINE-CLASS) and that it has been compiled with the inherited instance variable schools.

```
(all-instvars employees)    ⇒ (SCHOOLS NAME EMP-NO
                               MANAGER SALARY OVERTIME)
```

ALL-METHODS   *Procedure*

ALL-METHODS returns a list of all the methods of a SCOOPS class.

Format	(ALL-METHODS *class*)
Parameter	*class* — A SCOOPS class
Explanation	ALL-METHODS returns a list of the names of all the methods of *class*, including the inherited methods (if *class* is compiled or is in the inherited structure) and the gettable and settable methods.
	To exclude the inherited methods from the listing, use METHODS.
Examples	Assume that the class employees exists (as shown in the example for DEFINE-CLASS) and that it has been compiled with the inherited instance variable schools.

```
(all-methods employees)      ⇒ (GET-NAME GET-EMP-NO

                               GET-NO-OF-EMPLOYEES
                               GET-SALARY GET-SCHOOLS
                               GET-SOC-SEC-NO SET-NAME
                               SET-EMP-NO SET-MANAGER
                               SET-OVERTIME
                               SET-NO-OF-EMPLOYEES
                               SET-SCHOOLS SET-SOC-SEC-NO)
```

AND   *Special Form*

AND is a logical composition operator that connects expressions to form a compound predicate.

Format	(AND e*xp* ...)
Parameters	*exp* ... — Any Scheme expressions
Explanation	AND evaluates each *exp* from left to right, returning *false* as soon as one *exp* evaluates to *false*. Any remaining expressions are not evaluated. If all the expressions evaluate to *true* values, the value of the last expression is returned. If no expressions are passed to AND, *true* is returned.
Examples	(and (= 2 2) (> 2 1)) ⇒ *true* ;Value of last expression
	(and (= 2 2) (< 2 1)) ⇒ *false* ;Last expression is false.
	(and 1 2 'c '(f g)) ⇒ (f g) ;Value of last expression
	(and) ⇒ *true*

APPEND, APPEND!   *Procedure*

These procedures create one proper list from several lists.

Format	(APPEND *l* ...)
	(APPEND! *l* ...)
Parameters	*l* ... — The proper lists to be concatenated
Explanation	These procedures return a proper list consisting of the elements of l_1, followed by the elements of l_2, and so on. If only one *l* is given, it is returned. If no arguments are given, *false* is returned.
	With APPEND, the original lists are not affected. However, APPEND! modifies the original lists (except the last one) by changing the cdr component of the last pair in each list to point to the next list in the sequence.

Examples

```
(append! '(p q) '(r s) '(v))        ⇒ (P Q R S V)
(append '(p q) '(r s) '(v))         ⇒ (P Q R S V)
(define x '(a b))                    ⇒ unspecified value
(define y '(c d))                    ⇒ unspecified value
(append x y)                         ⇒ (A B C D)
x                                    ⇒ (A B)
y                                    ⇒ (C D)
(append! x y)                        ⇒ (A B C D)
x                                    ⇒ (A B C D)
y                                    ⇒ (C D)
```

APPLY   *Procedure*

APPLY invokes a procedure on a list of arguments.

Format	(APPLY *procedure* (*arg-list*))
Parameters	*procedure* — Any Scheme procedure
	arg-list — A proper list of Scheme objects of the form (*arg* ...)
Explanation	APPLY invokes *procedure*, passing each *arg* as an argument to the procedure. The result of the invocation is returned as the value of APPLY. This is equivalent to:
	(*procedure arg* ...)

Examples	(define a '(2 5))	⇒ *unspecified value*
	(apply + a)	⇒ 7
	(apply cdr (list a))	⇒ (5)
	(apply (lambda (n) (* n n)) (cdr a))	⇒ 25
	(define foo (lambda () "silly answer"))	⇒ *unspecified value*
	(apply foo '())	⇒ "silly answer"

APPLY-IF *Special Form*

APPLY-IF conditionally applies a specified procedure to the result of a predicate expression.

Format	(APPLY-IF *predicate procedure exp*)
Parameters	*predicate* — The condition to be evaluated
	procedure — The procedure to be applied to the value of *predicate* if *predicate* is true
	exp — The expression to be evaluated if *predicate* is false
Explanation	APPLY-IF first evaluates *predicate*. If the value of *predicate* is *true*, *procedure* is applied to the value of *predicate* and the resulting value is returned; otherwise, *exp* is evaluated and its value is returned. APPLY-IF is useful in conjunction with predicates that return meaningful *true* values. APPLY-IF is equivalent to the following:

```
(let ((temp1 predicate)
      (temp2 (lambda () exp)))
  (if temp1
      (procedure temp1)
      (temp2))).
```

Example	(apply-if (assq 'c '((a b)(c d)(e f)))
	(lambda (x) (cadr x))
	'should-not-get-here) ⇒ D

ARGS *Procedure*

ARGS returns a list of the arguments to a procedure in which a debugging breakpoint has occurred.

Format	(*ARGS*)
Explanation	*ARGS* returns a list of the arguments supplied to the procedure in progress when a break occurs. This procedure is meaningful only when a breakpoint is entered by the BREAK, BREAK-BOTH, BREAK-ENTRY, or BREAK-EXIT procedures.

Example   A procedure, named FIB, is defined as follows:

```
(define fib
  (lambda (n)
    (if (< n 2) 1
        (+ (fib (-1+ n))
           (fib (- n 2))))))      ⇒ unspecified value
```

Then a breakpoint is set to occur on entry to FIB as follows:

```
(break fib)                                    ⇒ unspecified value
```

Next, the FIB procedure is called. Notice that a breakpoint is entered when FIB is entered. At the breakpoint prompt ([Inspect]), the procedure *ARGS* is evaluated to get a list of arguments passed to FIB.

```
(fib 4)
  [BKPT encountered!] BREAK-ENTRY
  (#<PROCEDURE FIB> 4)
```

  [Inspect] *(Note: Press CTRL–V)* **Value of:** (*args*) ⇒ (4)

ASCII->SYMBOL   *Procedure*

ASCII->SYMBOL converts an ASCII code to a symbol.

Format   (ASCII->SYMBOL *n*)

Parameter   *n* — An integer within the ASCII code range of $0 \leq n \leq 255$

Explanation   ASCII->SYMBOL returns the symbol whose name is the character with an ASCII code of *n*.

Examples
```
(ascii->symbol 44)            ⇒ |,|
(ascii->symbol 123)           ⇒ {
(ascii->symbol 75)            ⇒ K
```

ASIN   *Procedure*

ASIN returns the arc sine of a number.

Format   (ASIN *num*)

Parameter   *num* — Any Scheme number between -1 and +1

Explanation   ASIN returns the arc sine of *num* in radians. This is a value between $-\pi/2$ and $\pi/2$, inclusive.

Examples	(asin −1)	⟹ −1.5707963267949
	(asin 0)	⟹ 0.
	(asin 1)	⟹ 1.5707963267949
	(asin 0.707108079859474)	⟹ 0.785400000000001

ASSERT

Special Form

ASSERT conditionally interrupts a procedure and enters the breakpoint command level.

Format (ASSERT *predicate message* ...)

Parameters *predicate* — The condition to be evaluated.

message ... — The messages printed when a breakpoint is entered. These messages usually indicate where the procedure was when the breakpoint occurred.

Explanation ASSERT first evaluates *predicate*. If the value of *predicate* is *true*, an unspecified value is returned. If the value is *false*, each *message* is printed and a breakpoint is entered.

For more information, see BKPT, INSPECT, and the *PC Scheme User's Guide — Student Edition*.

Examples A procedure, named FIB, is defined. In the ASSERT procedure, which is included in FIB, the *predicate* is (<> n 3) and the *message* arguments are "The variable n is" and n.

```
(define fib
  (lambda (n)
    (assert (<> n 3) "The variable n is " n)
    (if (< n 2) 1
        (+ (fib (-1+ n))
           (fib (- n 2))))))    ⟹ unspecified value
```

The FIB procedure is called. When the variable n eventually becomes 3, the assert *predicate* is false. Then the *message* is displayed, and a breakpoint is entered.

```
(fib 4)
 [ASSERT failure!]
 (assert ( ) "The variable n is "3)
[Inspect]
```

ASSOC, ASSQ, ASSV *Procedure*

These procedures return the first pair in a list of pairs whose car component matches a specified object.

Format	(ASSOC *obj alist*) (ASSQ *obj alist*) (ASSV *obj alist*)
Parameters	*obj* — Any Scheme object
	alist — A proper list in which each element is a pair
Explanation	These procedures return the first pair in *alist* whose car component is *obj*. If no pair in *alist* has *obj* in its car component, *false* is returned.
	To compare *obj* to the car component of each pair in *alist*, ASSOC uses EQUAL?, ASSQ uses EQ?, and ASSV uses EQV?.
Examples	(assoc 'a '((a 1) (b 2) (a 3))) ⇒ (A 1)
	(assv 'a '((a 1) (b 2) (a 3))) ⇒ (A 1)
	(assq 'a '((a 1) (b 2) (a 3))) ⇒ (A 1)
	(assoc 'd '((a 1) (b 2) (c 3))) ⇒ *false*
	(assv 'd '((a 1) (b 2) (c 3))) ⇒ *false*
	(assq 'd '((a 1) (b 2) (c 3))) ⇒ *false*
	(assoc '(a) '(((a)) ((b)) ((a c)))) ⇒ ((A))
	(assv '(a) '(((a)) ((b)) ((a c)))) ⇒ *false*
	(assq '(a) '(((a)) ((b)) ((a c)))) ⇒ *false*
	(assoc 5. '((2. 3.) (5. 7.) (11. 13.))) ⇒ (5. 7.)
	(assv 5. '((2. 3.) (5. 7.) (11. 13.))) ⇒ (5. 7.)
	(assq 5. '((2. 3.) (5. 7.) (11. 13.))) ⇒ *unspecified value*

ATAN

ATAN returns the arc tangent of its arguments.

Format	(ATAN *num₁* {*num₂*})
Parameters	*num₁* — Any Scheme number.
	num₂ — Any Scheme number. The argument *num₂* may be zero if *num₁* is not equal to *zero*. This argument is optional.
Explanation	ATAN calculates the arc tangent of its arguments and returns the result in radians.

- If only *num₁* is given, the value is the angle (in radians), whose tangent is *num₁*. This is a value between $-\pi/2$ and $\pi/2$, exclusive.

- If *num₂* is also given, the result is an angle whose tangent is equal to *num₁*/*num₂*. However, the signs of the two arguments are used to choose between two angles that differ by π and have the same tangent. The value is the signed angle between the X axis and the line from the origin to the point (*num₂*, *num₁*) and is always between $-\pi$ and π, exclusive. The following table shows the special cases of the result of ATAN:

Condition	Location	Result
num1=0 num2>0	Positive X axis	0
num1>0 num2>0	First Quadrant	$0 < result < \pi/2$
num1>0 num2=0	Positive Y axis	$\pi/2$
num1>0 num2<0	Second Quadrant	$\pi/2 < result < \pi$
num1=0 num2<0	Negative X axis	π
num1<0 num2<0	Third Quadrant	$-\pi < result < -\pi/2$
num1<0 num2=0	Negative Y axis	$-\pi/2$
num1<0 num2>0	Fourth Quadrant	$-\pi/2 < result < 0$
num1=0 num2=0	Origin	Error

Examples	(atan -1) ⟹ -0.785398163397448
	(atan 0) ⟹ 0.
	(atan 1) ⟹ 0.785398163397448
	(atan 1.73206060202403) ⟹ 1.0471999998
	(atan 5 2) ⟹ 1.19028994968253

ATOM?   *Procedure*

ATOM? determines whether an object is an atom.

Format	(ATOM? *obj*)
Parameter	*obj* — Any Scheme object
Explanation	ATOM? returns *true* if *obj* is not a pair; otherwise, *false* is returned. This is equivalent to:

```
(not (pair? obj))
```

For further information on pairs, see CONS and LIST.

Examples	(atom? (cons 'a 'b))	⟹ *false*
	(atom? (list->vector '(a b c)))	⟹ *true*
	(atom? 'a)	⟹ *true*

AUTOLOAD-FROM-FILE   *Procedure*

AUTOLOAD-FROM-FILE loads a file upon reference to an unbound variable.

Format	(AUTOLOAD-FROM-FILE *filespec var-list* {*env*})
Parameters	*filespec* — A string that names a file
	var-list — A list of variables
	env — An environment (an optional argument)
Explanation	AUTOLOAD-FROM-FILE loads *filespec* the first time any of the variables in *var-list* is referenced. The referenced variable must be unbound. The file is loaded into a particular environment specified by *env* or into the current environment if *env* is not specified. An unspecified value is returned.
Example	In the following example, if any of the variables in the list (test1 test2 test3) are referenced and are unbound, the file "e:\\test\\test.fsl" is loaded:

```
(autoload-from-file "e:\\test\\test.fsl"
  '(test1 test2 test3))          ⟹ unspecified value
```

#\BACKSPACE

#\BACKSPACE represents the ASCII backspace character.

Format	#\BACKSPACE
Explanation	#\BACKSPACE is the character object representing a backspace. When this object is printed to a port, the ASCII character code for backspace (8_{10}) is sent to that port. For instance, when this character is sent to the screen with WRITE-CHAR, DISPLAY, or PRINC, the cursor moves back one space.
Examples	(writeln "foo " #\backspace "bar") **foobar** $\Rightarrow$ *unspecified value*

BEGIN, BEGIN0

These special forms evaluate a sequence of expressions.

Format	(BEGIN *exp* ...) (BEGIN0 *exp*$_1$ ...)
Parameters	*exp* ... — Any Scheme expressions *exp*$_1$ ... — Any Scheme expressions
Explanation	These special forms evaluate each *exp* sequentially from left to right. BEGIN returns the value of the last *exp*; if *exp* is not specified, it returns the empty list. BEGIN0 returns the value of *exp*$_1$. These special forms are useful for sequencing operations with side effects, such as input and output.

Examples	(begin (display "4 plus 1 equals")
	      (display (1+ 4)))
	4 plus 1 equals 5 $\Rightarrow$ *unspecified value*
	
	(define y) $\Rightarrow$ *unspecified value*
	(begin0 (+ 5 6)
	      (set! y 99)) $\Rightarrow$ 11 ;y gets the value 99.
	y $\Rightarrow$ 99

BKPT   *Special Form*

BKPT interrupts a procedure and enters the breakpoint command level.

Format	(BKPT *message irritant*)
Parameters	*message* — Any Scheme expression. The value of *message* (normally a string) is printed when the breakpoint is encountered but before the breakpoint is entered.
	irritant — Any Scheme expression. The value of *irritant* (normally a value from the procedure in which the breakpoint occurs) is printed following *message*.
Explanation	BKPT causes a breakpoint. An unspecified value is returned. When BKPT is encountered in a procedure, the arguments *message* and *irritant* are printed, and then a breakpoint is entered.
	For more information on breakpoints, see INSPECT and the *PC Scheme User's Guide — Student Edition*.
Example	A procedure named FOO is defined and sets a breakpoint where the *message* is "The variable a is" and the *irritant* is a.

```
(define foo
  (lambda (a b)
    (bkpt "The variable a is" a)
    (+ a b 3)))                              ⇒ unspecified value
```

The FOO procedure is called and the BKPT procedure is executed. The *message* and *irritant* are displayed on the screen. Then the breakpoint is entered.

```
(foo 3 4)
  [BKPT encountered!] The variable a is
  3
[Inspect]
```

BOOLEAN?

BOOLEAN? determines if an object is either #T or #F.

Format	(BOOLEAN? *obj*)
Parameters	*obj* — Any Scheme object
Explanation:	BOOLEAN? returns *true* if *obj* is either #T or #F. Otherwise, *false* is returned.
Examples	(boolean? #T) ⇒ *true* (boolean? ´car) ⇒ false

BREAK, BREAK-BOTH, BREAK-ENTRY, BREAK-EXIT

These procedures install a breakpoint in a specified procedure.

Format	(BREAK *proc*) (BREAK-BOTH *proc*) (BREAK-ENTRY *proc*) (BREAK-EXIT *proc*)
Parameter	*proc* — A procedure. Since *proc* must evaluate to a procedure, it must be defined before a break procedure is used.
Explanation	These procedures break a specified procedure upon each entry to and/or exit from that procedure. An unspecified value is returned. Specifically:

- ■ BREAK — Breaks a procedure upon entry

- ■ BREAK-BOTH — Breaks a procedure upon entry and exit

- ■ BREAK-ENTRY — Breaks a procedure upon entry

- ■ BREAK-EXIT — Breaks a procedure upon exit

A break upon entry to a procedure works as follows: Each time the procedure *proc* is entered, a message containing the *proc* name and its arguments is printed. After the message is printed, a breakpoint is entered.

A break upon exit from a procedure works as follows: Each time the procedure *proc* is exited, a message containing the *proc* name, its arguments, and the value being returned from *proc* is printed. After the message is printed, a breakpoint is entered.

From either type of breakpoint, both *proc* and its arguments can be accessed by evaluating *PROC* and *ARGS*, respectively. Additionally, from an exit breakpoint, the value being returned can be accessed by evaluating *RESULT*.

For more information on breakpoints, see INSPECT and the *PC Scheme User's Guide — Student Edition*.

For information on removing a breakpoint from a specified procedure, see UNBREAK, UNBREAK-ENTRY, and UNBREAK-EXIT. To trace a procedure, use TRACE, TRACE-BOTH, TRACE-ENTRY, and TRACE-EXIT.

| Examples | The FIB procedure is defined as follows: |

```
(define fib
  (lambda (n)
    (if (< n 2) 1
        (+ (fib (-1+ n))
           (fib (- n 2))))))))          ⇒ unspecified value
```

Then a breakpoint is set to occur on entry to FIB.

```
(break-entry fib)                        ⇒ unspecified value
```

Next, the FIB procedure is called, and a breakpoint is entered upon entry to FIB.

```
(fib 1)
  [BKPT encountered!] BREAK-ENTRY
  (#<PROCEDURE fib> 1)
[Inspect]
```

C....R   *Procedure*

Each of the C....R procedures applies a sequence of the CAR and CDR procedures to a pair.

| Format | (C....R *pair*) |

| Parameter | *pair* — A pair |

| Explanation | C....R applies an appropriate sequence of the CAR and CDR procedures to *pair* and returns the result. The "...." may be any combination of the letters "a" (car) and "d" (cdr) up to four characters long. All of these procedures are evaluated from right to left. For example, (CwxyzR *pair*) is equivalent to (CwR (CxR (CyR (CzR *pair*)))), where w, x, y, and z are either "a" or "d". |

Examples	(cadr '(a b c))	⇒ B
	(cddar '((1 2 3) (4 5 6)))	⇒ (3)
	(cadddr '(a b c d e f g))	⇒ D

CALL-WITH-CURRENT-CONTINUATION, CALL/CC *Procedure*

These procedures invoke a specified procedure with the current continuation as its argument.

Format	(CALL-WITH-CURRENT-CONTINUATION *proc*) (CALL/CC *proc*)
Parameter	*proc* — A procedure of one argument
Explanation	CALL-WITH-CURRENT-CONTINUATION passes the current continuation as an argument to *proc*. The current continuation is a procedure of one argument and represents the remainder of the computation from the CALL-WITH-CURRENT-CONTINUATION application point. At any future time, the current continuation may be invoked with any value, with the effect that the value is taken as the value of the CALL-WITH-CURRENT-CONTINUATION application.
	The current continuation that is created by CALL-WITH-CURRENT-CONTINUATION has unlimited extent like any other procedure in Scheme. It may be stored in variables or data structures, and it may be called as many times as desired.
	An alternate name for CALL-WITH-CURRENT-CONTINUATION is CALL/CC.
Examples	The examples that follow show only the most common uses of CALL-WITH-CURRENT-CONTINUATION.
	The first example searches a list of numbers for the first negative value. When a negative value is encountered, the continuation is invoked to stop the search and return the value of the negative number.

```
(call-with-current-continuation
  (lambda (exit)
    (mapc (lambda (x)
            (if (negative? x)
                (exit x)))
          '(54 0 37 -3 245 19))
    #T))                                    ⟹ -3
```

In the next example, a continuation is used as an error escape. The list-length function counts the number of entries in a proper list. If an improper list is found, the continuation is invoked and returns #F as the result of the function.

```
(define list-length
  (lambda (obj)
    (call-with-current-continuation
     (lambda (return)
       ((rec loop (lambda (obj)
                    (cond ((null? obj) 0)
                          ((pair? obj)
                           (1+ (loop (cdr obj))))
                          (else (return #F)))))
        obj))))))
```
⟹ *unspecified value*

```
(list-length '(1 2 3 4))
```
⟹ 4

```
(list-length '(a b . c))
```
⟹ *false*

CALL-WITH-INPUT-FILE, CALL-WITH-OUTPUT-FILE   *Procedure*

These procedures open and close a file for input or output.

Format	(CALL-WITH-INPUT-FILE *filespec proc*) (CALL-WITH-OUTPUT-FILE *filespec proc*)
Parameters	*filespec* — A string
	proc — A procedure of one argument
Explanation	These procedures create a port by opening a new file named *filespec*. If the file cannot be opened, an error occurs. Otherwise, the procedure *proc* is called with the newly created port as its argument. If *proc* returns, the port is closed automatically and the value yielded by *proc* is returned. If *proc* does not return, Scheme does not close the port unless it can prove that the port is not to be used again.
	CALL-WITH-INPUT-FILE creates an input port from *filespec*. The file must already exist.
	CALL-WITH-OUTPUT-FILE creates an output port from *filespec*. The file need not necessarily exist. If the file exists, the data in it is overwritten.

Examples

```
(call-with-output-file "bounce.tmp"
  (lambda (p)
    (write 'boing! p)
    (newline p)
    #F))                                    ⇒ false

(call-with-input-file "bounce.tmp"
  (lambda (p)
    (read p)))                              ⇒ BOING!
```

CAR   *Procedure*

CAR returns the car component of a pair.

Format	(CAR *pair*)
Parameter	*pair* — A pair
Explanation	CAR returns the car component of *pair*. The car component is the first argument specified in the CONS procedure. When applied to the empty list, CAR returns an unspecified value.
	For related information, see CDR and CONS.

Examples

```
(car '(a b c))                  ⇒ A
(car (cons 'foo 'bar))          ⇒ FOO
(car '((a) b c d))              ⇒ (A)
(car '(1 . 2))                  ⇒ 1
(car '())                       ⇒ unspecified value
```

CASE   *Special Form*

CASE selects one of a series of clauses to evaluate based on the value of a controlling expresssion.

Format	(CASE *exp clause₁* ...)
Parameters	*exp* — Any Scheme expression. The value of *exp* determines which *clause* is evaluated.

clause₁ ... — Lists. Each *clause* is in the form (*selector exp₁* ..), where:

- *selector* is a nonpair or a list of nonpairs (not evaluated), including the optional keyword *else*.

- *exp₁* ... are the expressions to be evaluated if the corresponding selector is *true*.

Explanation	CASE first evaluates *exp* and then compares the value returned by *exp* with the *selector* of each *clause* until the comparison is *true*. The value of *exp* is compared to each *selector* using MEMV if *selector* is a list (a pair) and EQV? if *selector* is not a pair. Next, the expressions in the selected *clause* are evaluated from left to right, and the result of the last expression in the clause is returned as the result of the CASE special form. If no *selector* matches, an unspecified value is returned. To provide the effect of an *otherwise* clause, the special keyword *else* may be used as the *selector* for the last clause. If *else* is included and none of the preceding selectors evaluates to *true*, the expressions in the *else* clause are evaluated.

Examples

```
(case (* 2 3)
  ((2 3 5 7) 'prime)
  ((1 4 6 8 9) 'composite))              ⟹ COMPOSITE

(case (car '(c d))
  ((a) (car '(1 2 3)))
  ((b) (cdr '(4 5 6))))                  ⟹ unspecified value

(case 2
  (1 'one)
  ((2 3) 'two-and-one-half))            ⟹ TWO-AND-ONE-HALF

(case (car '(c d))
  ((a e i o u) (cadr '(consonant vowel)))
  ((y) 'y)
  (else (car '(consonant vowel))))       ⟹ CONSONANT
```

CDR

Procedure

CDR returns the cdr component of a pair.

Format	(CDR *pair*)
Parameter	*pair* — A pair
Explanation	CDR returns the cdr component of *pair*. The cdr component is the second argument specified in the CONS procedure. When applied to the empty list, the CDR procedure returns an unspecified value.
	For related information, see CAR and CONS.

Examples

```
(cdr '((a) b c d))      ⟹ (B C D)
(cdr '(1 . 2))          ⟹ 2
(cdr (cons 'foo 'bar))  ⟹ BAR
(cdr '())               ⟹ unspecified value
```

CEILING

Procedure

CEILING returns the smallest integer greater than or equal to its argument.

Format	(CEILING *num*)
Parameter	*num* — Any Scheme number
Explanation	CEILING returns the smallest integer greater than *num* if *num* is not an integer. If *num* is an integer, *num* is returned.
Examples	(ceiling 5.1) ⟹ 6
	(ceiling 5) ⟹ 5
	(ceiling −5.1) ⟹ −5

CHAR->INTEGER

Procedure

CHAR->INTEGER converts a character to its ASCII code.

Format	(CHAR->INTEGER *char*)
Parameter	*char* — Any character object
Explanation	CHAR->INTEGER returns the ASCII code of *char*.
Examples	(char->integer #\a) ⟹ 97
	(char->integer #\A) ⟹ 65
	(char->integer #\1) ⟹ 49
	(char->integer #\") ⟹ 34
	(char->integer #\backspace) ⟹ 8

CHAR-CI<?, CHAR-CI<=?, CHAR-CI=?, CHAR-CI>?, CHAR-CI>=?

Procedure

These procedures compare two characters, ignoring case.

Format	(CHAR-CI<? *char₁* *char₂*)
	(CHAR-CI<=? *char₁* *char₂*)
	(CHAR-CI=? *char₁* *char₂*)
	(CHAR-CI>? *char₁* *char₂*)
	(CHAR-CI>=? *char₁* *char₂*)
Parameters	*char₁* — Any character object
	char₂ — Any character object

Explanation	These procedures compare two characters using the specified relational operator and the order of the characters in the ASCII character set. Each procedure returns *true* if the comparison is *true*; otherwise, *false* is returned. The procedures are defined as follows:

CHAR-CI<?	Precedes
CHAR-CI<=?	Precedes or is the same as
CHAR-CI=?	Is the same as
CHAR-CI>?	Follows
CHAR-CI>=?	Follows or is the same as

Note that CI stands for case insensitive. Therefore, the comparison is performed as if all alphabetic characters were lowercase. Thus, special characters, such [, \,], ∧ , _ , and ' , which fall between the uppercase alphabet and the lowercase alphabet, would be less than any alphabetic character. This is an implementation detail on which programs should not depend.

See also CHAR<?, CHAR=?, CHAR=?, CHAR>?, and CHAR>=?.

Examples

(char-ci<? #\a #b)	⇒ *true*
(char-ci<=? #\b #\a)	⇒ *false*
(char-ci=? #\a #\A)	⇒ *true*
(char-ci>=? #\A #\\)	⇒ *true*
(char-ci>=? #\backspace #\return)	⇒ *false*

CHAR-DOWNCASE   *Procedure*

CHAR-DOWNCASE converts uppercase characters to lowercase characters.

Format	(CHAR-DOWNCASE *char*)
Parameter	*char* — Any character object
Explanation	CHAR-DOWNCASE returns the lowercase character of *char*. If *char* is not an uppercase alphabetic character, *char* is returned.
Examples	(char-downcase #\A) ⇒ #\a
	(char-downcase #\a) ⇒ #\a
	(char-downcase #\1) ⇒ #\1

CHAR-READY? *Procedure*

CHAR-READY? determines whether a character is ready on the input port.

Format (CHAR-READY? {*port*})

Parameter *port* — A port (an optional argument)

Explanation CHAR-READY? returns *true* if a character is ready on either *port* or the current input port if *port* is not specified; otherwise, *false* is returned. If CHAR-READY? returns *true*, the next READ-CHAR call on the given port is guaranteed to work. If the port is at the end of the file, CHAR-READY? returns an end–of–file object. You can use EOF-OBJECT? to determine whether an end-of-file object has been returned by CHAR-READY?.

Example
```
(define counter
  (lambda ()
    (letrec ((loop
               (lambda (n)
                 (if (char-ready?)
                     (let ((x (read-char)))
                       (display x)
                       (newline)
                       n)
                     (loop (1+ n)))))))
        (display "==> ")
        (loop 0))))
```
⟹ *unspecified value*

```
(counter)
==> 5
```
⟹ 99

CHAR-UPCASE *Procedure*

CHAR-UPCASE converts lowercase characters to uppercase characters.

Format (CHAR-UPCASE *char*)

Parameter *char* — Any character object

Explanation CHAR-UPCASE returns the uppercase character of *char*. If *char* is not a lowercase alphabetic character, *char* is returned.

Examples
```
(char-upcase #\a)          ⟹ #\A
(char-upcase #\A)          ⟹ #\A
(char-upcase #\1)          ⟹ #\1
```

CHAR<?, CHAR<=?, CHAR=?, CHAR>?, CHAR>=? *Procedure*

These procedures compare two characters, including case.

Format	(CHAR<? $char_1$ $char_2$)
	(CHAR<=? $char_1$ $char_2$)
	(CHAR=? $char_1$ $char_2$)
	(CHAR>? $char_1$ $char_2$)
	(CHAR>=? $char_1$ $char_2$)

Parameters $char_1$ — Any character object

$char_2$ — Any character object

Explanation These procedures compare two characters using the specified relational operator and the order of the characters in the ASCII character set. Each procedure returns *true* if the comparison is *true*; otherwise, *false* is returned. The procedures are defined as follows:

CHAR<?	Precedes
CHAR<=?	Precedes or is the same as
CHAR=?	Is the same as
CHAR>?	Follows
CHAR>=?	Follows or is the same as

Note that these procedures are case sensitive. See also CHAR-CI<?, CHAR-CI<=?, CHAR-CI=?, CHAR-CI>?, and CHAR-CI>=?.

Examples

(char<? #\a #\b)	⟹ *true*
(char<=? #\b #\a)	⟹ *false*
(char=? #\a #\A)	⟹ *false*
(char>=? #\A #\\)	⟹ *false*
(char>? #\backspace #\return)	⟹ *false*

CHAR? *Procedure*

CHAR? determines if its argument is a character object.

Format	(CHAR? *obj*)
Parameter	*obj* — Any Scheme object
Explanation	CHAR? returns *true* if *obj* is a character object and *false*, otherwise.

Examples		
	`(char? #\q)`	⇒ *true*
	`(char? #\return)`	⇒ *true*
	`(char? ´a)`	⇒ *false*
	`(char? "a")`	⇒ *false*
	`(char? 33)`	⇒ *false*

CLASS-COMPILED? *Procedure*

CLASS-COMPILED? determines whether a SCOOPS class has been compiled.

Format (CLASS-COMPILED? *class*)

Parameter *class* — A SCOOPS class

Explanation CLASS-COMPILED? returns *true* if *class* has been compiled and *false*, otherwise.

To compile a SCOOPS class, use COMPILE-CLASS.

Examples Assume that the class employees exists and that it has not been compiled.

`(class-compiled? employees)`	⇒ *false*
`(compile-class employees)`	⇒ *unspecified value*
`(class-compiled? employees)`	⇒ *true*

CLASS-OF-OBJECT *Procedure*

CLASS-OF-OBJECT returns the name of an object's SCOOPS class.

Format (CLASS-OF-OBJECT *object*)

Parameter *object* — An instance of a SCOOPS class

Explanation CLASS-OF-OBJECT returns the name of the class to which *object* belongs.

Example Assume that the class employees exists (as shown in the example for DEFINE-CLASS).

`(define empl (make-instance employees))`	⇒ *unspecified value*
`(class-of-object empl)`	⇒ EMPLOYEES

CLASSVARS
Procedure

CLASSVARS returns a list of the class variables defined in a SCOOPS class.

Format	(CLASSVARS *class*)
Parameter	*class* — A SCOOPS class
Explanation	CLASSVARS returns a list of the names of the class variables in *class*. This list does not include the inherited class variables.
	To include the inherited class variables in the listing, use ALL-CLASSVARS.
Examples	Assume that the class employees exists (as shown in the example for DEFINE-CLASS) and that it has been compiled with the inherited class variable soc-sec-no.

```
(classvars employees)                    ⟹  (NO-OF-EMPLOYEES)
```

CLEAR-GRAPHICS
Procedure

CLEAR-GRAPHICS erases all graphics from the screen and places the pen at the point (0,0).

Format	(CLEAR-GRAPHICS)
Parameters	None
Explanation	CLEAR-GRAPHICS clears all graphics from the graphics plane(s) by setting the color of all pixels to black. The text plane(s) remain unchanged. Also, the pen (an invisible pointer) is positioned at the center of the screen, which is point (0,0). An unspecified value is returned.

Other graphics procedures are as follows:

CLEAR-POINT
DRAW-BOX-TO
DRAW-FILLED-BOX-TO
DRAW-LINE-TO
DRAW-POINT
GET-PEN-COLOR
GET-PEN-POSITION
IS-POINT-ON?
POINT-COLOR
POSITION-PEN
SET-CLIPPING-RECTANGLE!
SET-PEN-COLOR!.

CLEAR-POINT   *Procedure*

CLEAR-POINT erases a point on the screen.

Format	(CLEAR-POINT *x y*)
Parameters	*x* — The screen x-coordinate (horizontal axis)
	y — The screen y-coordinate (vertical axis)
Explanation	CLEAR-POINT erases the point specified by the *x*- and *y*-coordinates by changing the color of the point to black. An unspecified value is returned.
	Other graphics procedures are DRAW-POINT, IS-POINT-ON?, and POINT-COLOR. For information on the range of values for the *x*- and *y*-coordinates, see the *PC Scheme User's Guide — Student Edition*.

CLOSE-INPUT-PORT, CLOSE-OUTPUT-PORT   *Procedure*

These procedures close a port.

Format	(CLOSE-INPUT-PORT *port*)
	(CLOSE-OUTPUT-PORT *port*)
Parameter	*port* — A port
Explanation	These procedures close *port*, with CLOSE-INPUT-PORT closing an input port and CLOSE-OUTPUT-PORT closing an output port. If *port* is associated with a file, that file is closed also. An unspecified value is returned.
Example	This example opens a file named aaa.s, prints the string to the file, and closes the file.

```
(let ((x (open-output-file "aaa.s")))
  (print "I'm Eddie, your shipboard computer."
         x)
  (close-output-port x))              ⟹ unspecified value
```

CLOSURE? *Procedure*

CLOSURE? determines if its argument is a procedure.

Format	(CLOSURE? *obj*)
Parameter	*obj* — Any Scheme object
Explanation	CLOSURE? returns *true* if *obj* is a procedure and *false*, otherwise.
	See also PROC?
Examples	

```
(closure? car)              ⟹ true
(closure? +)                ⟹ true
(closure? 'cdr)             ⟹ false
(closure? (lambda (x) x))   ⟹ true
```

COMPILE *Procedure*

COMPILE compiles a Scheme expression into object code.

Format	(COMPILE *exp*)
Parameter	*exp* — A Scheme expression
Explanation	COMPILE compiles *exp* into machine-dependent code. This code then may be executed using the EVAL procedure. COMPILE should be used on code that is going to be used again. For example, COMPILE is used in the implementation of COMPILE-FILE.
Example	In the example that follows, assume that foo.s defines fact (factorial).

```
(define simple-compile-file
  (lambda (file-in file-out)
    (let ((port-in (open-input-file file-in))
          (port-out (open-output-file file-out)))
      ((rec loop
         (lambda ()
           (let ((exp (read port-in)))
             (if (eof-object? exp)
                 (begin (close-input-port port-in)
                        (close-output-port port-out))
                 (let ((c-exp (compile exp)))
                   (write c-exp port-out)
                   (eval c-exp)
                   (loop)))))))))))        ⟹ unspecified value

(simple-compile-file "foo.s" "foo.so")     ⟹ unspecified value

(fact 5)                                   ⟹ 120
```

COMPILE-CLASS   *Special Form*

COMPILE-CLASS compiles the given SCOOPS class.

Format	(COMPILE-CLASS *class*)
Parameter	*class* — A SCOOPS class
Explanation	COMPILE-CLASS compiles *class*. An unspecified value is returned. The variables and methods of *class* are inherited from its mixins.
Example	Assume that the class employees exists (as shown in the example for DEFINE-CLASS) and that it has not been compiled.

```
(class-compiled? employees)        ⟹ false
(compile-class employees)          ⟹ unspecified value
(class-compiled? employees)        ⟹ true
```

COMPILE-FILE *Procedure*

COMPILE-FILE compiles and executes Scheme expressions stored in a file. The compiled object is saved in another file.

Format	(COMPILE-FILE *file-in file-out*)
Parameters	*file-in* — The name of the input file. This filename is a string.
	file-out — The name of the output file. This filename is a string.
Explanation	COMPILE-FILE, like LOAD, reads and executes the Scheme expressions it finds in *file-in*. Additionally, it writes the expressions in compiled form to *file-out*. An unspecified value is returned.
	Although expressions in compiled form are evaluated more efficiently when they are loaded by LOAD, they are, otherwise, the same as their original source forms.
Examples	Assume that the file FOURPLUS.S on the default disk drive contains the following lines:

```
(DEFINE (FOUR+ N) (ADDFOUR N))
(DISPLAY "Four+ loaded!")
```

The example for COMPILE-FILE is as follows:

```
(define four 4)                              ⇒ unspecified value

(macro addfour
  (lambda (x) (list '+ four (cadr x))))      ⇒ unspecified value

(compile-file "fourplus.s" "fourplus.so")
Four+ loaded!                                ⇒ unspecified value

(four+ 1)                                     ⇒ 5
(set! four 10000)                            ⇒ unspecified value
(load "fourplus.s")
Four+ loaded!                                ⇒ unspecified value

(four+ 1)                                     ⇒ 10001
(load "fourplus.so")
Four+ loaded!                                ⇒ unspecified value

(four+ 1)                                     ⇒ 5
```

COMPLEX?   *Procedure*

COMPLEX? determines whether its argument is a complex number.

Format	(COMPLEX? *obj*)
Parameter	*obj* — Any Scheme object
Explanation	COMPLEX? returns true if *obj* is a complex number and *false*, otherwise. In PC Scheme, complex numbers have not been implemented; therefore, COMPLEX? returns *true* if *obj* is any Scheme number and *false*, otherwise.
Examples	(complex? 4.5) ⟹ *true* (complex? "4.5") ⟹ *false* (complex? 0) ⟹ *true*

COND   *Special Form*

COND conditionally selects and evaluates one of a series of clauses.

Format	(COND *clause* ...)
Parameters	*clause* ... — A list of one or more expressions. Each *clause* is in the form (*guard exp* ...), where:

- *guard* is any Scheme expression, including the optional keyword *else*.

- *exp* ... are Scheme expressions that are evaluated only if the corresponding *guard* is true.

Explanation	COND consists of a series of clauses. The *guard* for each *clause* is evaluated until one of them is *true*. When a *guard* is *true*, each *exp* in that clause is evaluated in order; the result of the last expression in the selected *clause* is returned as the result of the entire COND form. If the selected *clause* contains only the *guard*, the value of the *guard* is returned. If all *guards* evaluate to *false*, the value returned by the COND form is unspecifed. To provide the effect of an *otherwise* clause, the special keyword *else* may be used as the *guard* for the last clause. Note that *else* always evaluates to *true*; therefore, if it is included and evaluated, its corresponding expressions are always evaluated.

With only one or two clauses, IF can be used instead.

Examples
```
(cond ((> 3 2) 'greater)
      ((< 3 2) 'less))        ⇒ GREATER

(cond ((> 3 3) 'greater)
      ((< 3 3) 'less)
      (else 'equal))          ⇒ EQUAL
```

CONS   *Procedure*

CONS creates a newly allocated pair.

Format   (CONS obj_1 obj_2)

Parameters obj_1 — Any Scheme object

                  obj_2 — Any Scheme object

Explanation   CONS returns a newly allocated pair whose car component is obj_1 and whose cdr component is obj_2. The pair is guaranteed to be unique (in the sense of EQ?). The procedures CAR and CDR are used to access the components of the pair.

                  For information on proper and improper lists, see LIST and LIST*.

Examples
```
(cons 'a '())          ⇒ (A)
(cons '(a) '(b c d))   ⇒ ((A) B C D)
(cons "a" '(b c))      ⇒ ("a" B C)
(cons 'a 3)            ⇒ (A . 3)
(cons '(a b) 'c)       ⇒ ((A B) . C)
```

CONS-STREAM   *Special Form*

CONS-STREAM creates a stream.

Format   (CONS STREAM obj_1 obj_2)

Parameters obj_1 — Any Scheme object

                  obj_2 — Any Scheme object

Explanation   CONS-STREAM returns a stream, which is an object consisting of two elements. The first element, known as the head and accessed by the HEAD procedure, is evaluated before it is stored in the stream. The second element, known as the tail, has its evaluation delayed until it is accessed by the TAIL procedure.

The CONS-STREAM special form is analogous to the following:

(cons obj_1 (delay obj_2))

The functions of CONS-STREAM, HEAD, and TAIL for streams are similar to the functions of CONS, CAR, and CDR for pairs. The primary difference is that the tail of a stream is often a delayed object whose value is itself a stream. This technique provides a convenient means of representing infinite sequences.

For other procedures that work with streams, see HEAD and TAIL.

Examples

```
(define (integers-from n)
  (cons-stream n (integers-from (1+ n))))    ⇒ unspecified value


(define (print-stream s)
  (display " ")
  (princ (head s))
  (newline)
  (print-stream (tail s)))                   ⇒ unspecified value

(print-stream (integers-from 14))
  14
  15
  .
  .
  .
```

CONTINUATION?   *Procedure*

CONTINUATION? determines if its argument is a continuation.

Format   (CONTINUATION? *obj*)

Parameter   *obj* — Any Scheme object

Explanation   CONTINUATION? returns *true* if *obj* is a continuation and *false*, otherwise.

Examples
```
(let ((k (call/cc (lambda (cont) cont))))
  (continuation? k))                        ⇒ true
(call/cc (lambda (k) (continuation? k)))    ⇒ true
(continuation? (lambda (k) k))              ⇒ false
```

COPY   *Procedure*

COPY makes an equivalent copy of an entire tree of pairs.

Format	(COPY *pair*)
Parameter	*pair* — A tree of pairs
Explanation	COPY returns a copy of *pair* such that when *pair* is compared to its copy with EQUAL?, *true* is returned. However, if *pair* is compared to its copy with EQ?, *false* is returned. The copy is formed from different cons-cells. Note that if *pair* is a circular list, an infinite loop is entered. If given an atom, just return it (note vectors are atoms).

Examples		
	(define x '(a b (c)))	⟹ *unspecified value*
	(eq? x x)	⟹ *true*
	(define y (copy x))	⟹ *unspecified value*
	y	⟹ (A B (C))
	(eq? x y)	⟹ *false*
	(equal? x y)	⟹ *true*

COS   *Procedure*

COS returns the cosine of a number.

Format	(COS *num*)
Parameter	*num* — Any Scheme number. This is an angle expressed in radians.
Explanation	COS returns the cosine of *num*.

Examples		
	(cos 0)	⟹ 1.
	(cos 1.0472)	⟹ 0.499997879272546
	(cos -5)	⟹ 0.283662185463226

CURRENT-COLUMN   *Procedure*

CURRENT-COLUMN returns the current column number of an output port.

Format	(CURRENT-COLUMN {*port*})
Parameter	*port* — An output port (an optional argument)
Explanation	CURRENT-COLUMN returns the current column associated with port (if specified) or the current output port. The next nonpair is printed in that column unless the port's (nonzero) line length would be exceeded. In this case, the nonpair would be printed on the next line, beginning in column 1.

Examples

```
(define newfile
   (open-output-file "newfile"))        ⟹ unspecified value
(current-column newfile)                ⟹ 1
(begin (write 'atom newfile)
       (current-column newfile))        ⟹ 5
```

CURRENT-INPUT-PORT   *Procedure*

CURRENT-INPUT-PORT returns the current default input port.

Format	(CURRENT-INPUT-PORT)
Explanation	CURRENT-INPUT-PORT returns the current default input port. This is the port used by CHAR-READY?, READ, READ-ATOM, READ-CHAR, and READ-LINE if no input port is specified.
Examples	(current-input-port) ⟹ CONSOLE

CURRENT-OUTPUT-PORT   *Procedure*

CURRENT-OUTPUT-PORT returns the current default output port.

Format	(CURRENT-OUTPUT-PORT)
Explanation	CURRENT-OUTPUT PORT returns the current default output port. This is the port used by DISPLAY, FRESH-LINE, NEWLINE, PRIN1, PRINC, WRITE, WRITE-CHAR, and WRITELN if no output port is specified.
Examples	(current-output-port) ⟹ CONSOLE

DEFINE *Special Form*

DEFINE binds and initializes a variable in an environment.

Format	(DEFINE *var exp*) (DEFINE *var*) (DEFINE *spec exp₁* ...)

Parameters ·   *var* — An identifier.

exp — Any Scheme expression.

spec — A proper or improper list of identifiers. It is an abbreviated notation for defining procedures; see the explanation of the third form below.

exp₁ ... — Any Scheme expressions.

Explanation   DEFINE binds and initializes a variable in an environment. An unspecified value is returned. DEFINE has the following three formats:

■ The first form, (DEFINE *var exp*), creates and initializes new instances of a variable. The variable *var* is intialized to the value of *exp*. DEFINE binds and initializes a variable in the current environment. When it appears at the top level, DEFINE adds variable definitions to the global environment. If the variable already exists, DEFINE has the effect of an assignment.

■ The second form, (DEFINE *var*), creates new instances of a variable. This form differs from the first form in that *var* is not initialized.

■ The third form for DEFINE, (DEFINE *spec exp₁* ...), is an abbreviated notation that permits a concise definition of procedure objects. When the first parameter is a list instead of an identifier, as in the following:

(DEFINE (*name var* ...) *exp₁* ...),

it can be interpreted one of two ways depending on the global variable PCS-INTEGRATE-DEFINE.

When the value of PCS-INTEGRATE-DEFINE is *false*, it will be interpreted as specified in the *Revised³ Scheme Report* as the following:

(DEFINE *name* (lambda (*var* ...) *exp₁* ...)).

When the value of PCS-INTEGRATE-DEFINE is *true*, it will be interpreted as the following:

(DEFINE *name* (NAMED-LAMBDA (*name var* ...) *exp₁* ...)).

In the above example, *name* is an identifier along with each *var* following it. The list of identifiers following *name* may take any of the forms permitted by LAMBDA or NAMED-LAMBDA, including a single identifier (*name . var*), an empty list (*name*), a proper list (*name a b*), or an improper list (*name a . b*).

It is possible to continue this process indefinitely by substituting a similar list in place of *name*. For example, (assuming PCS-INTEGRATE-DEFINE is *true*, the following:

(DEFINE (((FOO) A . B) C) exp₁ ...)

is equivalent to the following:

```
(DEFINE FOO
  (NAMED-LAMBDA (FOO)
    (LAMBDA (A . B)
      (LAMBDA (C) exp₁...)))))
```

DEFINE also may appear at the beginning of the body of a LAMBDA, LET, LET*, LETREC, or NAMED-LAMBDA special form, where it has the effect of extending the environment frame opened by the special form. In this case, an error results if the defined variable exists in the frame already, although bindings of the same name at higher lexical levels are permitted and are masked by the new definition.

For a related special form, see SET!.

Examples

The first two examples show the first format, (DEFINE var exp). The first example shows the binding of the variable ADD3 to a procedure that adds 3 to its argument. The second example binds a procedure FIRST to the procedure CAR.

```
(define add3 (lambda (x) (+ x 3)))    ⇒ unspecified value
(add3 4)                               ⇒ 7

(define first car)                     ⇒ unspecified value
(first '(a b))                         ⇒ A
```

The next example shows the format (DEFINE *spec exp₁*...). The recursive factorial procedure is defined.

```
(define (fact n)
  (if (<? n 2)
      1
      (* n (fact (-1+ n))))))          ⇒ unspecified value
(fact 5)                               ⇒ 120
```

The example that follows uses the format (DEFINE *(name var ...) exp₁ ...*). A procedure, ADDN, that returns a procedure is defined. The variables ADD2 and ADD99 are bound to the procedures returned by calling ADDN with arguments 2 and 99, respectively. ADD2 is called with 3 and returns 5 (2 is added to 3) as the result. ADD99 is called with 7 and returns 106 (99 is added to 7) as the result.

```
(define ((addn n) x) (+ x n))          ⇒ unspecified value
(define add2 (addn 2))                 ⇒ unspecified value
(add2 3)                               ⇒ 5
(define add99 (addn 99))               ⇒ unspecified value
(add99 7)                              ⇒ 106
```

The next example is an internal definition. Two procedures are defined locally to the LET special form using the internal DEFINE.

```
(let ((x 5))
  (define (bar a b)
    (+ (* a b) a))
  (define foo
    (lambda (y)
      (bar x y)))
  (foo (+ x 3)))                    ⇒ 45
```

The final example is similar to the previous one. However, FOO is bound but not initialized in the user initial environment, and (define foo ...) is changed to (set! foo ...). This change causes the side effect that the FOO procedure is bound in the user initial environment, thus allowing a call to the procedure from the top level.

```
(define foo)                        ⇒ unspecified value

(let ((x 5))
  (define (bar a b)
    (+ (* a b) a))
  (set! foo
    (lambda (y)
      (bar x y)))
  (foo (+ x 3)))                    ⇒ 45

(foo 10)                            ⇒ 55
```

DEFINE-CLASS   *Special Form*

DEFINE-CLASS defines a SCOOPS class.

Format   (DEFINE-CLASS *name* (*optional-attributes*) ...)

Parameters   *name* — The name of the SCOOPS class being defined.

optional-attributes ... — The description of the SCOOPS class consisting of any of the following:

■ CLASSVARS followed by the names of the class variables. A variable can be initialized by putting its name and initial value in a list. The initial value is evaluated when the class is compiled. If no initial value is specified, the variable remains unbound.

■ INSTVARS followed by the names of the instance variables. A variable can be initialized by putting its name and intial value in a list. The initial value is evaluated when the instance of the class is created. The initial value for an instance variable could be an active value.

- MIXINS followed by the names of the component classes.

- OPTIONS followed by the keywords GETTABLE-VARIABLES, SETTABLE-VARIABLES, or INITTABLE-VARIABLES. These keywords can be given either with arguments that are class and instance variables or without arguments, in which case the keyword refers to all the class and instance variables. To associate arguments with a keyword, put the keyword and its arguments in a list.

Explanation

DEFINE-CLASS defines a SCOOPS class, named *name*, consisting of *optional-attributes*. An unspecified value is returned.

Note that instance variables can have active values associated with them. These values are declared in *optional-attributes* after the keyword INSTVARS as follows:

(*name* (active *init-value getfn setfn*))

The value *init-value* is the initial value of *name*. Whenever *name* is accessed with GET-*name*, the current value of *name* is passed to *getfn* (a procedure of one argument), and the value returned by *getfn* is the value returned by GET-*name*. Whenever the value of *name* is changed with SET-*name*, the new value is passed to *setfn* (a procedure of one argument), and the value returned by *setfn* is the new value of *name*. Active values may be nested to an arbitrary depth by specifying another active value as the *init-value* of an active value.

Example

In this example, a class named employees is created. Its inherited classes will be personal-info and education-experience.

```
(define-class employees
  (classvars (no-of-employees 0))
  (instvars
    name emp-no manager salary (overtime 0))
  (mixins personal-info education-experience)
  (options
    (gettable-variables name emp-no no-of-employees)
      settable-variables
    inittable-variables))                    ⇒ unspecified value
```

DEFINE-INTEGRABLE *Special Form*

DEFINE-INTEGRABLE attempts to perform an in-line substitution for any symbol.

Format	(DEFINE-INTEGRABLE *name val*)
Parameters	*name* — A symbol that is to be replaced.
	val — Any Scheme object.
Explanation	DEFINE-INTEGRABLE is like DEFINE, except that the compiler has the option to substitute *val* for *name* whenever *name* occurs in a program. DEFINE-INTEGRABLE should be used only at the top level. If *val* cannot be evaluated (that is, if *val* is a special form), an error results. An unspecified value is returned.

Examples

```
(define-integrable di-less? <)        ⟹ unspecified value
(di-less? 1 2)                        ⟹ true
(di-less? 2 1)                        ⟹ false
(define (binop f n1 n2) (f n1 n2))    ⟹ unspecified value
(binop di-less? 1 2)                  ⟹ true
```

DEFINE-METHOD *Special Form*

DEFINE-METHOD defines a method for a SCOOPS class.

Format	(DEFINE-METHOD (*class method*) *lambdalist body*)
Parameters	*class* — A SCOOPS class
	method — The name of the method being defined
	lambdalist — The list of the formal parameters of the method
	body — The body of the method
Explanation	DEFINE-METHOD defines a method that determines the behavior of *class*. An unspecified value is returned. If a method with the same name exists already for *class*, this definition replaces the previous definition. Also, this definition applies to all subclasses of *class*.
Example	This example defines a class named employees and its methods. Notice that name, emp-no, salary, and overtime are instance variables of employees and thus are accessed directly instead of by using the get methods.

```
(define-class employees
  (classvars (no-of-employees 0))
  (instvars
    name emp-no manager salary (overtime 0))
  (mixins personal-info education-experience)
  (options
    (gettable-variables name emp-no no-of-employees)
      settable-variables
    inittable-variables))            ⟹ unspecified value

(define-method (employees earnings) ()
  (+ salary overtime))               ⟹ unspecified value

(define-method
  (employees earnings-greater-than) (val)
  (if (> (earnings) val)
      (writeln name " " emp-no)
      #f))                           ⟹ unspecified value

(define emp1
  (make-instance employees
    'name 'RALPH
    'emp-no 001
    'manager 'SAM
    'salary 100))                    ⟹ unspecified value

(send emp1 earnings-greater-than 99)
RALPH 1                              ⟹ false
```

DEFINE-STRUCTURE   *Special Form*

DEFINE-STRUCTURE allows the creation and use of record structures with named elements.

Format	(DEFINE-STRUCTURE *name slotdesc ...*) (DEFINE-STRUCTURE (*name* (INCLUDE *name1*)) *slotdesc ...*)
Parameters	*name* — A symbol. *slotdesc ...* — The slot names with optional default values. Therefore, *slotdesc* can be in one of two forms: *slotname* or (*slotname default-init*). The *slotname* must be a symbol and *default-init* must be a Scheme expression. *name1* — A symbol.
Explanation	DEFINE-STRUCTURE defines a record structure that has the components specified by *slotname*. An unspecified value is returned.

DEFINE-STRUCTURE generates the following:

- A constructor procedure, make-*name*, which creates an instance of *name*. If the *slotname* and its initial value are specified, that value may be given to the slot as an instance is created.

- An access procedure, *name-slotname*, for every *slotdesc*. These access forms are used to access the values of the components in the structure. Also, SET! may be used with an access form to alter the component of *name*. To do this, use the following syntax:

    (SET! (*name-slotname object*) *value*)

- A predicate procedure, *name?*, which takes one argument and returns *true* if the argument is an instance of *name* and *false*, otherwise.

The *default-init* is a Scheme expressions that is evaluated each time an instance of *name* is created; the result of the evaluation is used as the initial value of the slot. If no *default-init* is given, the initial contents of the slot are unspecified.

In the second format, only one INCLUDE option can be specified and *name1* must be the name of a previously defined structure. By using this format, a new structure definition can be built as an extension to an existing structure definition. The new structure has the same slots as the existing structure plus the ones defined. The access procedures for the existing structure also work on the new structure, and the new structure has access procedures *name-slotname* for components in the existing structure as well. Additionally, since the new structure becomes the subtype of the existing structure, the predicate of the existing structure recognizes the instances of the new structure.

Examples

The following example defines a structure named moving-object:

```
(define-structure moving-object
  x-vel (y-vel 0) mass)                    ⟹ unspecified value
(define obj1
  (make-moving-object 'x-vel 20 'mass 100)) ⟹ unspecified value
(moving-object-x-vel obj1)                 ⟹ 20
(set! (moving-object-y-vel obj1) 30)       ⟹ unspecified value
(moving-object-y-vel obj1)                 ⟹ 30
(moving-object? obj1)                      ⟹ true
```

The next example defines a structure named airplane that includes the structure moving-object. The airplane structure has five slots.

```
(define-structure
  (airplane (include moving-object))
  seats type)                              ⟹ unspecified value

(define b747
  (make-airplane 'type 'BOEING 'mass 100000)) ⟹ unspecified value
```

The following example shows that every airplane is a moving-object, but not every moving-object is an airplane:

```
(airplane? b747)           ⇒ true
(moving-object? b747)      ⇒ true
(airplane? obj1)           ⇒ false
```

The final example shows that access procedures for existing structures may be used also in a new structure.

```
(moving-object-mass b747)  ⇒ 100000
(airplane-mass b747)       ⇒ 100000
```

DELAY   *Special Form*

DELAY produces a delayed object.

Format	(DELAY *exp*)
Parameter	*exp* — Any Scheme expression
Explanation	DELAY returns a delayed object representing a suspended evaluation of *exp*. The first time this delayed object is forced (using FORCE), *exp* is evaluated in the environment in which it was written, and its value is returned. Subsequent forcing of the delayed object returns the same value. This is known as "memoizing."
	To produce an object which postpones the evaluation of *obj* but which is not memoized, use FREEZE. For more information on delayed objects, see FORCE, FREEZE, and THAW.
Examples	

```
(define a 10)      ⇒ unspecified value
(define b (delay a))  ⇒ unspecified value
(set! a 9)         ⇒ unspecified value
(force b)          ⇒ 9
(set! a 8)         ⇒ unspecified value
(force b)          ⇒ 9
```

DELAYED-OBJECT?   *Procedure*

DELAYED-OBJECT? determines if its argument is a delayed object.

Format	(DELAYED-OBJECT? *obj*)
Parameter	*obj* — Any Scheme object
Explanation	DELAYED-OBJECT? returns *true* if *obj* is an object created by the DELAY special form and *false*, otherwise.
Examples	(define x (delay (+ 5 5))) ⟹ *unspecified value*
	(delayed-object? x) ⟹ *true*
	(delayed-object? 5) ⟹ *false*

DELETE!, DELQ!   *Procedure*

These procedures return a list with all occurrences of a particular object removed.

Format	(DELETE! *obj list*)
	(DELQ! *obj list*)
Parameters	*obj* — The object to be removed from *list*
	list — The proper list from which *obj* is to be removed
Explanation	These procedures return a list in which all occurrences of *obj* in *list* are removed. DELETE! uses EQUAL? to compare *obj* to each element in *list*, while DELQ! uses EQ?.
	Note that these are destructive operations. The argument *list* may be destroyed during construction of the returned list. The returned list may not be EQ? to *list*. To capture the results of either DELETE! or DELQ!, you must bind the results of either command to a variable.
Examples	(define a '(a b c)) ⟹ *unspecified value*
	(define b (copy a)) ⟹ *unspecified value*
	(eq? a b) ⟹ *false*
	(equal? a b) ⟹ *true*
	(define c (list a 'c b)) ⟹ *unspecified value*
	c ⟹ ((A B C) C (A B C))
	(delete! a c) ⟹ (C)
	c ⟹ ((A B C) C)
	(set! c (list a 'c b)) ⟹ *unspecified value*
	(delq! a c) ⟹ (C (A B C))
	c ⟹ ((A B C) C (A B C))

DELETE-METHOD   *Special Form*

DELETE-METHOD deletes a method for a SCOOPS class.

Format	(DELETE-METHOD (*class method*))
Parameters	*class* — A SCOOPS class
	method — The name of the method being deleted
Explanation	DELETE-METHOD deletes *method* from *class*. An unspecified value is returned. If *method* is not defined in *class*, an error results. All the subclasses of *class* notice the deletion.
Examples	Assume that the class employees exists (as shown in the example for DEFINE-CLASS) with the method earnings (as shown in the example for DEFINE-METHOD). The following example deletes the method earnings from employees:

```
(delete-method (employee earnings))        ⇒ unspecified value
```

DESCRIBE   *Procedure*

DESCRIBE prints the description of a SCOOPS class or SCOOPS object.

Format	(DESCRIBE *class-or-object*)
Parameter	*class-or-object* — A SCOOPS class or an instance of a SCOOPS class
Explanation	DESCRIBE prints a description of *class-or-object* to the current output port. An unspecified value is returned.
	If *class-or-object* is a class, DESCRIBE prints the list of class variables, instance variables, and methods and tells whether the class has been compiled and whether the class has been inherited.
	If *class-or-object* is an instance of a class, DESCRIBE prints the names and the values of the class as well as the instance variables.
Example	Assume that the classes employees, personal-info, and education-experience exist, with personal-info having the single class variable soc-sec-no and education-experience having the instance variable schools.

```
(describe employees)
```

CLASS DESCRIPTION
==========================

```
    NAME             : EMPLOYEES
    CLASSVARS        : (SOC-SEC-NO NO-OF-EMPLOYEES)
    INSTANCE VARS    : (SCHOOLS NAME EMP-NO MANAGER SALARY
OVERTIME)
    METHODS          : (SET-NO-OF-EMPLOYEES SET-NAME
SET-EMP-NO SET-MANAGER SET-SALARY SET-OVERTIME
SET-SOC-SEC-NO SET-SCHOOLS GET-NAME GET-EMP-NO
GET-NO-OF-EMPLOYEES GET-SOC-SEC-NO GET-SCHOOLS)
    MIXINS           : (PERSONAL-INFO EDUCATION-EXPERIENCE)
    CLASS COMPILED : #T
    CLASS INHERITED : #T
```
                                            ⟹ *unspecified value*

DISPLAY   *Procedure*

DISPLAY writes an expression to an output port.

Format	(DISPLAY *exp* {port})
Parameters	*exp* — Any Scheme expression
	port — Optional argument that gives the output port to which *exp* is written
Explanation	DISPLAY writes the value of *exp* to either *port* or the current output port if *port* is not specified. An unspecified value is returned.
	Strings that are written are not enclosed in double quotes, and no characters are escaped within those strings. Also, special characters in symbols are not slashified.
	In general, DISPLAY is intended to produce human-readable output, and WRITE is intended for machine-readable output.

Examples

```
(display (+ 1 2))
3                                         ⟹ unspecified value

(display "Hi there.")
Hi there.                                 ⟹ unspecified value

(display '|abc|)
abc                                       ⟹ unspecified value
```

DO   *Special Form*

DO provides a generalized iteration capability.

Format	(DO ((*var* {*init* {*step*}}) ...) (*test exp* ...) *stmt* ...)
Parameters	*var* ... — Any Scheme identifier.

init ... — Any Scheme expressions. Each *init* is evaluated, and the result is used as the value of the corresponding *var*. This argument is optional.

step ... - Any Scheme expressions. Each *step* is evaluated, and the result is used as the value of the corresponding *var* for the next iteration. This optional argument can be specified only if *init* is specified.

test — Any Scheme expression. This expression is the predicate for stopping the iteration.

exp ... — Any Scheme expressions. These expressions are evaluated prior to exiting from the loop.

stmt ... — Any Scheme expressions. These expressions are evaluated in order each time *test* returns *false*.

Explanation   DO performs a general iteration. First, each *init* is evaluated in the environment of DO in an unspecified order, and each result is bound to a fresh copy of the corresponding *var*, thus creating an extended environment containing every *var*. Then the iteration phase begins.

On each iteration, *test* is evaluated first. If the result is *false*, each *stmt* is evaluated sequentially in the environment containing the *var* values. Next, each *step* is evaluated in the environment containing the *var* values, and the corresponding *var* is modified to hold the new value. Then *test* is evaluated again.

When *test* evaluates to *true*, the iteration stops. Each *exp* then is evaluated sequentially in the environment containing the *var* values. The value of the last *exp* is the value returned by DO. If no *exp* is present, DO returns the value of *test*.

The region set up by the binding of a *var* consists of the entire DO expression except for the *init* expressions.

If *step* is omitted, the corresponding *var* is not updated. The corresponding *init* may be omitted also, in which case the initial value is not specified.

Note that the following expression would cause an infinite loop:

```
(do ((var {init {step}}) ...)
    (#f)
  body)
```

Examples

This example prints the numbers 1 through 10 and returns 11 as its result:

```
(do ((i 1 (1+ i)))
    ((> i 10) i)
  (display " ")
  (display i))
1 2 3 4 5 6 7 8 9 10                          ⇒ 11
```

In the next example, a procedure of one argument, N, is created and bound to SIGMA. SIGMA runs a DO special form that adds the numbers from 1 to N.

```
(define sigma
  (lambda (n)
    (do (( i 0 (1+ i))
         (sum 0 (+ sum i)))
        ((> i n) sum))))              ⇒ unspecified value

(sigma 5)                                    ⇒ 15
```

DOS-CALL   *Procedure*

DOS-CALL executes DOS commands.

Format

(DOS-CALL *filespec parameters* {*int*})

Parameters

filespec — A string that names a file. It must have an extension of .EXE or .COM.

parameters — A string. It is passed to the DOS command.

int — An integer. This optional argument specifies the number of paragraphs of memory to be freed to run the DOS command. (In PC Scheme, a paragraph is 16 bytes.)

Explanation

DOS-CALL executes the DOS command specified by *filespec* with the arguments specified by *parameters*. An unspecified value is returned.

Using DOS-CALL is advantageous in situations where time is not critical (for example, when you want to run a database program and are not planning to use PC Scheme until the database program has finished). You can pass parameters to DOS-CALL on the command line, but values can be returned from DOS-CALL only via files.

Before executing the DOS command, Scheme stores *int* paragraphs of its memory on disk. If *int* is not specified, all paragraphs of the Scheme heap are stored on disk. If *filespec* contains the name of an executable program, Scheme then loads the other program as a DOS child process, and executes the program.

After the DOS command has executed, Scheme restores its memory image from disk and resumes execution.

DOS-CALL results in one of the following three actions, depending on whether *filespec* and *parameters* are specified:

- If *filespec* contains the fully qualified pathname of an executable file, it is invoked and the *parameters* string is passed to it. Since DOS will not search the path declaration to locate the file, either the file must reside in the default directory, or the *filespec* must include the name of the directory in which the file is located.

- If *filespec* is a null string, a new copy of DOS is started and the command passed in *parameters* is executed. After the execution is complete, control returns to Scheme.

- If both *filespec* and *parameters* are null strings, DOS-CALL exits to COMMAND.COM and stops there until the DOS command EXIT is entered. Then Scheme restores its memory image from disk and resumes execution.

WARNING: The DOS facility underlying the PC Scheme DOS-CALL feature must be used with great care to avoid damage to the system and the directory structure on your disks. Please read the next two paragraphs carefully before using DOS-CALL.

When executing within DOS during an invocation of DOS-CALL, do not delete any file that currently is open for input or output by your Scheme program. DOS allows you to delete a file that is active, but a subsequent write to that file may destroy your disk's directory structure. For example, if you are using the TRANSCRIPT-ON capability of PC Scheme at the time you invoke DOS-CALL, do not delete the transcript file and return to Scheme. Turn off the transcript with a call to TRANSCRIPT-OFF before invoking DOS-CALL.

Some DOS tasks execute and stay resident in memory when they terminate. An example of such a task is the DOS PRINT command. If such a task is executed using DOS-CALL, Scheme cannot restore its memory without overwriting the resident task. When this situation is detected, PC Scheme issues the message "DOS-CALL error: Unable to restore PC Scheme memory." This error condition causes PC Scheme to terminate and return control to DOS. If you wish to execute a DOS task that terminates and stays resident, you must invoke it before you enter PC Scheme so that it does not have to be loaded at the time of the DOS-CALL.

Example   (dos-call "" "size *.fsl")

.
. ; Screen is cleared.
.

MS-DOS File Size Utility version 2.12

ralph.fsl   48
peat.fsl   32

2 files, total of 80 bytes

.
. ;The Scheme window is restored
. ;along with the Scheme memory

⇒ *unspecified value*

DOS-CHDIR   *Procedure*

DOS-CHDIR allows you to change to another directory.

Format   (DOS-CHDIR *directoryspec*)

Parameter   *directoryspec* — A string that specifies a new directory name. The string may contain drive and path specifications, but it must not contain wildcard characters. Remember that, in Scheme, the backslash character (\) causes an escape sequence. You must, therefore, specify two backslash characters (\\) in a character string if you want one backslash to appear in the directory name.

Explanation   DOS-CHDIR changes the current default directory to *directoryspec*. If successful, the procedure returns the name of the previous directory. If not successful (the specified directory does not exist), the procedure returns the name of the current directory.

Example   In the following example, assume that the current directory is *e:\pcs*:

(dos-chdir "e:\\")   ⇒ "E:\\PCS"

DOS-CHANGE-DRIVE   *Procedure*

DOS-CHANGE-DRIVE allows you to change to another drive.

Format	(DOS-CHANGE-DRIVE *drivespec*)
Parameter	*drivespec* — A string that names a drive
Explanation	DOS-CHANGE-DRIVE changes the current default disk drive to *drivespec*. The procedure returns a #T message whether or not the drive actually exists. Note that this procedure is compatible with the way DOS currently operates.
Example	(dos-change-drive "a:")　　　　　⇒ *true*

DOS-DELETE   *Procedure*

DOS-DELETE allows you to delete files.

Format	(DOS-DELETE *filespec*)
Parameter	*filespec* — A string that names a file. The string may contain drive and path specifications, but it must not contain wildcard characters. Remember that, in Scheme, the backslash character (\) causes an escape sequence. You must, therefore, specify two backslash characters (\\) in a character string if you want one backslash to appear in the filename.
Explanation	DOS-DELETE returns 0 if it successfully deletes the file. Anything else indicates a DOS error.
Example	In the following example, assume that the file *temp.exe* exists on the *e:* drive: (dos-delete "e:temp.exe")　　　　　⇒ 0

DOS-DIR *Procedure*

DOS-DIR returns a list of the filenames from a DOS directory.

Format	(DOS-DIR *filespec*)
Parameter	*filespec* — A string that names a file. It may contain DOS wildcard characters.
Explanation	DOS-DIR returns a list of the filenames that match *filespec*. Any directory names that are returned as a result of the procedure have the suffix <DIR>.
Examples	Assume that the e:\test\ directory contains the following files and a subdirectory called SUB1:

ADVENTUR.S   EXAMPLE.S
EXAMPLE.DOC   PROB1.S
EXAMPLE.FSL   SCHEME.INI

The following examples show the use of DOS-DIR:

```
(dos-dir
  "e:\\test\\*.s")        ⇒ ("ADVENTUR.S" "EXAMPLE.S"
                                "PROB1.S")
(dos-dir
  "e:\\test\\*.obj")      ⇒ false
(dos-dir
  "e:\\test\\*.*")        ⇒ ("ADVENTUR.S" "EXAMPLE.S"
                                "EXAMPLE.DOC" "PROB1.S"
                                "EXAMPLE.FSL" "SCHEME.INI"
                                "SUB1 <DIR>")
```

DOS-FILE-COPY *Procedure*

DOS-FILE-COPY allows you to copy files.

Format	(DOS-FILE-COPY *sourcefilespec destinationfilespec*)
Parameters	*sourcefilespec* — A string that names a file. The string may contain drive and path specifications, but it must not contain wildcard characters. The file named by *sourcefilespec* must already exist. Remember that in Scheme the backslash character (\) causes an escape sequence. You must, therefore, specify two backslash characters (\\) in a character string if you want one backslash to appear in the filename.
	destinationfilespec — A string that follows the same conventions as *soucefilespec*, except that the file named by *destinationfilespec* is created if it does not already exist and is replaced by *soucefilespec* if it does.

Explanation	DOS-FILE-COPY returns 0 if it successfully copies the file. Anything else indicates a DOS error.
Example	In the following example, assume that the file *temp.exe* exists in the current directory:

```
(dos-file-copy "temp.exe" "temp.xxx")  ⇒ 0
```

DOS-FILE-SIZE
Procedure

DOS-FILE-SIZE gives you the size of a file.

Format	(DOS-FILE-SIZE *filespec*)
Parameter	*filespec* — A string that names a file. The string may contain drive and path specifications, but it must not contain wildcard characters. Remember that in Scheme the backslash character (\) causes an escape sequence. You must, therefore, specify two backslash characters (\\) in the character string if you want one backslash to appear in the filename.
Explanation	DOS-FILE-SIZE returns an integer that represents the size of *filespec* in bytes.
Example	(dos-file-size "temp.exe") ⇒ 189

DOS-RENAME
Procedure

DOS-RENAME allows you to change the names of files.

Format	(DOS-RENAME *currentfilespec newfilespec*)
Parameters	*currentfilespec* — A string that names a file. The string may contain drive and path specifications, but it must not contain wildcard characters. The file named by *currentfilespec* must already exist. Remember that in Scheme the backslash character (\) causes an escape sequence. You must, therefore, specify two backslash characters (\\) in the character string if you want one backslash to appear in the filename.
	newfilespec — A string that names a file. The string cannot contain drive or path specifications, nor can it contain wildcard characters.

Explanation	DOS-RENAME returns 0 if it successfully renames the file. Anything else indicates a DOS error.
Example	(dos-rename "temp.old" "temp.new") $\Rightarrow$ 0

DRAW-BOX-TO   *Procedure*

DRAW-BOX-TO draws the outline of a rectangle on the screen.

Format	(DRAW-BOX-TO x y)
Parameters	x — The screen x-coordinate (horizontal axis) of a corner of the box
	y — The screen y-coordinate (vertical axis) of the same corner of the box
Explanation	DRAW-BOX-TO draws a rectangle outline using the current pen position as one corner of the box and x- and y-coordinates as the diagonally opposite corner. The rectangle is drawn in the current color, and the pen moves to the x- and y-coordinate. An unspecified value is returned.
	To draw a solid rectangle, use DRAW-FILLED-BOX-TO.

DRAW-FILLED-BOX-TO   *Procedure*

DRAW-FILLED-BOX-TO draws a solid rectangle on the screen.

Format	(DRAW-FILLED-BOX-TO x y)
Parameters	x — The screen x-coordinate (horizontal axis) of a corner of the box
	y — The screen y-coordinate (vertical axis) of the same corner of the box
Explanation	DRAW-FILLED-BOX-TO draws a solid rectangle using the current pen position as one corner of the box and the x- and y-coordinates as the diagonally opposite corner. The rectangle is drawn and filled in with the current color, and the pen moves to the x- and y-coordinate. An unspecified value is returned.
	To draw only the outline of a rectangle. use DRAW-BOX-TO.

DRAW-LINE-TO   *Procedure*

DRAW-LINE-TO draws a line on the screen.

Format	(DRAW-LINE-TO *x y*)
Parameters	*x* — The screen *x*-coordinate (horizontal axis).
	y — The screen *y*-coordinate (vertical axis).
Explanation	DRAW-LINE-TO draws a line from the current pen position to the position given by the *x*- and *y*-coordinates and moves the pen to the point specified by those coordinates. The pen is an invisible pointer that is initially in the middle of the screen at position (0,0). The line is drawn in the current color. DRAW-LINE-TO returns an unspecified value.
	To move the pen without drawing a line, use POSITION-PEN. To change the color, use SET-PEN-COLOR!. For information on the range of values for the *x*- and *y*-coordinates, see the *PC Scheme User's Guide — Student Edition*.

DRAW-POINT   *Procedure*

DRAW-POINT draws a point on the screen but does not move the pen.

Format	(DRAW-POINT *x y*)
Parameters	*x* — The screen *x*-coordinate (horizontal axis)
	y — The screen *y*-coordinate (vertical axis)
Explanation	DRAW-POINT draws a point at the position specified by the x- and y-coordinates. The pen, an invisible pointer that is initially in the middle of the screen at position (0,0), does not move. The color of the point is the current color. DRAW-POINT returns an unspecified value.
	Other graphics procedures are CLEAR-POINT and SET-PEN-COLOR!. For information on the range of values for the x- and y-coordinates, see the *PC Scheme User's Guide — Student Edition*.

EDIT *Procedure*

EDIT invokes the structure editor.

Format	(EDIT *pair*)
Parameter	*pair* — A tree of pairs
Explanation	EDIT invokes the structure editor so that *pair* can be modified. Do not specify any procedures in *pair*, since you cannot use EDIT to modify procedures. After the changes are made and the editor is exited, the modified *pair* is returned. For more information, see the *PC Scheme User's Guide — Student Edition.*

EDWIN *Procedure*

EDWIN invokes the text editor.

Format	(EDWIN)
Parameters	None
Explanation	EDWIN invokes the text editor, which is a version of the EMACS editor for personal computers. EDWIN is an interactive, real-time, display-oriented editor and is integrated into the PC Scheme system. For more information, see the *PC Scheme User's Guide — Student Edition.*

EMPTY-STREAM? *Procedure*

EMPTY-STREAM? determines if a stream contains any elements.

Format	(EMPTY-STREAM? *stream*)
Parameter	*stream* — A stream
Explanation	EMPTY-STREAM? returns *true* if the *stream* has no elements. Otherwise, *false* is returned. If the argument is not a stream, an unspecified value is returned.
	For further information on streams, see CONS-STREAM, HEAD, and TAIL.
Examples	(empty-stream? (cons-stream nil nil)) ⟹ *false* (empty-stream? the-empty-stream) ⟹ *true*

ENGINE-RETURN   *Procedure*

ENGINE-RETURN returns a value from an engine procedure that completed successfully.

Format	(ENGINE-RETURN *val*)
Parameter	*val* — Any Scheme object
Explanation	ENGINE-RETURN invokes an engine procedure that completed successfully and returns the value of *val* as the result of the engine.
	ENGINE-RETURN must be invoked from within an engine. If it is not, an error occurs.
	For information on creating an engine, see MAKE-ENGINE.
Example	In this example, an engine, ENGINE, is created. It runs for 5 ticks, and a new engine is returned. Then the new engine runs for 5 ticks, and the answer is returned.

```
(define fib
  (lambda (n)
    (if (< n 2)
        1
        (+ (fib (-1+ n))
           (fib (- n 2)))))))          ⇒ unspecified value

(define engine
  (make-engine
    (lambda () (engine-return (fib 10))))) ⇒ unspecified value

(define ans
  (let loop ((engine engine))
    (engine 5
            (lambda (value ticks) value)
            loop)))                        ⇒ unspecified value

ans                                        ⇒ 89
```

ENVIRONMENT-BINDINGS   *Procedure*

ENVIRONMENT-BINDINGS allows examination of the first frame of an environment.

Format	(ENVIRONMENT-BINDINGS *env*)
Parameter	*env* — An environment
Explanation	ENVIRONMENT-BINDINGS returns an associative list containing the names and values of the variables in the first frame of *env*.
	ENVIRONMENT-PARENT may be used to examine successive frames of an environment.

Examples

```
(define e (make-environment
              (define x 1)
              (define y 2)
              (define z 3)))          ⇒ unspecified value

(environment-bindings e)             ⇒ ((x . 1) (y . 2)
                                          (z . 3))
```

ENVIRONMENT-PARENT   *Procedure*

ENVIRONMENT-PARENT returns the parent frame of an environment.

Format	(ENVIRONMENT-PARENT *env*)
Parameter	*env* — An environment
Explanation	ENVIRONMENT-PARENT returns the parent frame of *env*.
	To get a list of the variables in the first frame, use the procedure ENVIRONMENT-BINDINGS.

Examples

```
(define e
  (let ((x 5))
    (let ((y 10))
      (the-environment))))           ⇒ unspecified value

(environment-bindings e)             ⇒ ((y . 10))

(environment-bindings
  (environment-parent e))            ⇒ ((x . 5))
```

ENVIRONMENT?   *Procedure*

ENVIRONMENT? determines if its argument is an environment.

Format	(ENVIRONMENT? *obj*)
Parameter	*obj* — Any Scheme object
Explanation	ENVIRONMENT? returns *true* if *obj* is an environment and *false*, otherwise.
Examples	(environment? '((not really) (an environment))) ⟹ *false* (environment? (the-environment)) ⟹ *true* (environment? (make-environment (define a 1))) ⟹ *true*

EOF-OBJECT?   *Procedure*

EOF-OBJECT? determines whether its argument is an end-of-file object.

Format	(EOF-OBJECT? *obj*)
Parameter	*obj* — Any Scheme object
Explanation	EOF-OBJECT? returns *true* if *obj* is an end-of-file object and *false*, otherwise.
Examples	(define port (open-input-string "5")) ⟹ *unspecified value* (read port) ⟹ 5 (eof-object? (read port)) ⟹ *true*

EQ?   *Procedure*

EQ? indicates whether its arguments are identical.

Format	(EQ? obj_1 obj_2)
Parameters	obj_1 — Any Scheme object
	obj_2 — Any Scheme object
Explanation	EQ? returns *true* if obj_1 is identical in all respects to obj_2. However, if there is any way at all that obj_1 and obj_2 can be distinguished, EQ? returns *false*. Note that objects maintain their identity even if they are fetched from or stored into variables or data structures.

Examples	`(eq? 'a 'a)`	⇒ *true*
	`(eq? 'a 'b)`	⇒ *false*
	`(eq? (cons 'a 'b) (cons 'a 'b))`	⇒ *false*
	`(let ((x (read))`	
	`  (eq? (cdr (cons 'b x)) x))`	⇒ *true*

The next three examples compare lists, strings, and numbers. Since whether they return true or not is implementation-dependent, it is recommended that code not be written that is dependent on the returned value. EQV? or the appropriate data type predicate (such as = or STRING=?) should be used instead of EQ?.

`(eq? '(a (b) c) '(a (b) c))`	⇒ *unspecified value*
`(eq? "abc" "abc")`	⇒ *unspecified value*
`(eq? 2 2)`	⇒ *unspecified value*

EQUAL? *Procedure*

EQUAL? determines if two arguments are identical or are equivalent numbers, lists, characters, strings, or vectors.

Format	(EQUAL? *obj₁* *obj₂*)

Format: $(EQUAL?\ obj_1\ obj_2)$

Parameters	*obj₁* — Any Scheme object
	obj₂ — Any Scheme object

obj_1 — Any Scheme object

obj_2 — Any Scheme object

Explanation EQUAL? returns *true* if obj_1 and obj_2 are identical objects (they satisfy the EQ? predicate) or if they are equivalent numbers, lists, characters, strings, or vectors. Two objects generally are considered to be equivalent if they print the same. If the objects are not identical or equivalent, *false* is returned. The EQUAL? procedure may not terminate if its arguments are circular data structures.

Because EQUAL? performs such a general comparison, other faster and more specific comparison procedures, such as EQ? and EQV?, normally are preferred where applicable.

Examples	`(equal? 'a 'a)`	⇒ *true*
	`(equal? 'a 'b)`	⇒ *false*
	`(equal? '(a) '(a))`	⇒ *true*
	`(equal? '(a (b) c) '(a (b) c))`	⇒ *true*
	`(equal? "abc" "abc")`	⇒ *true*
	`(equal? 2 2)`	⇒ *true*
	`(equal? (make-vector 5 'a)`	
	`        (make-vector 5 'a))`	⇒ *true*

EQV?   *Procedure*

EQV? determines if two arguments are identical or are equivalent numbers or characters.

Format	(EQV? obj_1 obj_2)
Parameters	obj_1 — Any Scheme object
	obj_2 — Any Scheme object
Explanation	EQV? returns true if obj_1 and obj_2:

- Are identical objects (satisfy the EQ? predicate)

- Are numbers and are equal according to the = procedure

- Are characters and are equal according to the CHAR=? procedure

- Are strings and are equal according to the STRING=? procedure

Otherwise, *false* is returned.

Examples	(eqv? 'a 'a)	⟹ *true*
	(eqv? 'a 'b)	⟹ *false*
	(eqv? '(a) '(a))	⟹ *false*
	(eqv? '(a (b) c) '(a (b) c))	⟹ *false*
	(eqv? "abc" "abc")	⟹ *true*
	(eqv? 2 2)	⟹ *true*
	(eqv? (make-vector 5 'a)	
	(make-vector 5 'a))	⟹ *false*

ERROR   *Special Form*

ERROR prints an error message and enters a breakpoint.

Format	(ERROR *message irritant* ...)
Parameters	*message* — A string to be printed when an error occurs. This message usually explains why the error procedure was called.
	irritant ... — Any Scheme object.
Explanation	This procedure signals an error, prints *message*, and prints each *irritant*. Then a breakpoint is entered.

Examples

```
(define henhouse
  (lambda (animal)
    (if (eq? animal 'chicken)
        'ok
        (error "Chickens threatened by" animal))))
```
⟹ *unspecified value*

```
(henhouse 'chicken)
```
⟹ OK

```
(henhouse 'wolf)
  [ERROR encountered!] Chickens threatened by
  WOLF
[Inspect]
```

#\ESCAPE
Character Object

#\ESCAPE represents the ASCII escape character.

Format   #\ESCAPE

Explanation   #\ESCAPE is the character object representing an escape. When printed to a port, the ASCII character for ESCAPE (27_{10}) is sent to that port.

EVAL
Procedure

EVAL evaluates an expression in a particular environment.

Format   (EVAL *exp* {*env*})

Parameters   *exp* — Any Scheme expression, including compiled Scheme expressions

env — Any environment

Explanation   EVAL evaluates *exp* in *env*. If *env* is not specified, the current global environment is used. The value of *exp* is returned.

Examples
```
(define x 99)                          ⟹ unspecified value
(define y 100)                         ⟹ unspecified value
(define env
  (let ((x 4) (y 5))
    (the-environment)))                ⟹ unspecified value
(define a (compile '(+ x y )))         ⟹ unspecified value
(eval '(+ x y) env)                    ⟹ 9
(eval a env)                           ⟹ 9
```

EVEN? *Procedure*

EVEN? determines whether an integer is even.

Format	(EVEN? *int*)
Parameter	*int* — An integer
Explanation	EVEN? returns *true* if *int* is even — that is, if (REMAINDER *int* 2) is zero. Otherwise, *false* is returned.
Examples	(even? 2) $\Rightarrow$ *true* (even? 1) $\Rightarrow$ *false* (even? -4) $\Rightarrow$ *true* (even? 0) $\Rightarrow$ *true* (even? 4.) $\Rightarrow$ *error*

EXACT? *Procedure*

EXACT? determines whether a number is exact.

Format	(EXACT? *num*)
Parameter	*num* — Any Scheme number
Explanation	EXACT? returns *true* if *num* is an exact number and *false*, otherwise. In PC Scheme, the exact property of numbers has not been implemented; therefore, EXACT? always returns *false*.
Examples	(exact? 42) $\Rightarrow$ *false* (exact? -4.39) $\Rightarrow$ *false* (exact? 0) $\Rightarrow$ *false*

EXIT *Procedure*

EXIT exits from Scheme and returns to the operating system.

Format	(EXIT)
Parameters	None
Explanation	EXIT is used to exit from the Scheme environment and return to the operating system.

EXP

EXP calculates the natural antilogarithm of a number.

Format   (EXP *num*)

Parameter   *num* — Any Scheme number

Explanation   EXP calculates and returns the value of e^{num}.

Examples
```
(exp 0)              ⇒ 1.
(exp .5)             ⇒ 1.64872127070013
(exp 1)              ⇒ 2.71828182845905
(exp 10)             ⇒ 22026.4657948071
```

EXPLODE

Procedure

EXPLODE returns the individual symbols in its argument.

Format   (EXPLODE *obj*)

Parameter   *obj* — A symbol, string, or integer

Explanation   EXPLODE returns a list of one-character symbols representing the characters in the printed representation of *obj*.

Examples
```
(explode
  "Test String")
            ⇒ (T |e| |s| |t| | | S |t| |r| |i| |n| |g|)
(explode
  '|@weird atom!|
            ⇒ (@ |w| |e| |i| |r| |d| | | |a| |t| |o| |m| !)
(explode 1234)
            ⇒ (|1| |2| |3| |4|)
(explode '(a b c))
            ⇒ unspecified value
```

EXPT

Procedure

EXPT is the general exponential procedure.

Format   (EXPT *num₁* *num₂*)

Parameters	num_1 — Any Scheme number
	num_2 — Any Scheme number
Explanation	EXPT calculates and returns the value of $num_1{}^{num2}$.
Examples	(expt 0 0) ⟹ 1
	(expt 2 4) ⟹ 16
	(expt 2 −4) ⟹ 0.0625
	(expt 10 0.5) ⟹ 3.16227766016838

#F *Constant*

#F is the boolean truth value representing a *false* condition.

Format	#F
Explanation	#F is the boolean value for a *false* condition. Since #F is self-evaluating, it does not need to be quoted in programs.
	#!FALSE is provided for historical reasons only. New code should use #F.

NOTE: #T prints as #T, and #F prints as ( ).

Examples	(eq? #F ´#F) ⟹ *true*
	#F ⟹ *false*

FALSE *Variable*

FALSE is a variable with an initial value of #F.

Format	FALSE
Explanation	FALSE is set originally to #F. Since FALSE is a variable, its value may be changed.
	New code should be written using the constant #F.
Examples	(eq? false #F) ⟹ *true*
	(let ((false 0))
	(eq? false #F)) ⟹ *false*

FAST-LOAD   *Procedure*

FAST-LOAD loads into Scheme a file that is in fast-load format.

Format	(FAST-LOAD *filespec*)
Parameter	*filespec* — A string that names a fast-load (fsl) file
Explanation	FAST-LOAD reads and evaluates the expressions in *filespec*. An unspecified value is returned. The file must be in fast-load format.
Example	Assume that a file called FOURPLUS.S on the default disk drive has been converted to a fast-load file called FOURPLUS.FSL. Assume also that FOURPLUS.S contains the following lines:

```
(DEFINE (FOUR+ N) (+ N 4))
(DISPLAY "Four+ loaded!")
```

The following example shows the use of FAST-LOAD:

```
(fast-load "fourplus.fsl")
Four+ loaded!                                ⇒ unspecified value
(four+ 1)                                    ⇒ 5
```

FILE-EXISTS?   *Procedure*

FILE-EXISTS? determines if a specified file exists.

Format	(FILE-EXISTS? *filespec*)
Parameter	*filespec* — A string that names the file whose existence is to be verified
Explanation	FILE-EXISTS? returns *true* if *filespec* is a file and *false*, otherwise. The *filespec* is passed as a string to the operating system without parsing and may contain drive and pathname qualifiers and an extension.

Example	`(file-exists? "E:\\Goodstuff\\stuff")` ⇒ *true*
	`; assuming that stuff exists in this directory on this`
	`; drive`

FLOAT   *Procedure*

FLOAT converts its argument to a floating point number.

Format	(FLOAT *num*)
Parameter	*num* — Any Scheme number
Explanation	FLOAT converts *num* to a floating point number and returns the result. If *num* is already a floating point number, *num* is returned.

Examples

```
(float 1)                            ⟹ 1.
(float 1.5)                          ⟹ 1.5
(float -2)                           ⟹ -2.
(float 12345678901234567890)         ⟹ 1.23456789012346e19
```

FLOAT?   *Procedure*

FLOAT? determines whether its argument is a floating point number..

Format	(FLOAT? *obj*)
Parameter	*obj* — Any Scheme object
Explanation	FLOAT? returns *true* if *obj* is a floating point number and *false*, otherwise.

Examples

```
(float? 5)                           ⟹ false
(float? 3.)                          ⟹ true
(float? 3.0)                         ⟹ true
(float? 67.35)                       ⟹ true
(float? 'x)                          ⟹ false
```

FLOOR   *Procedure*

FLOOR returns the largest integer that is not larger than its argument.

Format	(FLOOR *num*)
Parameter	*num* — Any Scheme number
Explanation	FLOOR returns the largest integer not greater than *num* if *num* is not an integer. If *num* is an integer, *num* is returned.
Examples	(floor 5.1) ⇒ 5
	(floor 5) ⇒ 5
	(floor −5.1) ⇒ −6

FLUID   *Special Form*

FLUID returns the fluid binding of a variable.

Format	(FLUID *var*)
Parameter	*var* — The variable to be looked up in the fluid environment
Explanation	FLUID returns the fluid binding of *var*. If *var* is not in the fluid environment, an error results.
	For information on fluid bindings, see FLUID-LAMBDA and FLUID-LET.
Examples	(let ((x 5))
	(fluid-let ((x 99))
	(list x (fluid x)))) ⇒ (5 99)

FLUID-BOUND?   *Special Form*

FLUID-BOUND? determines if a variable is bound in the fluid environment.

Format	(FLUID-BOUND? *var*)
Parameter	*var* — The variable being searched for in the fluid environment. It is not evaluated.
Explanation	FLUID-BOUND? returns *true* if *var* is in the fluid environment and *false*, otherwise.

For information on fluid bindings, see FLUID-LAMBDA and FLUID-LET.

Examples	`((fluid-lambda (x)` `     (fluid-bound? x)) 5)`	$\Rightarrow$ *true*
	`(fluid-let ((x 4))` `     (fluid-bound? y))`	$\Rightarrow$ *false*

FLUID-LAMBDA   *Special Form*

FLUID-LAMBDA creates a procedure with fluidly bound parameters.

Format

(FLUID-LAMBDA (*var* ...) *exp*$_1$ ...)

Parameters

var...— A proper list of identifiers. Each *var* is bound to a location in the fluid environment where a value is stored when the procedure returned by the FLUID-LAMBDA special form is called. The total number of identifiers must equal the total number of actual arguments.

exp$_1$ ... — The expressions that are evaluated in the fluid environment.

Explanation

FLUID-LAMBDA returns a procedure characterized by three elements:

■ A formal argument list, (*var* ...)

■ A procedure body, *exp*$_1$ ...

■ The lexical environment in effect when the FLUID-LAMBDA special form is evaluated

When the procedure created by FLUID-LAMBDA is called, it is processed as follows:

1. Any arguments passed to the procedure are evaluated.

2. The fluid environment is extended to include each *var*, and the evaluated arguments are bound to their corresponding *var*.

3. The body of the procedure, *exp*$_1$ ..., is evaluated in the extended fluid environment and lexical environment.

4. The value of the last *exp* evaluated is returned as the result of the procedure call.

To refer to a formal parameter from the body of a fluid procedure, use the FLUID special form.

For more information on fluid environments, see FLUID and FLUID-LET.

Example

```
(define foo
  (let ((x 3))
    (fluid-lambda (x)
      (+ x (fluid x))))))          ⟹ unspecified value

(foo 5)                            ⟹ 8
```

FLUID-LET   *Special Form*

FLUID-LET evaluates a series of expressions in an extended fluid environment.

Format	(FLUID-LET ((*var form*) ...) *exp*$_1$ ...)
Parameters	*var* ... — Identifiers. Each *var* creates a new binding in the fluid environment.
	form ... — Any Scheme expressions. The value of each *form* becomes the value of its corresponding *var*.
	exp$_1$ ...— Any Scheme expressions. Each *exp* is evaluated in the extended fluid environment.
Explanation	FLUID-LET is a binding construct that extends the current fluid environment and evaluates its body in that environment. Specifically, this special form:

1. Evaluates each *form* (in some unspecified order)

2. Fluidly binds each *form* to its corresponding *var*

3. Evaluates each *exp* in the extended fluid environment, returning the value of the last *exp*

4. Unbinds each *var* before returning

FLUID-LET is essentially equivalent to the following:

((FLUID–LAMBDA (*var* ...) *exp1* ...) *form* ...)

Examples

```
(define foo (lambda () (add1 (fluid a))))    ⟹ unspecified value

(fluid-let ((a 5) (b 7))
  (* (fluid b) (foo)))                        ⟹ 42

(let ((x 3))
  (fluid-let ((x 5))
    (+ x (fluid x))))                         ⟹ 8
```

FLUSH-INPUT   *Procedure*

FLUSH-INPUT clears an input port's buffer.

Format	(FLUSH-INPUT {*port*})
Parameter	*port* — An input port (an optional argument)
Explanation	FLUSH-INPUT discards any characters up to and including the next end-of-line sequence in the input buffer that are associated with *port*, if it is given, or with the current input port. An unspecified value is returned.
Example	Assume that the file "TREES" contains the following two lines:

   I THINK THAT I SHALL NEVER SEE
   A POEM LOVELY AS A TREE

FLUSH-INPUT could be used as follows:

```
(define trees (open-input-file "trees"))        ⇒ unspecified value
(read trees)                                    ⇒ I
(read trees)                                    ⇒ THINK
(flush-input trees)                             ⇒ unspecified value
(read trees)                                    ⇒ A
(read trees)                                    ⇒ POEM
```

FOR-EACH   *Procedure*

FOR-EACH applies a procedure to each element of a list.

Format	(FOR-EACH *procedure list*)
Parameters	*procedure* — A procedure of one argument
	list — A proper list
Explanation	FOR-EACH applies *procedure* to each element of *list*. The order of application is from left to right. An unspecified value is returned.
	To return the results of the applications, use MAP.
Examples	

```
(for-each display '("one" "after" "another"))
oneafteranother                                          ⇒ unspecified value

(define x 0)                                             ⇒ unspecified value
(for-each (lambda (n)(set! x n)) '(1 2 3 4 ))
                                                         ⇒ unspecified value
x                                                        ⇒ 4
```

FORCE *Procedure*

FORCE evaluates a delayed object.

Format	(FORCE *delayed-obj*)
Parameter	*delayed-obj* — An object created using the DELAY procedure
Explanation	FORCE evaluates *delayed-obj*. If the object has been forced previously, the previous result is used; if not, the object is evaluated and its result is saved for future use (memoized) and returned.
	For more information on delayed objects, see DELAY.

Examples		
	(define a 10)	⟹ *unspecified value*
	(define b (delay a))	⟹ *unspecified value*
	(set! a 9)	⟹ *unspecified value*
	(force b)	⟹ 9
	(set! a 8)	⟹ *unspecified value*
	(force b)	⟹ 9

FREESP *Procedure*

FREESP returns the number of bytes that are currently available in memory.

Format	(FREESP)
Explanation	FREESP returns the number of bytes that are currently unallocated in memory. To determine the maximum amount of memory available, do a garbage collection to deallocate all unused memory. Note that if you execute consecutive FREESP procedures, you will not get the same value for the number of bytes that are available in memory. This inconsistency occurs because PC Scheme saves all input (and results) on the history maintained by the system's top-level function, and your entering (freesp) is itself considered input. To clear this history, you must use the SCHEME-RESET procedure.
Example	(freesp) ⟹ *unspecified value*

FREEZE *Special Form*

FREEZE returns a thunk.

Format	(FREEZE *exp*₁ ...)
Parameters	*exp*₁ ... — Scheme expressions that are evaluated when the thunk is invoked
Explanation	FREEZE returns a thunk (a procedure of no arguments). Each time THAW is used with this thunk, each *exp* argument is evaluated in sequence in the thunk's environment (the environment in which the thunk was frozen). This special form is equivalent to the following: (lambda ( ) *exp*₁ ...) For information on evaluating the thunk, see THAW.
Example	(define foo (let ((x 5)) (freeze x))) ⟹ *unspecified value* (+ 99 (thaw foo)) ⟹ 104

FRESH-LINE *Procedure*

FRESH-LINE conditionally outputs an end-of-line character sequence.

Format	(FRESH-LINE { *port*})
Parameters	*port* — An output port (an optional agreement)
Explanation	FRESH-LINE outputs an end-of-line character sequence to either *port*, if it is specified, or the current output port, only if the port is not already at the beginning of a line. An unspecified value is returned.
Example	(begin (writeln "foo") (fresh-line) (display "bar")) foo bar ⟹ *unspecified value* (begin (writeln "foo") (newline) (display "bar")) foo bar ⟹ *unspecified value*

GC

Procedure

GC causes a garbage collection.

Format	(GC {*compact?*})
Parameter	*compact?* — This optional argument is only available in PC Scheme. If it is #T, then the compaction phase of garbage collection is invoked. Otherwise, the normal garbage collection phase is invoked.
Explanation	GC causes a garbage collection and returns an unspecified value. If *compact?* is specified and #T the compaction phase of garbage collection is invoked. In PC Scheme, this phase will normally take twice as long as the normal garbage collection phase. Note, however, that garbage collection normally occurs automatically whenever necessary.
	For more information on garbage collection, see the *PC Scheme User's Guide — Student Edition*.
Examples	(gc) ⟹ *unspecified value*
	(gc #T) ⟹ *unspecified value*

GCD

Procedure

GCD returns the greatest common divisor of a set of integers.

Format	(GCD *int* ...)
Parameters	*int* ... — Integers
Explanation	GCD returns the nonnegative integer that is the greatest common divisor of its integer arguments (*int* ...).
Examples	(gcd 49 28 98) ⟹ 7
	(gcd) ⟹ 0

GENSYM *Procedure*

GENSYM generates a new symbol.

Format	(GENSYM {*x*})
Parameter	*x* — A string or a nonnegative integer. There are three possibilities for this argument:

- If *x* is a string, it is used as the prefix for the symbols generated on the current and all succeeding calls to GENSYM.

- If *x* is a nonnegative integer, it sets the counter value that is used as the suffix for the generated symbol.

- If *x* is omitted, the counter is incremented, and the counter value is used as the suffix for the generated symbol.

Explanation GENSYM generates and returns a new, uninterned symbol. If *x* is a string, the new print name starts with this string. This string becomes the default prefix until another string is specified. If no string is ever specified, the default string is "G". In either case, the name ends with the current value of the internal counter. This counter is incremented each time a symbol is generated, thus ensuring unique symbols. These symbols, often called gensyms, are seldom seen by the user. The argument *x* is usually omitted.

An uninterned symbol is one which is never identical (in the sense of the EQ? predicate) to any symbol read by the Scheme reader, even those with the same printed representation.

Examples
```
(gensym)                ⇒ G0
(gensym "start-")       ⇒ |start-1|
(gensym 55)             ⇒ |start-55|
(gensym)                ⇒ |start-56|
```

GETCV *Special Form*

GETCV returns the value of a SCOOPS class variable.

Format	(GETCV *class var*)
Parameters	*class* — A SCOOPS class
	var — The name of a class variable defined in *class*
Explanation	GETCV returns the value of *var* in *class*. If *class* has not been compiled or *var* has not been described as gettable in DEFINE-CLASS, an error results.

Examples   Assume that the class employees has been defined (as shown in the example for DEFINE-CLASS).

```
(setcv employees no-of-employees 1000)   ⇒ unspecified value
(getcv employees no-of-employees)         ⇒ 1000
```

GET-FILE-POSITION   *Procedure*

GET-FILE-POSITION gets the location of a file's file-pointer.

Format   (GET-FILE-POSITION *port*)

Parameters   *port* — A Scheme port object created by a prior call to OPEN-OUPUT-FILE, OPEN-INPUT-FILE, or OPEN-EXTEND-FILE

See also SET-FILE-POSITION!

Examples   Assume the file STUFF.S on the default disk drive consists of the following:

THIS IS A TEST OF THE RANDOM ACCESS FEATURE.

Examples of the use of GET-FILE-POSITION follows:

```
(define p (open-input-file "stuff.s"))   ⇒ unspecified value
(set-file-position! p 10 0)               ⇒ unspecified value
(read p)                                  ⇒ TEST
(get-file-position p)                     ⇒ 14
(read-char p)                             ⇒ #\SPACE
```

GET-PEN-COLOR   *Procedure*

GET-PEN-COLOR returns the drawing color used by the graphics pen.

Format   (GET-PEN-COLOR)

Parameters   None

Explanation   GET-PEN-COLOR returns an integer value that represents the current color used by the graphics pen. For information on valid colors, see the *PC Scheme User's Guide — Student Edition*.

See also SET-PEN-COLOR!.

GET-PEN-POSITION   *Procedure*

GET-PEN-POSITION returns the graphics pen's current position.

Format	(GET-PEN-POSITION)
Parameters	None
Explanation	GET-PEN-POSITION returns the graphics pen's current position as the pair (x . y). X represents the x-coordinate (horizontal axis) and y the y-coordinate (vertical axis) of the display screen.
	See also POSITION-PEN.

GETPROP   *Procedure*

GETPROP returns the value of a specific property from the property list of a symbol.

Format	(GETPROP *name prop*)
Parameters	*name* — A symbol name
	prop — A symbol identifying the property to be found
Explanation	GETPROP returns the value of *prop* found in the property list associated with *name*. The procedure EQ? is used for the comparison. If *prop* is not found, *false* is returned.
	Other property list procedures are PROPLIST, PUTPROP, and REMPROP.
Examples	(putprop ´lemon ´sour ´taste) ⟹ *unspecified value*
	(getprop ´lemon ´taste) ⟹ SOUR
	(remprop ´lemon ´taste) ⟹ *unspecified value*
	(getprop ´lemon ´taste) ⟹ ( )

GET-VIDEO-MODE

GET-VIDEO-MODE returns the current screen display mode.

Format	(GET-VIDEO-MODE)
Parameters	None
Explanation	GET-VIDEO-MODE returns the current screen display mode number. This number indicates the way text and/or graphics are displayed on the screen. Refer to the chapter on graphics in the *PC Scheme User's Guide — Student Edition* for an explanation of the mode number.
	To change the display mode, use SET-VIDEO-MODE!.

GRAPHICS-COLORS

Variable

GRAPHICS-COLORS is a list of the available screen colors with their corresponding numbers.

Format	*GRAPHICS-COLORS*
Explanation	*GRAPHICS-COLORS* is a list that associates names of available screen colors with numbers. The number may be used as an argument to the procedure SET-PEN-COLOR!.
	For information on the valid colors, see the *PC Scheme User's Guide — Student Edition*.

HEAD

Procedure

HEAD returns the first element of a stream.

Format	(HEAD *stream*)
Parameter	*stream* — A stream
Explanation	HEAD returns the first element of *stream*.
	For other procedures that work with streams, see CONS-STREAM and TAIL.
Examples	(define spider (cons-stream ´cephalothorax ´abdomen)) ⟹ *unspecified value*
	(head spider) ⟹ CEPHALOTHORAX

IF *Special Form*

IF conditionally evaluates one of two alternate expressions.

Format	(IF *condition consequent* {*alternative*})
Parameters	*condition* — Any Scheme expression. The value of *condition* determines whether *consequent* or *alternative* is evaluted.
	consequent — Any Scheme expression
	alternative — Any Scheme expression
Explanation	IF first evaluates *condition*. If *condition* yields *true*, *consequent* is evaluated and its value is returned. Otherwise, *alternative*, if it is specified, is evaluated and its value is returned. If *condition* is *false* and no *alternative* is specified, the value returned by the expression is unspecified.
	To choose among more than two alternatives, use CASE or COND.

Examples		
(if (>? 3 2) 'yes 'no)	⟹	YES
(if (>? 2 3) 'yes 'no)	⟹	NO
(if (>? 3 2) (− 3 2) (+ 3 2))	⟹	1
(if (memq 'a '(a b c)) 'found-it)	⟹	FOUND-IT
(if (>? 2 3) 'yes)	⟹	*unspecified value*

IMPLODE *Procedure*

IMPLODE creates a symbol from the objects in a list.

Format	(IMPLODE *list*)
Parameter	*list* — A list of objects each of which may be a symbol, string, character, or integer.
Explanation	IMPLODE returns a symbol whose print name is formed by concatenating the print names of the first character of each object in *list*. Any integer in *list* is converted to its ASCII equivalent.
	For information on the complementary procedure, see EXPLODE.

Examples		
(implode '(v a r))	⟹	VAR
(implode '("hi" mom))	⟹	|hM|
(implode '(a b c 44))	⟹	|ABC,|

INEXACT? *Procedure*

INEXACT? determines whether a number is an inexact number.

Format	(INEXACT? *num*)
Parameter	*num* — Any Scheme number
Explanation	INEXACT? returns *true* if *num* is not an inexact number and *false*, otherwise. In PC Scheme, the inexact property of numbers has not been implemented; therefore, INEXACT? always returns *true*.
Examples	(inexact? 42) ⇒ *true*
	(inexact? −4.39) ⇒ *true*
	(inexact? 0) ⇒ *true*

INPUT-PORT *Fluid Variable*

INPUT-PORT defines the current default input port of the system.

Format	(FLUID INPUT-PORT)
Explanation	This fluid variable is used by functions such as READ or READ-CHAR, which are defined as using the current default input port. The initial value of the variable is set to the console. You can redefine the current default input port by rebinding INPUT-PORT. The procedure WITH-INPUT-FROM-FILE makes the redefinition automatically for input statements within its body. The procedure SCHEME-RESET resets INPUT-PORT to the current value of STANDARD-INPUT. The procedure RESET has no effect on INPUT-PORT.

Examples

```
; The following is typed into the console window
(begin
  (define w (make-window "Window" #T))
    (window-set-size! w 10 35)
    (window-set-position! w 10 40)
    (window-clear w)
    (set-fluid! input-port w)
    (set-fluid! output-port w))

; The remaining forms are typed into the new window
(eq? (current-input-port) w)     ⇒ true
                                 ; verify ports are the same
(read-char)                      ⇒ #\x
                                 ; (assuming x was pressed)
                                 ; input occurred in console window
(read-char 'console)             ⇒ #\x
                                 ; (assuming x was pressed)
                                 ; input occurred in console  window
(reset)                          ; initializes the top-level but stays in
                                 ; this window
(scheme-reset)                   ; resets Scheme; includes setting
                                 ; default ports back to console
                                 ; window
```

INPUT PORT?   *Procedure*

INPUT PORT? determine if its argument is an input port.

Format	(INPUT-PORT? *obj*)
Parameter	*obj* — Any Scheme object
Explanation	INPUT-PORT? returns *true* if *obj* is an input port and *false*, otherwise.
	To create an input port for a file, use CALL-WITH-INPUT-FILE or OPEN-INPUT-FILE.

Examples

```
; Assuming temp.s exists
(define p1 (open-input-file "temp.s"))   ⇒ unspecified value
(input-port? p1)                          ⇒ true
(input-port? (current-input-port))        ⇒ true
(input-port? 5)                           ⇒ false
```

INSPECT   *Procedure*

INSPECT is an interactive debugging utility.

Format	(INSPECT {*env*})
Parameter	*env* — An environment (an optional argument)
Explanation	INSPECT allows the inspection of certain Scheme data structures such as environments and procedures, thus providing helpful information for debugging. Note that INSPECT is called every time a breakpoint is entered. It also may be called from the Scheme top level.
	Since the function of INSPECT is implementation-dependent, see the *PC Scheme User's Guide — Student Edition* for more information.

INSTVARS   *Procedure*

INSTVARS returns a list of the instance variables defined in a SCOOPS class.

Formats	(INSTVARS *class*)
Parameter	*class* — A SCOOPS class

Explanation	INSTVARS returns a list of the names of the instance variables defined in *class*. This list does not include the inherited instance variables.
	To include the inherited instance variables in the listing, use the procedure ALL-INSTVARS.
Examples	Assume that the class employees exists as shown in the example for DEFINE-CLASS.

```
(instvars employees)    ⇒ (NAME EMP-NO MANAGER SALARY
                                OVERTIME)
```

INTEGER->CHAR   *Procedure*

INTEGER->CHAR converts an ASCII code to a character.

Format	(INTEGER->CHAR *n*)
Parameter	*n* — An integer in the range $0 \leq n \leq 255$
Explanation	INTEGER->CHAR returns the character object whose ASCII code is *n*.
Examples	`(integer->char 44)` ⇒ #\, `(integer->char 123)` ⇒ #\{ `(integer->char 75)` ⇒ #\K

INTEGER->STRING   *Procedure*

INTEGER->STRING converts an integer to a string.

Format	(INTEGER->STRING *int base*)
Parameters	*int* — An integer
	base — An integer that is the base *int* is converted to before it is converted to a string
Explanation	INTEGER->STRING returns a string that is the printed expression of *int* in *base*.
Examples	`(integer->string 1234 8)` ⇒ "2322" `(integer->string 1234 10)` ⇒ "1234" `(integer->string 1234 16)` ⇒ "4D2" `(integer->string #x1234 8)` ⇒ "11064" `(integer->string #x1234 10)` ⇒ "4660" `(integer->string #x1234 16)` ⇒ "1234"

INTEGER?

INTEGER? determines whether its argument is an integer.

Format	(INTEGER? *obj*)
Parameter	*obj* — Any Scheme object
Explanation	INTEGER? returns *true* if *obj* is an integer and *false*, otherwise.
Examples	(integer? 1) ⇒ *true*
	(integer? 1.5) ⇒ *false*
	(integer? –1) ⇒ *true*
	(integer? "foo") ⇒ *false*

IS-POINT-ON?

Procedure

IS-POINT-ON? indicates whether a particular graphics point on the screen is on (not black).

Format	(IS-POINT-ON? *x y*)
Parameters	*x* — The screen *x*-coordinate (horizontal axis)
	y — The screen *y*-coordinate (vertical axis)
Explanation	IS-POINT-ON? returns *true* if the point at the position specified by the *x*- and *y*-coordinates is on and returns *false*, otherwise. Since the screen color is black, a point must be one of the other colors to be on and visible.
	Other graphics procedures are CLEAR-POINT, DRAW-POINT, and POINT-COLOR. For information on the values of the *x*- and *y*-coordinates, see the *PC Scheme User's Guide — Student Edition*.

LAMBDA

Special Form

LAMBDA returns an instance of a procedure object.

Format	(LAMBDA *formals* *exp*₁ ...)

Parameters   *formals* — A single identifier or a list of identifiers. The *formals* can be one of three types:

- *(var ...)* — A proper list of identifiers. Each *var* is bound to a corresponding value when the procedure returned by the LAMBDA special form is called. The total number of identifiers must equal the total number of actual arguments.

- *var* — An identifier that is bound to a location where a value is stored. The actual arguments specified when the procedure is called are gathered into a list and then bound to *var*.

- $(var_1 ... . var_n)$ — An improper list of identifiers. Each *var* is bound to a value when the procedure returned by the LAMBDA special form is called. Each *var*, except var_n, must match to an actual argument when the procedure created by the LAMBDA special form is called. Any additional arguments are gathered into a list and bound to var_n.

exp_1 ... — The expressions that are evaluated in the extended environment when the procedure is called.

Explanation   LAMBDA returns a procedure characterized by three elements:

- A formal argument specifier, *formals*

- A procedure body, exp_1 ...

- The environment in effect when the LAMBDA special form is evaluated

When the procedure created by LAMBDA is called, it is processed as follows:

1. All arguments passed to the procedure are evaluated.

2. The environment associated with the procedure is extended to include the *formals*, and the evaluated arguments are bound to the *formals*.

3. The body of the procedure, exp_1 ..., is evaluated in the extended environment.

4. The value of the last *exp* evaluated is returned as the result of the procedure call.

Each evaluation of the LAMBDA special form returns a different instance of the procedure object.

For a related special form, see NAMED-LAMBDA.

Examples   The first example shows that a procedure is returned.

```
(lambda (x) (+ x x))                    ⇒ #<PROCEDURE>
```

The next example shows the procedure being applied to an actual argument of 4; 8 is returned as the result of the procedure.

```
((lambda (x) (+ x x)) 4)                    ⇒ 8
```

In the next example, the procedure is bound to the REVERSE-SUBTRACT variable. Then the REVERSE-SUBTRACT procedure is applied to the arguments 7 and 10, and the result from the procedure is returned.

```
(define reverse-subtract
   (lambda (x y) (- y x)))                  ⇒ unspecified value

(reverse-subtract 7 10)                     ⇒ 3
```

Next, a procedure is bound to the FOO variable. Note that the value 4, which is stored in the location bound by x, is associated with the procedure when the LAMBDA special form is evaluated. Therefore, the value 4 is used instead of the value 99, which is bound to x in the global environment.

```
(define x 99)                               ⇒ unspecified value

(define foo)
   (let ((x 4))
      (lambda (y) (+ x y))))                ⇒ unspecified value

(foo 6)                                     ⇒ 10
```

The next procedure illustrates the format (LAMBDA *var exp...*). This procedure binds the list (3 4 5 a) to the variable x and returns the value of x as the result of the procedure.

```
((lambda x x) 3 4 5 'a)                     ⇒ (3 4 5 A)
```

The next example shows the format (LAMBDA (*var₁ ... . varₙ*) *exp ...*). It binds 3 to x, 4 to y, and (5 A) to z (which is an illustration of the *Rest* construct). The value of z is returned as the result.

```
((lambda (x y . z) z) 3 4 5 'a)            ⇒ (5 A)
```

LAST-PAIR   *Procedure*

LAST-PAIR returns the last pair in a list.

Format   (LAST-PAIR *list*)

Parameter   *list* — A proper or improper list

Explanation	LAST-PAIR returns the last pair in *list*. The last pair is defined to be a pair whose cdr component is not a pair. Therefore LAST-PAIR can be defined as follows:

```
(define last-pair
 (lambda (x)
  (if (pair? (cdr x))
      (last-pair (cdr x))
      x)))
```

Examples	`(last-pair '(a b c))`	⇒ (C)
	`(last-pair '(a b . c))`	⇒ (B . C)

LCM   *Procedure*

LCM returns the least common multiple of a set of integers.

Format	(LCM *int ...*)
Parameters	*int ...* — Integers
Explanation	LCM returns the nonnegative integer that is the least common multiple of its integer arguments (*int ...*).
Examples	`(lcm 32 -36)` ⇒ 288
	`(lcm)` ⇒ 1

LENGTH   *Procedure*

LENGTH returns the number of elements in a proper list.

Format	(LENGTH *list*)
Parameter	*list* — A proper list
Explanation	LENGTH returns the number of elements in *list*.
Examples	`(length '())` ⇒ 0
	`(length '(a b c))` ⇒ 3
	`(length '(a (b) (c d e f)))` ⇒ 3
	`(length '(a b . c))` ⇒ *unspecified value*

LET   *Special Form*

LET evaluates expressions in an extended lexical environment.

Format	(LET ((*var* *form*) ...) *exp* ...) (LET *name* ((*var* *form*) ...) *exp* ...)
Parameters	*var* ... — Identifiers. Each *var* is bound to the value of its corresponding form.
	form ... — Any Scheme expressions.
	exp ... — Any Scheme expressions. Each *exp* is evaluated in the extended environment.
	name — A name given to the LET expression, thus allowing recursive calls to the LET special form. This argument is optional.
Explanation	LET is a binding construct that extends the current lexical environment and evaluates its body in that environment. Specifically, this special form:

1. Evaluates each *form* in the current environment (in some unspecified order)

2. Binds each *var* to the value of the corresponding form

3. Evaluates each *exp* in the extended environment, returning the value of the last *exp*

The binding of each *var* has *exp* ... as its scope.

LET is equivalent to the following:

((LAMBDA (*var* ...) *exp* ...) *form* ...)

Giving a *name* to a LET special form is allowed, thus permitting LET to be called iteratively or recursively. A named LET is equivalent to the following:

((NAMED–LAMBDA (*name* *var* ...) *exp* ...) *form* ...)

The LET, LET*, and LETREC special forms give Scheme a block structure. Note that in LET, the *form* ... arguments are not within the scope of the *var* ... being bound. To allow bound *vars* to refer to each other, use either LETREC or LET*, as appropriate. FLUID-LET is used to bind fluid variables.

Examples	The following example looks up the variables X and Y in the current lexical environment and returns their product:

```
(let ((x 2) (y 3))
  (* x y))                                      ⟹ 6
```

In the next example, the procedure FOO is defined locally in the second LET. Note that the binding of X used is from the outer LET.

```
(let ((x 2) (y 3))
  (let ((foo (lambda (z)
               (+ x y z)))
        (x 7))
    (foo 4)))                          ⟹ 9
```

In the next example of a named LET, FOO calls itself recursively with two arguments. The first is bound to X and the second is bound to Y.

```
(let foo ((x 5) (y 4))
  (if (< y 1) x
      (foo (+ x y) (-1+ y))))          ⟹ 15
```

LET*   *Special Form*

LET* evaluates expressions in an incrementally extended lexical environment.

Format	(LET* ((*var form*) ...) *exp* ...)
Parameters	*var* ... — Identifiers. Each *var* is bound to the value of its corresponding form.
	form ... — Any Scheme expressions.
	exp ... — Any Scheme expressions. Each *exp* is evaluated in the extended environment.
Explanation	LET* is a binding construct that incrementally extends the current lexical environment. Unlike LET, the initial variable bindings are performed serially where each new binding is evaluated in an extended environment that includes the previous variables. Specifically, this special form:

1. Evaluates each *form* in the current lexical environment extended with the bindings of each previously specified *var*, and then binds its corresponding var to its value

2. Evaluates the body, *exp* ..., in the extended environment, returning the value of the last *exp*

To define variables using slightly different environments for the binding, use LET or LETREC.

Examples	The first example shows x being used in the binding of y. This use is valid since x is evaluated after y is bound.

```
(let* ((x 3) (y (+ x 4)))
  (+ x y))                             ⟹ 10
```

In the next example, note that within FOO, the x bound by the LET* is used instead of the x bound by the LET.

```
(let ((x 99))
  (let* ((x 2)
         (y 3)
         (foo (lambda (z)
                (+ x y z))))
    (foo 4)))                          ⇒ 9

(let ((x 2))
  (let* ((x (* x x))
         (y (* x x)))
    (+ x y)))                          ⇒ 20
```

LETREC   *Special Form*

LETREC evaluates expressions in a lexical environment extended with mutually referential bindings.

Format   (LETREC ((*var* *form*) ...) *exp* ...)

Parameters   *var* ...— Identifiers. Each *var* is bound to the value of its corresponding *form*.

                    form ... — Any Scheme expressions.

                    exp ...— Any Scheme expressions. Each *exp* is evaluated in the extended environment.

Explanation   LETREC is similar to LET except that the initializing forms are evaluated in an environment that has been extended to include every *var*, thus making mutual recursion possible. Specifically, this special form:

1. Extends the environment with a new binding for each *var*

2. Evaluates each *form* in the resulting environment (in some unspecified order)

3. Assigns to each *var* the result of the corresponding form

4. Evaluates each *exp* sequentially in the resulting environment, returning the value of the last *exp*

Each binding of a *var* has the entire LETREC special form as its scope, making it possible to define mutually recursive procedures.

One restriction on LETREC is very important: it must be possible to evaluate each *form* without referring to the value of a *var* directly. If this restriction is violated, the effect is undefined, and an error may be signalled during evaluation of the forms. Typically, the forms are LAMBDA expressions, and the restriction is satisfied automatically.

This example shows that the x defined by the LETREC is used instead of the x defined by the LET:

```
(let ((x 2) (y 3))
  (letrec ((foo (lambda (z)
                  (+ x y z)))
           (x 7))
    (foo 4)))                        ⟹ 14
```

This example illustrates two mutually recursive procedures:

```
(lectrec ((even? (lambda (n)
                   (if (zero? n)
                       #T
                       (odd? (-1+ n)))))
          (odd? (lambda (n)
                  (if (zero? n)
                      #F
                      (even? (-1+ n))))))
  (even? 88))                        ⟹ true
```

LINE-LENGTH   *Procedure*

LINE-LENGTH returns the line length of an output port.

Format   (LINE-LENGTH {*port*})

Parameter   *port* — An output port (an optional argument)

Explanation   LINE-LENGTH returns the line length associated with *port*, if it is given, or with the current output port. The default line length is 80 for all output ports. A value of zero indicates unlimited line length.

Examples   (define lengthy (open-output-file "lengthy"))

                                                              ⟹ *unspecified value*
                    (line-length lengthy)   ⟹ 80
                    (set-line-length! 15 lengthy)   ⟹ *unspecified value*
                    (line-length lengthy)   ⟹ 15

LIST   *Procedure*

LIST creates a proper list from its arguments.

Format   (LIST *obj* ...)

Parameters   *obj* ...— Any Scheme objects

Explanation	LIST returns a proper list whose elements are the arguments (*obj* ...) in the specified order.
	To form a list where the cdr component of the last pair is the last object specified, use LIST*. For more information on lists and pairs, see CAR, CDR, and CONS.
Examples	(list 'a (+ 3 4) (car '(a b c))) ⟹ (A 7 A) (list 'a) ⟹ (A) (list) ⟹ ()

LIST*   *Procedure*

LIST* creates a dotted list from its arguments.

Format	(LIST* *obj*$_1$ ... *obj*$_n$)
Parameters	*obj*$_1$ ... *obj*$_n$— Any Scheme objects
Explanation	List* uses CONS to create a pair whose car component is *obj*$_1$ and whose cdr component is (LIST* obj$_2$ ... *obj*$_n$). This pair is returned as the result of LIST*. With only two arguments, LIST* behaves in the same way as CONS. If LIST* is applied to a single argument, that argument is returned.
	For more information on lists and pairs, see CAR, CDR, CONS, and LIST.
Examples	(list* 'a 'b 'c) ⟹ (A B . C) (list* '(a b) 'c '(d e)) ⟹ ((A B) C D E) (list* 'a 'b) ⟹ (A . B) (list* 'a) ⟹ A

LIST-REF   *Procedure*

LIST-REF returns a specific element of a list.

Format	(LIST-REF *list n*)
Parameters	*list* — A list
	n — A nonnegative integer
Explanation	LIST-REF returns the nth element of *list*, where the index of the first element is zero. If n is greater than or equal to the length of a proper list, the empty list is returned. If n is greater than or equal to the length of an improper list, an error occurs.
	See also LIST-TAIL.

Examples	(list-ref '(a b c) 0)	⇒ A
	(list-ref '(a b c) 2)	⇒ C
	(list-ref '(a b c) 4)	⇒ ()
	(list-ref '(a b . c) 1)	⇒ B
	(list-ref '(a b . c) 2)	⇒ *error*

```
(define x                 ;Creates a circular list
  (let ((tmp '(a b c)))
    (set-cdr! (cddr tmp) tmp)))        ⇒ unspecified value

(list-ref x 1000)                       ⇒ A
```

LIST-TAIL   *Procedure*

LIST-TAIL returns a sublist of a list.

Format	(LIST-TAIL *list n*)

Parameters   *list* — A list

n — A nonnegative integer

Explanation   LIST-TAIL returns the nth pair of *list*, where the index of the first element is zero. If *n* is greater than or equal to the length of a proper list, the empty list is returned. If *n* is greater than or equal to the length of an improper list, an error occurs.

See also LIST-REF.

Examples	(list-tail '(a b c) 0)	⇒ (A B C)
	(list-tail '(a b c) 2)	⇒ (C)
	(list-tail '(a b c) 4)	⇒ ( )
	(list-tail '(a b . c) 1)	⇒ (B . C)
	(list-tail '(a b . c) 2)	⇒ C

LIST->STREAM   *Procedure*

LIST->STREAM converts a list to a stream.

Format	(LIST->STREAM *list*)

Parameter   *list* — A proper list

Explanations   LIST->STREAM returns a finite stream that corresponds to *list*. The head of the stream corresponds to the car component of the list, and the tail of the stream represents the rest of the list.

To create a list from a stream, use STREAM->LIST.

Examples	`(define l (list->stream '(a b c)))`	⟹ *unspecified value*
	`(head l)`	⟹ A
	`(head (tail l))`	⟹ B
	`(head (tail (tail l)))`	⟹ C
	`(tail (tail (tail l)))`	⟹ #(THE-EMPTY-STREAM)

LIST->STRING *Procedure*

LIST->STRING converts a list of characters to a string.

Format	`(LIST->STRING list)`
Parameter	*list* — A proper list of characters
Explanations	LIST->STRING returns a string made up of the characters in *list*.
	The inverse operation is STRING->LIST.
Examples	`(list->string '(#\a #\3 #\. #\Z))` ⟹ `"a3.Z"`
	`(list->string '(#\S #\c #\h #\e #\m #\e))` ⟹ `"Scheme"`

LIST->VECTOR *Procedure*

LIST->VECTOR creates a new vector from a proper list.

Format	`(LIST->VECTOR list)`
Parameter	*list* — A proper list.
Explanation	LIST->VECTOR returns a newly created vector whose elements are the elements of *list*. The new vector has the same length as *list*.
	To create a list from a vector, use VECTOR->LIST. Related vector procedures are VECTOR-REF and VECTOR-SET!.
Examples	`(define a (list->vector '(a b c d e)))` ⟹ *unspecified value*
	`(vector-ref a 1)` ⟹ B
	`(vector-length a)` ⟹ 5

LOAD   *Procedure*

LOAD loads a file into Scheme.

Format	(LOAD *filespec*)
Parameter	*filespec* — A string that names a file
Explanation	LOAD reads and evaluates the expressions in *filespec*. An unspecified value is returned. The file may be in source format; or if COMPILE-FILE has been used, it may be in compiled or fast-load format.
Example	Assume that the file FOURPLUS.S on the default disk drive contains the following lines:

```
(DEFINE (FOUR+ N) (+ N 4))
(DISPLAY "Four+ loaded!")
```

The following example shows the use of LOAD:

```
(load "fourplus.s")
Four+ loaded!                      ⇒ unspecified value
(four+ 1)                          ⇒ 5
```

LOG   *Procedure*

LOG returns the logarithm of a number.

Format	(LOG n_1 {n_2})
Parameters	n_1 — Any Scheme number
	n_2 — Any Scheme number (an optional argument)
Explanation	LOG returns the logarithm of the specified numbers. If n_2 is given, the procedure returns the value of $\log_{n_2} n_1$; otherwise, the procedure returns the value of the natural logarithm $\log_e n_1$.

Examples

```
(log 1)                            ⇒ 0
(log (exp1))                       ⇒ 1.
(log 100 10)                       ⇒ 2.
(log 500 10)                       ⇒ 2.69897000433602
(log 500)                          ⇒ 6.21460809842219
```

MACRO

MACRO creates new special forms.

Format	(MACRO *name expander*)
Parameters	*name* — The name of the new special form
	expander — A procedure of one argument that does the expanding
Explanation	MACRO declares *name* to be the keyword of a new special form called a macro. When such a macro is encountered during evaluation, the evaluator replaces the entire macro expression with its expansion by calling *expander* and passing it the macro expression as its argument. Then the evaluation takes place. Note, however, that if a macro is self-referential, it is possible that the expansion may never end. MACRO returns an unspecified value.
	See also SYNTAX.

Examples

```
(macro add3
  (lambda (e)
    (list '+
          (cadr e)
          3)))                    ⇒ unspecified value
(add3 0)                          ⇒ 3
(add3 -7)                         ⇒ -4

(macro iterate
  (lambda (e)
    (let ((name (cadr e))
          (initial-bindings (caddr e))
          (body (cdddr e)))
      `((rec ,name
          (lambda
            ,(mapcar car initial-bindings)
            ,@body))
        ,@(mapcar cadr initial-bindings)))))
                                  ⇒ unspecified value

(iterate loop ((x 5) (y 10))
        (if (negative? x)
            '()
            (begin
              (print (list x y))
              (loop (sub1 x) (add1 y)))))

(5 10)
(4 11)
(3 12)
(2 13)
(1 14)
(0 15)
```

MAKE-ENGINE *Procedure*

MAKE-ENGINE creates an object that is called an engine.

Format	(MAKE-ENGINE *thunk*)
Parameter	*thunk* — A procedure of no arguments
Explanation	MAKE-ENGINE creates and returns a Scheme object called an engine. The argument is a *thunk* that represents a computation to be performed. The value of the computation becomes the argument to ENGINE-RETURN, which notifies the engine that the computation has completed and, in turn, passes back the value.

An engine is a procedure of three arguments:

1. *ticks* — A positive integer. This number is the amount of time the engine runs. The length of a *tick* is implementation-dependent.

2. *success-continuation* — A procedure of two arguments. The first argument receives the result of evaluating *thunk*. The other argument is the number of *ticks* remaining.

3. *failure-continuation* — A procedure of one argument that represents the new engine. The new engine is a procedure that continues execution where the previous engine stopped.

The computation embodied by *thunk* will be started when the engine is executed. The computation proceeds for a number of *ticks*. If the computation completes inside the given number of ticks, the *success-continuation* is invoked with the result of evaluating *thunk* and the number of ticks remaining. If the computation did not finish before the ticks ran out, a new engine is created. The new engine will continue the execution of *thunk* where the previous engine stopped. The *failure-continuation* is invoked with the new engine as its argument.

Each time the same engine is invoked, its evaluation begins in the same place. The result of either *success-continuation* or *failure-continuation* is returned as the result of the invoked engine.

An engine may not call an engine.

For information on invoking *success-continuation* and returning a value, see ENGINE-RETURN.

Example   In the example that follows, a Fibonacci number is calculated using an engine. After defining the Fibonacci function, the success and failure functions are defined, and the engine that begins the computation is created and assigned to the variable engine. The begin form then executes the engine and, if the computation completes, the result of success becomes the value of engine; if the computation does not complete before the ticks run out, the result of failure becomes the value of engine, and is the new engine that will continue the evaluation. Because machine speeds vary and the length of a tick is implementation-dependent, the begin form may need to be re-executed several times before the answer becomes available.

```
(define fib
  (lambda (n)
    (if (< n 2)
        1
        (+ (fib (-1+ n))
           (fib (- n 2)))))))          ⇒ unspecified value

(define success
  (lambda (value ticks) value))        ⇒ unspecified value

(define failure
  (lambda (new-engine) new-engine))    ⇒ unspecified value

(define engine
  (make-engine
    (lambda () (engine-return (fib 15))))) ⇒ unspecified value

(begin (define engine (engine 10 success failure)) engine)
                                ⇒ #<PROCEDURE MAKE-ENGINE>
                                  while the computation has not
                                  completed
                                ⇒ 987  when the thunk completes
```

MAKE-ENVIRONMENT   *Special Form*

MAKE-ENVIRONMENT creates an environment object.

Format   (MAKE-ENVIRONMENT *exp* ...)

Parameters   *exp* ... — Any Scheme expressions

Explanation   MAKE-ENVIRONMENT returns a new environment object, which is formed by extending the current environment. Each *exp* is evaluated in the extended environment and typically adds variable bindings (via DEFINE) to the extended environment. MAKE-ENVIRONMENT is essentially equivalent to the following:

(LET ( ) *exp* ... (THE-ENVIRONMENT))

See also THE-ENVIRONMENT.

Example	(define dinosaurs ´extinct) ⟹ *unspecified value*

```
(define dinosaurs ´extinct)        ⟹ unspecified value
(define alternate-earth
  (make-environment
    (define dinosarus ´thriving)))
                              ⟹ unspecified value
(access dinosaurs (the-environment))
                              ⟹ EXTINCT
(environment-bindings alternate-earth)
                        ⟹((DINOSAURS . THRIVING))
```

MAKE-INSTANCE   *Special Form*

MAKE-INSTANCE creates an instance of a SCOOPS class.

Format	(MAKE-INSTANCE *class var init-val ...*)
Parameters	*class* — A SCOOPS class
	var ... — The variables in *class* whose values are to be initialized
	init-val .. — The initial values for each *var*
Explanation	MAKE-INSTANCE evaluates *var* and *init-val* and then returns an instance of *class*, which is an environment. This special form can be used to specify initial values for instance variables that have been described as inittable in DEFINE-CLASS.

Example

```
(define-class employees
  (classvars (no-of-employees 0))
  (instvars
    name emp-no manager salary (overtime 0))
  (mixins personal-info education-experience)
  (options
    (gettable-variables name emp-no no-of-employees)
    settable-variables
    inittable-variables))          ⟹ unspecified value

(define-method (employees earnings) ()
  (+ salary overtime))             ⟹ unspecified value

(define-method)
  (employees earnings-greater-than) (val)
  (if (>? (earnings) val)
      (writeln name " " emp-no)
      #F))                         ⟹ unspecified value

(define emp1
  (make-instance employees
    'name 'RALPH
    'emp-no 001
    'manager 'SAM
    'salary 100))                  ⟹ unspecified value

(send emp1 earnings-greater-than 99)
RALPH 1                            ⟹ false
```

MAKE-STRING   *Procedure*

MAKE-STRING creates and initializes a string.

Format   (MAKE-STRING *size {fillchar}*)

Parameters   *size* — An integer representing the number of characters in the string. For PC Scheme, this integer is in the range $0 \leq size \leq 16380$.

fillchar — A character.

Explanation   MAKE-STRING returns a newly allocated string of length *size* where all the characters are *fillchar*. If *fillchar* is not specified, then the contents of the string are unspecified.

Examples
```
(make-string 5 #\X)               ⟹ "XXXXX"
(make-string 1 #\0)               ⟹ "0"
(make-string 0 #\?)               ⟹ ""
```

MAKE-VECTOR   *Procedure*

MAKE-VECTOR creates a vector.

    Format   (MAKE-VECTOR *size* {*initval*})

    Parameters   *size* — An integer indicating the number of elements in the vector. For PC Scheme, this integer is in the range $0 \leq size \leq 10921$.

                       initval — Any Scheme object. Its value is placed in each element of the new vector. This argument is optional.

    Explanation   MAKE-VECTOR returns a newly allocated vector with *size* elements. If *initval* is given, each element of the newly created vector is initialized to *initval*; otherwise, each element initially has an unspecified value.

                       Related vector procedures are VECTOR-LENGTH, VECTOR-REF, and VECTOR-SET!.

    Example

```
(define a (make-vector 8 '(1)))  ⇒ unspecified value
a                                ⇒ #((1) (1) (1) (1) (1) (1)
(1) (1))
(vector-set! a 3 'b)             ⇒ unspecified value
a                                ⇒ #((1) (1) (1) B (1) (1) (1) (1))
```

MAKE-WINDOW   *Procedure*

MAKE-WINDOW creates a Scheme window object.

    Format   (MAKE-WINDOW {*label* {*border?*}})

    Parameters   *label* — A string to be used as the window's label. A null string or *false* may be used to indicate that no label is desired. The label is printed in the upper left-hand corner of the border. This argument is optional.

                       border? — A boolean value. A *true* value indicates that the window is to have a border. The border is drawn in the character positions just outside the data portion of the window. This optional argument can be specified only if *label* is specified.

Explanation	MAKE-WINDOW creates and returns a window object representing the entire console screen. The screen is not changed by this operation. To display the window on the screen, use WINDOW-CLEAR.
	For further information on changing a window's attributes, position, and size, see WINDOW-SET-ATTRIBUTE!, WINDOW-SET-POSITION!, and WINDOW-SET-SIZE!, respectively.
	For more information on windows, see the *PC Scheme User's Guide — Student Edition*.

MAP   *Procedure*

MAP applies a procedure to each element of a list and returns the results.

Format	(MAP *procedure list*)
Parameters	*procedure* — A procedure of one argument
	list — A proper list
Explanation	MAP applies *procedure* to each element of *list* in an unspecified order. A list containing the results of the evaluations is returned.
	To apply the procedure without returning the results, use FOR-EACH.
Examples	(map car '((a 1) (b 2) (c 3) (d 4))) ⟹ (A B C D) (map (lambda (y) (+ y y)) '(1 2 3 4 5 6 7)) ⟹ (2 4 6 8 10 12 14)

MAPC   *Procedure*

MAPC applies a procedure to each element of a list.

Format	(MAPC *procedure list*)
Parameters	*procedure* — A procedure of one argument
	list — A proper list
Explanation	MAPC applies *procedure* to each element of *list* in order from left to right. An unspecified value is returned.
	MAPC is an alternate name for FOR-EACH and has been retained for historical reasons.
	To return the results of the applications, use MAP or MAPCAR.

Examples	`(mapc display '("one" "after" "another"))`
	oneafteranother $\Rightarrow$ *unspecified value*
	`(define x 0)` $\Rightarrow$ *unspecified value*
	`(mapc (lambda (n)(set! x n)) '(1 2 3 4))`
	$\Rightarrow$ *unspecified value*
	`x` $\Rightarrow$ 4

MAPCAR
Procedure

MAPCAR applies a procedure to each element of a list and returns the results.

Format	(MAPCAR *procedure* *list*)
Parameters	*procedure* — A procedure of one argument
	list — A proper list
Explanation	MAPCAR applies *procedure* to each element of *list* in an unspecified order. A list containing the results of the evaluation is returned.
	MAPCAR is an alternate name for MAP and has been retained for historical reasons.
	To apply the procedure without returning the results, use FOR-EACH or MAPC.
Examples	`(mapcar car '((a 1) (b 2) (c 3) (d 4)))`
	$\Rightarrow$ (A B C D)
	`(mapcar (lambda (y) (+ y y))`
	`'(1 2 3 4 5 6 7))` $\Rightarrow$ (2 4 6 8 10 12 14)

MAX
Procedure

MAX returns the largest value among its arguments.

Format	(MAX *num*$_1$ ...)
Parameters	*num*$_1$ ... — Any Scheme numbers
Explanation	MAX returns the largest value among its arguments. If only *num*$_1$ is given, *num*$_1$ is returned.

Examples	(max 3 583.26 9.46)	$\Rightarrow$ 583.26
	(max 5 10 15 -20)	$\Rightarrow$ 15
	(max 4)	$\Rightarrow$ 4
	(max 12345678901234567 8900000 25.3)	
		$\Rightarrow$ 12345678901234567 8900000

MEMBER, MEMQ, MEMV *Procedure*

These procedures return the sublist beginning with the occurrence of a specific object in a proper list.

Format	(MEMBER *obj* *list*)
	(MEMQ *obj* *list*)
	(MEMV *obj* *list*)
Parameters	*obj* — Any Scheme object
	list — A proper list
Explanation	These procedures search for the first occurrence of *obj* in *list* with MEMBER using EQUAL? for comparison, MEMQ using EQ?, and MEMV using EQV?. If *obj* is found, the sublist containing *obj* as its first element is returned. If *obj* is not found in *list*, *false* is returned.

Examples	(member 'a '(a b c))	$\Rightarrow$ (A B C)
	(memq 'a '(a b c))	$\Rightarrow$ (A B C)
	(memv 'a '(a b c))	$\Rightarrow$ (A B C)
	(member 'b '(a b c))	$\Rightarrow$ (B C)
	(memq 'b '(a b c))	$\Rightarrow$ (B C)
	(memv 'b '(a b c))	$\Rightarrow$ (B C)
	(member 'a '(b c d))	$\Rightarrow$ *false*
	(memq 'a '(b c d))	$\Rightarrow$ *false*
	(memv 'a '(b c d))	$\Rightarrow$ *false*
	(member (list 'a) '(b (a) c))	$\Rightarrow$ ((A) C)
	(memq (list 'a) '(b (a) c))	$\Rightarrow$ *false*
	(memv (list 'a) '(b (a) c))	$\Rightarrow$ *false*
	(member 101 '(100 101 102))	$\Rightarrow$ (101 102)
	(memq 101 '(100 101 102))	$\Rightarrow$ *unspecified value*
	(memv 101 '(100 101 102))	$\Rightarrow$ (101 102)

METHODS   *Procedure*

METHODS returns a list of the methods defined in a SCOOPS class.

Format	(METHODS *class*)
Parameter	*class* — A SCOOPS class
Explanation	METHODS returns a list of the names of the methods defined in *class*. This list does not include the inherited methods.
	To include the inherited methods in the listing, use ALL-METHODS.
Example	Assume that the class employees exists (as shown in the example for DEFINE-CLASS) and that it has been compiled with the inherited instance variable schools and the inherited class variable soc-sec-no.

```
(methods employees)       ⇒(GET-NAME GET-EMP-NO
                            GET-NO-OF-EMPLOYEES
                            GET-SALARY SET-EMP-NO
                            SET-MANAGER SET-OVERTIME
                            SET-NO-OF-EMPLOYEES)
```

MIN   *Procedure*

MIN returns the smallest value among its arguments.

Format	(MIN *num$_1$* ...)
Parameters	*num$_1$* ... — Any Scheme numbers
Explanation	MIN returns the smallest value among its arguments. If only *num$_1$* is given, *num$_1$* is returned.

Examples	(min 3 583.26 9.46)	⇒ 3
	(min 5 10 15 −20)	⇒ −20
	(min 4)	⇒ 4

MINUS

MINUS changes the sign of a number.

Format	(MINUS *num*)
Parameter	*num* — Any Scheme number
Explanation	MINUS changes the sign of its argument from positive to negative or vice versa and returns that number as its value. A zero argument is not changed.
Examples	(minus −3) $\Rightarrow$ 3
	(minus 0) $\Rightarrow$ 0
	(minus 2.3) $\Rightarrow$ −2.3

MIXINS

MIXINS returns a list of the mixins of a SCOOPS class.

Format	(MIXINS *class*)
Parameter	*class* — A SCOOPS class.
Explanation	MIXINS returns a list of the mixins of *class*.
Examples	Assume that the class employees exists (as shown in the example for DEFINE-CLASS).

(mixins employees) $\Rightarrow$ (PERSONAL-INFO EDUCATION-EXPERIENCE)

MODULO

MODULO divides two integers and returns the remainder.

Format	(MODULO int_1 int_2)
Parameters	int_1 — An integer that is the dividend
	int_2 — An integer that is the divisor
Explanation	MODULO divides int_1 by int_2 and returns the remainder. If int_2 is zero, an error is signalled. The value returned by MODULO always has the sign of int_2.

Note that MODULO and REMAINDER differ only when either the dividend or the divisor is negative. MODULO always has the sign of the divisor, and REMAINDER always has the sign of the dividend.

To find the integer quotient, use QUOTIENT.

Examples		
(modulo 13 4)		$\Rightarrow$ 1
(modulo -13 4)		$\Rightarrow$ 3
(modulo 13 -4)		$\Rightarrow$ -3
(modulo -13 -4)		$\Rightarrow$ -1

NAME->CLASS   *Procedure*

NAME->CLASS returns the SCOOPS class with the specified name.

Format	(NAME->CLASS *class*)
Parameter	*class* — The name of a SCOOPS class
Explanation	NAME->CLASS returns the SCOOPS class with the name *class*.
Example	Assume that the class employees exists (as shown in the example for DEFINE-CLASS).

(name->class 'employees) $\Rightarrow$ *scoops-class*

NAMED-LAMBDA   *Special Form*

NAMED-LAMBDA returns an instance of a procedure object.

Format	(NAMED-LAMBDA *formals* exp_1 ...)
Parameters	*formals* — A proper or improper list of identifiers. Each type of *formals* mentioned below contains *name* as its first element. The identifier *name* is bound to the procedure created by NAMED-LAMBDA. The binding occurs at the same time the remaining variables are bound, as discussed below. The *formals* can be one of two types:

■ (*name* *var* ...) — A proper list of identifiers. Each *var* is bound to a corresponding value when the procedure returned by the NAMED-LAMBDA special form is called. The total number of identifiers must equal the total number of actual arguments.

■ (*name* *var$_1$* ... . *var$_n$*) — An improper list of identifiers. Each *var* is bound to a value when the procedure returned by the NAMED-LAMBDA special form is called. Each *var*, except *var$_n$*, must match to an actual argument when the procedure created by the NAMED-LAMBDA special form is called. Any additional arguments are gathered into a list and bound to *var$_n$*. If only *var$_1$* is specified (*name* . *var$_1$*), all the arguments are gathered into a list and are bound to *var$_1$*.

exp$_1$ ... — The expressions that are evaluated in the extended environment when the procedure is called.

Explanation   NAMED-LAMBDA returns a procedure characterized by three elements:

■ A formal argument specifier, *formals*

■ A procedure body, *exp$_1$* ...

■ The environment in effect when the NAMED-LAMBDA special form is evaluated.

When the procedure created by NAMED-LAMBDA is called, it is processed as follows:

1. All arguments passed to the procedure are evaluated.

2. The environment associated with the procedure is extended to include the *formals*, *name* is bound to the procedure created by NAMED-LAMBDA, and the evaluated arguments are bound to the remaining *formals*. (You may use the Rest construct if you wish.)

3. The body of the procedure, *exp$_1$* ..., is evaluated in the extended environment.

4. The value of the last *exp* evaluated is returned as the result of the procedure call.

Each evaluation of the NAMED-LAMBDA special form returns a different instance of the procedure object.

NAMED-LAMBDA is equivalent to REC.

In comparison to LAMBDA, the fact that NAMED-LAMBDA has the added variable *name* has subtle effects on the behavior and performance (execution speed) of self-recursive procedure definitions. For example, consider the following two definitions of the factorial function:

```
(define fact
  (named-lambda (fact n)
    (if (= n 1) 1 (* n (fact (- n 1))))))

(define fact
  (lambda (n)
    (if (= n 1) 1 (* n (fact (- n 1))))))
```

The self-reference to FACT in the first version is satisfied by the lexical binding of FACT inherent in a NAMED-LAMBDA. However, in the second version, FACT is a globally bound variable whose value is looked up each time the *else* clause of the IF is executed. This process permits the value of that binding to be changed at runtime, which may be meaningful in other cases, but not meaningful here. Also, the second version executes somewhat slower than the first version.

Examples

```
(define fact
  (named-lambda (fact n)
    (if (= n 0) 1 (* n (fact (-1+ n)))))))    ⇒ unspecified value
(fact 3)                                       ⇒ 6
(define another-fact fact)                     ⇒ unspecified value
(set! fact 99)                                 ⇒ unspecified value
(another-fact 3)                               ⇒ 6
```

NEGATIVE?   *Procedure*

NEGATIVE? determines whether a number is less than zero.

Format   (NEGATIVE? *num*)

Parameter   *num* — Any Scheme number

Explanation   NEGATIVE? returns *true* if *num* is less than zero and *false*, otherwise.

Examples
```
(negative? -5.53)                              ⇒ true
(negative? 5)                                  ⇒ false
(negative? 0)                                  ⇒ false
(negative? -0)                                 ⇒ false
(negative? 'foo)                               ⇒ error
```

#\NEWLINE   *Character Object*

#\NEWLINE is a single character that represents the line delimiter.

Format   #\NEWLINE

Explanation   #\NEWLINE is the character object that represents the appropriate end-of-line sequence. When this object is printed to a port, the ASCII character code for carriage return (13_{10}) is sent to that port, followed by the ASCII character for linefeed (10_{10}). For instance, when this character is sent to the screen with WRITE-CHAR, DISPLAY, or PRINC, the cursor moves to the beginning of the next line.

Examples	(writeln "foo" #\newline "bar")
	foo
	bar	⟹ *unspecified value*

NEWLINE *Procedure*

NEWLINE outputs an end-of-line character sequence.

Format	(NEWLINE {*port*})
Parameter	*port* — A port (an optional argument)
Explanation	NEWLINE outputs an end-of-line character sequence to *port*, if it is specified, or to the current output port. An unspecified value is returned.
Examples	(begin
	(display "abcd")
	(newline)
	(display "wxyz"))
	abcd
	wxyz ⟹ *unspecified value*

NIL *Constant or Variable*

NIL is an identifier equated with '( ) (the empty list).

Format	NIL
Explanation	Whether NIL is a constant or a variable depends on the boolean variable PCS-INTEGRATE-T-AND-NIL. If PCS-INTEGRATE-T-AND-NIL is *true*, NIL is considered to be equivalent to '( ); otherwise, NIL is a variable defined in the user global environment. New code should use the constants '( ) or #F, as appropriate.

Examples	(eq? nil #F)	⟹ *true*
	(set! pcs-integrate-t-and-nil #F)	⟹ *unspecified value*
	(let ((nil 3))	
	(eq? nil '( )))	⟹ *false*
	(set! pcs-integrate-t-and-nil #T)	⟹ *unspecified value*
	(let ((nil 3))	
	(eq? nil '( )))	⟹ *error*

NOT   *Procedure*

NOT logically negates its arguments.

Format	(NOT *obj*)
Parameter	*obj* — Any Scheme object
Explanation	NOT returns *true* if *obj* is *false* and returns *false*, otherwise. Note that the empty list and the boolean value #F are indistinguishable.
Examples	(not #F) $\Rightarrow$ *true* (not #T)) $\Rightarrow$ *false* (not (memq 'a '(a b c))) $\Rightarrow$ *false* ; MEMQ returns a *true* value. (not 'foo) $\Rightarrow$ *false*

NULL?   *Procedure*

NULL? indicates whether an object is the empty list.

Format	(NULL? *obj*)
Parameter	*obj* — Any Scheme object
Explanation	NULL? returns *true* if *obj* is the empty list and *false*, otherwise. Note that the empty list and the boolean value #F are indistinguishable.
Examples	(null? '()) $\Rightarrow$ *true* (null? #F) $\Rightarrow$ *true* (null? (cdr '(a))) $\Rightarrow$ *true* (define ex '(a b d)) $\Rightarrow$ *unspecified value* (null? ex) $\Rightarrow$ *false*

NUMBER?   *Procedure*

NUMBER? determines whether its argument is a number.

Format	(NUMBER? *obj*)
Parameter	*obj* — Any Scheme object
Explanation	NUMBER? returns *true* if *obj* is a Scheme number and *false*, otherwise.

Examples	(number? 42)	⟹ *true*
	(number? −4.39)	⟹ *true*
	(number? 0)	⟹ *true*
	(number? '(1 2 3))	⟹ *false*
	(number? "1")	⟹ *false*
	(number? #\1)	⟹ *false*

NUMBER->STRING
Procedure

NUMBER->STRING converts a number to a string in a specified format.

Format (NUMBER->STRING *num format*)

Parameters *num* — Any Scheme number.

format — A list representing the format of the number. The possible formats are as follows:

- (INT) — Express *num* as an integer.

- (FIX *n*) — Express *num* as a fixed radix point value where *n* specifies the number of places to the right of the radix point.

- (FLO *n*) — Express *num* as a floating radix point value where *n* is the total number of places to be displayed.

- (SCI *n* *m*) — Express *num* in exponential notion where *n* specifies the total number of places to be displayed and *m* specifies the number of places to the right of the radix point.

- (HEUR) — Express *num* heuristically using the minimum number of digits required to get an expression, such that when the expression is coerced back to a number, the original machine representation is produced.

Explanation NUMBER->STRING returns a string that is the printed expression of *num* in *format*.

Examples

(number->string 1234 '(int))	⟹ "1234"
(number->string 1234.56789 '(fix 3))	
	⟹ "1234.568"
(number->string (/ 13 7) '(flo 5))	
	⟹ "1.8571"
(number->string (expt 3.14159 90)	
'(sci 5 4))	⟹ "5.5393E44"
(number->string (expt 3.14159 90)	
'(heur))	⟹ "5.53930817569592E44"

OBJECT-HASH, OBJECT-UNHASH *Procedure*

These procedures use a hashing function to associate an object with a unique integer. The association is stored in the object-hash table.

Format	(OBJECT-HASH *obj*) (OBJECT-UNHASH *int*)
Parameters	*obj* — Any Scheme object
	int — An integer
Explanation	Based on a hashing function, an object is associated with a unique integer. The association between the object and the integer is a weak reference because the association is maintained only as long as the object is pointed to by some Scheme object. Objects that are no longer referenced are removed from the object-hash table during garbage collection.

- OBJECT-HASH assigns an integer to *obj* and records the relationship in the object-hash table. Objects that are identical (in the sense of EQ?) are assigned the same integer.

- OBJECT-UNHASH returns the object associated with *int*, provided some other reference to *obj* exists. If no association exists, *false* is returned.

Examples	(define x ´(a b c)) ⟹ *unspecified value* (define y (object-hash x)) ⟹ *unspecified value* (display (object-unhash y)) ⟹ *unspecified value* (ABC) (define x #F) ⟹ *unspecified value* ;Kill reference (gc) ⟹ *unspecified value* (object-unhash y) ⟹ (ABC) ; y is in top-level history (scheme-reset) ⟹ *unspecified value* ;remove y from history [**PCS-DEBUG-MODE is OFF**] (object-unhash y) ⟹ *false* ; association no longer exists

---

ODD? *Procedure*

ODD? determines whether an integer is odd.

Format	(ODD? *int*)
Parameter	*int* — An integer
Explanation	ODD? returns *true* if *int* is odd — that is, if (REMAINDER *int* 2) is non-zero. If *int* is not odd, *false* is returned. If the argument is not an integer, an error occurs.

Examples	(odd? 1)	$\Rightarrow$ *true*
	(odd? 2)	$\Rightarrow$ *false*
	(odd? 0)	$\Rightarrow$ *false*
	(odd? -3)	$\Rightarrow$ *true*
	(odd? 3.0)	$\Rightarrow$ *error*

OPEN-BINARY-INPUT-FILE, OPEN-BINARY-OUTPUT-FILE   *Procedure*

These procedures open a file for binary input or output.

Format	(OPEN-BINARY-INPUT-FILE *filespec*)
	(OPEN-BINARY-OUTPUT-FILE *filespec*)
Parameters	*filespec* — A string that names a file
Explanation	These procedures open a file for reading or writing binary data. The data being read or written is interpreted by the input/output routines (i.e., carriage return, etc.).

- OPEN-BINARY-INPUT-FILE opens *filespec* for binary input. A newly allocated port for the opened *filespec* is returned.

- OPEN-BINARY-OUTPUT-FILE opens *filespec* for binary output. A newly allocated port for the opened *filespec* is returned.

OPEN-EXTEND-FILE, OPEN-INPUT-FILE,   *Procedure*
OPEN-INPUT-STRING, OPEN-OUTPUT-FILE

These procedures open a file for input or output.

Format	(OPEN-EXTEND-FILE *filespec*)
	(OPEN-INPUT-FILE *filespec*)
	(OPEN-INPUT-STRING *string*)
	(OPEN-OUTPUT-FILE *filespec*)
Parameters	*filespec* — A string that names a file
	string — A string
Explanation	These procedures open a file for input or output. However, they work differently as described here.

- OPEN-EXTEND-FILE opens *filespec* for output. A newly allocated port for the opened *filespec* is returned. If the file exists, the output is appended to the end of the file. If the file does not exist, it is created.

- OPEN-INPUT-FILE opens *filespec*, which is an existing file, for input. A newly allocated port for the opened *filespec* is returned.

- OPEN-INPUT-STRING creates and returns a input port whose buffer contains *string*. With this procedure, a string of characters can be converted into S-expressions using the READ procedure.

- OPEN-OUTPUT-FILE creates and opens a new output file named *filespec*. If a file by that name exists, its contents are overwritten. A newly allocated port for the opened *filespec* is returned.

Examples

```
(define bounce (open-output-file "bounce"))  ⇒ unspecified value
(begin (write 'boing! bounce)
       (newline bounce))                     ⇒ unspecified value
(close-output-port bounce)                   ⇒ unspecified value
(define bounce (open-input-file "bounce"))   ⇒ unspecified value
(read bounce)                                ⇒ BOING!

(define evaluate-string
  (lambda (s)
    (let* ((sp (open-input-string s))
           (ans (eval (read sp))))
      (close-input-port sp)
      ans)))                                 ⇒ unspecified value
(define s "(+ 3 5)")                         ⇒ unspecified value
(evaluate-string s)                          ⇒ 8
```

OR   *Special Form*

OR is a logical composition operator that connects expressions to form a compound predicate.

Format   (OR *exp* ...)

Parameters   *exp* ... — Any Scheme expressions

Explanation   OR evaluates each *exp* from left to right, returning the value of the first *exp* that is not *false*. Any remaining expressions are not evaluated. If all expressions evaluate to *false*, *false* is returned. If no arguments are passed to OR, *false* is returned.

Examples

```
(or (= 2 2) (> 2 1))                ⇒ true ;Value of first expression
(or (< 2 1) (= 2 2))                ⇒ true ;Value of second expression
(or #F #F #F)                       ⇒ false
(or (memq 'b '(a b c)) (/ 3 0))     ⇒ (b c) ;Note that division by
                                            ;zero did not occur.
(or)                                ⇒ false
```

OUTPUT-PORT

Fluid Variable

OUTPUT-PORT defines the current default output port of the system.

Format	(FLUID OUTPUT-PORT)
Explanation	This fluid variable is used by functions such as DISPLAY, WRITE, and WRITE-CHAR, which are defined to use the current default output port. The initial value of the variable is set to the console. You can redefine the current default output port by rebinding OUTPUT-PORT. The procedure WITH-OUTPUT-TO-FILE makes the redefinition automatically for output statements within its body. The procedure SCHEME-RESET resets OUTPUT-PORT to the current value of STANDARD-OUTPUT. The procedure RESET has no effect on OUTPUT-PORT.

Examples

```
; The following is typed into the console window
(begin
  (define w (make-window "Window" #T))
    (window-set-size! w 10 35)
    (window-set-position! w 10 40)
    (window-clear w)
    (set-fluid! input-port w)
    (set-fluid! output-port w))

; The remaining forms are typed into the new window
(eq? (current-output-port) w)         ⇒ true
                                      ; verify ports are the same
(display "Hi there")                  ⇒ unspecified value
                                      ; (displays the string in window)
(display "Hi there" 'console)         ⇒ unspecified value
                                      ; (displays the string in window)
(reset)                               ; reinitializes the top level but
                                        stays in this window
(scheme-reset)                        ; resets Scheme; includes setting
                                        default ports back to console
                                        window
```

OUTPUT-PORT?

Procedure

OUTPUT-PORT? determines if its argument is an output port.

Format	(OUTPUT-PORT? *obj*)
Parameter	*obj* — Any Scheme object
Explanation	OUTPUT-PORT? returns *true* if *obj* is an output port and *false,* otherwise. To create an output port for a file, use CALL-WITH-OUTPUT-FILE, OPEN-EXTEND-FILE, or OPEN-OUTPUT-FILE.

Examples

```
(define p1 (open-output-file "temp.s"))   ⟹ unspecified value
(output-port? p1)                          ⟹ true
(output-port? (current-output-port))       ⟹ true
(output-port? 5)                           ⟹ false
```

#\PAGE

#\PAGE represents the ASCII form feed character.

Format   #\PAGE

Explanation   #\PAGE is the character object representing a form feed. When this object is printed to a port, the ASCII character for form feed (12_{10}) is sent to that port. For instance, when this character occurs in a file and that file is later printed, the printer prints at the beginning of the next page any characters after the form feed.

Examples
```
(define port
   (open-output-file "foo.bar"))    ⟹ unspecified value
(display "foo" port)                ⟹ unspecified value
(display #\page port)               ⟹ unspecified value
(display "bar" port)                ⟹ unspecified value
(close-output-port port)            ⟹ unspecified value
```

When foo.bar is printed to a printer, "foo" prints at the top of the first page and "bar" prints at the top of the next page.

PAIR?

Procedure

PAIR? indicates whether its argument is a pair.

Format   (PAIR? *obj*)

Parameter   *obj* — Any Scheme object

Explanation   PAIR? returns *true* if *obj* is a pair and *false*, otherwise.

Examples
```
(pair? '(a . b))        ⟹ true
(pair? '(a b c))        ⟹ true
(pair? '())             ⟹ false
(pair? (vector 'a 'b))  ⟹ false
```

PCS-DEBUG-MODE   *Variable*

PCS-DEBUG-MODE enables and disables debug mode.

Format	PCS-DEBUG-MODE
Explanation	PCS-DEBUG-MODE is a compile-time variable that enables debug mode when set to *true* and disables debug mode, otherwise. If an expression is compiled or evaluated with PCS-DEBUG-MODE set to *true,* debugging information is produced and stored with the compiled object code.

PCS-DEBUG-MODE is set initially to *false*, thus disabling debug mode. Note that enabling debug mode makes more information available at runtime at the expense of execution speed.

PCS-DEBUG-MODE is specific to PC Scheme.

PCS-INTEGRATE-DEFINE   *Variable*

PCS-INTEGRATE-DEFINE controls the compiler interpretation of DEFINE, when used to define procedure objects.

Format	PCS-INTEGRATE-DEFINE
Explanation	The defining form (DEFINE (*name var* ...) *exp*[1] ...) is an abbreviated notation that permits a concise definition of procedure objects. When PCS-INTEGRATE-DEFINE is *true*, the compiler will interpret it as if it were written

(DEFINE *name* (NAMED-LAMBDA (*name var* ...) *exp*[1] ...))

otherwise it will be interpreted as specified in the *Revised[3] Scheme Report* as

(DEFINE *name* (LAMBDA (*var* ...) *exp*[1] ...)).

The default value for PCS-INTEGRATE-DEFINE is *true*.

PCS-INTEGRATE-INTEGRABLES   *Variable*

PCS-INTEGRATE-INTEGRABLES controls whether the values of integrable variables are integrated during compilation.

Format	PCS-INTEGRATE-INTEGRABLES

Explanation	If PCS-INTEGRATE-INTEGRABLES is *true*, the compiler integrates (compiles in-line) the values of variables defined with DEFINE-INTEGRABLE. Otherwise, the compiler sets up a procedure call for each of the variables. PCS-INTEGRATE-INTEGRABLES is set originally to *true*.

PCS-INTEGRATE-INTEGRABLES is specific to PC Scheme.

PCS-INTEGRATE-PRIMITIVES   *Variable*

PCS-INTEGRATE-PRIMITIVES controls the integration of primitives during compilation.

Format	PCS-INTEGRATE-PRIMITIVES
Explanation	If PCS-INTEGRATE-PRIMITIVES is *true*, the compiler integrates (compiles in-line) primitives like + and CAR; otherwise, the compiler sets up a procedure call for each primitive. PCS-INTEGRATE-PRIMITIVES is set originally to *true*.

PCS-INTEGRATE-PRIMITIVES is specific to PC Scheme.

PCS-INTEGRATE-T-AND-NIL   *Variable*

PCS-INTEGRATE-T-AND-NIL controls whether the identifiers T and NIL are constants or variables.

Format	PCS-INTEGRATE-T-AND-NIL
Explanation	If PCS-INTEGRATE-T-AND-NIL is *true*, T and NIL are considered to be identical to the constants #T and #F, respectively. Otherwise, T and NIL are considered to be variables whose original values are the constants #T and #F, respectively. PCS-INTEGRATE-T-NIL is set originally to *true*.

PCS-INTEGRATE-T-AND-NIL is specific to PC Scheme.

PI   *Variable*

PI is the ratio of a circle's circumference to its diameter.

Format	PI
Explanation	PI is the ratio of a circle's circumference to its diameter.

Example	pi	⇒ 3.14159265358979
	(cos pi)	⇒ −1.
	(tan (/ pi 4))	⇒ 1.

POINT-COLOR *Procedure*

POINT-COLOR returns a point's color value.

Format	(POINT-COLOR)
Parameters	None
Explanation	POINT-COLOR returns an integer value that represents the color of the point at the current graphics pen position. For information on valid colors, see the *PC Scheme User's Guide — Student Edition*.

PORT? *Procedure*

PORT? determines if an object is a port.

Format	(PORT? *obj*)
Parameter	*obj* — Any Scheme object
Explanation	PORT? returns *true* if *obj* is a port and *false,* otherwise.

Window objects are represented by port data objects.

To create a port for a file, use OPEN-EXTEND-FILE, OPEN-INPUT-FILE, or OPEN-OUTPUT-FILE. To create a port to read from a string, use OPEN-INPUT-STRING.

Examples

```
(define wastebasket
    (open-output-file "nul"))          ⇒ unspecified value
(port? 'port)                          ⇒ false
(port? "nul")                          ⇒ false
(port? wastebasket)                    ⇒ true
(port? (current-input-port))           ⇒ true
```

POSITION-PEN

POSITION-PEN moves the graphics pen to a different point on the screen.

Format	(POSITION-PEN *x* *y*)
Parameters	*x* — The screen x-coordinate (horizontal axis)
	y — The screen y-coordinate (vertical axis)
Explanation	POSITION-PEN sets the current pen position to the point specified by the *x*- and *y*-coordinates. The pen, which is an invisible pointer, is initially at position (0,0). An unspecified value is returned.
	To move the pen and draw a line between the starting and ending points, use DRAW-LINE-TO. To draw a point without moving the pen, use DRAW-POINT. For information on the value of the *x*- and *y*-coordinates, see the *PC Scheme User's Guide — Student Edition*.

POSITIVE?

POSITIVE? determines whether a number is greater than zero.

Format	(POSITIVE? *num*)
Parameter	*num* — Any Scheme number
Explanation	POSITIVE? returns *true* if *num* is greater than zero and *false*, otherwise.
Examples	(positive? 5) ⟹ *true*
	(positive? −5.53) ⟹ *false*
	(positive? 4.1) ⟹ *true*
	(positive? 0) ⟹ *false*
	(positive? 'foo) ⟹ *error*

PP   *Procedure*

PP prints an expression, indenting as necessary to show the structure.

Format   (PP *exp* {*port* {*width*}})

Parameters   *exp* — The value to be printed.

                        port — An optional argument that specifies the output port to which *exp* is output. If *port* is *false*, the current output is used.

                        width — An optional argument that gives the number of characters the pretty printer prints on a line. If *width* is not specified, the default value is the smaller of 72 and the line length of either *port* or the current output port if *port* is *false*. Note that *width* can be specified only if *port* is specified.

Explanation   PP is the pretty printer, which prints the value of *exp* in a format that shows its structure clearly. The procedure prints *exp* to the specified *port* using the line length specified by *width*. This procedure typically is used to print lists. An unspecified value is returned.

                        Procedures defined in debug mode (see PCS-DEBUG-MODE) have their defining source expression stored with the procedure object. Therefore, PP can pretty print such procedures in source form.

Examples   ```
(set! pcs-debug-mode #T)   ⇒ unspecified value

(define (fact n)
  (if (< n 2)
      1
      (* n (fact (-1+ n))))))   ⇒ unspecified value

(pp fact)
#<PROCEDURE FACT>=
(lambda (n)
  (if (< n 2)
      1
      (* n (fact (-1+ n)))))))   ⇒ unspecified value
```
```

PRIN1, PRINC   *Procedure*

These procedures print an expression to a port.

Format	(PRIN1 *exp* {*port*})
	(PRINC *exp* {*port*})
Parameters	*exp* — Any Scheme expression. This argument is evaluated and then its value is printed.
	port — An optional argument that specifies the output port.
Explanation	These procedures print the value of *exp* to either *port* or the current output port if *port* is not specified. An unspecified value is returned. PRIN1 and PRINC work differently, as explained here.

■ PRIN1 is an alternate name for WRITE. It is intended to be used for subsequent machine readability. Strings that are written are enclosed in double quotes, and special characters (backslash and double quotes) within the string are escaped by backslashes. PRIN1 slashifies special characters in symbols.

■ PRINC is an alternate name for DISPLAY. It typically is used to produce human readable output. Strings that are written are not enclosed in double quotes, and no characters are escaped within those strings. PRINC does not slashify special characters in symbols.

Examples

```
(prin1 (+ 1 2))
3                                               ⇒ unspecified value

(princ (+ 1 2))
3                                               ⇒ unspecified value

(prin1 "Hi there.")
"Hi there."                                     ⇒ unspecified value

(princ "Hi there.")
Hi there.                                       ⇒ unspecified value

(prin1 '|abc| )
|abc|                                           ⇒ unspecified value

(princ '|abc| )
abc                                             ⇒ unspecified value
```

PRINT

PRINT prints an expression to the next line on an output port.

Format	(PRINT *exp* {*port*})
Parameters	*exp* — Any Scheme expression. This argument is evaluated and then its value is printed.
	port — An optional argument that specifies the output port.
Explanation	PRINT prints the value of *exp* (using WRITE) to either *port* or the current output port if *port* is not specified. The value is preceded by an end-of-line character sequence and is followed by a space. An unspecified value is returned.
Examples	`(begin (display "Here is 42 on a newline:")`
	`       (print "42")`
	`       (display "Notice the space after 42."))`
	Here is 42 on a newline:
	"42" Notice the space after 42. ⟹ *unspecified value*

PRINT-LENGTH

PRINT-LENGTH returns the number of characters needed to print a value.

Format	(PRINT-LENGTH *obj*)
Parameter	*obj* — Any Scheme object
Explanation	PRINT-LENGTH returns the number of characters needed by DISPLAY to print *obj*. This procedure is useful if you are developing your own formatting procedure.
Examples	`(print-length 42)` ⟹ 2
	`(print-length "a b c")` ⟹ 5
	`(print-length '|12 qv@,|)` ⟹ 7
	`(print-length +)` ⟹ 14
	`(print +)`
	#<PROCEDURE +> ⟹ *unspecified value*

PROC   *Procedure*

PROC pretty prints the procedure in which a debugging breakpoint has occurred.

Format	(*PROC*)
Explanation	*PROC* pretty prints the source of the procedure in progress when a break occurs. An unspecified value is returned. This procedure is meaningful only with PCS-DEBUG-MODE on and when a breakpoint is entered by the BREAK, BREAK-BOTH, BREAK-ENTRY, or BREAK-EXIT procedures.
Example	Debug mode is turned on and a procedure named FIB is defined.

```
(set! pcs-debug-mode #T)                    ⇒ unspecified value

(define fib
  (lambda (n)
    (if (< n 2) 1
        (+ (fib (-1+ n))
           (fib (- n 2)))))))            ⇒ unspecified value
```

Then breakpoints for entry and exit are set using BREAK-BOTH.

```
(break-both fib)                            ⇒ unspecified value
```

Next, the FIB procedure is called, and the entry breakpoint is entered. When the breakpoint prompt ([Inspect]) is displayed, the *PROC* procedure is evaluated and the FIB procedure is returned. Then press CTRL-G to continue FIB, and the exit breakpoint is entered. When the breakpoint prompt is displayed, the *PROC* procedure is evaluated again and the FIB procedure is returned.

```
(fib 1)
 [BKPT encountered!] BREAK-EXIT
 ((#<PROCEDURE fib> 1) -> 1)
[Inspect]  (Note: Press CTRL-V) Value of:  (*proc*)
 #<PROCEDURE FIB> =
(lambda (n)
  (if (< n 2) 1
      (+ (fib (-1+ n))
         (fib (- n 2)))))))            ⇒ unspecified value
```

PROC? *Procedure*

PROC? determines if its argument is a procedure or continuation.

Format	(PROC? *obj*)
Parameter	*obj* — Any Scheme object
Explanation	PROC? returns *true* if *obj* is a procedure or continuation and *false*, otherwise. Note that an object is a continuation if PROC? returns *true* and CLOSURE? returns *false*.

See also CLOSURE? and CONTINUATION?.

Examples

```
(proc? car)                     ⇒ true
(proc? +)                       ⇒ true
(proc? ´cdr)                    ⇒ false
(proc? (lambda (x) x))          ⇒ true

(define here
  (call-with-current-continuation
    (lambda (k) k)))            ⇒ unspecified value
(proc? here)                    ⇒ true
```

PROCEDURE? *Procedure*

PROCEDURE? determines if its argument is a procedure.

Format	(PROCEDURE? *obj*)
Parameters	*obj* — Any Scheme object
Explanation	PROCEDURE? returns *true* if *obj* is a procedure and *false*, otherwise. See also PROC?, CLOSURE?, and CONTINUATION?.

Examples

```
(procedure? car)               ⇒ true
(procedure? ´car)              ⇒ false
(procedure? (Lambda(x) x)))    ⇒ true
```

PROCEDURE-ENVIRONMENT   *Procedure*

PROCEDURE-ENVIRONMENT accesses the environment closed over by a procedure.

Format	(PROCEDURE-ENVIRONMENT *procedure*)
Parameter	*procedure* — A Scheme procedure
Explanation	PROCEDURE-ENVIRONMENT returns the environment closed over by *procedure*. It also may access the environment closed over by a delayed object (created using DELAY). For more information on delayed objects, see DELAY.

Examples

```
(define proc
  (let ((a 1) (b 2))
    (lambda (x
      (+ a b x))))                    ⟹ unspecified value

(define env
  (procedure-environment proc))       ⟹ unspecified value

(environment-bindings env)            ⟹ ((a . 1) (b . 2))
```

PROPLIST   *Procedure*

PROPLIST returns the property list of a symbol.

Format	(PROPLIST *name*)
Parameter	*name* — A symbol
Explanation	PROPLIST returns the property list associated with *name*. If *name* is not associated with a property list, the empty list is returned.

The list returned by PROPLIST should not be modified using SET-CAR!, SET-CDR!, and so on, since this could affect the implementation of property lists adversely.

The property list associated with *name* is a list containing the currently defined properties for *name* and the values associated with each property. Both *name* and the properties are symbols.

See also GETPROP, PUTPROP, and REMPROP.

Examples

;Assume the symbol BLUE-WHALE has an empty property list.

```
(proplist 'blue-whale)                  ⟹ ()
(define sea 'ocean)                      ⟹ unspecified value
(putprop 'blue-whale 'krill 'eats)       ⟹ unspecified value
(putprop 'blue-whale sea 'dwells-in)     ⟹ unspecified value
(proplist 'blue-whale)                   ⟹ (DWELLS-IN OCEAN
                                             EATS KRILL)
```

PUTPROP   *Procedure*

PUTPROP adds a value to the property list of a symbol.

Format	(PUTPROP *name val prop*)
Parameters	*name* — A symbol
	val — The value to be added to the symbol's property list
	prop — A symbol identifying the property name
Explanation	PUTPROP adds the value of *val* to the *name* property list under the property *prop*. If *prop* already exists, the new value replaces the previous value. An unspecified value is returned.
	See related procedures GETPROP, PROPLIST, and REMPROP.

Examples

;Assume the symbol BLUE-WHALE has an empty property list.

```
(proplist 'blue-whale)                  ⟹ ()
(define sea 'ocean)                      ⟹ unspecified value
(putprop 'blue-whale 'krill 'eats)       ⟹ unspecified value
(putprop 'blue-whale sea 'dwells-in)     ⟹ unspecified value
(proplist 'blue-whale)                   ⟹ (DWELLS-IN OCEAN
                                             EATS KRILL)

(putprop 'blue-whale 'fish 'eats)        ⟹ unspecified value
(proplist ' blue-whale)                  ⟹ (DWELLS-IN OCEAN
                                             EATS FISH)
```

QUASIQUOTE   *Special Form*

QUASIQUOTE contructs a list, even if only part of the desired structure is known in advance.

Format	(QUASIQUOTE *pattern*) `pattern
Parameters	*pattern* — Any Scheme object, but usually a list or vector

---

Explanation	QUASIQUOTE, like QUOTE, returns its argument unevaluated if no commas or the special forms UNQUOTE or UNQUOTE-SPLICING appear within the *pattern*.

The expression (QUASIQUOTE *pattern*) may be abbreviated as '*pattern*. The two notations are identical in all respects.

If a comma appears within *pattern,* the expression following the comma is evaluated, and its result is inserted into the structure instead of the comma and the expression. The notation (UNQUOTE *expression*) is an alternate notation for ,*expression* and the two are identical in all respects.

If an at-sign (@) immediately follows a comma, the expression after the at-sign must evaluate to a list. The opening and closing parenthesis of the list are stripped away, and the elements of the list are inserted in place of the comma/at-sign/expression sequence. The notation (UNQUOTE-SPLICING *expression*) is an alternate notation for ,@*expression* and the two are identical in all respects.

UNQUOTE (,) and UNQUOTE-SPLICING (,@) are only valid within quasiquote expressions.

Quasiquote forms may be nested. Substitutions are made only for unquoted components appearing at the same nesting level as the outermost quasiquote. The nesting level increases by one inside each successive quasiquotation, and decreases by one inside each unquotation.

Examples

```
`(a ,(+ 2 3) ,@(map 1+ '(4 5 6)) b)         ⇒ (A 3 5 6 7 B)
(QUASIQUOTE
   (a
    (UNQUOTE (+ 2 3))
    (UNQUOTE-SPLICING (map 1+ '(4 5 6)))
    b))                                      ⇒ (A 3 5 6 7 B)
`#(10 5 ,(sqrt 4) ,@(map sqrt '(16 9)) 8)  ⇒ (10 5 2 4 3 8)

`(a `(b ,(+ 1 2) ,(foo ,(+ 1 3) d) e) f)   ⇒ (a '(b .(+ 1 2)
                                               ,(foo 4 d) e) f)


(macro first
   (lambda (x)
     `(car ,(cadr x))))                     ⇒ unspecified value
(first '(a b c))                            ⇒ A
(car '(a b c))                              ⇒ A
```

QUOTE
Special Form

QUOTE returns its argument unevaluated.

Format	(QUOTE *obj*) '*obj*
Parameter	*obj* — Any Scheme object
Explanation	QUOTE returns its argument unevaluated. This notation is used to include literal constants in Scheme code. The expression (QUOTE *obj*) may be abbreviated as '*obj*. The two notations are equivalent in all respects.

Examples

(quote a)	⟹ A
(quote #(a b c))	⟹ #(A B C)
(quote (+ 1 2))	⟹ (+ 1 2)
'a	⟹ A
'#(a b c)	⟹ #(A B C)
'(+ 1 2)	⟹ (+ 1 2)
'(quote a)	⟹ (QUOTE A)
''a	⟹ (QUOTE A)
(string=? "abc" '"abc")	⟹ *true*
(eq? #T '#T)	⟹ *true*
(=? 145932 '145932)	⟹ *true*

QUOTIENT
Procedure

QUOTIENT divides two integers and returns the integer quotient.

Format	(QUOTIENT *int₁* *int₂*)
Parameters	*int₁* — An integer that is the dividend
	int₂ — An integer that is the divisor
Explanation	QUOTIENT divides *int₁* by *int₂* and returns the integer quotient. If *int₂* is zero, an error results.
	To find the remainder, use MODULO or REMAINDER.

Examples

(quotient 10 2)	⟹ 5
(quotient −5 −3)	⟹ 1
(quotient 0 3)	⟹ 0
(quotient 5 −2)	⟹ −2

RANDOM *Procedure*

RANDOM returns a pseudo-random integer.

Format	(RANDOM *num*)
Parameter	*num* — A positive integer
Explanation	RANDOM returns a pseudo-random integer between zero and *num* - 1, inclusive.

Examples

```
(define roll-dice
  (lambda ()
    (let ((die1 (1+ (random 6)))
          (die2 (1+ (random 6))))
      (writeln "You rolled a " die1
        " and a " die2)
      (+ die1 die2))))                   ⟹ unspecified value

(roll-dice)
You rolled a 3 and a 2                   ⟹ 5
(roll-dice)
You rolled a 5 and a 6                   ⟹ 11
```

RANDOMIZE *Procedure*

RANDOMIZE seeds the random number generator.

Format	(RANDOMIZE *number*)
Parameters	*number* — Any Scheme number such that -2^{32} < number < 2^{32}

Explanation PC Scheme starts each session with the random number generator initialized to a preset seed value, so the sequence of pseudo-random numbers that RANDOM produces will be the same each time. RANDOMIZE is used to change the seed value so different sequences are generated.

Either integer or floating-point numbers can be used as seed values. Any given seed value produces a set sequence of random numbers, so two uses of the same seed value will generate the same sequence each time. This repeatability is useful while testing code that involves random numbers.

The number 0 is not used as a seed; instead, the seed value is derived from the time-of-day clock. Therefore, two uses of 0 as a seed value are unlikely to generate the same sequence. A finished program that uses random numbers will probably want to use the 0 seed so that the seed value itself is randomly initialized from the clock.

Numbers outside the specified range are mapped into the 0 seed. An unspecified value is returned.

Examples

This initial set of examples uses seed values of 39583 and 39583.7254, respectively. Each one generates its own sequence of numbers. When the seed value is repeated, so is its sequence.

```
(randomize 39583)       ⟹ unspecified value
(random 100)            ⟹ 76
(random 100)            ⟹ 25
(randomize 39583.7254)  ⟹ unspecified value
(random 100)            ⟹ 72
(random 100)            ⟹ 87
(randomize 39583)       ⟹ unspecified value
(random 100)            ⟹ 76
(random 100)            ⟹ 25
```

The following examples are seeded from the time-of-day clock, so the sequences are not repeatable.

```
(randomize 0)             ⟹ unspecified value
(random 100)              ⟹ 58
(random 100)              ⟹ 23
(randomize 0)             ⟹ unspecified value
(random 100)              ⟹ 80
(random 100)              ⟹ 45
(randomize (- (expt 2 33)))  ⟹ unspecified value
(random 100)              ⟹ 15
(random 100)              ⟹ 22
```

RATIONAL?   *Procedure*

RATIONAL? determines whether its argument is a rational number.

Format   (RATIONAL? obj)

Parameter   *obj* — Any Scheme number

Explanation   RATIONAL? returns *true* if *obj* is a rational number and *false*, otherwise. In PC Scheme, rational numbers have not been implemented; therefore, RATIONAL? returns *true* if *obj* is an integer and *false*, otherwise.

Examples
```
(rational? 42)       ⟹ true
(rational? -4.39)    ⟹ false
(rational? 0)        ⟹ true
(rational? '(1 2 3)) ⟹ false
(rational? "1")      ⟹ false
```

READ   *Procedure*

READ reads Scheme data objects.

Format	(READ {*port*})
Parameter	*port* — A port (an optional argument)
Explanation	READ reads and returns a Scheme data object from *port*. If *port* is not specified, the procedure reads from the current input port. When the end of the file is reached, an end-of-file object is returned. If the end of the file is reached while reading a list, READ returns the list as if a right parenthesis was read for each left parenthesis unmatched at the time.
	To test for end-of-file objects returned by READ, use EOF-OBJECT?.
Examples	Assume that the file STUFF.S on the default disk drive consists of the following lines:

A FEW ATOMS
AND ((A LIST) (OF LISTS))

Examples of the use of READ are as follows:

```
(define p (open-input-file "stuff.s")) ⟹ unspecified value
(read p)                               ⟹ A
(read p)                               ⟹ FEW
(flush-input p)                        ⟹ unspecified value
(read p)                               ⟹ AND
(read p)                               ⟹((A LIST) (OF LISTS))
(read p)                               ⟹ end-of-file
```

READ-ATOM   *Procedure*

READ-ATOM reads a Scheme atom.

Format	(READ-ATOM {*port*})
Parameter	*port* — A port (an optional argument)
Explanation	READ-ATOM reads and returns an atom from *port*. If *port* is not specified, the procedure reads from the current input port. If the upcoming characters represent a sequence that is special to READ, such as an unescaped left parenthesis or unescaped ',@' pair, READ-ATOM distinguishes these sequences by returning the symbol formed from those characters in a list of one element.

When the end of the file is reached, an end-of-file object is returned. To test for end-of-file objects returned by READ-ATOM, use EOF-OBJECT?.

Examples   Assume that the file STUFF.S on the default disk drive consists of the following lines:

A FEW ATOMS
AND ((A LIST) (OF LISTS))

Examples of the use of READ-ATOM are as follows:

```
(define p (open-input-file "stuff.s"))    ⇒ unspecified value
(read-atom p)                             ⇒ A
(flush-input p)                           ⇒ unspecified value
(read-atom p)                             ⇒ AND
(read-atom p)                             ⇒ (|(|)
(read p)                                  ⇒ (A LIST)
(read p)                                  ⇒ (OF LISTS)
(read-atom p)                             ⇒ (|)|)
(read-atom p)                             ⇒ end-of-file
```

READ-CHAR   *Procedure*

READ-CHAR reads a character.

Format   (READ-CHAR {*port*})

Parameter   *port* — A port (an optional argument)

Explanation   READ-CHAR reads and returns a character from *port*. If *port* is not specified, the procedure reads from the current input port. If the port is the console or a window, the character is not echoed.

Examples   Assume that the file STUFF.S on the default disk drive consists of the following lines:

A FEW ATOMS
AND ((A LIST) (OF LISTS))

Examples of the use of READ-CHAR are as follows:

```
(define p (open-input-file "stuff.s"))    ⇒ unspecified value
(read-char p)                             ⇒ #\A
(read-char p)                             ⇒ #\SPACE
(flush-input p)                           ⇒ unspecified value
(read p)                                  ⇒ AND
(read-char p)                             ⇒ #\SPACE
(read-char p)                             ⇒ #\(
```

READ-LINE   *Procedure*

READ-LINE reads a line of characters.

Format	(READ-LINE {*port*})
Parameter	*port* — A port (an optional argument)
Explanation	READ-LINE reads a sequence of characters from *port*, starting at the current position and running up to the next end-of-line or end-of-file, and returns it as a *string*. If *port* is not specified, the procedure reads from the current input port. If the port is the console or a window, the character is not echoed. When the end of the file is reached, an end-of-file object is returned.
	To test for end-of-file objects returned by READ-LINE, use EOF-OBJECT?.
Examples	Assume that the file STUFF.S on the default disk drive consists of the following lines:

A FEW ATOMS
AND ((A LIST) (OF LISTS))

Examples of the use of READ-LINE are as follows:

```
(define p (open-input-file "stuff.s"))  ⟹ unspecified value
(read-line p)                           ⟹ "A FEW ATOMS"
(read p)                                ⟹ AND
(read-char p)                           ⟹ #\SPACE
(read-char p)                           ⟹ #\(
(read-line p)                           ⟹"(A LIST)
                                              (OF LISTS))"
(read p)                                ⟹ #!EOF
```

REAL?   *Procedure*

REAL? determines whether its argument is a real number (not complex).

Format	(REAL? *obj*)
Parameter	*obj* — Any Scheme object
Explanation	REAL? returns *true* if *obj* is a real number and *false*, otherwise. In PC Scheme, real numbers have not been implemented; therefore, REAL? returns *true* if *obj* is any Scheme number and *false*, otherwise.

Examples	(real? 42)	⇒ *true*
	(real? -4.39)	⇒ *true*
	(real? 0)	⇒ *true*
	(real? '(1 2 3))	⇒ *false*
	(real? "1")	⇒ *false*
	(real? #\1)	⇒ *false*

REC   *Special Form*

REC allows a self-recursive expression to refer to itself independently of its binding.

Format	(REC *var exp*)
Parameters	*var* — A scheme identifier
	exp — Any Scheme expression
Explanation	REC is useful for defining recursive procedures. This special form binds *var* locally to *exp* and returns the value of *exp*. The value returned by REC is the value of *exp*. REC is equivalent to the following:

(LETREC ((*var exp*)) *var*)

If *exp* is a procedure, then REC is equivalent to NAMED-LAMBDA.

Examples The need for REC is shown in this first set of examples. Clearly, the occurrence of FOO within the definition of the procedure FOO was intended to be self-recursive; however, because of the renaming, the function returning SOMETHING-ELSE is actually used. REC prevents this problem and also allows slightly better code to be compiled.

```
(define foo
  (lambda (arg)
    (if (zero? arg)
  1
        (* 2 (foo (-1+ arg))))))) ⇒ unspecified value
(define bar foo)                  ⇒ unspecified value
(bar 4)                           ⇒ 16
(set! foo (lambda (arg) 'something-else)) ⇒ unspecified value
(bar 4)                           ⇒ error
```

In the next example, REC is used for self-recursion. Therefore, the rebinding of FOO does not affect the recursion calls as it does in the previous example.

```
(define foo
  (rec foo
    (lambda (arg)
      (if (zero? arg)
1        (* 2 (foo (-1+ arg)))))))     ⟹ unspecified value
(define bar foo)                        ⟹ unspecified value
(bar 4)                                 ⟹ 16
(set! foo (lambda (arg) 'something-else)) ⟹ unspecified value
(bar 4)                                 ⟹ 16
```

REMAINDER   *Procedure*

REMAINDER divides two integers and returns the remainder.

Format	(REMAINDER int_1 int_2)
Parameters	int_1 — An integer that is the dividend
	int_2 — An integer that is the divisor
Explanation	REMAINDER divides int_1 by int_2 and returns the remainder. If int_2 is zero, a divide-by-zero error is signalled. The value returned by REMAINDER always has the sign of int_1 .
	Note that MODULO and REMAINDER differ only when either the dividend or the divisor is negative. MODULO always has the sign of the divisor, and REMAINDER always has the sign of the dividend.
	To find the integer quotient, use QUOTIENT.
Examples	(remainder 13 4) ⟹ 1
	(remainder -13 4) ⟹ -1
	(remainder 13 -4) ⟹ 1
	(remainder -13 -4) ⟹ -1

REMPROP

REMPROP deletes a property from the property list of a symbol.

Format	(REMPROP *name prop*)
Parameters	*name* — A symbol with an associated property list
	prop — A symbol identifying the property to be removed from the specified property list
Explanation	REMPROP deletes *prop* and any value associated with it from *name*. It returns an unspecified value.
	See related procedures GETPROP, PROPLIST, and PUTPROP.

Examples

```
(putprop 'coffee 'yes 'caffeine?)          ⇒ unspecified value
(getprop 'coffee 'caffeine?)               ⇒ YES
(define decaffeinate
   (lambda (sym) (remprop sym 'caffeine?)))  ⇒ unspecified value
(decaffeinate 'coffee)                     ⇒ unspecified value
(getprop 'coffee 'caffeine?)               ⇒ false
```

RENAME-CLASS

RENAME-CLASS renames a SCOOPS class.

Format	(RENAME-CLASS (*class new-name*))
Parameters	*class* — A SCOOPS class
	new-name — The new name for the SCOOPS class
Explanation	RENAME-CLASS renames *class* as *new-name*. An unspecified value is returned.
Examples	Assume that the class employees exists (as shown in the example for DEFINE-CLASS).

```
(rename-class (employees slaves))    ⇒ unspecified value
```

RESET   *Procedure*

RESET returns the system to the currently defined top-level read-eval-print loop.

Format	(RESET)
Parameters	None
Explanation	RESET aborts further evaluation of the pending forms and restarts the system by beginning execution of the top-level read-eval-print loop that is bound to the fluid identifier SCHEME-TOP-LEVEL. The fluid variables INPUT-PORT and OUTPUT-PORT are not rebound. RESET does not affect the global environment.
	For a discussion of the top level, refer to the description of the fluid variable SCHEME-TOP-LEVEL.

Examples

```
(define simple-read-eval-print-loop
  (named-lambda (loop)
    (newline)
    (write '==>)
    (let ((ans (eval (read))))
      (write ans)
      (loop))))                               ⇒ unspecified value

(fluid-let ((scheme-top-level simple-read-eval-print-loop))
  (reset))                                    ⇒ unspecified value
==> (car '(a b c))                            ⇒ A

==> (scheme-reset)
[PCS-DEBUG-MODE is OFF]
[1]
```

RESET-SCHEME-TOP-LEVEL   *Procedure*

RESET-SCHEME-TOP-LEVEL binds the fluid identifier SCHEME-TOP-LEVEL to the system's top-level read-eval-print loop.

Format	(RESET-SCHEME-TOP-LEVEL)
Parameters	None
Explanation	RESET-SCHEME-TOP-LEVEL binds the fluid identifier SCHEME-TOP-LEVEL to the system's top-level read-eval-print loop. This procedure does not itself begin execution of the top level.

Refer to the description of the fluid variable SCHEME-TOP-LEVEL for a more complete discussion of the top level.

Examples
In the following example, the function new-top-level is defined. It saves the history list of the current top level and creates a continuation, assigned to the fluid variable q, that will exit the new top level. The RESET-SCHEME-TOP-LEVEL reassigns SCHEME-TOP-LEVEL from its tentative nil value to the system's top level, and RESET activates the new top level.

```
(define (new-top-level)
  (print "((fluid q)) quits new top level")
  (let ((prev-history (getprop '%pcs-stl-history
        %pcs-stl-history)))
    (call/cc
      (lambda (k)
        (fluid-let ((scheme-top-level nil)
                    (q lambda () (k nil))))
          (reset-scheme-top-level)
          (reset))))
    (putprop '%pcs-stl-history prev-history %pcs-stl-
        history)
    #t))                                      ⇒ unspecified value


(cdr '(a b c))                                ⇒ (b c)
(new-top-level)                               ⇒unspecified value
```

The new top level is a new instantiation of the system top level. Note that the system prompt has started over at the value of [1].

"((fluid q)) quits new top level"
[PCS-DEBUG-MODE is OFF]
```
(cdr '(a b c))                                ⇒ (b c)
```

Finally, we exit the new top level by invoking the continuation. The continuation takes you back to just after the CALL/CC. The PUTPROP restores the history list to its former state, and the system prompt counter continues from where it was interrupted.

```
((fluid q))                                   ⇒ #T
```

RESULT   *Procedure*

RESULT returns the value returned by the procedure in which a debugging breakpoint has occurred.

Format   (*RESULT*)

Explanation   *RESULT* returns the result about to be returned by the procedure in progress when a break occurs. This procedure is meaningful only when a breakpoint is entered by the BREAK-BOTH (exit only) or BREAK-EXIT procedures.

Examples   A procedure, named FIB, is defined as follows:

```
(define fib
  (lambda (n)
    (if (< n 2) 1
        (+ (fib (-1+ n))
           (fib (- n 2))))))         ⟹ unspecified value
```

Then an exit breakpoint is set using BREAK-EXIT, as follows:

```
(break-exit fib)                     ⟹ unspecified value
```

The FIB procedure is called, and a breakpoint is entered when FIB is exited. When the breakpoint prompt ([Inspect]) is displayed, the *RESULT* procedure is evaluated; it returns the value being returned by FIB.

```
(fib 4)
  [BKPT encountered!] BREAK-EXIT
  ((#<PROCEDURE fib> 1) -> 1)
[Inspect]  (Note: Press CTRL–V) Value of: (*result*)  ⟹ 1
```

#\RETURN   *Character Object*

#\RETURN represents the ASCII carriage return character.

Format   #\RETURN

Explanation   #\RETURN is the character object representing a carriage return. When this object is printed to a port, the ASCII character for carriage return (13_{10}) is sent to that port. For instance, when this character is sent to the screen with WRITE-CHAR, DISPLAY, or PRINC, the cursor moves to the beginning of a new line.

If #\RETURN is sent to a printer, the line printed just before #\RETURN is overwritten by the line printed just after #\RETURN.

#\RETURN differs from #\NEWLINE in that #\NEWLINE is a single character that outputs the appropriate end-of-line sequence, but #\RETURN always outputs the ASCII carriage return character.

Examples
```
(writeln "foo" #\return "bar")
foo
bar                                  ⟹ unspecified value
```

REVERSE

Procedure

REVERSE returns a list containing the elements of its arguments in reverse order.

Format	(REVERSE *list*)
Parameter	*list* — A proper list
Explanation	REVERSE returns a proper list consisting of the elements of *list* in reverse order. The original list is not affected.
Examples	(reverse '(a b c))　　　　　　　⟹ (C B A) (reverse '(a (b c) d (e (f))))　⟹ ((E (F)) D (B C) A)

REVERSE!

Procedure

REVERSE! destructively reverses the order of the elements in a proper list.

Format	(REVERSE! *list*)
Parameter	*list* — A proper list
Explanation	REVERSE! destructively reverses *list* and returns a proper list consisting of the elements of *list* in reverse order.
Examples	(define x '(a b c))　⟹ *unspecified value* (reverse! x)　　　　 ⟹ (C B A) x　　　　　　　　　 ⟹ (A)

ROUND

Procedure

ROUND rounds a number to the closest integer.

Format	(ROUND *num*)
Parameter	*num* — A real number or integer
Explanation	ROUND returns the integer closest to *num*.

If *num* is positive, it is:

■ Rounded up for fractions greater than .5

■ Rounded to the nearest even integer for fractions equal to .5

■ Rounded down for fractions less than .5

If *num* is negative, it is:

■ Rounded down for fractions greater than .5

■ Rounded to the nearest even integer for fractions equal to .5

■ Rounded up for fractions less than .5

Examples		
(round 3.75)	⇒	4
(round 3.50)	⇒	4
(round 3.49)	⇒	3
(round -9.4)	⇒	-9

#\RUBOUT   *Character Object*

#\RUBOUT represents the ASCII delete character.

Format   #\RUBOUT

Explanation   #\RUBOUT is the character object representing a delete. When this object is printed to a port, the ASCII character for delete (63_{10}) is sent to that port.

Example   In the example that follows, #\RUBOUT maps into ⌂.

```
(writeln "foo" #\rubout "bar")
foo⌂bar                                        ⇒ unspecified value
```

RUNTIME   *Procedure*

RUNTIME returns the time of day as an integer value.

Format   (RUNTIME)

Parameters   None

Explanation	RUNTIME returns the time of day expressed as an integral number in some units of time. The units of time are implementation-dependent. PC Scheme uses hundredths of a second.
Example	The following example is a general timing special form:

```
(syntax (timer proc)
  (let ((start (runtime))
        (end 0))
     proc
     (set! end (runtime))
     (if (< end start) ;If true, timing went past midnight.
         (/ (+ (- (* 24 60 60 100) start) end) 100)
         (/ (- end start) 100))))          ⟹ unspecified value

(define (fact n)
  (if (< n 2) 1 (* n (fact (-1+ n))))))    ⟹ unspecified value

(timer (fact 100))                         ⟹ elapsed-time
```

SCHEME-RESET   *Procedure*

SCHEME-RESET unconditionally resets the system back to a known initial state.

Format	(SCHEME-RESET)
Parameters	None
Explanation	Execution of the pending forms is aborted. SCHEME-RESET resets the fluid environment to its initial state, without affecting the global lexical environment. The fluid variables INPUT-PORT and OUTPUT-PORT are rebound to the values of STANDARD-INPUT and STANDARD-OUTPUT, respectively, the fluid variable SCHEME-TOP-LEVEL is rebound to the system's top-level read-eval-print loop, and other fluid bindings are lost. Finally, the system's top level resumes execution.

Refer to the description of the fluid variable SCHEME-TOP-LEVEL for a more complete discussion of the top level. |
| **Examples** | |

```
(set-fluid! scheme-top-level
  (named-lambda (loop)
    (newline)
    (display "Your wish, sire? ")
    (write (eval (read)))
    (loop)))                               ⟹ unspecified value
```

Your wish, sire? (scheme-reset)
[PCS-DEBUG-MODE is OFF]
[1]

SCHEME-TOP-LEVEL

Fluid Variable

SCHEME-TOP-LEVEL is bound to the value of the top-level read-eval-print loop.

Format

(FLUID SCHEME-TOP-LEVEL)

Explanation

SCHEME-TOP-LEVEL is a fluid variable that is bound to the value of the top-level read-eval-print loop. The value is a procedure of no arguments. If the variable takes on any other kind of value, an error occurs whenever a RESET is called.

Since it is a variable, the value of SCHEME-TOP-LEVEL can be changed, thus allowing different top-level read-eval-print loops to be run.

The function bound to SCHEME-TOP-LEVEL can have its loop coded explicitly. Or the function can perform an action and return, in which case the system calls the value of SCHEME-TOP-LEVEL again, forcing the function to loop.

Rebinding SCHEME-TOP-LEVEL does not in itself make the new top level active, since the system must invoke the variable as a function. Two ways can be used to make the top level active. The first way is to set up a binding using the FLUID-LET or FLUID-LAMBDA procedures, and then call RESET. The second way is to use SET-FLUID! to replace the current binding, and then either call RESET or exit the current top-level function (letting the system invoke RESET for you).

To restore the system to its own top level, use RESET-SCHEME-TOP-LEVEL to change the binding of SCHEME-TOP-LEVEL to its original value, and then activate SCHEME-RESET as indicated in the previous paragraph. SCHEME-RESET can also be used, but it not only resets the top level, it reinitializes other parts of PC Scheme back to a known state, too.

Examples

The following is an example of a top level with an explicitly coded loop:

```
(define rep-with-loop
  (named-lambda (loop)
    (newline)
    (display '|rep-with-loop ==>|)
    (write (eval (read)))
      (loop)))                          ⟹ unspecified value

(fluid-let
  ((scheme-top-level rep-with-loop))
  (reset))

rep-with-loop ==>  (cdr '(a b c))            ⟹ (B C)


rep-with-loop ==>  (scheme-reset)

[PCS–DEBUG–MODE is OFF]
[1]
```

The following example shows a top level without an explicitly coded loop:

```
(define rep-without-loop
  (lambda ()
    (newline)
    (display '|rep-without-loop ==>|)
    (write (eval (read)))))        ⟹ unspecified value

(fluid-let
  ((scheme-top-level rep-without-loop))
  (reset))

rep-without-loop ==>  (cdr '(a b c))        ⟹ (B C)

rep-without-loop ==>  (scheme-reset)
```

[PCS-DEBUG-MODE is OFF]
[1]

SEND   *Special Form*

SEND sends a message to an object in a SCOOPS class.

Format   (SEND *object msg arg* ...)

Parameters   *object* — An instance of a SCOOPS class

                      msg — The name of the message to be sent

                      arg ... — The arguments to the method associated with the message

Explanation   SEND sends *msg* to *object*, applies the method associated with *msg* to the
                      arguments (*arg* ...), and returns the result of the application. SEND evaluates
                      object and its arguments (*arg* ...) but does not evaluate *msg*. The maximum
                      number of arguments to the method that can be specified in SEND is 8. If
                      object cannot handle *msg*, an error results.

                      See also SEND-IF-HANDLES.

| **Examples** | ```
(define-class employees
  (classvars (no-of-employees 0))
  (instvars
    name emp-no manager salary (overtime 0))
  (mixins personal-info education-experience)
  (options
    (gettable-variables name emp-no no-of-employees)
    settable-variables
    inittable-variables))
``` | ⇒ *unspecified value* |

```
(define-method (employees earnings) ()
  (+ salary overtime))
```
⇒ *unspecified value*

```
(define-method
  (employees earnings-greater-than) (val)
  (if (>? (earnings) val)
      (writeln name " " emp-no)
      #F))
```
⇒ *unspecified value*

```
(define emp1
  (make-instance employees
    'name 'RALPH
    'emp-no 001
    'manager 'SAM
    'salary 100))
```
⇒ *unspecified value*

`(send emp1 get-name)`	⇒ RALPH
`(send emp1 earnings)`	⇒ 100
`(send emp1 set-overtime 100)`	⇒ *unspecified value*
`(send emp1 earnings)`	⇒ 200

SEND-IF-HANDLES   *Special Form*

SEND-IF-HANDLES sends a message to a SCOOPS object only if the object can handle the message.

Format	(SEND-IF-HANDLES *object msg arg* ...)
Parameters	*object* — An instance of a SCOOPS class
	msg — The name of the message to be sent
	arg ... — The arguments to the method associated with the message
Explanation	SEND-IF-HANDLES sends *msg* to *object* only if *object* can handle *msg*, applies the method associated with *msg* to the arguments (*arg* ...), and returns the result of the application. SEND-IF-HANDLES evaluates *object* and its arguments (*arg* ...) but does not evaluate *msg*. The maximum number of arguments to the method that can be specified in SEND-IF-HANDLES is 8. If *object* cannot handle *msg*, *false* is returned.

See also SEND.
```

| **Examples** | ```
(define-class employees
  (classvars (no-of-employees 0))
    (instvars
     name emp-no manager salary (overtime 0))
  (mixins personal-info education-experience)
  (options
    (gettable-variables name emp-no no-of-employees)
    settable-variables
    inittable-variables))
``` | $\Rightarrow$ *unspecified value* |

```
(define-method (employees earnings) ()
  (+ salary overtime))
```                                                        $\Rightarrow$ *unspecified value*

```
(define-method
  (employees earnings-greater-than) (val)
  (if (>? (earnings) val)
      (writeln name " " emp-no)
      #F))
```                                                        $\Rightarrow$ *unspecified value*

```
(define emp1
  (make-instance employees
    'name 'RALPH
    'emp-no 001
    'manager 'SAM
    'salary 100))
```                                                        $\Rightarrow$ *unspecified value*

```
(send-if-handles emp1 get-name)
```                     $\Rightarrow$ RALPH
```
(send-if-handles emp1 earnings)
```                     $\Rightarrow$ 100
```
(send-if-handles emp1 set-overtime 100)
```             $\Rightarrow$ *unspecified value*
```
(send-if-handles emp1 earnings)
```                     $\Rightarrow$ 200
```
(send-if-handles emp1 get-value)
```                    $\Rightarrow$ *false*

SEQUENCE   *Special Form*

SEQUENCE evaluates the expressions in sequence. The value of the last expression is returned.

Format   (SEQUENCE exp_1 ...)

Parameters exp_1 ... — Any Scheme expressions

Explanation   SEQUENCE is an alternate name for BEGIN. It evaluates each *exp* sequentially from left to right and returns the value of the last *exp*. This special form sequences side effects, such as input and output. If *exp* is not specified, the empty list is returned.

To evaluate expressions and return the value of the first one, use BEGIN0.

SEQUENCE is provided for historical reasons only. New code should use BEGIN.
```

| Example | ```
(sequence (display "4 plus 1 equals ")
          (display (1+ 4)))
```
4 plus 1 equals 5 $\Rightarrow$ *unspecified value* |

---

**SET!** *Special Form*

SET! changes the value of a variable.

| Format | ```
(SET! var exp)
(SET! (FLUID var) exp)
(SET! (VECTOR-REF vec n) exp)
(SET! (ACCESS sym₁ ... env) exp)
``` |

Parameters

var — An identifier

exp — Any Scheme expression

vec — A vector

n — A nonnegative integer

sym₁ ... — Symbols

env — An environment

Explanation

SET! changes the value of *var* to be the value of *exp*. An unspecified value is returned. If the first argument to SET! is a symbol, SET! changes the value of that symbol in the current environment. If the first argument is not a symbol, it is expanded as a macro. After the expansion is complete, SET! is in one of four formats.

The first form, (SET! *var exp*), changes the value of *var* to that of *exp* in the current environment. The *exp* is evaluated but the *var* is not. However, if *var* has not been bound previously, an error results. For more information on binding *var*, see DEFINE, LAMBDA, LET, LET*, LETREC, and NAMED-LAMBDA.

The second form, (SET! (FLUID *var*) *exp*), finds *var* in the fluid environment and changes its value to that of *exp*. If *var* cannot be found in the fluid environment, an error results. For more information on fluids, see FLUID, FLUID-LAMBDA, FLUID-LET, and FLUID-SET!.

The third form, (SET! (VECTOR-REF *vec n*) *exp*), changes the value of the nth position in *vec* to that of *exp*. For more information on vectors, see MAKE-VECTOR, VECTOR-REF, and VECTOR-SET!.

7-154 *Alphabetic Catalog of Language Elements*   *TI Scheme Language Reference Manual — Student Edition*

The fourth form, (SET! (ACCESS sym_1 ... env) exp), changes the value of sym_1 in env if only sym_1 is specified. If more than one sym is specified, ACCESS gets the value of sym_n in env. This value must be an environment. Next, sym_{n-1} is looked up in that environment and an environment is returned. Then sym_{n-2} is looked up in that environment and so on. When sym_1 is looked up in the environment returned when sym_2 is looked up, SET! changes the value of sym_1 to the value of exp. If a sym_1 cannot be found in the environment, the environment is extended with sym_1 and initialized to the value of exp.

Examples

This example changes the value of FOO in the user-initial-environment:

```
(define foo 5)                      ⇒ unspecified value
foo                                 ⇒ 5
(set! foo 99)                       ⇒ unspecified value
foo                                 ⇒ 99
```

The next example creates a procedure, ACCUMULATOR, with local state. When ACCUMULATOR is called with an argument, it changes the local state variable FOO to FOO plus the argument.

```
(define accumulator
  (let ((foo 0))
    (lamdba (n)
      (set! foo (+ foo n))
      foo)))                        ⇒ unspecified value
(accumulator 2)                     ⇒ 2
(accumulator 5)                     ⇒ 7

(fluid-let ((a 5))
  (writeln (fluid a))
  (set! (fluid a) 77)
  (fluid a))                        ⇒ 5
                                    ⇒ 77

(define vec (vector 1 2 3 4 5 6 7)) ⇒ unspecified value
(set! (vector-ref vec 3) 'a)        ⇒ unspecified value
vec                                 ⇒ #(1 2 3 A 5 6 7)
```

SET-CAR! *Procedure*

SET-CAR! changes the car component of a pair.

Format	(SET-CAR! *pair obj*)
Parameters	*pair* — A pair
	obj — Any Scheme object
Explanation	SET-CAR! replaces the car component of *pair* with *obj*. An unspecified value is returned.
	To replace the cdr component, use SET-CDR!.

Examples

```
(define a '(a b c))          ⟹ unspecified value
(define b a)                 ⟹ unspecified value
a                            ⟹ (A B C)
b                            ⟹ (A B C)
(set-car! b '(1 2))          ⟹ unspecified value
b                            ⟹ ((1 2) B C)
a                            ⟹ ((1 2) B C)
```

SET-CDR! *Procedure*

SET-CDR! changes the cdr component of a pair.

Format	(SET-CDR! *pair obj*)
Parameters	*pair* — A pair
	obj — Any Scheme object
Explanation	SET-CDR! replaces the cdr component of *pair* with *obj*. An unspecified value is returned.
	To replace the car component, use SET-CAR!.

Examples

```
(define a '(a b c))          ⟹ unspecified value
(define b a)                 ⟹ unspecified value
a                            ⟹ (A B C)
b                            ⟹ (A B C)
(set-cdr! b '(1 2))          ⟹ unspecified value
b                            ⟹ (A 1 2)
a                            ⟹ (A 1 2)
```

SET-CLIPPING-RECTANGLE!   *Procedure*

SET-CLIPPING-RECTANGLE! sets the screen's clipping rectangle.

Format	(SET-CLIPPING-RECTANGLE! *x1 y1 x2 y2*)
Parameters	*x1* — The screen x-coordinate (horizontal axis) of the top left corner of the clipping rectangle.
	y1 — The screen y-coordinate (vertical axis) of the top left corner of the clipping rectangle.
	x2 — The screen x-coordinate (horizontal axis) of the bottom right corner of the clipping rectangle.
	y2 — The screen y-coordinate (vertical axis) of the bottom right corner of the clipping rectangle.
Explanation	SET-CLIPPING-RECTANGLE sets the corners of the clipping rectangle. The rectangle itself is not displayed, but the output from drawing functions is displayed on the screen only if it lies inside the rectangle.
	For more information concerning graphics and clipping, see the *PC Scheme User's Guide — Student Edition*.

SETCV   *Special Form*

SETCV changes the value of a SCOOPS class variable.

Format	(SETCV *class var exp*)
Parameters	*class* — A SCOOPS class
	var — The name of a class variable defined in *class*
	exp — The value to be stored in *var*
Explanation	SETCV stores the value of *exp* in the *var* in *class*. An unspecified value is returned. If *class* has not been compiled or *var* has not been described as settable in DEFINE-CLASS, an error results.
Examples	Assume that the class employees has been defined as shown in the example for DEFINE-CLASS.

```
(setcv employees no-of-employees 1000)    ⇒ unspecified value
(getcv employees no-of-employees)         ⇒ 1000
```

SET-FILE-POSITION!   *Procedure*

SET-FILE-POSITION! positions the file pointer to any byte offset within a file.

Format	(SET-FILE-POSITION! *port num-bytes location*)
Parameters	*port* — A Scheme port object created by a prior call to OPEN-OUTPUT-FILE, OPEN-INPUT-FILE, or OPEN-EXTEND-FILE.
	num-bytes — The number of bytes to move in the file, either positive or negative.
	location — An integer value indicating the start position from which *num-bytes* is valid.

        0 — Set file position *num-bytes* from the beginning of the file.

        1 — Set file position *num-bytes* from the current file position.

        2 — Set file position *num-bytes* from the end of file, including the end-of-file object.

Explanation	SET-FILE-POSITION! allows you to randomly access data within a file.
	See also GET-FILE-POSITION.
Examples	Assume the file STUFF.S on the default disk drive consists of the following:

THIS IS A TEST OF THE RANDOM ACCESS FEATURE.

Examples of the use of SET-FILE-POSITION! follow:

```
(define p (open-input-file "stuff.s"))    ⟹ unspecified value
(set-file-position! p 10 0)               ⟹ unspecified value
(read p)                                  ⟹ TEST
(set-file-position! p 16 2)               ⟹ unspecified value
(read p)                                  ⟹ ACCESS
(read-char p)                             ⟹ #\SPACE
```

SET-FLUID!   *Special Form*

SET-FLUID! changes the fluid binding of a variable.

Format	(SET-FLUID! *var obj*)
Parameters	*var* — A variable in the fluid environment
	obj — The value to be stored

Explanation	SET-FLUID! changes the fluid binding of *var* to the value of *obj*. If *var* is not fluidly bound, an error results. SET-FLUID! returns an unspecified value.	

Examples

```
(define make-synthetic-fuel
  (fluid-lambda (x)
    (set-fluid! x 'oil)
    (fluid x)))                          ⇒ unspecified value
(make-synthetic-fuel 'water)            ⇒ OIL
(make-synthetic-fuel 'alcohol)          ⇒ OIL
```

SET-LINE-LENGTH! *Procedure*

SET-LINE-LENGTH! changes the line length of an output port.

Format

(SET-LINE-LENGTH! *num* {*port*})

Parameters

num — A nonnegative integer

port — A output port (an optional argument)

Explanation

SET-LINE-LENGTH! changes the line length associated with either *port*, if it is specified, or the current output port to *num*. If *num* is 0, no column position is maintained and end-of-line sequences are no longer inserted automatically. SET-LINE-LENGTH! returns an unspecified value.

A port's line length is used by the Scheme output routines to determine where to break lines. However, since the output routines do not split the printed representation of an individual symbol across lines, it is possible to produce output lines that are longer than a port's line length. For example, if DISPLAY is used to print a character string with 90 characters to a port whose line length is 80, an output of 90 characters (plus the end-of-line sequence) results.

Examples

```
(define lengthy (open-output-file "lengthy"))
                                        ⇒ unspecified value
(line-length lengthy)                   ⇒ 80
(set-line-length! 15 lengthy)           ⇒ unspecified value
(line-length lengthy)                   ⇒ 15
```

SET-PALETTE! *Procedure*

SET-PALETTE! affects the colors used in graphics procedures.

Format

```
(SET-PALETTE! color  mapping)          ; TIPC, IBM EGA
(SET-PALETTE! ground  colors)          ; IBM CGA
```

Parameters	*color* — The number used as an identifier for a color.
	mapping — The new number to be associated with that color
	ground — Either background (0) or foreground (1)
	colors — Either the new background color (0-127) or the palette selection (0 or 1) for the foreground
Explanation	On the TIPC or the TI Business-Pro computer in TI mode, or with an EGA on the IBM or the TI Business-Pro computer in IBM mode, SET-PALETTE! modifies the mapping used to display the various colors on the screen. An unspecified value is returned.
	With a CGA on the IBM or the TI Business-Pro computer in IBM mode, SET-PALETTE! may be used to change the background color or to change the color palette used for the foreground. An unspecified value is returned.
	Refer to the chapter on graphics in the *PC Scheme User's Guide — Student Edition* for a description of how this procedure operates on a particular computer.

SET-PEN-COLOR! *Procedure*

SET-PEN-COLOR! changes the drawing color used by the graphics pen.

Format	(SET-PEN-COLOR! *color*)
Parameter	*color* — The new color. This value may be a color name or a number corresponding to a color.
Explanation	SET-PEN-COLOR! changes the current color used by the pen to *color*. An unspecified value is returned. All graphics are drawn in this color until it is changed. The default color used by the pen is white.
	Other graphics procedures are DRAW-BOX-TO, DRAW-FILLED-BOX-TO, DRAW-LINE-TO, and DRAW-POINT. For information on valid colors, see the *PC Scheme User's Guide — Student Edition*.

SET-VIDEO-MODE! *Procedure*

SET-VIDEO-MODE! changes the screen display mode.

Format	(SET-VIDEO-MODE! *mode-number*)
Parameter	*mode-number* — An integer between -16,384 and +16,383, inclusive

Explanation	SET-VIDEO-MODE! changes the way text and/or graphics are displayed on the screen. An unspecified value is returned.
	The way a particular mode changes the display varies between computers. See the chapter on graphics in the *PC Scheme User's Guide — Student Edition* for more information. See also GET-VIDEO-MODE.

SIN *Procedure*

SIN returns the sine of a number.

Format	(SIN *num*)
Parameter	*num* — Any Scheme number. This is an angle expressed in radians.
Explanation	SIN returns the sine of *num*.
Examples	(sin 0) ⟹ 0. (sin 0.7854) ⟹ 0.707108079859474 (sin 1.0472) ⟹ 0.866026628183543

SORT! *Procedure*

SORT! sorts lists and vectors.

Format	(SORT! *sortee {pred}*)
Parameters	*sortee* — A list or a vector.
	pred — A predicate procedure of two arguments. For example, < sorts *sortee* in ascending order and > sorts it in descending order.
Explanation	SORT! destructively orders *sortee* according to *pred*. It returns the sorted list or vector.
Examples	(define v1 (vector 1 3 5 2 4 6)) ⟹ *unspecified value* (set! v1 (sort! v1 <?)) ⟹ *unspecified value* v1 ⟹ #(1 2 3 4 5 6) (set! v1 (sort! v1 >?)) ⟹ *unspecified value* v1 ⟹ #(6 5 4 3 2 1) (define s1 (string->list "acsrgbql")) ⟹ *unspecified value* (set! s1 (sort! s1 char<?)) ⟹ *unspecified value* (list->string s1) ⟹ "abcglqrs" (set! s1 (sort! s1 char>?)) ⟹ *unspecified value* (list->string s1) ⟹ "srqlgbca"

#\SPACE

Character Object

#\SPACE represents the ASCII space character.

Format	#\SPACE
Explanation	#\SPACE is the character object representing a space. When this object is printed to a port, the ASCII character for space (32_{10}) is sent to that port. For instance, when this character is sent to the screen with WRITE-CHAR, DISPLAY, or PRINC, the cursor moves forward one space.
Examples	`(writeln "foo" #\space "bar")` **foo bar** ⇒ *unspecified value*

SQRT

Procedure

SQRT returns the square root of a number.

Format	(SQRT *num*)
Parameter	*num* — Any nonnegative Scheme number
Explanation	SQRT coerces *num* to a real number and then returns the positive square root of that real number.
Examples	`(sqrt 1)` ⇒ 1. `(sqrt 2)` ⇒ 1.4142135623731 `(sqrt 10)` ⇒ 3.16227766016838

STANDARD-INPUT   *Variable*

STANDARD-INPUT defines the original input port of the system.

Format	STANDARD-INPUT
Explanation	STANDARD-INPUT is set initially to be the keyboard, which is the normal input port. Since STANDARD-INPUT is a variable, its value may be changed. The value of the fluid variable INPUT-PORT is reset to STANDARD-INPUT whenever the system's top-level function is invoked. SCHEME-RESET will always reset INPUT-PORT, but RESET does not. STANDARD-INPUT can be used to read from the console no matter what the current input port is unless it has been reassigned.
Examples	`(input-port? standard-input)` ⟹ *true* `(read standard-input)` `hello-there` ⟹ HELLO-THERE

STANDARD-OUTPUT   *Variable*

STANDARD OUTPUT defines the original output port of the system.

OUTPUT - PORT

Format	STANDARD-OUTPUT
Explanation	STANDARD-OUTPUT is set initially to the screen, which is the normal output port. Since STANDARD-OUTPUT is a variable, its value may be changed. The value of the fluid variable OUTPUT-PORT is reset to STANDARD-OUTPUT whenever the system's top-level function is invoked. SCHEME-RESET will always reset INPUT-PORT, but RESET does not. STANDARD-OUTPUT can be used to write to the console no matter what the current output port is unless it has been reassigned.
Examples	`(output-port? standard-output)` ⟹ *true* `(display "a bit of text" standard-output)` **a bit of text** ⟹ *unspecified value*

STREAM? *Procedure*

STREAM? determines if its argument is a stream.

Format	(STREAM? *obj*)
Parameter	*obj* — Any Scheme object
Explanation	STREAM? returns *true* if *obj* is a stream and *false*, otherwise.
	To create a stream, use CONS-STREAM.
Examples	`(define s (cons-stream 'a the-empty-stream))`

```
(define s (cons-stream 'a the-empty-stream))
                                        ⟹ unspecified value
(stream? s)                             ⟹ true
(stream? the-empty-stream)              ⟹ true
(stream? '(a b c))                      ⟹ false
```

STREAM->LIST *Procedure*

STREAM->LIST converts a finite stream to a list.

Format	(STREAM->LIST *stream*)
Parameter	*stream* — A finite stream
Explanation	STREAM->LIST returns a list whose elements are the elements of *stream*. The first element of the list is the head of *stream*, the second element is the head of the tail of *stream*, and so on.
	To create a stream from a list, use LIST->STREAM.
Examples	

```
(define s (cons-stream 'a the-empty-stream))
                                        ⟹ unspecified value
(stream->list s)                        ⟹ (A)
(stream->list (cons-stream 'b s))       ⟹ (B A)
(stream->list (list->stream '(x y z)))  ⟹ (X Y Z)
```

STRING->LIST   *Procedure*

STRING->LIST converts a string into a list of character objects.

Format	(STRING->LIST *string*)
Parameter	*string* — A string
Explanation	STRING->LIST returns a list of the character objects in *string*.
Examples	(string->list "Scheme") ⟹ (#\S #\c #\h #\e #\m #\e) (string->list "a3 Z") ⟹ (#\a #\3 #\SPACE #\Z)

STRING->NUMBER   *Procedure*

STRING->NUMBER converts a string into a number of the specified format.

Format	(STRING->NUMBER *string exactness radix*)
Parameters	*string* — A Scheme string
	exactness — A symbol representing whether the number is to be exact or inexact. PC Scheme presently implements all numbers as inexact.
	'E — Exact 'I — Inexact
	radix — a symbol representing the radix of string.
	'B — Binary 'D — Decimal 'O — Octal 'X — Hexadecimal
Explanation	STRING->NUMBER returns a number for string represented in *radix*.
Examples	(STRING->NUMBER "1001" 'I 'B) ⟹ 9 (STRING->NUMBER "64" 'I 'O) ⟹ 52 (STRING->NUMBER "64" 'I 'X) ⟹ 100

STRING->SYMBOL   *Procedure*

STRING->SYMBOL converts a string to a symbol.

Format   (STRING->SYMBOL *string*)

Parameter   *string* — A string

Explanation   STRING->SYMBOL returns the interned symbol of *string*. No case coercion
                is performed.

                See also STRING->UNINTERNED-SYMBOL and SYMBOL->STRING.

Examples   In the first two examples, note that the symbol is converted to uppercase
                letters; however, the case of the string does not change. Because of the case
                conversion, the result of the comparison in the third example is *false*.

                `'mISSISSIppi`   ⇒ `MISSISSIPPI`

                `(string->symbol "mISSISSIppi"`   ⇒ `|mISSISSIppi|`

                `(eq? 'mISSISSIppi`
                `    (string->symbol "mISSISSIppi"))`   ⇒ *false*

                `(eq? 'JollyWog`
                `    (string->symbol`
                `      (symbol->string 'JollyWog)))`   ⇒ *true*

STRING->UNINTERNED-SYMBOL   *Procedure*

STRING->UNINTERNED-SYMBOL converts a string into an uninterned symbol.

Format   (STRING->UNINTERNED-SYMBOL *string*)

Parameter   *string* — A string

Explanation   STRING->UNINTERNED-SYMBOL returns an uninterned symbol, which is
                is created from *string*.

                An uninterned symbol is one that is never identical (in the sense of the EQ?
                predicate) to any symbols read by the Scheme reader, even those with the
                same printed representation.

                See also STRING->SYMBOL.

| Examples | ```
(define foo
  (string->uninterned-symbol "alpha")) ⇒ unspecified value
foo                                     ⇒ |alpha|
(eq? foo 'alpha)                        ⇒ false
``` |
|---|---|

STRING-APPEND   *Procedure*

STRING-APPEND concatenates two or more strings.

Format	(STRING-APPEND *string* ...)
Parameters	*string* ... — Strings
Explanation	STRING-APPEND creates and returns a string that is the concatenation of the supplied string arguments (*string* ...). If only one *string* is supplied, a copy of *string* is returned. If no arguments are supplied, the empty string is returned.
| Examples | ```
(string-append "xyz" "123" "abc")  ⇒ "xyz123abc"
(string-append "" "MNO-PQR")        ⇒ "MNO-PQR"
(string-append)                     ⇒ ""
``` |

STRING-CI<?, STRING-CI=?   *Procedure*

These procedures compare two strings, ignoring case.

Format	(STRING-CI<? *string₁* *string₂*)
	(STRING-CI=? *string₁* *string₂*)
Parameters	*string₁* — A string
	string₂ — A string
Explanation	These procedures compare $string_1$ and $string_2$ character by character using the ASCII character codes.

- STRING-CI<? returns *true* if one of the following conditions is true:

    - A character in $string_1$ is less than the corresponding character in $string_2$, and all previous characters in $string_1$ are equal to the corresponding characters in $string_2$, ignoring case.

    - The length of $string_1$ is less than the length of $string_2$, and the characters in $string_1$ are equal to the corresponding characters in $string_2$.

    Otherwise, STRING-CI<? returns *false*.

- STRING-CI=? returns *true* if both of the following conditions are true:

    - Each character in *string₁* is equal to the corresponding character in *string₂*, ignoring case.

    - The length of *string₁* is the same as the length of *string₂*.

    Otherwise, STRING-CI=? returns *false*.

    Note that CI stands for case-insensitive. Therefore, the comparisons are performed as if all alphabetic characters were lowercase. Thus, special characters, such as [, \,], ^ , _, and ', which fall between the uppercase alphabet and the lowercase alphabet, would be less than any alphabetic character. This fact is an implementation detail on which programs should not depend.

    To include case sensitivity in the comparison, use STRING<?, STRING<=?, STRING=?, STRING>?, and STRING>=?.

Examples

```
(string-ci<? "string-a" "string-B")   ⇒ true
(string-ci<? "mnopq" "MNOPQR")        ⇒ true
(string-ci=? "sTring" "string")       ⇒ true
(string-ci<? "sTring" "strin'")       ⇒ false
(string-ci=? "sTrin" "string")        ⇒ false
```

STRING-COPY
Procedure

STRING-COPY returns a copy of a string.

Format   (STRING-COPY *string*)

Parameter   *string* — A string

Explanation STRING-COPY returns a new string that is a copy of *string*.

Examples

```
(define st1 "A string")              ⇒ unspecified value
(define st2 st1)                     ⇒ unspecified value
(eq? st1 st2)                        ⇒ true
(define st3 (string-copy st1))       ⇒ unspecified value
(eq? st1 st3)                        ⇒ false
(eqv? st1 st3)                       ⇒ true
```

STRING-FILL!
Procedure

STRING-FILL! replaces each character in a string with a specified value.

Format   (STRING-FILL! *string fillchar*)

Parameters	*string* — A string
	fillchar — A character
Explanation	STRING-FILL! replaces each character in *string* with *fillchar*. An unspecified value is returned. Note that the original *string* is modified without being copied.
	See also SUBSTRING-FILL!.
Examples	(define st (make-string 5 #\X)) ⟹ *unspecified value*
	(string-fill! st #*) ⟹ *unspecified value*
	st ⟹ "*****"

STRING-LENGTH

Procedure

STRING-LENGTH returns the number of characters in a string.

Format	(STRING-LENGTH *string*)
Parameter	*string* — A string
Explanation	STRING-LENGTH returns the number of characters in *string*.
Examples	(string-length "aardvark") ⟹ 8
	(string-length "a b") ⟹ 3
	(string-length "") ⟹ 0

STRING-NULL?

Procedure

STRING-NULL? determines if its argument is a null string.

Format	(STRING-NULL? *string*)
Parameter	*string* — A string
Explanation	STRING-NULL? returns *true* if the length of *string* is zero and returns *false*, otherwise.
Examples	(string-null? "") ⟹ *true*
	(string-null? "ab") ⟹ *false*
	(string-null? " ") ⟹ *false*

STRING-REF   *Procedure*

STRING-REF returns a specific character from a string.

Format	(STRING-REF *string index*)
Parameters	*string* — A string
	index — A nonnegative integer
Explanation	STRING-REF returns the *index* element of *string*. The index of the first character of *string* is zero, and the index of the last character is one less than the length of *string*.
Examples	(define st "abcde") ⟹ *unspecified value*
	(string-ref st 0) ⟹ #\a
	(string-ref st 3) ⟹ #\d

STRING-SET!   *Procedure*

STRING-SET! replaces a specified character in a string.

Format	(STRING-SET! *string index char*)
Parameters	*string* — A string
	index — A nonnegative integer
	char — A character object
Explanation	STRING-SET! replaces the *index* element of *string* with *char*. An unspecified value is returned. The index of the first character of *string* is zero, and the index of the last character is one less than the length of *string*.
Examples	(define st "alpha") ⟹ *unspecified value*
	(string-set! st 3 #\i) ⟹ *unspecified value*
	st ⟹ "alpia"

STRING<?, STRING<=?, STRING=?, STRING>?, STRING>=?   *Procedure*

These procedures compare two strings, including case.

Format   (STRING<? $string_1$ $string_2$)
                          (STRING<=? $string_1$ $string_2$)
                          (STRING=? $string_1$ $string_2$)
                          (STRING>? $string_1$ $string_2$)
                          (STRING>=? $string_1$ $string_2$)

Parameters $string_1$ — A string

                    $string_2$ — A string

Explanation   These procedures compare $string_1$ and $string_2$ character by character using the ASCII character codes, including case.

- STRING<? returns *true* if one of the following is true:

  - A character in $string_1$ is less than the corresponding character in $string_2$, and all previous characters in $string_1$ are equal to the corresponding characters in $string_2$.

  - The length of $string_1$ is less than the length of $string_2$, and the characters in $string_1$ are equal to the corresponding characters in $string_2$.

  Otherwise, STRING<? returns *false*.

- STRING<=? returns *true* if one of the following is true:

  - A character in $string_1$ is less than the corresponding character in $string_2$, and all previous characters in $string_1$ are equal to the corresponding characters in $string_2$.

  - The length of $string_1$ is less than or equal to the length of $string_2$, and the characters in $string_1$ are equal corresponding characters in $string_2$.

  Otherwise, STRING<=? returns *false*.

- STRING=? returns *true* if both of the following are true:

  - Each character in $string_1$ is equal to the corresponding character in $string_2$.

  - The length of $string_1$ is the same as the length of $string_2$.

  Otherwise, STRING=? returns *false*.

- STRING>? returns *true* if one of the following is true:

    - A character in $string_1$ is greater than the corresponding character in $string_2$, and all previous characters in $string_1$ are equal to the corresponding characters in $string_2$.

    - The length of $string_1$ is greater than the length of $string_2$, and the characters in $string_1$ are equal to the corresponding characters in $string_2$.

    Otherwise, STRING>? returns *false*.

- STRING>=? returns *true* if one of the following is true:

    - A character in $string_1$ is greater than the corresponding character in $string_2$, and all previous characters in $string_1$ are equal to the corresponding characters in $string_2$.

    - The length of $string_1$ is greater than or equal to the length of $string_2$, and the characters in $string_1$ are equal to the corresponding characters in $string_2$.

    Otherwise, STRING>=? returns *false*.

    To compare two strings ignoring case, use STRING-CI<? or STRING-CI=?.

Examples	`(string<? "ABCD" "ZBCD")` ⇒ *true*
	`(string<=? "abc" "abcd")` ⇒ *true*
	`(string>? "abcd" "MNOP")` ⇒ *true*
	`(string>? "abc" "ABC")` ⇒ *true*
	`(string>=? "MNOP" "abcde")` ⇒ *false*

STRING? *Procedure*

STRING? determines if its argument is a string.

Format	(STRING? *obj*)
Parameter	*obj* — Any Scheme object
Explanation	STRING? returns *true* if *obj* is a string and *false*, otherwise.
Examples	`(string? "a string")` ⇒ *true*
	`(string? "")` ⇒ *true*
	`(string? 'no-string)` ⇒ *false*

SUB1
Procedure

SUB1 subtracts 1 from its argument.

Format	(SUB1 *num*)
Parameter	*num* — Any Scheme number
Explanation	This procedure is the same as −1+. SUB1 subtracts one from *num* and returns the result.
Examples	(sub1 8) ⇒ 7 (sub1 −14) ⇒ −15

SUBSTRING
Procedure

SUBSTRING returns a string that is all or part of another string.

Format	(SUBSTRING *string start end*)
Parameters	*string* — A string.
	start — An integer. The substring starts in position *start*.
	end — An integer. The substring ends in position *end*−1.
Explanation	SUBSTRING returns a string that contains the characters of *string* beginning with position *start* and ending with position *end*−1.
Examples	(substring "abcdefg" 2 6) ⇒ "cdef" (substring "abcdefg" 0 1) ⇒ "a" (substring "abcdefg" 0 7) ⇒ "abcdefg"

SUBSTRING-CI<?, SUBSTRING-CI=?,
Procedure

These procedures compare two substrings, ignoring case.

Format	(SUBSTRING-CI<? $string_1$ $start_1$ end_1 $string_2$ $start_2$ end_2) (SUBSTRING-CI=? $string_1$ $start_1$ end_1 $string_2$ $start_2$ end_2)
Parameters	$string_1$ — A string.
	$start_1$ — An integer. The first substring starts in position $start_1$, where $0 \leq start_1 < end_1 \leq$ length of $string_1$.

end_1 — An integer. The first substring ends in position $end_1 - 1$, where $0 \leq start_1 < end_1 \leq$ length of $string_1$.

$start_2$ — A string. It may be the same string as $string_1$.

$start_2$ — An integer. The second substring starts in position $start_2$, where $0 \leq start_2 < end_2 \leq$ length of $start_2$.

end_2 — An integer. The second substring ends in position $end_2 - 1$, where $0 \leq start_2 < end_2 \leq$ length of $start_2$.

Explanation

These procedures compare the substring of $string_1$ specified by $start_1$ and end_1 to the substring of $string_1$ specified by $start_2$ and end_2 using the ASCII character codes.

■ SUBSTRING-CI<? returns *true* if one of the following conditions is true:

- A character in the first substring is less than the corresponding character in the second substring, and all previous characters in the first substring are equal to the corresponding characters in the second substring, ignoring case.

- The length of the first substring is less than the length of the second substring, and the characters in the first substring are equal to the corresponding characters in the second substring, ignoring case.

Otherwise, SUBSTRING-CI<? returns *false*.

■ SUBSTRING-CI=? returns *true* if both of the following conditions are true:

- Each character in the first substring is equal to the corresponding character in the second substring, ignoring case.

- The length of the first substring is equal to the length of the second substring.

Otherwise, SUBSTRING-CI=? returns *false*.

Note that CI stands for case-insensitive. Therefore, the comparisons are performed as if all alphabetic characters were lowercase. Thus, special characters, such as [, \,], ∧, _, and ', which fall between the uppercase alphabet and the lowercase alphabet, would be less than any alphabetic character. This fact is an implementation detail on which programs should not depend.

To include case sensitivity in the comparison, use SUBSTRING<? and SUBSTRING=?.

Examples

```
(define st1 "ABCDEFG")          ⇒ unspecified value
(define st2 "abcdefg")          ⇒ unspecified value
(substring-ci<? st2 0 4 st1 0 5)   ⇒ true
(substring-ci=? st1 1 3 st2 1 4)   ⇒ false
(substring-ci<? st2 1 5 "abcgefd" 1 5)   ⇒ true
```

SUBSTRING-FILL! *Procedure*

SUBSTRING-FILL! replaces a sequence of characters in a string with a specified value.

Format	(SUBSTRING-FILL! *string start end fillchar*)
Parameters	*string* — A string.
	start — An integer. The substring starts in position *start*, where $0 \leq start < end \leq$ length of *string*.
	end — An integer. The substring ends in position *end*-1, where $0 \leq start < end \leq$ length of *string*.
	fillchar — A character.
Explanation	SUBSTRING-FILL! replaces each character in the specified substring with *fillchar*. An unspecified value is returned. The substring begins in position *start* of *string* and ends in position *end*-1. Note that the original *string* is modified without being copied.
	See also STRING-FILL!.
Examples	

```
(define st1 (make-string 5 #\A))     ⟹ unspecified value
st1                                  ⟹ "AAAAA"
(substring-fill! st1 1 4 #\*)        ⟹ unspecified value
st1                                  ⟹ "A***A"
(substring-fill! st1 2 3 #\!)        ⟹ unspecified value
st1                                  ⟹ "A*!*A"
```

SUBSTRING-FIND-NEXT-CHAR-IN-SET, SUBSTRING-FIND-PREVIOUS-CHAR-IN-SET *Procedure*

These procedures find the character in a string that is a member of a specified set of characters.

Format	(SUBSTRING-FIND-NEXT-CHAR-IN-SET *string start end charset*)
	(SUBSTRING-FIND-PREVIOUS-CHAR-IN-SET *string start end charset*)
Parameters	*string* — A string.
	start — An integer. The substring of *string* to be examined starts in position *start*, where $0 \leq start < end \leq$ length of *string*.

end — An integer. The substring of *string* to be examined ends in position *end*-1, where $0 \leq start < end \leq$ length of *string*.

charset — A character or a string containing characters.

Explanation	These procedures search all or part of *string* and return the index of the first character in *string* that is a member of *charset* using CHAR=? for comparison. If no character in the substring of *string* is found in *charset*, *false* is returned. The direction of the search depends on which procedure is used, as described here.

- SUBSTRING-FIND-NEXT-CHAR-IN-SET searches *string* forwards from *start* to *end*-1.

- SUBSTRING-FIND-PREVIOUS-CHAR-IN-SET searches *string* backwards from *end*-1 to *start*.

Examples
```
(define charset "abc")                    ⇒ unspecified value
(define s "I am here, but who Cares.")    ⇒ unspecified value
(substring-find-next-char-in-set
   s 0 24 charset)                        ⇒ 2
(substring-find-previous-char-in-set
   s 0 24 charset)                        ⇒ 20
(substring-find-next-char-in-set
   s 0 24 #\5)                            ⇒ false
```

SUBSTRING-MOVE-LEFT!, SUBSTRING-MOVE-RIGHT! *Procedure*

These procedures copy a substring into the same or another string.

Format

(SUBSTRING-MOVE-LEFT! *string₁* *start₁* *end₁* *string₂* *start₂*)

(SUBSTRING-MOVE-RIGHT! *string₁* *start₁* *end₁* *string₂* *start₂*)

Parameters

$string_1$ — A string.

$start_1$ — An integer. The first substring starts in position $start_1$, where $0 \leq start_1 < end_1 \leq$ length of $string_1$.

end_1 — An integer. The first substring ends in position end_1-1, where $0 \leq start_1 < end_1 \leq$ length of $string_1$.

$string_2$ — A string. It may be the same as $string_1$.

$start_2$ — An integer. The second substring starts in position $start_2$, where $0 \leq start_2 < (start_2 + (end_1 - start_1 - 1)) \leq$ length of $string_2$.

Explanation   These procedures copy the characters in $string_1$ to $string_2$. An unspecified value is returned. The direction in which the characters are moved in the source substring depends on which procedure is used.

- SUBSTRING-MOVE-LEFT! starts copying from the $start_1$ position (from the left). Specifically, it copies the characters in $string_1$ from position $start_1$ to end_1-1 to $string_2$ beginning in position $start_2$. The characters from position $start_2$ through $start_2 + (end_1 - start_1 - 1)$ in $string_2$ are replaced one at a time.

- SUBSTRING-MOVE-RIGHT! starts copying from the end_1-1 position (from the right). Specifically, it copies the characters in $string_1$ from position $end_1 - 1$ to $start_1$ to $string_2$ beginning in position $start_2 + (end_1 - start_1 - 1)$. The characters from position $start_2 + (end_1 - start_1 - 1)$ through $start_2$ are replaced one at a time.

Note that SUBSTRING-MOVE-LEFT! and SUBSTRING-MOVE-RIGHT! are equivalent if the source and destination substrings do not overlap.

Examples

```
(define st1 "ABLE-ELBA")              ⇒ unspecified value
(define st2
  "able was I ere I saw elba")        ⇒ unspecified value
(substring-move-left! st1
  5 9 st2 21)                         ⇒ unspecified value
st2                                   ⇒"able was I ere I
                                         saw ELBA"
(define st4 "abcdefg")                ⇒ unspecified value
(substring-move-left! st4
  2 6 st4 0)                          ⇒ unspecified value
st4                                   ⇒ "cdefefg"
(define st5 "abcdefg")                ⇒ unspecified value
st5                                   ⇒ "abcdefg"
(substring-move-right! st5
  2 6 st5 0)                          ⇒ unspecified value
st5                                   ⇒ "efefefg"
```

SUBSTRING<?, SUBSTRING=?   *Procedure*

These procedures compare two substrings, including case.

Format   (SUBSTRING<? $string_1$ $start_1$ end_1 $string_2$ $start_2$ end_2)
                    (SUBSTRING=? $string_1$ $start_1$ end_1 $string_2$ $start_2$ end_2)

Parameters	$string_1$ — A string.

$start_1$ — An integer. The first substring starts in position $start_1$, where $0 \leq start_1 < end_1 \leq$ length of $string_1$.

end_1 — An integer. The first substring ends in position end_1-1, where $0 \leq start_1 < end_1 \leq$ length of $string_1$.

$string_2$ — A string. It may be the same string as $string_1$.

$start_2$ — An integer. The second substring starts in position $start_2$, where $0 \leq start_2 < end_2 \leq$ length of $string_2$.

end_2 — An integer. The second substring ends in position end_2-1, where $0 \leq start_2 < end_2 \leq$ length of $string_2$.

Explanation

These procedures compare the substring of $string_1$ specified by $start_1$ and end_1 to the substring of $string_2$ specified by $start_2$ and end_2 using the ASCII character codes, including case.

■ SUBSTRING<? returns *true* if one of the following conditions is true:

- A character in the first substring is less than the corresponding character in the second substring, and all previous characters in the first substring are equal to the corresponding characters in the second substring.

- The length of the first substring is less than the length of the second substring, and the characters in the first substring are equal to the corresponding characters in the second substring.

Otherwise, SUBSTRING<? returns *false*.

■ SUBSTRING=? returns *true* if both of the following conditions are true:

- Each character in the first substring is equal to the corresponding character in the second substring.

- The length of the first substring is equal to the length of the second substring.

Otherwise, SUBSTRING=? returns false.

To compare two substrings ignoring case, use SUBSTRING-CI<? and SUBSTRING-CI=?.

Examples

```
(substring<? "ABCDE" 1 4 "BCDEF" 0 4)      ⟹ true
(substring<? "ABCD" 1 3 "abcd" 1 3)         ⟹ true
(substring<? "ABCDEF" 1 4 "ABCDZZ" 1 4)    ⟹ false
(substring=? "house" 0 2 "whole" 1 3 )      ⟹ true
(substring=? "foo" 0 3 "food" 0 3)          ⟹ true
(substring=? "foo" 0 3 "fOOd" 0 3)          ⟹ false
```

SYMBOL->ASCII   *Procedure*

SYMBOL->ASCII converts the first character of a symbol name to its ASCII code.

Format	(SYMBOL->ASCII *symbol*)
Parameter	*symbol* — A symbol
Explanation	SYMBOL->ASCII returns the ASCII value of the first character of *symbol*.

Examples

```
(symbol->ascii 'k)          ⇒ 75  ;k is mapped to uppercase.
(symbol->ascii '{)          ⇒ 123
(symbol->ascii 'lo)         ⇒ 76  ;l is mapped to uppercase.
(symbol->ascii '|lo|)       ⇒ 108 ;l is left in lowercase.
```

SYMBOL->STRING   *Procedure*

SYMBOL->STRING converts a symbol to a string.

Format	(SYMBOL->STRING *symbol*)
Parameter	*symbol* — A symbol
Explanation	SYMBOL->STRING returns the printed representation of *symbol* as a string. No case coercion is performed.
	The inverse operation is STRING->SYMBOL.

Examples

```
(quote flying-fish)          ⇒ FLYING-FISH
(symbol->string 'flying-fish) ⇒ "FLYING-FISH"
(symbol->string 'Martin)     ⇒ "MARTIN"
(symbol->string
    (string->symbol "Malvina")) ⇒ "Malvina"
```

SYMBOL?   *Procedure*

SYMBOL? indicates whether an object is a symbol.

    Format   (SYMBOL? *obj*)

    Parameter   *obj* — Any Scheme object

    Explanation   SYMBOL? returns *true* if *obj* is a symbol and returns *false*, otherwise.

    Examples

```
(symbol? 'foo)           ⇒ true
(symbol? (car '(a b)))   ⇒ true
(symbol? "bar")          ⇒ false
```

SYNTAX   *Special Form*

SYNTAX creates new special forms from patterns and expansions of the patterns.

    Format   (SYNTAX *pattern expansion*)

    Parameters   *pattern* — A list structure of symbols. The first element of the list structure must be a symbol. This gives a pattern for the special form call; the symbol names the special form.

                    expansion — Any Scheme expression. Given the pattern, the new special form expands to this expression.

    Explanation   SYNTAX creates a new special form, or macro, whose keyword is the first element of *pattern*. An unspecified value is returned. To create the expander procedure of the macro, each symbol in *pattern* is recognized in *expansion* and is replaced by its position in *pattern*. If an improper list in *pattern* ends with a symbol, this symbol is recognized as the rest of the list.

                    Note that SYNTAX is a variation of MACRO.

    Examples   The first example creates a new special form called FIRST, which takes the car of its argument.

```
(syntax (first x) (car x))   ⇒ unspecified value

(first '(a b c))             ⇒ A
```

The next example shows the destructuring ability of SYNTAX.

```
(syntax (hi ((a b)(c d) . e))
        (quote ((d b)(a c)(a b c d . e))))
                                    ⇒ unspecified value

(hi ((1 2)(3 4) 5 6 7))             ⇒ ((4 2) (1 3)

(1 2 3 4 5 6 7))
```

The last example shows how to create a special form that creates special forms. A new special form, named MY-ALIAS, is created; MY-ALIAS creates a new special form named NAME1. NAME1 is expanded to be replaced by NAME2.

```
(syntax (my-alias name1 name2)
        (syntax (name1 args) (name2 args)))
                                    ⇒ unspecified value

(my-alias second cadr)             ⇒ unspecified value

(second '(a b c))                  ⇒ B
```

T   *Constant or Variable*

T is an identifier equated with #T.

Format	T
Explanation	Whether T is a constant or a variable depends on the boolean variable PCS-INTEGRATE-T-AND-NIL. If PCS-INTEGRATE-T-AND-NIL is *true*, T is considered to be identical to the constant #T; otherwise, T is a variable defined in the user global environment and is initialized to the value #T. New code should use the constant #T.

Examples

```
(eq? t #T)                         ⇒ true
(set! pcs-integrate-t-and-nil #F)  ⇒ unspecified value
(let ((t 3))
  (eq? t #T))                      ⇒ false

(set! pcs-integrate-t-and-nil #T)  ⇒ unspecified value
(let (t 3))
  (eq? t #T))                      ⇒ error
```

#\TAB   Character   *Object*

#\TAB represents the ASCII tab character.

Format	#\TAB
Explanation	#\TAB is the character object representing a tab. When this object is printed to a port, the ASCII character for tab (9_{10}) is sent to that port. For instance, when this character is sent to the screen with WRITE-CHAR, DISPLAY, or PRINC, the cursor moves to the next tab position. Tab positions are every eight columns.
Examples	(writeln "foo" #\tab "bar") **foo bar** ⇒ *unspecified value*

TAIL   *Procedure*

TAIL returns all but the first element of a stream.

Format	(TAIL *stream*)
Parameter	*stream* — A stream
Explanation	TAIL returns the tail (all but the first element) of *stream*. For other procedures that work with streams, see CONS-STREAM and HEAD.
Examples	(define x (cons-stream 'a 'b)) ⇒ *unspecified value* (tail x) ⇒ B

TAN   *Procedure*

TAN returns the tangent of a number.

Format	(TAN *num*)
Parameter	*num* — Any Scheme number. This is an angle expressed in radians.
Explanation	TAN returns the tangent of *num*.
Examples	(tan 0) ⇒ 0. (tan 0.5236) ⇒ 0.577351901726381 (tan 1.0472) ⇒ 1.73206060282403

THAW *Procedure*

THAW invokes a procedure that has no arguments.

Format	(THAW *thunk*)
Parameter	*thunk* — A procedure with no arguments
Explanation	THAW invokes *thunk* and returns its value.
	For information on creating a *thunk*, see FREEZE.
Examples	(define popsicle (freeze 'fruit-juice)) ⇒ *unspecified value*
	(thaw popsicle) ⇒ FRUIT-JUICE
	(popsicle) ⇒ FRUIT-JUICE

THE-EMPTY-STREAM *Variable*

THE-EMPTY-STREAM is a variable that represents an empty stream.

Format	THE-EMPTY-STREAM
Explanation	THE-EMPTY-STREAM is set initially to a stream that has no elements.
	For more information on streams, see CONS-STREAM, HEAD, and TAIL.
Examples	(define strm
	(cons-stream 'strm-head the-empty-stream))
	⇒ *unspecified value*
	(stream->list strm) ⇒ (STRM-HEAD)
	(stream? the-empty-stream) ⇒ *true*
	(empty-stream? the-empty-stream) ⇒ *true*

THE-ENVIRONMENT *Procedure*

THE-ENVIRONMENT returns the current lexical environment.

Format	(THE-ENVIRONMENT)
Parameters	None
Explanation	THE-ENVIRONMENT returns the lexical environment in effect at the point of the call.

See also MAKE-ENVIRONMENT.

Examples
```
(define surface-environment (the-environment))
                                          ⇒ unspecified value
(define nastiest-predator 'tiger)         ⇒ unspecified value

(define ocean-environment
  (let ((nastiest-predator 'shark))
    (the-environment)))                   ⇒ unspecified value

(access nastiest-predator surface-environment)
                                          ⇒ TIGER
(access nastiest-predator ocean-environment)
                                          ⇒ SHARK
```

THE-NON-PRINTING-OBJECT   *Variable*

THE-NON-PRINTING-OBJECT does not print at Scheme top level.

Format   *THE-NON-PRINTING-OBJECT*

Explanation   *THE-NON-PRINTING-OBJECT* is set originally to an internal value that is recognized by the Scheme read-eval-print loop, causing nothing to be printed. When this variable is used as the result of a top-level procedure, the result does not print.

Examples
```
(begin (display "This will return the ")
       (display "non-printing object and ")
       (newline)
       (display "the result will not be printed.")
       *the-non-printing-object*)
```
This will return the non-printing object and
and the result will not be printed.
⇒

TRACE, TRACE-BOTH, TRACE-ENTRY, TRACE-EXIT   *Procedure*

These procedures install tracing breakpoints in a specified procedure.

Format   (TRACE *proc*)
                (TRACE-BOTH *proc*)
                (TRACE-ENTRY *proc*)
                (TRACE-EXIT *proc*)

Parameter   *proc* — A procedure. Since *proc* must evaluate to a procedure, it must be defined before a tracing procedure is used.

Explanation   These procedures trace each entry to or exit from a specified procedure. An unspecified value is returned. Specifically, the procedures work as follows:

- TRACE — Traces each entry to a procedure

- TRACE-BOTH — Traces each entry to and exit from a procedure

- TRACE-ENTRY — Traces each entry to a procedure

- TRACE-EXIT — Traces each exit from a procedure

Tracing the entry to a procedure works as follows: each time the procedure *proc* is entered, a message containing the *proc* name and its arguments is printed.

Tracing the exit from a procedure works as follows: each time the procedure *proc* is exited, a message containing the *proc* name, its arguments, and the value returned by *proc* is printed.

When PCS-DEBUG-MODE is off and a self-recursive procedure that uses NAMED-LAMBDA or REC such as the following is traced, only the first call (outer call) is traced:

```
(DEFINE name (NAMED-LAMBDA (name ...) ... (name ...)
                          ...))
```

To remove tracing information from a procedure, use UNTRACE, UNTRACE-ENTRY, or UNTRACE-EXIT. To install general-purpose break-points in a procedure, see BREAK, BREAK-BOTH, BREAK-ENTRY, and BREAK-EXIT.

Examples   A recursive factorial procedure named FACT is defined as follows:

```
(define fact
  (lambda (n)
    (if (< n 2) 1 (* n (fact (-1+ n)))))))
```
⟹ *unspecified value*

Next, the FACT procedure is called and the answer is returned.

```
(fact 3)
```
⟹ 6

Then the TRACE-BOTH procedure is called to trace each entry to and exit from FACT.

```
(trace-both fact)
```
⟹ *unspecified value*

Now the FACT procedure is called again. Since FACT is a recursive procedure, it is called three times, once with 3 as its argument, once with 2 as its argument, and once with 1 as its argument as shown by the messages displayed on the screen. It is also exited from 3 times, once with the value of 1, once with the value of 2, and once with the value of 6 as shown.

```
(fact 3)
  >>> Entering #<PROCEDURE FACT>
    Argument 1: 3
  >>> Entering #<PROCEDURE FACT>
    Argument 1: 2
  >>> Entering #<PROCEDURE FACT>
    Argument 1: 1
  <<< Leaving #<PROCEDURE FACT> with value 1
    Argument 1: 1
  <<< Leaving #<PROCEDURE FACT> with value 2
    Argument 1: 2
  <<< Leaving #<PROCEDURE FACT> with value 6
    Argument 1: 3                              ⇒ 6
```

TRANSCRIPT-OFF, TRANSCRIPT-ON   *Procedure*

These procedures control the printing of a transcript file.

Format	(TRANSCRIPT-OFF)
	(TRANSCRIPT-ON *filespec*)
Parameter	*filespec* — A string that names a file
Explanation	These procedures determine whether or not console input and output (I/O) are recorded in a transcript file.
	TRANSCRIPT-ON causes all console I/O to be recorded in *filespec*. An unspecified value is returned. If *filespec* already exists, the transcript output is appended to the end of the file.
	TRANSCRIPT-OFF turns off the automatic recording of console I/O and closes the transcript file (*filespec*). An unspecified value is returned.
	The default setting for transcript mode is off.

Examples

```
(transcript-on "trans.fil")          ⇒ unspecified value
(print "transcript test")
"transcript test"                    ⇒ unspecified value
(+ 3 2)                              ⇒ 5
(transcript-off)                     ⇒ unspecified value
```

After the above session has been completed, the file trans.fil contains the following:

```
OK
[2] (print "transcript test")
"transcript test"
[3] (+ 3 2)
5
[4] (transcript-off)
```

In this example, [2], [3], and [4] are Scheme prompts.

#T   *Constant*

#T is the boolean truth value representing a true condition.

Format	#T
Explanation	#T is the boolean value for a true condition. Since #T is self-evaluating, it does not need to be quoted in programs.
	#!TRUE is provided for historical reasons only. New code should use #T.

NOTE: #T prints as #T, and #F prints as ( ).

Examples	(eq? #T '#T)	⇒ *true*
	#T	⇒ *true*

TRUE   *Variable*

TRUE is a variable with an initial value of #T.

Format	TRUE	
Explanation	TRUE is set originally to #T. Since TRUE is a variable, its value may be changed.	
	Write new code using the constant #T.	
Examples	(eq? true #T)	⇒ *true*
	(let ((true 1))	
	(eq? true #T))	⇒ *false*

TRUNCATE

Procedure

TRUNCATE returns the integer component of a number.

Format   (TRUNCATE *num*)

Parameter   *num* — Any Scheme number

Explanation   TRUNCATE returns the integer part of *num* by rounding *num* towards zero.

Examples

```
(truncate 3.5)        ⇒ 3
(truncate -3.5)       ⇒ -3
(truncate 7)          ⇒ 7
```

UNADVISE, UNADVISE-ENTRY, UNADVISE-EXIT

Procedure

These procedures remove advice from a specified procedure.

Format
```
(UNADVISE  {proc})
(UNADVISE-ENTRY  {proc})
(UNADVISE-EXIT  {proc})
```

Parameter   *proc* — A procedure. Since *proc* must evaluate to a procedure, it must be defined before using UNADVISE, UNADVISE-ENTRY, or UNADVISE-EXIT.

Explanation   These procedures remove the entry and exit advice from *proc* including tracing and breakpoints. An unspecified value is returned. Specifically, the procedures work as follows:

- UNADVISE — Removes both entry and exit advice. This is equivalent to calling both UNADVISE-ENTRY and UNADVISE-EXIT.

- UNADVISE-ENTRY — Removes entry advice.

- UNADVISE-EXIT — Removes exit advice.

If *proc* is not specified, the default is all advised procedures.

For information on giving advice to a specified procedure, see ADVISE-ENTRY, ADVISE-EXIT, BREAK, BREAK-BOTH, BREAK-ENTRY, BREAK-EXIT, TRACE, TRACE-BOTH, TRACE-ENTRY, and TRACE-EXIT.

Examples   A procedure named FOO is defined as follows:

```
(define foo (lambda (a b) (+ a b 3)))     ⇒ unspecified value
```

The procedures ADVISE-ENTRY and ADVISE-EXIT are called next with the FOO procedure and with advice of (lambda (p a e) ...) and (lambda (p a r e) ...), respectively.

```
(advise-entry foo
  (lambda (p a e)
    (writeln "The procedure " p
             " is being called with "
             a)))                              ⟹ unspecified value

(advise-exit foo
  (lambda (p a r e)
    (writeln "When the procedure " p
             " is called with " a
             ", it returns " r)
    r))                                        ⟹ unspecified value
```

Now, when the FOO procedure is called, the entry and exit messages are displayed and the value is returned.

```
(foo 3 4)
```
The procedure #\<PROCEDURE foo\>
is being called with (3 4)
When the procedure #\<PROCEDURE foo\>
is called with (3 4), it returns 10   ⟹ 10

Next, UNADVISE is called to turn off all advice. Then, when the FOO procedure is called, no advice is displayed.

```
(unadvise foo)                                 ⟹ unspecified value

(foo 3 4)                                      ⟹ 10
```

UNBOUND?

Special form

UNBOUND? determines whether a variable is bound in an environment.

Format	(UNBOUND? *sym*₁ {... *env*})
Parameters	*sym*₁ ... — Symbols (not evaluated)
	env — An environment (evaluated)
Explanation	UNBOUND? checks an environment to see if *sym* is bound in that environment.
	If an environment is not specified, UNBOUND? returns *true* if *sym* is not bound in the current environment and *false*, otherwise.
	If *env* and only one *sym* are specified, UNBOUND? returns *true* if *sym* is not bound in *env*.

If *env* and more than one *sym* are specified, the value of sym_n in *env* is obtained. This value must be an environment. Next, sym_{n-1} is looked up in that environment and an environment is returned. Then sym_{n-2} is looked up in that environment and so forth. When sym_1 is looked up in the environment returned when sym_2 is looked up, UNBOUND? returns *true* if sym_1 is not bound in that environment and returns *false*, otherwise.

Examples

```
(define env1
    (make-environment (define x 5)))   ⟹ unspecified value (de-
fine env2
    (make-environment (define y env1))) ⟹ unspecified value
(unbound? x env1)                      ⟹ false
(unbound? y env1)                      ⟹ true
(unbound? y env2)                      ⟹ false
(unbound? x y env2)                    ⟹ false
```

UNBREAK, UNBREAK-ENTRY, UNBREAK-EXIT   *Procedure*

These procedures remove a breakpoint from a specified procedure.

Format

```
(UNBREAK proc)
(UNBREAK-ENTRY proc)
(UNBREAK-EXIT proc)
```

Parameter

proc — A procedure. Since *proc* must evaluate to a procedure, it must be defined before any procedure that removes a breakpoint is used.

Explanation

These procedures discontinue the entering of a breakpoint on entry to or exit from *proc*. An unspecified value is returned. Specifically, the procedures work as follows:

- UNBREAK — Discontinues breaking a procedure upon entry and exit. This is equivalent to calling both UNBREAK-ENTRY and UNBREAK-EXIT.

- UNBREAK-ENTRY — Discontinues breaking a procedure upon entry.

- UNBREAK-EXIT — Discontinues breaking a procedure upon exit.

If *proc* is not specified, the default is all procedures.

For information on including a breakpoint in a procedure, see BREAK, BREAK-BOTH, BREAK-ENTRY, and BREAK-EXIT.

Examples

A procedure, named FOO, is defined.

```
(define foo
    (lambda (a b)
        (+ a b 3)))                    ⟹ unspecified value
```

Next, a break upon entry is set by calling BREAK-ENTRY.

(break-entry foo)   ⟹ *unspecified value*

Now the FOO procedure is called and an entry breakpoint is executed.

```
(foo 5 6)
  [BKPT encountered!] BREAK-ENTRY
  (#<PROCEDURE foo> 5 6)
[Inspect] . . .
```

After Scheme is returned to the top-level read-eval-print loop, the UNBREAK procedure is called. Then FOO is called and no break occurs.

(unbreak foo)   ⟹ *unspecified value*
(foo 4 3)   ⟹ 10

UNQUOTE   *Special Form*

UNQUOTE is a special form valid only within QUASIQUOTE expressions.

Format	(UNQUOTE *expression*) ,*expression*
Parameters	*expression* — Any Scheme expression
Explanation	When appearing within a QUASIQUOTE pattern, *expression* is evaluated and its result is inserted into the quasiquote structure instead of the unquote expression. (UNQUOTE *expression*) may be abbreviated as ,*expression*. The two notations are equivalent in all respects.
Examples	See QUASIQUOTE.

UNQUOTE-SPLICING   *Special Form*

UNQUOTE-SPLICING is a special form valid only within QUASIQUOTE expressions.

Format	(UNQUOTE-SPLICING *expression*) @*expression*
Parameters	*expression* — Any Scheme expression

Explanation	When appearing within a QUASIQUOTE pattern, *expression* must evaluate to a list. The opening and closing parenthesis of the list are stripped away, and the elements of the list are inserted in place of the unquote-splicing sequence.
	(UNQUOTE-SPLICING *expression*) may be abbreviated as ,@*expression*. The two notations are equivalent in all respects.
Examples	See QUASIQUOTE.

UNTRACE, UNTRACE-ENTRY, UNTRACE-EXIT   *Procedure*

These procedures remove tracing information from a specified procedure.

Format	(UNTRACE *proc*) (UNTRACE-ENTRY *proc*) (UNTRACE-EXIT *proc*)
Parameter	*proc* — A procedure. Since *proc* must evaluate to a procedure, it must be defined before any procedure that removes tracing is used.
Explanation	These procedures discontinue tracing the entry to or exit from *proc*. An unspecified value is returned. Specifically, the procedures work as follows:

- ■ UNTRACE — Discontinues tracing a procedure upon entry and exit. This is equivalent to calling both UNTRACE-ENTRY and UNTRACE-EXIT.

- ■ UNTRACE-ENTRY — Discontinues tracing a procedure upon entry.

- ■ UNTRACE-EXIT — Discontinues tracing a procedure upon exit.

If *proc* is not specified, the default is all procedures.

For information on including tracing information in a procedure, see TRACE, TRACE-BOTH, TRACE-ENTRY, and TRACE-EXIT.

Examples	A recursive factorial procedure, named FACT, is defined.

```
(define fact
  (lambda (n)
    (if (< n 2) 1 (* n (fact (-1+ n))))))
                                            ⇒ unspecified value
```

Now the FACT procedure is called and the answer is returned.

```
(fact 3)                                    ⇒ 6
```

Then the TRACE-BOTH procedure is called to trace the entry to and exit from FACT.

```
(trace-both fact)                        ⇒ unspecified value
```

Next, the FACT procedure is called again. Since FACT is a recursive procedure, it is called three times, once with 3 as its argument, once with 2 as its argument, and once with 1 as its argument as shown by the messages. FACT also is exited three times, once with 1 returned, once with 2 returned, and once with the final value of 6 returned.

```
(fact 3)
 >>> Entering #<PROCEDURE FACT>
   Argument 1: 3
 >>> Entering #<PROCEDURE FACT>
   Argument 1: 2
 >>> Entering #<PROCEDURE FACT>
   Argument 1: 1
 <<< Leaving #<PROCEDURE FACT> with value 1
   Argument 1: 1
 <<< Leaving #<PROCEDURE FACT> with value 2
   Argument 1: 2
 <<< Leaving #<PROCEDURE FACT> with value 6
   Argument 1: 3                          ⇒ 6
```

To stop the tracing, the UNTRACE procedure is called. Now when FACT is called again, no tracing is done.

```
(untrace fact)                           ⇒ unspecified value
(fact 4)                                 ⇒ 24
```

USER-GLOBAL-ENVIRONMENT   *Variable*

USER-GLOBAL-ENVIRONMENT is bound to the environment that contains system-defined variables.

Format   USER-GLOBAL-ENVIRONMENT

Explanation   USER-GLOBAL-ENVIRONMENT is bound to the environment that defines system variables. This environment is the parent of the USER-INITIAL-ENVIRONMENT.

Examples
```
(define brand-new-value 42)              ⇒ unspecified value
(set! (access brand-new-value
              user-global-environment)
        99)                              ⇒ unspecified value
(access brand-new-value user-global-environment)
                                         ⇒ 99
(access read user-global-environment)    ⇒ #<PROCEDURE read>
(eq? (environment-parent user-initial-environment)
     user-global-environment)            ⇒ true
read                                     ⇒ #<PROCEDURE read>
```

USER-INITIAL-ENVIRONMENT

Variable

USER-INITIAL-ENVIRONMENT is the standard top-level environment.

Format	USER-INITIAL-ENVIRONMENT
Explanation	USER-INITIAL-ENVIRONMENT is bound to the environment in which typed expressions are evaluated. This environment is empty initially.
	See also USER-GLOBAL-ENVIRONMENT.

Examples

```
(let ((brand-new-value 99))
  (set! (access brand-new-value
               user-initial-environment)
        42))                              ⟹ unspecified value
brand-new-value                           ⟹ 42
(eq? (environment-parent user-initial-environment)
     user-global-environment)            ⟹ true
```

VECTOR

Procedure

VECTOR creates a new vector containing the specified elements.

Format	(VECTOR obj_1 ...)
Parameters	obj_1 ... — Any Scheme objects
Explanation	VECTOR returns a new vector whose elements are the values of the specified objects in order. The number of elements in the new vector is the same as the number of arguments.
	Related vector procedures are VECTOR-REF and VECTOR-SET!.
Examples	(vector 'a 1 2 (list 'a 'b 'c)) ⟹ #(A 1 2 (A B C))

VECTOR->LIST

Procedure

VECTOR->LIST creates a list from a vector.

Format	(VECTOR->LIST *vector*)
Parameter	*vector* — A vector
Explanation	VECTOR->LIST returns a proper list of the objects contained in *vector*.

To create a vector from a proper list, use LIST–>VECTOR. Other related vector procedures are MAKE-VECTOR, VECTOR, VECTOR-REF, and VECTOR-SET!.

Examples

```
(define a (vector 'a 'b 'c 3))    ⟹ unspecified value
a                                  ⟹ #(A B C 3)
(vector->list a)                   ⟹ (A B C 3)
```

VECTOR-FILL!   *Procedure*

VECTOR-FILL! replaces each element of a vector with a specified value.

Format   (VECTOR-FILL! *vector fill*)

Parameters   *vector* — A vector

               fill — Any Scheme object

Explanation   VECTOR-FILL! replaces each element of vector with the value of *fill*. An unspecified value is returned.

               For related vector procedures, see MAKE-VECTOR, VECTOR-REF, and VECTOR-SET!.

Examples

```
(define a (vector 'a 'b 1 2))     ⟹ unspecified value
a                                  ⟹ #(A B 1 2)
(vector-fill! a 5)                 ⟹ unspecified value
a                                  ⟹ #(5 5 5 5)
```

VECTOR-LENGTH   *Procedure*

VECTOR-LENGTH returns the number of elements in a vector.

Format   (VECTOR-LENGTH *vector*)

Parameter   *vector* — A vector

Explanation   VECTOR-LENGTH returns the number of elements in *vector*.

               For related vector procedures, see MAKE-VECTOR, VECTOR-REF, and VECTOR-SET!.

Examples

```
(define a (vector 'a 'b 1 2))     ⟹ unspecified value
a                                  ⟹ #(A B 1 2)
(vector-length a)                  ⟹ 4
```

VECTOR-REF   *Procedure*

VECTOR-REF returns a specific element from a vector.

Format	(VECTOR-REF *vector index*)
Parameters	*vector* — A vector
	index — A nonnegative integer
Explanation	VECTOR-REF returns the element of *vector* from the position specified by *index*. The index of the first element of *vector* is zero, and the index of the last element is one less than the number of elements in *vector*.
	For related vector procedures, see MAKE-VECTOR and VECTOR-SET!.
Examples	(define a (vector 'a 'b 1 2)) ⟹ *unspecified value*
	(vector-ref a 0) ⟹ A
	(vector-ref a 2) ⟹ 1
	(vector-ref a 3) ⟹ 2
	(vector-length a) ⟹ 4

VECTOR-SET!   *Procedure*

VECTOR-SET! replaces a specific element in a vector.

Format	(VECTOR-SET! *vector index obj*)
Parameters	*vector* — A vector
	index — A nonnegative integer
	obj — Any Scheme object
Explanation	VECTOR-SET! stores the value of *obj* in the element of *vector* specified by *index*. An unspecified value is returned. The index of the first element of *vector* is zero, and the index of the last element is one less than the number of elements in *vector*.
	For related vector procedures, see MAKE-VECTOR and VECTOR-REF.
Examples	(define a (make-vector 4 'a)) ⟹ *unspecified value*
	a ⟹ #(A A A A)
	(vector-set! a 2 99) ⟹ *unspecified value*
	a ⟹ #(A A 99 A)

VECTOR?   *Procedure*

VECTOR? indicates whether an object is a vector.

Format	(VECTOR? *obj*)
Parameter	*obj* — Any Scheme object
Explanation	VECTOR? returns *true* if *obj* is a vector and returns *false*, otherwise.
	For related vector procedures, see MAKE-VECTOR, VECTOR-REF, and VECTOR-SET!.
Examples	(vector? (vector 1 2 3)) ⟹ *true*
	(vector? (list 1 2 3)) ⟹ *false*

WHEN   *Special Form*

WHEN conditionally evaluates a sequence of expressions.

Format	(WHEN *predicate exp₁* ...)
Parameters	*predicate* — Any Scheme expression.
	exp₁ ... — Any Scheme expressions. These form the body of WHEN.
Explanation	WHEN evaluates *predicate*. If the value of *predicate* is *true*, each *exp* is evaluated in order; otherwise, they are ignored. Since the body of the WHEN special form is evaluated for its effect, an unspecified value is returned.

Examples

```
(define sugar-bowl 'sugar)                  ⟹ unspecified value
(define salt-shaker 'salt)                  ⟹ unspecified value
(define nobody-is-looking #F)               ⟹ unspecified value
(define play-joke
  (lambda ()
    (let ((cup '()))
      (when nobody-is-looking
          (set! cup salt-shaker)
          (set! salt-shaker sugar-bowl)
          (set! sugar-bowl cup)))))         ⟹ unspecified value
(play-joke)                                 ⟹ unspecified value
sugar-bowl                                  ⟹ SUGAR
(set! nobody-is-looking #T)                 ⟹ unspecified value
(play-joke)                                 ⟹ unspecified value
sugar-bowl                                  ⟹ SALT
```

WINDOW-CLEAR

WINDOW-CLEAR clears a window.

Procedure

Format	(WINDOW-CLEAR *window*)
Parameter	*window* — A Scheme window
Explanation	WINDOW-CLEAR clears the area described by *window* and draws a border (if one is specified by *window*). The cursor is positioned in the upper left-hand corner of the window, which is location (0,0). This procedure is used to display a window on the screen. An unspecified value is returned.
	To create a window, use MAKE-WINDOW.
	For more information on windows, see the *PC Scheme User's Guide — Student Edition*.

WINDOW-DELETE

WINDOW-DELETE deletes a window.

Procedure

Format	(WINDOW-DELETE *window*)
Parameter	*window* — A Scheme window
Explanation	WINDOW-DELETE clears the area described by *window* as well as the area covered by its border. An unspecified value is returned.
	To create a window, use MAKE-WINDOW.
	For more information on windows, see the *PC Scheme User's Guide — Student Edition*.

WINDOW-GET-ATTRIBUTE

WINDOW-GET-ATTRIBUTE returns the current value of an attribute for a window.

Procedure

Format	(WINDOW-GET-ATTRIBUTE *window name*)

Parameters	*window* — A Scheme window.

name — An attribute name. The following are valid attribute names:

- 'BORDER-ATTRIBUTES — The video attributes used to draw the border of *window*. Attributes include such features as color, intensity, flashing characters, reverse video, and underlining. The value returned is an integer between 0 and 255, inclusive, and is hardware-dependent. Consult the *PC Scheme User's Guide — Student Edition* for more information.

- 'TEXT-ATTRIBUTES — The video attributes used for the text in the data portion of *window*. Attributes include such features as color, intensity, flashing characters, reverse video, and underlining. The value returned is an integer between 0 and 255, inclusive, and is hardware-dependent. Consult the *PC Scheme User's Guide — Student Edition* for more information.

- 'WINDOW-FLAGS — The least significant bit of the value returned is the wrap/clip attribute. If the integer returned is even, lines longer than the line length of *window* are clipped (truncated); otherwise, lines longer than the line length are wrapped (continued) on subsequent lines. Bits other than the least significant bit are reserved.

Explanation	WINDOW-GET-ATTRIBUTE returns an integer representing the current value of *name* for *window*.

To specify the attributes of a window, use WINDOW-SET-ATTRIBUTE!.

For more information on windows, see the *PC Scheme User's Guide — Student Edition*.

WINDOW-GET-CURSOR   *Procedure*

WINDOW-GET-CURSOR returns the position of the cursor in a window.

Format	(WINDOW-GET-CURSOR *window*)
Parameter	*window* — A Scheme window
Explanation	WINDOW-GET-CURSOR returns the current position of the cursor in *window* as a dotted pair (line . column). The line and column positions are relative to the upper lefthand corner of *window*.

To position the cursor in a *window*, use WINDOW-SET-CURSOR!.

For more information on windows, see the *PC Scheme User's Guide — Student Edition*.

WINDOW-GET-POSITION

Procedure

WINDOW-GET-POSITION returns the position of a window.

Format	(WINDOW-GET-POSITION *window*)
Parameter	*window* — A Scheme window
Explanation	WINDOW-GET-POSITION returns the coordinates of the upper lefthand corner of *window* (excluding the border) as a dotted pair (line . column). The upper lefthand corner of the screen is (0,0).
	To specify the window's location, use WINDOW-SET-POSITION!.
	For more information on windows, see the *PC Scheme User's Guide — Student Edition*.

WINDOW-GET-SIZE

Procedure

WINDOW-GET-SIZE returns the size of a window.

Format	(WINDOW-GET-SIZE *window*)
Parameter	*window* — A Scheme window
Explanation	WINDOW-GET-SIZE returns the number of lines and columns of *window* as a dotted pair (lines . columns).
	To specify the window's size, use WINDOW-SET-SIZE!.
	For more information on windows, see the *PC Scheme User's Guide — Student Edition*.

WINDOW-POPUP

Procedure

WINDOW-POPUP puts a temporary window on the screen.

Format	(WINDOW-POPUP *window*)
Parameter	*window* — A Scheme window
Explanation	WINDOW-POPUP saves the data that will be covered by *window* (for future restoration), draws the border of *window* (if one is specified), and clears *window*. An unspecified value is returned.

NOTE: Pop-up windows must be maintained in a last in, first out manner. Also, I/O operations should not be performed to windows that currently are covered by pop-up windows.

To remove a pop-up window from the screen, use WINDOW-POPUP-DELETE.

For more information on windows, see the *PC Scheme User's Guide — Student Edition*.

WINDOW-POPUP-DELETE   *Procedure*

WINDOW-POPUP-DELETE removes a pop-up window from the screen.

Format	(WINDOW-POPUP-DELETE *window*)
Parameter	*window* — A Scheme pop-up window
Explanation	WINDOW-POPUP-DELETE deletes *window* and restores the data on the screen when *window* was created. An unspecified value is returned.

NOTE: Pop-up windows must be maintained in a last in, first out manner.

To create a pop-up window, use WINDOW-POPUP.

For more information on windows, see the *PC Scheme User's Guide — Student Edition*.

WINDOW-RESTORE-CONTENTS   *Procedure*

WINDOW-RESTORE-CONTENTS restores the text and border attributes of a window.

Format	(WINDOW-RESTORE-CONTENTS *window contents*)
Parameters	*window* — A Scheme window
	contents — Data and character attributes captured by WINDOW-SAVE-CONTENTS
Explanation	WINDOW-RESTORE-CONTENTS restores *contents* in *window*. An unspecified value is returned.
	For more information on windows, see the *PC Scheme User's Guide — Student Edition*.

WINDOW-SAVE-CONTENTS   *Procedure*

WINDOW-SAVE-CONTENTS returns the text and border attributes of a window.

Format	(WINDOW-SAVE-CONTENTS *window*)
Parameter	*window* — A Scheme window
Explanation	WINDOW-SAVE-CONTENTS captures and returns the contents (text and border attributes) in the area described by *window* (including the border if one is specified).
	The contents may be restored in the window with the WINDOW-RESTORE-CONTENTS procedure.
	For more information on windows, see the *PC Scheme User's Guide — Student Edition*.

WINDOW-SET-ATTRIBUTE!   *Procedure*

WINDOW-SET-ATTRIBUTE! changes an attribute of a window.

Format	(WINDOW-SET-ATTRIBUTE! *window* *name* *value*)
Parameters	*window* — A Scheme window.
	name — An attribute name. The following are valid attribute names:

- ■ 'BORDER-ATTRIBUTES — The video attributes used to draw the border of *window*. Attributes include such features as color, intensity, flashing characters, reverse video, and underlining.

- ■ 'TEXT-ATTRIBUTES — The video attributes used for the text in the data portion of *window*. Attributes include such features as color, intensity, flashing characters, reverse video, and underlining.

- ■ 'WINDOW-FLAGS — The least significant bit represents the wrap/clip attribute. If *value* is even, lines longer than the line length of *window* are clipped (truncated); otherwise, lines longer than the line length are wrapped (continued) on subsequent lines. Bits other than the least significant bit are reserved.

	value — An integer between 0 and 255, inclusive. This value is hardware-dependent. Consult the *PC Scheme User's Guide — Student Edition* for more information.
Explanation	WINDOW-SET-ATTRIBUTE! changes the attribute (*name*) of *window* to *value*. An unspecified value is returned. The display does not change until the next I/O operation to *window* is performed.

> **WARNING**: Setting an attribute to an invalid value may cause undesirable side effects.

See also WINDOW-GET-ATTRIBUTE.

For more information on windows, see the *PC Scheme User's Guide — Student Edition*.

WINDOW-SET-CURSOR!   *Procedure*

WINDOW-SET-CURSOR! changes the position of the cursor in a window.

Format	(WINDOW-SET-CURSOR! *window cursor-line cursor-column*)
Parameters	*window* — A Scheme window.
	cursor-line — An integer representing the line number in *window*. A value of *false* may be used to leave the cursor on the same line.
	cursor-column — An integer representing the column number in *window*. A value of *false* may be used to leave the cursor in the same column.
Explanation	WINDOW-SET-CURSOR! changes the current position of the cursor in *window* to *cursor-line* and *cursor-column*. An unspecified value is returned. The line and column position of the upper lefthand corner of *window* is (0,0).

See also WINDOW-GET-CURSOR.

For more information on windows, see the *PC Scheme User's Guide — Student Edition*.

WINDOW-SET-POSITION!   *Procedure*

WINDOW-SET-POSITION! changes the position of a window.

Format	(WINDOW-SET-POSITION! *window ul-line ul-col*)
Parameters	*window* — A Scheme window.
	ul-line — An integer representing the upper left vertical position of *window*. A value of *false* can be used to leave the vertical position unchanged.
	ul-col — An integer representing the upper left horizontal position of *window*. A value of *false* can be used to leave the horizontal position unchanged.

Explanation   WINDOW-SET-POSITION! changes the location of the upper lefthand corner (excluding the border) of *window* to (*ul-line, ul-col*). An unspecified value is returned. The display does not change until the next I/O operation to *window* is performed. The upper lefthand corner of the screen is (0,0).

See also WINDOW-GET-POSITION.

For more information on windows, see the *PC Scheme User's Guide — Student Edition.*

WINDOW-SET-SIZE!   *Procedure*

WINDOW-SET-SIZE! changes the dimensions of a window.

Format   (WINDOW-SET-SIZE! *window n-lines n-cols*)

Parameters   *window* — A Scheme window.

n-lines — An integer representing the number of lines in *window*. A value of *false* may be used to leave the number of lines unchanged.

n-cols — An integer representing the number of columns in *window*. A value of *false* may be used to leave the number of columns unchanged.

Explanation   WINDOW-SET-SIZE! changes the dimensions of *window* to be *n-lines* by *n-cols*. An unspecified value is returned. The display does not change until the next I/O operation to *window* is performed.

See also WINDOW-GET-SIZE!.

For more information on windows, see the *PC Scheme User's Guide — Student Edition.*

WINDOW?   *Procedure*

WINDOW? determines if its argument is a window.

Format   (WINDOW? *obj*)

Parameter   *obj* — Any Scheme object

Explanation   WINDOW? returns *true* if *obj* is a port object for a window and *false,* otherwise.

WITH-INPUT-FROM-FILE, WITH-OUTPUT-TO-FILE   *Procedure*

These procedures open and close a file for input or output.

Format	(WITH-INPUT-FROM-FILE *filespec thunk*) (WITH-OUTPUT-TO-FILE *filespec thunk*)
Parameters	*filespec* — A string that names a file
	thunk — A procedure of no arguments
Explanation	These procedures create the specified type of port using *filespec* and change the default value of the appropriate current port to be the newly created port. Next, *thunk* is evaluated. When the evaluation is complete, the new port is closed, and the default value of the current port is reset to its original value. The value of *thunk* is returned.
	These procedures attempt to close the new port and restore the previous default value whenever the current continuation changes in such a way as to make it doubtful that the *thunk* will ever return.
	WITH-INPUT-FROM-FILE opens an input port using *filespec*. The file must exist already. The new port becomes the current input port.
	WITH-OUTPUT-TO-FILE opens an output port using *filespec*. The file need not exist. If the file exists, the information in it is overwritten. The new port becomes the current output port.

Examples

```
(with-output-to-file "bounce.tmp"
  (lambda ()
    (write 'boing!)
    #F))                          ⇒ false

(with-input-from-file "bounce.tmp"
  (lambda ()
    (read)))                      ⇒ BOING!
```

WRITE   *Procedure*

WRITE prints its argument to a port.

Format	(WRITE *exp* {*port*})
Parameters	*exp* — Any Scheme expression. This argument is evaluated and then its value is printed.
	port — An optional argument that specifies the output port.

Explanation	WRITE prints the *value* of *exp* to either *port* or the current output port if *port* is not specified. An unspecified value is returned.

Strings that are written are enclosed in double quotes, and special characters (backslash and double quotes) within the string are escaped by backslashes. WRITE slashifies special characters in symbols.

In general, DISPLAY is intended for producing human-readable output; while WRITE is intended for machine-readable output.

Examples	`(write (+ 1 2))`	
	3	⟹ *unspecified value*
	`(write "Hi there.")`	
	"Hi there."	⟹ *unspecified value*
	`(write '|abc|)`	
	|abc|	⟹ *unspecified value*

WRITE-CHAR *Procedure*

WRITE-CHAR prints its argument to a port.

Format	(WRITE-CHAR *char* {*port*})
Parameters	*char* — A Scheme character
	port — An optional argument that specifies the output port
Explanation	WRITE-CHAR prints the character representation of *char* (not the written representation) to either *port* or the current output port if *port* is not specified. An unspecified value is returned.

Examples

```
(define write-odd-chars
  (rec loop
    (lambda (string index)
      (cond ((= index (string-length string))
             (newline))
            ((odd? index)
             (write-char
               (string-ref string index))
             (loop string (+ 2 index)))
            (else (loop string (1+ index)))))))
```
⟹ *unspecified value*

```
(define s "abcdefg")
```
⟹ *unspecified value*

```
(write-odd-chars s 0)
bdf
```
⟹ *unspecified value*

```
(string-set! s 3 #\backspace)
```
⟹ *unspecified value*

```
(write-odd-chars s 0)
f
```
⟹ *unspecified value*

WRITELN   *Procedure*

WRITELN writes its arguments to the current output port.

Format   (WRITELN *obj*₁ ...)

Parameters   *obj*₁ ... — Objects that are evaluated and then printed

Explanation   WRITELN prints the value of each *obj* in order to the current output port
                    using DISPLAY. After all the arguments are printed, WRITELN calls
                    NEWLINE to end the line. WRITELN returns an unspecified value.

Examples
```
(begin (writeln 'abc 1 2 " abc")
       (display "def"))
  ABC12 abc
  def
```
⟹ *unspecified value*

ZERO?

ZERO? determines whether a number is zero.

Format	(ZERO? *num*)
Parameter	*num* — Any Scheme number
Explanation	ZERO? returns *true* is *num* is zero and *false*, otherwise.
Examples	(zero? 0) ⇒ *true*
	(zero? 5) ⇒ *false*
	(zero? −.3) ⇒ *false*

BIBLIOGRAPHY

[1]   Abelson, Harold, and Sussman, Gerald Jay with Sussman, Julie. *Structure and Interpretation of Computer Programs*. Cambridge, MA: MIT Press, 1985.

[2]   Bobrow, D.G., and Stefik, M.J. *The LOOPS Manual*. Palo Alto, CA: Xerox Corporation, 1983.

[3]   Church, Alonzo. "The Calculi of Lambda Conversion." *Annals of Mathematics Studies 6* (1941).

[4]   Fessenden, Carol; Clinger, William; Friedman, Daniel P.; and Haynes, Christopher. "Scheme 311 Version 4 Reference Manual." Indiana University Computer Science Department Technical Report No. 137 (February 1983).

[5]   Friedman, Daniel P., and Haynes, Christopher T. "Constraining Control." In *Conference Record of the Twelfth Annual ACM Symposium on Principles of Programming Languages*. January 1985, pp. 245–254.

[6]   Friedman, Haynes, Kohlbecker, and Wand. "Fundamental Abstractions of Programming Languages and Their Implementation." *Programming Language: Abstractions and Their Implementations*. To appear.

[7]   Friedman, Daniel P.; Haynes, Christopher T.; Kohlbecker, Eugene; and Wand, Mitchell. "Scheme 84 Interim Reference Manual." Indiana University Computer Science Department Technical Report No. 153 (January 1985).

[8]   Greif, Irene, and Hewitt, Carl. *Actor Semantics of Planner-73*. Working paper 81, MIT AI Lab, Cambridge, MA. 1975.

[9]   Haynes, Christopher T., and Friedman, Daniel P. "Engines Build Process Abstractions." In *Conference Record of the 1984 ACM Symposium on LISP and Functional Programming*. August 1984, pp. 18-24.

[10] Haynes, Christopher T., and Friedman, Daniel P. "An Abstraction of Timed Preemption." Indiana University Computer Science Department Technical Report No. 178 (August 1985).

[11] Haynes, Christopher T.; Friedman, Daniel P.; and Kohlbecker, Eugene. "Programming with Continuations." Indiana University Computer Science Department Technical Report No. 151 (November 1983).

[12] Haynes, Christopher T.; Friedman, Daniel P.; and Wand, Mitchell. "Continuations and Coroutines." In *Conference Record of the 1984 ACM Symposium on LISP and Functional Programming*. August 1984, pp. 293-298.

[13] Landin, Peter. "A Correspondence Between ALGOL 60 and Church's Lambda Notation: Part I." In *Communications of the ACM*, 8(2). February 1965, pp. 89-101.

[14] Massachusetts Institute of Technology. *MIT Scheme Manual*. 7th ed. Cambridge, MA: Massachusetts Institute of Technology, 1984.

[15] Rees, Jonathon A.; Adams, Norman I., IV; and Meehan, James R. *The T Manual*. 4th ed. 1984.

[16] Rees, Jonathon A., and Clinger, W., eds. "Revised[3] Report on the Algorithmic Language Scheme." Massachusetts Institute of Technology AI Memo No. 848a (September, 1986).

[17] Reynolds, John. "Definitional Interpreters for Higher Order Programming Languages." In *ACM Conference Proceedings*. 1972, pp. 717-740.

[18] Steele, Guy L. *COMMON LISP: The Language*. Bedford, MA: Digital Press, 1984.

[19] Steele, Guy L. "Rabbit: a Compiler for Scheme." Massachusetts Institute of Technology AI Technical Report No. 474 (May 1978).

[20] Steele, Guy Lewis, Jr., and Sussman, Gerald Jay. "The Art of the Interpreter, or The Modularity Complex (Parts Zero, One, and Two)." Massachusetts Institute of Technology AI Memo No. 453 (May 1978).

[21] Steele, Guy Lewis, Jr., and Sussman, Gerald J. "The Revised Report on Scheme, a Dialect of LISP." Massachusetts Institute of Technology AI Memo No. 452 (January 1978).

[22] Sussman, Gerald Jay, and Steele, Guy Lewis, Jr. "Scheme: an Interpreter for Extended Lambda Calculus." Massachusetts Institute of Technology AI Memo No. 349 (December 1975).

[23] Texas Instruments. *PC Scheme User's Guide — Student Edition*. Austin: Texas Instruments, 1988.

[24] Wand, Mitchell. "Continuation-based Multiprocessing." In *Conference Record of the 1980 LISP Conference*. August 1980, pp. 19-28.

[25] Weinreb, D.; Moon, D.; and Stallman, R. *Lisp Machine Manual*. Cambridge, MA: Massachusetts Institute of Technology, 1983.

INDEX

numbers
1+ procedure, description of 7-5

symbols
! suffix 3-6
character 2-2
#F:
  boolean object 4-1
  constant, description of 7-71
  literal 3-5
#!NULL constant 3-5
#T:
  boolean object 4-1
  constant, description of 7-187
  literal 3-5
#\BACKSPACE character object,
      description of 7-19
#\ESCAPE character object,
      description of 7-68
#\NEWLINE character object,
      description of 7-114–7-115
#\PAGE character object,
      description of 7-122
#\RETURN character object,
      description of 7-146
#\RUBOUT character object,
      description of 7-148
#\SPACE character object,
      description of 7-162
% identifier 3-6
' character 2-2
'() constant, description of 7-2
(character 2-2
) character 2-2
* procedure, description of 7-2
+ procedure, description of 7-3
, character 2-2
- procedure, description of 7-3
-1+ procedure, description of 7-4
-> infix 3-6
/ procedure, description of 7-4
; character 2-5
< procedure, description of 7-5–7-6
<= procedure, description of 7-5–7-6
<> procedure, description of 7-5–7-6
= procedure, description of 7-5–7-6
> procedure, description of 7-5–7-6
>= procedure, description of 7-5–7-6
? suffix 3-6
@ character 2-2
[character 2-2
\ character 2-2
] character 2-2
' character 2-2
{ character 2-2
| character 2-2
} character 2-2

a
ABS procedure 4-5
  description of 7-6
ACCESS procedure 3-4, 4-14
  description of 7-6–7-7
ACOS procedure 4-5
  description of 7-7
ACTIVE keyword 5-3
active values 5-3–5-4
  definition 5-3
ADD1 procedure, description of 7-7
ADVISE-ENTRY procedure,
      description of 7-8–7-9
ADVISE-EXIT procedure,
      description of 7-8–7-9
ALIAS special form,
      description of 7-9
ALL-CLASSVARS procedure,
      description of 7-10
ALL-INSTVARS procedure,
      description of 7-10
ALL-METHODS procedure,
      description of 7-11
alphabetic characters, case sensitivity 2-2
AND special form 3-7
  description of 7-11
APPEND procedure 4-8
  description of 7-12
APPEND! procedure, description of 7-12
applicative order evaluation 3-1
APPLY procedure, description of 7-12–7-13
APPLY-IF special form 3-7
  description of 7-13